Animal Learning

Introductions to Modern Psychology

General Editor: Max Coltheart
Birkbeck College, University of London

Animal Learning
An Introduction

Stephen Walker

Routledge & Kegan Paul
London and New York

For LPBW

First published in 1987 by
Routledge & Kegan Paul Ltd
11 New Fetter Lane, London EC4P 4EE

Published in the USA by
Routledge & Kegan Paul Inc.
in association with Methuen Inc.
29 West 35th Street, New York, NY 10001

Set in Baskerville, 11 on 12 pt
by Input Typesetting Ltd, London
and printed in Great Britain
by R. Clay & Co. Ltd.
Bungay, Suffolk

Library of Congress Cataloging-in-Publication Data

Walker, Stephen F.
Animal learning.

(Introductions to modern psychology)
Bibliography: p.
Includes index.
1. Learning in animals. I. Title. II. Series.
QL785.W1438 1987   156'.315   86-28046
ISBN 0-7102-0482-5
ISBN 0-7102-1152-X (pbk.)

Contents

Figures

Acknowledgments

I should like to thank the following authors and publishers for their permission to make use of copyright illustrations. The relevant figure numbers from the list above arc given at the end of each citation.

Academic Press, Orlando, Florida
Grant, D. S. (1976). Effect of sample presentation time on long-delay matching in the pigeon. *Learning and Motivation*, 7, 580–90. (9.2)
Gray, J. A. (1975). *Elements of a Two-Process Theory of Learning*. (7.2)

American Association for the Advancement of Science, Washington DC
Hawkins, R. D., Abrams, T. W., Carew, T. J. and Kandel, E. R. (1983). A cellular mechanism for classical conditioning in *Aplysia*: Activity-dependent amplification of pre-synaptic facilitation. *Science, 219*, 400–5. (3.3)

American Journal of Psychology, **Champaign, Illinois**
Crespi, L. P. (1942). Quantitative variation in incentive and performance in the white rat. *American Journal of Psychology, 55*, 467–517. (5.3)

American Psychological Association, Washington, DC
Davis, M. and Wagner, A. R. (1969). Habituation of startle response under incremental sequence of stimulus intensities. *Journal of Comparative and Physiological Psychology, 67*, 486–92. (2.2)

Groves, P. M. and Thompson, R. F. (1970). Habituation: A dual-process theory. *Psychological Review*, *77*, 419–50. (2.2)

Hall, G. and Pearce, J. M. (1979). Latent inhibition of a CS during CS-US pairings. *Journal of Experimental Psychology: Animal Behaviour Processes*, *5*, 31–42. (4.2)

Hanson, H. M. (1959). Effects of discrimination training on stimulus generalization. *Journal of Experimental Psychology*, *58*, 321–34. (8.1)

Sands, S. F. and Wright, A. A. (1980). Serial probe recognition performance by a rhesus monkey and a human with 10- and 20-item lists. *Journal of Experimental Psychology: Animal Behaviour Processes*, *6*, 386–96. (9.4)

Santiago, H. C. and Wright, A. A. (1984). Pigeon memory: *same/different* concept learning, serial probe recognition acquisition, and probe delay effects on the serial position function. *Journal of Experimental Psychology: Animal Behaviour Processes*, *10*, 498–512. (9.5)

Thorndike, E. L. (1898). Animal Intelligence: an experimental study of the associative processes in animals. *Psychological Review, Monograph Supplements*, *2(8)*, 1–109. (5.1, 5.2)

Woods, S. C. (1976). Conditioned hypoglycemia. *Journal of Comparative and Physiological Psychology*, *90*, 1164–8. (3.4)

Wright, A. A., Santiago, H. C. and Sands, S. F. (1984). Monkey memory: *same/different* concept learning, serial probe recognition acquisition, and probe delay effects on the serial position function. *Journal of Experimental Psychology: Animal Behaviour Processes*, *10*, 513–29. (9.5)

E. J. Brill, Leiden
Tinbergen, N. and Perdeck, A. C. (1950). On the stimulus situation releasing the begging response in the newly-hatched herring-gull chick (*Larus argentatus* Pont). *Behaviour*, *3*, 1–39. (1.3)

Journal of General Psychology, **Washington, DC**
Krueger, R. C. and Hull, C. L. (1931). An electro-chemical parallel to the conditioned reflex. *Journal of General Psychology*, *5*, 262–9. (3.3)

Lawrence Erlbaum Associates Ltd, Hillsdale, NJ
Wagner, A. R. (1976). Priming in STM: an information-processing mechanism for self-generated or retrieval-generated depression in performance. In Tighe, T. J. and Leaton, R. N. (eds.), *Habituation*, 95–128. (4.3)

McGraw-Hill Book Company Inc, New York
Harlow, H. F. (1959). Learning set and error factory theory. In Koch, S. (ed.), *Psychology: A Study of a Science, Volume 2*. 492–537. (8.4)

Perceptual and Motor Skills, Missoula, Montana
Gossette, R. L. and Hood, P. (1968). Successive discrimination reversal measures as a function of variation of motivational and incentive levels. *Perceptual and Motor Skills, 26*, 47–52. (8.3)

Pergamon Journals Ltd, Oxford
Overman, W. H. and Doty, R. W. (1980). Prolonged visual memory in macaques and man. *Neuroscience, 5*, 1825–31. (9.3)

Pion Ltd, London
Morgan, M. J., Fitch, M. D., Holman, J. G. and Lea, S. E. G. (1976). Pigeons learn the concept of an 'A'. *Perception, 5*, 57–66. (8.2)

John Wiley, New York
Miller, N. E. (1944). Experimental studies of conflict. In Hunt, J. McV. (ed.), *Personality and the Behaviour Disorders, Vol. I*. Ronald Press: New York, 431–65. (7.1)

1 Theoretical and historical issues

'When one says "a man learns", you agree that this is the least and first of sentences, do you not?'

Eleatic Stranger, Plato's *Sophist*

Innate and acquired knowledge

The most famous and influential pages ever written about learning were designed to show that conventional and obvious theories about learning are wrong. Plato's dialogue *Meno*, written more than 2,000 years ago, has the philosopher Socrates conducting an improvised experiment in order to convince Meno, a rich young aristocrat, that the most expensive and expert lessons can teach nothing that is not already innately known, though hidden, and therefore already present in the learner. The example Socrates chose was a simplified version of Pythagoras' Theorem, which I trust readers will remember from their schooldays. If not, so much the better, since those who believe they do not already know the theorem will be in a good position to judge Plato's theory, which is that they have learned it all before in a previous life. More knowledgeable readers must make an effort to put themselves in the shoes of Meno's young slaveboy, the subject of the original experiment, who had been born and bred in his master's household and, we are assured, had been taught no geometry whatever.

The starting point of the experiment is the square ABCD, which Socrates drew in the sand, shown here in Figure 1.1, which has sides 2 feet long. By drawing in the cross lines the

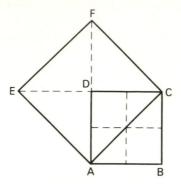

Figure 1.1   *The square on the diagonal.*
See text.

slaveboy, who can count, and also knows that 2 x 2 is 4, is able to deduce from the diagram that a square with a 2–foot side has an area of 4 square feet. That is the easy part. The hard question, which Socrates now puts, is how can we draw a square with twice the area of the first one, that is, a square with an area of 8 square feet? That's obvious, says the slave-boy, drawing a square with a side twice as long. But more drawing in the sand quickly demonstrates that a square with a 4–foot side is too big, since its area is 16 square feet. The slaveboy then makes a compromise guess of a square with a 3–foot side, but gives up on seeing that this gives 9 square feet. This is an important stage in the experiment, since Socrates starts the question over again from scratch, asking the slaveboy a series of easy questions, which ends with the correct answer to the difficult question. Shortening the series a little, one can say: look at the square ABCD, isn't it cut in half by the line AC? In that case, if the area of ABCD is 4, and it is cut in half by AC, what is the area of the triangle ADC? And wouldn't you say that the big square AEFC is made up of sections just like ADC? How many of these sections are there? So there are 4 of these sections in the big square AEFC, and just 2 of the same sections in ABCD? And what is the relation of 4 to 2? Double, now says the slaveboy. So how many square feet in the big square then? 8 feet, says the slaveboy. But which line do we know is the side of the 8–feet square? The slaveboy points to AC. Ah, then says Socrates, the technical name for that is the diagonal, so it would be your personal opinion that the square on the diagonal of the original square is double the original area. That is so, Socrates.

Socrates takes this to mean that the slave boy has spontaneously blurted out Pythagoras' theorem due to his innate knowledge of it. (It is possible to use similar techniques to prove that the square on the hypoteneuse equals the sum of the squares on the sides of any rectangle, but it would take a good deal more drawing in the sand: see Figure 1.2). Since no one had told the slaveboy about geometry in his present life, he must have learned about it in a previous life. But in any previous life we could have performed the same experiment. Therefore, the soul is infinitely immortal, at least in a backwards direction, and in fact Socrates generalizes from

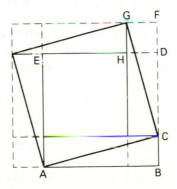

Figure 1.2 *Is Pythagoras' theorem innate?*
There are various ways in which one can see a general proof of Pythagoras' theorem in this figure, which is more elaborate than that drawn by Socrates in Plato's 'Meno'. The outer square contains the square on the hypoteneuse of ABC with 4 triangles like ABC. The same outer square is made up of the square on AB (ABDE) plus a square on CB (DFGH) plus 4 triangles the size of ABC. Taking away the 4 extra triangles in each case leads one to discover Pythagoras' theorem. But does this mean that everyone is born already knowing the theorem?

this argument to conclude that the Soul is immortal in the future as well. It was thus a very serious point, and not just a demonstration of educational techniques.

There are many other philosophical implications of course, but for our purposes Plato's theory of learning – that all learning consists of the recollection of already known innate ideas – provides an extreme example of a nativist (or rationalist) view, in which the role of information input from personal experience of the environment is minimized. The notion that the soul has learned everything that there is to know in previous lives, including those in a wide variety of animal species, did not remain academically respectable for very long, though it retains a certain popular appeal, but if previous lives are interpreted metaphorically as the influence of past evolution on genetically inherited characteristics then one could say that there are modern nativist theories, in the field of human sociobiology, which approach Plato's in their emphasisis on predetermined factors in psychology.

There has of course never been any shortage of opposition to Socrates' interpretation of the slaveboy experiment, and to the Platonic nativist position more generally. Both Socrates and Plato were in many ways reactionaries, whose views happened to stick – the belief that human life was ruled by customs and conventions, and that skills of all kinds could be taught on a commercial basis by professional teachers, was the received wisdom being attacked by Socrates. One of the participants in the discussion of learning with Meno, Anytus, shortly afterwards brought Socrates to trial and extracted the death penalty, though it is likely that this had more to do with politics than with the argument over learning, since Anytus was a politician who had just been involved in the restoration of democracy to Athens after a brief but extremely violent coup by the 'Thirty Tyrants', many of whom were Socrates' relatives or former pupils. (The explicit conclusion at the end of the discussion with Meno is that political rulers obtain their ability to rule by divine right, no matter how annoying this might be is to democrats such as Anytus.)

The substantial theoretical opposition to Plato's arguments for innate ideas was supplied soon afterwards by Aristotle, who can safely be counted as an 'empiricist', that is, as a theorist who believes that learning and the acquisition of knowledge depend upon information flowing into the mind from the outside world, during one's lifetime and definitely not before that. In a brief discussion of memory, Aristotle specifically says that when anyone learns something for the first time, or hears or sees something new, no recollection of innate knowledge is involved (*De Memoria*, 451a, 20). On the contrary, he argued that the mind is capable of thinking a range of thoughts, just as a blank writing tablet or piece of paper is capable of having all sorts of things potentially written on it (*De Amina*, 430a, 5). This has proved to be a very enduring image for empiricist theories, which are the standard form for learning theories. Obviously there is a world of difference between Plato's theory, that everyone's head comes complete with an encyclopedia of information which needs only to be accessed by an appropriate question, and Aristotle's alternative that although we may eventually acquire an enormous amount of information, the pages of our internal encyclopedia are all blank to start out with. Exactly how the information from the outside world can come to be encoded and stored and understood internally is of course something for much further debate. It is very useful for me that in the places where Aristotle discusses these details, he usually refers to animal as well as human psychology. His basic assumptions are that information is gathered from the environment by sense perception, or an innate faculty of discrimination; in some animals sense perceptions may persist as a simple form of memory; in others a more complete memory for events is found; and in people deliberate searching and reconstruction of memories, and inferences from perception by the power of reasoning, allow for the acquisition of knowledge from the experience of life. It is hardly surprising that with this sort of naturalistic approach Aristotle specifically disagreed with Socrates' emphasis on innate or universal ideas, even for mathematical concepts. (See Book A, chapter 1 of Aristotle's *Metaphysics* for sensation and memory in animals; Books M and N for disagreement with Socrates – 1078b; and *Posterior Analytics*, Book II, chapter xix for perception and memory.)

This very ancient difference of opinion about the relative importance of internal and external sources of knowledge and influences on behaviour has been the source of many kinds of argument, but the same issue, be it put as nature versus nurture, genetics versus culture, or learning versus instinct, is arguably still the single most contentious theoretical problem in the learning theories of today. Before looking at some slightly later developments in this innate encyclopedia versus blank pages contrast, I should perhaps add the cautionary note that, although it is easiest to understand the issue in terms of extremes, even extreme theorists usually modify their position to compromise on difficult cases.

We now move on rather quickly however, missing out a period of 2,000 years, from the empiricism of Aristotle in the fourth century BC to the development of it by Locke (1632–1704). To Aristotle's image of the blank tablet, or *tabula rasa*, Locke added that of the mind as, at birth, an empty cabinet, waiting to be filled with ideas (Locke, 1689/1982, p. 55) and is primarily responsible for the most popular empiricist model of the mind of a child as plain white paper devoid of all characters (p. 104). This alone should make his disagreement with Plato's assumptions clear enough, but Locke was extraordinarily thorough in dismissing all claims that the human mind is governed by any innate principles, or primary notions, brought into the world at birth. Children and idiots, he says, plainly have far fewer ideas than a rational adult, and if innate ideas can only be uncovered by mature reason, there does not seem much point in having them innate. Locke particularly disagrees with the idea that if someone accedes to a certain mathematical demonstration, this means that the mathematical principle involved was innate. Children have to learn, gradually, their numbers, before they can even agree that 3 plus 4 equals 7 (and also have to understand both the name and the concept of equality). More complicated mathematical demonstrations, such as, of course, Socrates' square on the diagonal, simply demonstrate that good teaching from another person is far more useful than any innate impression on its own – it is the nature of the things contained in the demonstration which are persuasive. It is much harder to construct the demonstration than just to agree with it, and Locke does not think that many of the mathetmaticians that he knew would want to agree that all the diagrams that they had drawn were just copies of innate blueprints engraved on everyone's mind

(p. 60). For social behaviour, and moral and religious principles, the great diversity of accepted practices during the history of mankind and in various cultures, persuaded Locke that there were no common factors. Perhaps he overestimated the prevalence of cannibalism, expecially of children, and thus overstated the argument against any parental instinct for preserving and cherishing offspring, but the variousness of both social and intellectual ideas across human cultures and across historical periods remains as a challenge to present-day sociobiologists (e.g. Lumsden and Wilson, 1981).

Few learning theorists today would be as extreme as Locke, in limiting babies to only very faint ideas of hunger, thirst, warmth and pain, which they may have felt in the womb; but whether or not children, of say 5 or 6, have access to innate ideas of impossibility, identity, and a whole being necessarily bigger than one of its parts, is still a subject for investigation in developmental psychology. Locke said children had neither these nor any innate idea of the existence of God or the duty to worship him, keeping about as rigorously as anyone ever has to the blank paper model of human nature. It is difficult to say why Locke opposed innate mental principles so vigorously, but one can hardly ignore the fact that an English king was beheaded while Locke was growing up, and another was run out of the country the year before the publication in 1689 of Locke's major work. Locke came from a Puritan and Parliamentarian family, and was firmly identified with the democratic and Whig side of the political issues of his time. Immediately after his psychological *Essay*, he published two political treatises; the first attacked the Divine right of Kings, and the second promoted the ideals of natural equality, the acquisition of property by individual effort, and rationally argued checks and balances in government which, it is sometimes held, eventually became enshrined in the constitution of the United States of America (Russell, 1946). It is not too far-fetched to presume that Locke's distrust of innate principles, and firm belief in the ability of all rational individuals to work things out for themselves, reflect political liberalism as well as psychological empiricism.

By the rigour of his opposition to innate ideas, Locke set himself the problems of a learning theorist, and it is worth looking briefly at his solutions. If the mind begins as a blank, how is it ever filled? As Locke put it, 'Whence comes it by that vast store, which the busy and boundless fancy of man has painted on it, with an almost endless variety? Whence has it all the materials of reason and knowledge?' He gives immediately the learning theorist's answer: 'To this I answer, in one word, from Experience.' That is all very well, but a number of details have to be specified, and there have always been difficulties in saying exactly what should go where, and in what order, on the blank paper. Like Aristotle, Locke said that the original source of all ideas was sensation, that is information received from seeing, hearing, touching, tasting and smelling the outside world. This is one fountain of experience, and the second is an internal sense, or reflection, since perceiving the operation of our own minds in doubting, believing, thinking, reasoning and willing is an equally important source of mental life. Human reflection is largely dependent on language, of course, but Locke followed in the tradition of allowing animals a share in the earlier stages of learning. Sensation, or the faculty of perception, he thought was common to all animals, and indeed was what separated animals from vegetables, but many members of the animal kingdom could be assumed to have very obscure and dull perceptions, since their sensory organs are wisely adapted to their ecological state and condition: we may reasonably conclude, says Locke, that the quickness and variety of the sensations of an oyster or a cockle do not match those of people, or of other higher animals. However, the prime importance given to perception in Locke's theory is illustrated by his (surely extreme) suggestion that a human being whose sensory input was restricted to the small dull level of a cockle or an oyster would be prevented from exceeding these molluscs in any other form of intelligence – 'notwithstanding all that is boasted of innate principles' (Locke, 1689/1982, pp. 148–9).

Perception alone could lead no further, and could certainly not produce learning, unless it was combined with some kind of retention of perceived information. Habituation and conditioned reflexes can be the simplest forms of retention, but in Locke's theory the main form of retention considered is a full-blown model of human memory. In this, a simple perceived idea can first of all be kept 'in view', by contemplation, for some period of time but, as in modern theories of short-term memory, only a small number of items can be kept in view at once, and thus all ideas are at some point put out of view, in a long-term repository. Once they are there, they may be revived or retrieved for further contemplation in the future. All ideas in the long-term store are subject to 'constant decay': those which make the deepest impression, and last longest, are those given motivational significance by pleasure or pain, but repetition, and attention, also help to fix ideas in memory in Locke's theory. Retrieval of an idea from memory is often an active and willed process, but at other times, Locke notes (pp. 150–3), items in memory return to mind 'of their own accord'; or are 'tumbled out of their dark cells' and brought to light by tempestuous passions. Taken together, memory processes are essential to all other cognitive processes, and in fact Locke attributes stupidity in general to extreme slowness in the retrieval of ideas from the memory.

This is fairly typical as an empiricist model of memory; a peculiarity of Locke's is that he assumes that it applies to many other animals, as well to the human species. This is peculiar partly because it minimizes the role of verbal coding in human memory, but much recent experimental research supports the view that birds and mammals have well-developed memory systems (see chapters 8 and 9). Locke himself was impressed with the memory of imitating birds for previously heard sounds, the more so because in the case of artificial sounds imitation does not seem to be of any use in 'the bird's preservation' (Locke, 1689/1982, p. 155).

It is worth noting that a more sophisticated treatment of the problem of retrieval of information from memory was considered and rejected by Plato. One of the theories discussed by Socrates was the one of an imprint-receiving lump of wax, which could be bigger in some people than in others, of harder or softer consistency, and a source of fallibility in memory if the wax is too small or too soft, leading imprints to become crowded on top of one another or smudged (*Theaetetus*, 191–94). But this does not allow for the difference between stored and retrieved memories. We can in some sense have memories without using them in the same way that one can have clothes without wearing them; the metaphor which Socrates develops from this is that of an aviary, which starts off empty. Someone goes out and catches large numbers of wild birds and puts them in his aviary – in this sense he has got them. But if he wants to hold and look at a particular one he has the new problem of retrieving it from within the aviary, and he may find that in some cases this is very difficult, or that if some of the birds fly in groups he catches the wrong one, and so on. In this context Socrates says that the aviary/memory store is empty at birth – during life one fills one's memory store with pieces of knowledge as one might fill one's aviary with birds, but there are analogous problems with retrieving the items from the store. The most interesting point made by Plato was that the identification of items used in retrieval may be different from the identification used when catching them in the first place – but he eventually rejects the metaphor altogether on the unrealistic grounds that if one knew enough about a memory to be able to retrieve it from the store there would be no need to carry the retrieval process any further.

Whatever the other details of a theory of perception and memory, it must include the assumption that representations perceived or remembered can be distinguished as same or different: Locke calls this discernment, and says it depends on, among other things, attention and the acuity of the sense organs – in modern theories the concept of discrimination learning in some ways corresponds to this (see chapter 8). A separate cognitive operation in Locke's theory is comparison of ideas with respect to time, place, and other individual features – this is rather like relational as opposed to absolute discrimination, and is the point, curiously, where Locke begins to distinguish human intellectual processes from those of animals, since he believed that animals only compared very concrete features of objects. After that, according to Locke, even foxes and dogs begin to fall far short of human cognition, because they do not compose large complex ideas by combining together simple ones. Children first slowly get ideas fixed in their memories by repeated sensations, then gradually learn the verbal signs of speech, and in order not to have an endless list of names for each slightly different sensory experience they abstract general ideas from particular experiences and objects. Abstraction, according to Locke, is completely absent in all animals. He was not necessarily right about this, but the important point here is that both people and animals are supposed to gradually build up experience, based on sensation, with human cognition achieved by the addition of extra stages of gradual experience over and above purely animal learning.

This would seem to be an empiricist learning theory of a particularly extreme type, but even Locke surreptitiously includes some nature along with nurture, as is made clear in his discussion of the association of ideas. For Locke most learning and thinking took place because certain ideas have 'natural correspondence and connexion' with others: physical similarity would be the simplest reason why two sensations could be connected together, but it was an essential function of human rationality to produce inherently reasonable relationships among ideas. However, says Locke, if you observe other people closely, you will almost always find some particular thing about them that is rather odd, and in fact many other people are completely unreasonable. This is because some ideas can become connected together by accident or custom, and once this process has started, it becomes very difficult to stop (1689/1982, p. 395). The examples include adults making themselves sick by eating too much honey, and afterwards feeling ill even when just hearing the name of honey; children learning to fear the dark by being told stories which connect darkness to goblins; and the rare case of a young man who practised complicated dance-steps in a room with a large trunk in it, and afterwards found that he could only dance properly either in that same room, or in a room that had a trunk in a similar position. But mental associations between ideas at random were thought by Locke to be very common, especially in perverse sects of religion or philosophy, and the foundation of almost all the errors in the world.

This is a very unusual treatment of the association of ideas, and not one much adhered to after Locke, but the general belief that random conjunctions of stimuli may have unexpected and unwanted after-effects is common in several recent theories of the role of conditioning experiences in the origins of neurosis. In Greek theories association of ideas was, on the contrary, a generally beneficial mental technique. In Aristotle's treatment (e.g. Sorabji, 1972) the association of ideas is discussed as a process of recollection, for use, for instance, in memorizing and remembering speeches. Recollection is a matter of a train of ideas in constant succession, and in getting to the next idea in the sequence we are likely to move to something that is similar, opposite or in some sense close to the current, one. But arbitrariness of associations can be made use of by the mnemonic method of loci: Greeks memorizing speeches often deliberately associated ideas in the speech with positions in a well-known room, so that when giving the speech they could imagine moving round the room, and be reminded of the point they wanted to make.

The theory of how one is reminded of something was not just a matter of practical mnemonics for Plato, but a crucial part of his theory of innate ideas. First, he said, one could be reminded of something despite dissimilarity – a lover who saw a lyre might visualize the boy he loved who normally played it. Second, one could be reminded by similarity – when seeing a picture of person X, one will recollect the person X themselves. But in this case one will be just as aware of the difference between the cue and the recollection – one may see a very bad caricature of Mrs Thatcher, and contemplate the real Mrs Thatcher, without being tempted to think that the cartoon *is* Mrs Thatcher. Socrates goes on from this to the innateness of abstract concepts. If we look at two almost equal sticks, we are reminded of the concept of equality, but we do not think the sticks themselves are identical to the concept – among other things, someone else might say the sticks were not equal (the Platonic version of the social psychological experiment of Asch, 1956). We must have had prior knowledge of equality in order to be reminded of it by the almost equal sticks, and since all sense perceptions of equality must be inferior to the ideal concept of equality, in order to ever be reminded of absolute equality we must have had knowledge of it before we were born, thus our soul had to exist before birth, and, Socrates concludes, after death as well. Deducing immortality from the association of ideas is of course far-fetched, and the argument appears rushed, and in a sense this is understandable, as the discussion is supposed to take place just prior to Socrates' execution: but the importance given to recollection in Platonic theory is probably one reason for Aristotle's emphasis on the topic (Sorabji, 1972).

After Locke, the principle of the association of ideas was developed in a quite different direction by Hume (1711–76), who was an extremist on all psychological and philosophical issues, but as a political historian an amiable Tory. Like Locke, Hume assumed that the origin of ideas was in sense impressions, and like Aristotle he assumed that progress from one idea to another in a train of thought would be based on connections due to similarity, contiguity and habitual sequence. But, taking a very radical step of his own, he denied that any particular kind of relation between ideas is more natural or inevitable than another, or that it is possible for human reason to provide logical relations between experienced ideas in any way independent of the quite arbitary associations between ideas arising from individual circumstances. Thus, in Hume, learning from experience is second to nothing else in its influence on mental life, and, in this sense, he can be regarded as the progenitor of many other learning theories. Another very modern feature of Hume's theorizing was his reduction of all psychological mechanisms to the sequence of one event being followed by another, which he usually referred to as 'cause and effect'. He achieved considerable notoriety by arguing that we have no logical justification for reasoning that bread will be nourishing in the future, because it has been so in the past – what matters for present purposes is not whether he was right about this, but Hume's alternative, psychological explanation, that we expect things to happen in the future as we have experienced them in the past, but because of an irrational process of habit: 'All inferences from experience, therefore, are the effects of custom, not of reasoning' (1777/1970, p. 43). Hume's only concession to any innately accurate process of reasoning was to divide human thought into two categories: 'relations of ideas', which are completely independent of empirical evidence, and thus confined, in his view, to pure mathematics; and 'matters of fact', which include everything else. All matters of fact can be reduced to one sense impression having followed another, which is described as cause and effect. This allows Hume to give a one-word answer to virtually all psychological questions: '*What is the nature of all our reasonings concerning matter of fact?* – the relation of cause and effect. *What is the foundation of all our reasonings and conclusions concerning that relation?* It may be replied in one word, Experience' (1777/1970, p. 32, original italics).

Perhaps the most significant aspect of Hume's writing for twentieth-century learning theories was that the key feature of learning from experience was applied universally, and no hard and fast line was drawn between its effects on the human species and its effects on other animals. Thus, 'It is certain that the most ignorant and stupid peasants – nay infants, nay even brute beasts – improve by experience, and learn the qualities of natural objects, by observing the effects which result from them' (1777/1970, p. 39). It seemed obvious to Hume that domestic animals such as horses or greyhounds learned from experience, and became more cunning and less impetuous as they got older; and that systematic training with reward and punishment could induce animals to behave in an arbitrary and unnatural manner. He did not pretend that these animals should therefore be assumed to be capable of argument or reasoning, but since he believed that neither children, nor mankind in general, nor even philosophers in their non-professional moments, were guided by pure reasoning, there was less cause for Hume to specify animal inadequacies in this respect than there was for Locke or Aristotle.

There were, however, some exceptions to the universal of unreasoning custom and habit, even for Hume – these were the abstract schemes of quantity and number, which did not require empirical evidence. It was worthwhile Hume believed, to reason out Pythagoras' Theorem, but he did not therefore suppose that there was anything innate about it. 'That *the square of the hypoteneuse is equal to the squares of the other two sides*, cannot be known, let the terms be ever so exactly defined, without a train of reasoning and enquiry' (1777/1970, p. 163). Hume remained, however, extremely sceptical about the value of what he called 'a priori reasoning', if it was not combined with matter-of-fact evidence. Nothing could be learned, he believed, from purely logical manipulations, such as saying 'where there is no property, there is no injustice', with injustice defined as a violation of property, since this was nothing more than an imperfect kind of definition. And for matter-of-fact, realistic knowledge of the world, Hume suggested that thinking things out from first principles in the traditional philosophical way – his 'a priori' reasoning – was completely useless: one could never know whether a stone would fall up or down, or whether one billiard ball hitting another would stop, fly off at an angle, or return in a straight line, on purely a priori grounds, unless one had practical or experimental evidence to go on. Thus he felt that the only possible sources of knowledge were abstract reasoning with a numerical basis, or experimental evidence based on experience. This seems to be a reasonable approximation to modern scientific practice, and therefore should not have caused much of a stir on methodological grounds, but both its philosophical necessity and its psychological truth have been repeatedly questioned.

Both the philosophical and the psychological reactions against Hume were begun by Kant (1724–1804), who as a consequence is frequently referred to as one of the most influential of modern thinkers. Although he is as famous for the obscurity of his writing as he is for the weight of his conclusions, Kant's elaboration of the whole nature/nurture question had a considerable influence in the early development of experimental psychology (Boring, 1950), and distinctions not unlike those he used have become increasingly important in modern learning theory. The starting point is the distinction between Hume's 'relations of ideas' and 'matters of fact'. Kant's terms were 'analytic' and 'synthetic'. Roughly speaking the former are logical necessities, such as 'a rose is a rose', 'a tall man is a man', or 'something large takes up a lot of room', and possibly also $2 + 2 = 4$ and Pythagoras' theorem; while the other category is of experienced facts such as 'today is Thursday', 'the present prime minister's first name is Margaret.' The distinction is partly based on amount of new factual content: if a sports commentator says 'Liverpool have just won the European cup on penalties', a good deal of new information has been conveyed to the listener; on the other hand, if, as often happens, the commentator has nothing new to say, he may fill in time with analytical judgments, such as 'but this game isn't over until the final whistle's blown' or 'this race is going to be won by the runner who runs fastest from start to finish'.

To anyone with empiricist sympathies, it seems rather unlikely that even logical necessities should be in any way innate, and almost inconceivable that experienced or reported matters of fact, such as may be found in daily newspapers or *The Guinness Book of Records*, should be influenced at all by knowledge that is inherited. But, if anything, it seems more likely that logical necessities might contain some germ of an innate principle than that unlearned expectations are contained in matters of fact. It is the contribution of Kant that stresses the importance of innate first principles, even for the perception of matters of fact. Plato came close to claiming that everyone was influenced by innate concepts of such things as tables and beds, and even of individuals, the argument going that if you are able to perceive Margaret Thatcher, you have to know what it is that you are perceiving before you can perceive it, and therefore the concept of Margaret Thatcher is innate, but this sort of view is rarely defended (though see Fodor, 1980). The Kantian position seems to be much more of a compromise, since he has no doubt that 'all knowledge begins from experience'; it is just that there are innate categories which are 'keys to possible experiences' and which might reasonably be regarded as part of the innate organization of the perceptual apparatus, such as the distinction between one and many objects, and the experience of succession in time (Kant, 1781/1979, pp. 25, 219). Even in Aristotle's or Hume's theory of learning from experience, there has to be some intuitive means of first understanding sense perceptions, or of recording that one sensation has followed another in time. Thus to rely *only* on experience, and nothing else at all by way of innate mental organization, is unrealistic, even for experienced perceptual facts. However, in terms of modern learning theories, which, unlike Kant's, but like Hume's, attempt to account for learning as it occurs in species other than our own, it is necessary to take into account even stronger kinds of innate matters of fact. Bertrand Russell's instructive example was that a dog may become excited either because it observes its master putting on his hat (in anticipation of going out for a walk) or (instinctively) because it smells a rabbit. Russell's belief was that if the dog became capable of talking like a philosopher it would say as regards the smell of rabbit, 'wherever there is this smell, there is something edible', and as regards the hat, 'my master's putting on his hat is an invariable antecedent to his going out'. Moreoever, if the dog was asked *how* it knew these things 'he would say, in the latter case, that he had observed it, and in the former, that it was a synthetic *a priori* intuition' (Russell, 1940, p. 248).

Clearly, the greater the evidence for instinctive organization of behaviour, the more plausible it is to assume that perceived events correspond to innate principles, and that animals recognize their natural foods, or fellow species-members, as conforming to some kind of 'innate releasing mechanism', as present-day ethologists have suggested (Tinbergen, 1951). Even David Hume recognized this, and, in order to defend the continuity between human and other species, said that learing from experience was itself an instinct, and that avoidance of being burned by fire in man was as much an instinct as that by which a bird incubates eggs (1777/1970, p. 108). This is probably not true, but illustrates the fact that even an arch-empiricist like Hume could not avoid getting instinctive processes mixed up in his learning theory. In subsequent chapters it will become apparent that the degree to which any species brings innate dispositions to bear on its reactions to experience is still a matter of intense experimental and theoretical investigation.

Darwinian evolution

Questions of both learning and instinct and, above all, of the relation between human and animal psychology, were given a new impetus by the rapid growth of biological knowlege in the nineteenth century, and in particular by the widely discussed Darwinian theory of evolution. As it is now understood, evolutionary theory tends to emphasize first and foremost genetically inherited characteristics, and therefore innate and instinctive determinants of both animal and human psychology, as is illustrated by the 'selfish gene' axioms of modern sociobiology (Hamilton, 1964; Dawkins, 1976; Wilson, 1975). But, increasingly, the study of behavioural ecology and particularly concern with the foraging techniques of individual species is leading to theories in which the biological utilities of the learning process are fully recognized (Krebs and Davies, 1983; Kamil and Roitblat, 1985; Lea, 1981, 1984a).

It is important to establish that one conceivable and initially popular relation between learning and evolution is now known to be biologically impossible. Darwin himself incorporated into his own speculations (especially in discussing emotional expression) Lamarck's suggestion that useful habits acquired by parents could be passed on to their offspring by a biological form of inheritance. Thus, Darwin suggested that 'some instincts have been developed simply through long-continued and inherited habit', and that this explained why some instinctive behaviours appeared now to be superfluous or counter-productive. Dogs which now scratch the ground without burying anything might be repeating a movement 'originally followed by some remote progenitor of the dog-genus for a definite purpose' (Darwin, 1872/1965, pp. 42–4). Darwin was mistaken about this. Behavioural evolution must take place by the other mechanism he suggested – 'through the preservation of variations of pre-existing instincts – that is, through natural selection' (Darwin, 1872/1965, pp. 42 and 44). There is a certain appeal to the notion that the personal achievements of one generation can be passed on to the next, perhaps because a parent who had arduously acquired a knowledge of statistics, or a foreign language, might wish that this could be transferred to their offspring. But there is no biological mechanism by which information can be moved from the brain to the testicles or the ovaries of the parent. This was suspected by Weissman at the turn of the century, and is confirmed by all known biochemistry (Maynard-Smith, 1975; Dawkins, 1982). It applies not only to complex psychological information, but equally to habits discussed by Darwin such as the laying back of the ears by animals when fighting (which serves a protective function), and to purely physical results of the environment on growth and maturation.

Thus all instinctive programming of behaviour, and all innate influences on learning, must result from the selection of individuals most favoured by random variation in the instinctive and innate influences themselves. This allows, however, for a spectrum of behaviour-controlling mechanisms, with many unexpected combinations of inherited predisposition and learned individual initiative. At one extreme, perception can be regarded as the equivalent to the opening of a lock by a certain innate key – all that can be perceived in this case being whether or not the innate key is present. At the other extreme, quite artificial and novel stimulus information can be correctly categorized, though no doubt this process depends to some degree on built-in capacities. Most of human perception is surely of the latter kind – we have no difficulty in recognizing an electric typewriter or a television screen when we see one, though no genetic assistance for this particular task could possibly have been inherited from the effects of selection on previous generations. It is also the case that domestic and laboratory animals can learn to respond appropriately to stimuli from human artifacts, which they equally are in no sense genetically programmed to deal with. However, in many species, and not only in behaviourally simple animals, it is possible to find cases where sensory perception seems to correspond more closely to the lock-and-key model. In a very similar way, using the keyboard of a typewriter is a motor behaviour that cannot have been inherited or directly affected by evolution (and, although other animals do not type, they may be trained to ride bicycles and so on), but from the human knee jerk to the wriggling of worms it is possible to find patterns of movement that are undoubtedly inherited, and some of these, especially those required for the construction of nests or shelters (in either wasps or weaver-birds), may be both complex in themselves and complex in their relation to environmental stimulation.

Ticks and Toads

Ticks are arachnid arthropods, which have a very simple style of life, even by comparison with their close relatives the spiders, since they are specialized as parasitic bloodsuckers.

A tick may stay clinging to a twig, perhaps for months, until exposed to a low concentration of butyric acid, a component of the smell of a mammal, released from skin glands. It then drops, falling on to the mammal, attaches itself to the mammals' skin, and gorges itself with blood. When fully fed, it may have a strong tendency to climb upwards when on vertical surfaces, but this would be largely due to the fact that its body is swollen with blood behind the region of the legs, so that the mechanical force of gravity will keep the tick's body oriented in an upward direction (Fraenkel and Gunn, 1940). Thus the climbing up to a high position in a tree, and the falling off on to a mammal below, are greatly facilitated, if not wholly determined, by two rudimentary innate influences (namely, the reflexive response to butyric acid, and the physical tendency to crawl upwards when full).

Somewhat more complicated lock-and-key systems appear to control the feeding responses of frogs and toads. They do not have tracking eye movements, but respond to moving visual stimuli of a particular size and shape with a stereotyped sequence of responses. In the common toad *Bufo bufo*, studied by Ewert (1982), this consists of first orienting the whole body towards the stimulus, approaching it, and then snapping, swallowing and gulping after binocular fixation. By putting toads inside glass cylinders and presenting standard visual stimuli outside the cylinder, Ewert and others have isolated certain innate stimulus preferences. For instance, a stripe moving in the direction of its long axis is likely to elicit prey-catching activities, in proportion to its length, but the same stripe, moving perpendicularly to its long axis, is not. Ewert (1976, 1982) refers to this as the 'worm/antiworm' phenomenon. Since it occurs immediately after metamorphosis, and can be traced to the selective response of cells in the ganglion layer of the retina and further on in the toad's visual pathway, it seems undeniable that this form of perceptual categorization is inherited and is not learned from individual experience of worms. Many other forms of response to visual stimuli by frogs and toads, including the direction and distance of jumps away from threat, appear to be innately programmed (Ingle, 1982). A large South American toad, *Ceratophrys ornata*, sits hidden in vegetation until a moving stimulus the size of a small rodent appears, whereupon it leaps towards the stimulus with open mouth, ready to swallow a whole mouse or lizard. In captivity it has been known to eat whole rats, and since it operates according to the rule of the larger the approaching stimulus the better, and fails to distinguish between its normal prey and the human hand, it has to be approached with caution by the human observer (Grzimek, 1974).

Learned modifications to innate releasing mechanisms

The chemical stimulus which results in the falling of the tick, and the visual stimulus which elicits worm-catching behaviour in the common toad, could well be used to support the concept of the innate releasing mechanism, or IRM, introduced by Tinbergen (1951) in his book *The Study of Instinct*. An example used by Tinbergen himself was the reaction of infant herring gulls to cardboard models which bore varying degrees of resemblance to a real herring gull profile (see Figure 1.3). Adult herring gulls have yellow beaks with a prominent red dot at the end, to which infant 'begging' responses are directed: grey bills with a prominent dot are preferred to grey bills with no dot, and there is a preference for the dot to be red in addition to this. Since other gull species with slightly different adult appearance have roughly corresponding infant preferences, it seems reasonable to assume that innate templates or filters are responsible for the species-specific differences (Hailman, 1962; Weidman, 1961). The very first responses of all newborns are not likely to be much influenced by learning, despite empiricist arguments like that of Kuo (1924, 1932) which claimed that the embryo has learned what is necessary: and in the case of nestling birds, the example of the cuckoo provides an undeniable example of innate behaviour patterns. The infant cuckoo, as soon as it is hatched, laboriously manoeuvres all other eggs and nestlings out over the brim of the nest. It must then make begging responses, consisting partly of gaping of the mouth, which impel parental feeding by the unwitting host species. But the later and more impressive example of its unlearned perceptual abilities is that it must, when adult, be able to

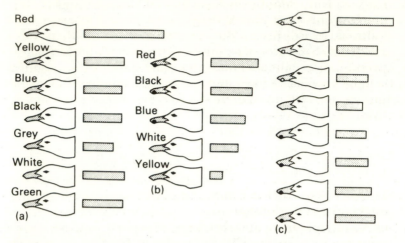

Figure 1.3   *Innate visual preferences in herring gulls.*
Three sets of model heads used to elicit pecking responses from herring gull chicks, with bars showing the relative amount of pecking elicited by each model. In (a) bill colour was varied; in (b) the colour of a patch on a yellow bill was varied; and in (c) the black/white contrast of the patch against a grey bill was varied. After Tinbergen and Perdeck (1950).

recognize a fellow member of its own species, of the opposite sex. It would therefore be foolish to deny the possibility of a very large measure of inherited control over the reactions of individual birds, in certain species. But this does not mean that *all* birds species employ the same measure of innate control, or that individual learning cannot be added on to initial innate preferences.

Tinbergen's own experimental work provides ample evidence of learned modifications to such initial preferences. For instance Tinbergen and Kuenen (1957), in their experiments on the reactions to artificial stimuli of nestling thrushes, observed that if a very natural, adult thrush-like stimulus was presented with no following feeding experience, the infants very soon refused to respond to it, whereas if an artificial non-preferred stimulus was followed by food, the young birds began to respond to it as if it was the natural releaser. It is undoubtedly the case that a great deal of perceptual learning takes place during the early life of many nestling ('altricial') bird species. Both herring gulls (Tinbergen, 1953) and terns (Stevenson *et al.*, 1970) learn to recognize their own parents' vocal calls after only a few days. Other social learning is more gradual (Klinghammer, 1967), and several passerine species, for instance bullfinches (Nicolai, 1959) and canaries (Marler and Waser, 1977) have their song production strongly influenced by their own auditory experience.

Imprinting and social learning

It is well known that non-nestling, 'precocial' birds such as ducks, geese, or domestic chicks, undergo a very rapid form of social learning, and become 'imprinted' on the visual impression of moving objects present in the first few days of their experience, whether or not these correspond closely to the appearance of their natural parents. This is apparently a specialized learning process, since is it time-constrained, not easily reversed, and not influenced in the expected direction by external rewards and punishments, but clearly, if young birds become 'imprinted' on the human form (Lorenz, 1967) or on an experimental football (Hess, 1959; Bateson, 1966, 1979), then perceptual information from the environment has become inserted into the animal's cognitive system, in a thoroughly empiricist way.

Although this kind of early social learning is most obvious in birds, and possibly more specialized, a combination of early innate preferences and more protracted individual learning of social recognition is typical of mammals. Experiments on the taming of wild animals and observations of domesticated species make it clear that, while there may be innate components of social recognition, visual, auditory and olfactory, the social experiences of individuals strongly determine their social behaviour. This is best illustrated by the experiments of Harlow (1958; Harlow and Suomi, 1970) who demonstrated that deprivation of normal interaction with a natural mother led to thoroughly abnormal behaviour in rhesus monkeys, only partly alleviated by the substitution of a cloth 'surrogate mother'. Similarly, for human infants, though human ethologists would expect that response to eye contact and response to the sounds of the human voice are to some extent innate in human babies, no one would suppose that the experiences of a human infant are not a profound influence on all aspects of its future behaviour.

Individual learning and foraging

For the naturalistic study of animal behaviour, an increasingly significant theoretical base is provided by mathematical analysis of the efficiency of various patterns of food-seeking, or foraging, and the attempt to relate these to ecological factors such as the amount of variability in food distribution over space and time, the number of different types of food available, and so on (Krebs and Davies, 1983; Kamil and Sargent, 1981; Charnov, 1976). It goes almost without saying that there is massive innate influence (and perhaps here it is appropriate to call it innate determination) on what foods a particular species will seek, and how it will go about seeking them. Swallows will scythe through the air for insects, sparrow-hawks will catch sparrows, antelope will graze, and lions will hunt antelopes. The swallow does not have to learn to be a swallow, and it is quite possible that this particular species does not have to learn a great deal about its foraging strategies. However, there are some bird species which apparently have to learn even the basics of their trade, and a great many other species in which minute-to-minute and day-to-day knowledge about food locations and types is essential to the success of their foraging forays.

A species which seems to be born ill-prepared for its main task in life is the oyster-catcher. This may be connected with the fact that this bird, in Britain, does not eat oysters, which are in short supply and expensive, but mussels, which are relatively abundant. Although young oyster-catchers are mobile soon after birth, like ducklings and chicks, they are not able to feed themselves for at least six weeks, and sometimes not for six months, after hatching (Norton-Griffiths, 1967, 1969). By the time the young are fledged, at six weeks, they are fairly good at probing for worms in sand or mud with their long beaks, but they are still 'hopelessly inefficient' at opening up mussels or other molluscs, or at dealing with crabs. If the main available food is mussels or crabs, they thus have to follow their parents to the feeding ground for the food to be presented to them ready-to-eat.

During the months that this continues, the young are not merely growing stronger but are also gradually learning the techniques necessary for feeding themselves. The evidence for this is partly that some never learn, and die, and partly that, with mussels, two quite distinct techniques are used in foraging by adult birds. For mussels covered by shallow water, the bird searches for one which is open, and stabs into it with its beak, cutting through the muscle which would otherwise close the shell. But for mussels fully uncovered by the retreating tide, and therefore tightly closed, the adult pulls one loose, carries it to a hard patch of sand, and hammers it open at the weakest point, which is the flat undersurface. The point is that individual adults specialize in one or other of these methods, and that their offspring appear to learn from example, and adopt the particular technique most favoured by their parents (Norton-Griffiths, 1969).

Clearly skills in bill use might be refined by practice, even if the rudiments are innately given, as is true for the motor performance of flying in birds. Other kinds of learning are involved in perceptual search and identification. An animal has to be able to recognize when it has found what it is looking for, and it may search more effectively if it knows what it is looking for: the term 'search image' is sometimes used to explain selective response to certain types of prey (Tinbergen, 1981; Croze, 1970; Drent, 1982). The observable facts are 'that animals may show selective responsiveness to particular stimulus patterns and that the effective patterns may be determined by previous experience with them or related patterns' (Hinde, 1970, p. 125). In part, the concept of a search image overlaps with more general hypotheses about pattern recognition (see chapter 9), but the natural utilities of searching behaviour are most directly reflected in the way that expectancies of food-finding may vary with induction from recent experience. Croze (1970) simply showed that crows, which normally show little interest in half-shells of mussels lying on sand, immediately began turning them over after he had laid out a row of shells with pieces of meat alongside them, and then had hidden pieces of meat under the shells. Krebs *et al.* (1972) gave great tits the semi-natural task of foraging for meal worms hidden in an aviary which contained 18 each of the following types of hiding place: large cups filled with torn-up paper; half ping-pong balls filled with sawdust; wooden poles with a small hole drilled in the top, covered with masking tape. Only one meal worm was hidden for a particular test, and whichever bird in a group found this had a strong tendency to try other hiding places of the same type.

Apart from search images of a particular kind of prey, or a particular kind of prey location, a number of other decisions made during foraging involve short- or long-term learning about features of the environment. Drent (1982) discusses the different time scales involved in decisions made by parent starlings feeding their young, which were studied by J. M. Tinbergen (1981). On setting out from the nest these birds had to aim either close to the colony, where they could easily find leatherjacket grubs, or much further away, where they could less easily find much more palatable caterpillars. On the whole they preferred to go for the higher-quality but difficult-to-get caterpillars, unless their large brood was very hungry, when they more often brought back the easy-to-get but less desirable leatherjackets. For either type of prey individual birds had to select a 'macro-patch', this is, a general region to fly to to begin searching, and also a 'micro-patch' – not looking for too long on one particular leaf, for instance, before moving on to the next. A final decision, which also might be determined to some extent by trial and error, is how much food to collect before flying back to the nest. This sort of psychological problem as set to individuals of a particular species by its behavioural ecology, is a very active area of current research, and even the briefest examination of it emphasizes how much room is left for learning from experience in behaviours that at first sight look largely instinctive (Boice, 1984; Fragaszy and Mason 1983; Leger *et al.* 1983). Lea (1981, 1984a) has gone so far as to suggest that learning as a process is a device evolved by animals as an aid to their foraging activities.

Ideas versus reflexes and explanations versus descriptions

The current emphasis in naturalistic and evolutionary analyses of animal learning may be in terms of decision-making, information-processing, and cognition, but this has not always been so. Darwin and his collaborator Romanes (1883, 1886) tended to get carried away by anecdotal evidence for very highly intelligent behaviour in parrots, sheepdogs and farm animals, and the desire for a sounder scientific base for theories of learning in animals prompted Morgan (1894) to propose what is now known as 'Lloyd Morgan's canon': 'In no case may we interpret an action as the outcome of the exercise of a higher psychical faculty, if it can be interpreted as the exercise of one which stands lower on the psychological scale'. This implies a rule of always choosing the simplest possible explanation – the scientific law of parsimony – which has much to recommend it. There is a problem, however, in defining simplicity, and in deciding exactly what range of evidence must be included under any particular explanation – the universal application of Lloyd Morgan's canon does not solve all theoretical issues. Interest in the phenomena of learning, both human and animal, has been closely connected with a running argument about the level of explanation to be applied to the phenomena, which cuts across the nature/nurture issue, and which is not over yet.

The course of the argument has gone roughly like this: at the turn of the century Pavlov in Russia and Thorndike in America were independently trying to establish a rigorous and scientific approach to learning, which would make use of laboratory experiments with animals, but which could also be widely applied to human behaviour, particularly in the psychology of education and in the treatment of mental illness. Shortly afterwards J. B. Watson formally proposed that the study of learning and conditioning and indeed the rest of psychology as well (which he took to be largely determined by learning and conditioning), should embrace the programme of behaviourism, and thus become 'a purely objective experimental branch of natural science' (Watson, 1914/1967, p. 1). In all these developments, the emphasis was on what could be directly and quantitatively *measured*, with explanations for the measurements kept as parsimonious as possible, and therefore differing as little as possible from the measurements themselves. Thus theories were couched in terms of conditioned reflexes, physiological processes closely tied to reflexes, and simple habits, or stimulus-response connections (stimuli and responses both being directly observable: see Boakes 1984: *From Darwin to Behaviourism*). A considerable amount of progress was made in finding experimental techniques to test such theories, and the mathematical principles of behaviour put forward by Hull (1943, 1952) were extremely influential in their day. However, the behaviourist and stimulus-response approach has fairly obvious limitations, especially, but not only, as applied to human learning. In particular, the theoretical issues associated with attention, perception and memory were largely ignored by Hull. In terms of the Darwinian and evolutionary explanation of animal psychology, the extreme empiricism of behaviourism meant that all species of animal were taken to be equal as collections of spinal reflexes. Differences between species were therefore ignored, or denied as a matter of principle, and thus the role of learning processes in the natural life of a species was not often considered. Even for the experimental evidence from a single domesticated species – the laboratory rat – the strictly stimulus-response theorists were vunerable to criticism, and the work of Tolman (1932, 1959), probed at these weak points.

Tolman himself advocated a 'purposive behaviourism', which sounds like a contradiction in terms. What he did in practice was to seek soundly based experimental evidence for explanations of animal learning which invoke inner and unobservable psychological processes, such as the mental inspection of 'cognitive maps' and the formation of 'expectancies' as to future events (Tolman, 1948). By and large, the study of animal learning after about 1970 follows either Tolman or Darwin, or both. Laboratory research on domesticated species seeks to support theoretical models of animal learning which presume that internal representation of outer events are encoded, sorted, retrieved and rehearsed in the animal's memory (Hulse *et al.*, 1978; Spear and Miller, 1981;

Roitblat *et al.*, 1984), while more naturalistic studies attempt to relate the cognitive capacities and proclivities of a given species to the behavioural ecology of its conditions of life – a thoroughly Darwinian enterprise.

Human and animal learning

Both the emphasis on cognition and the emphasis on the specializations of particular species bring up the question of the relation between human and animal learning. Few apart from Hume (1777/1970), Hull (1943, 1952) and Skinner (1953, 1972) have ever proposed that the relation should be one of identity. If nothing else, the ordinary human use of spoken language means that the content of what a person is potentially able to learn has little in common with the content of what is learned in any other species' natural life, or in the most carefully contrived animal experiment. Most modern learning theorists would therefore accept that the acquisition of knowledge by human individuals must differ in some very striking ways from the learning processes available to any sub-human species. There are, however, a number of reasons why questions about animal learning should continue to be asked.

1 The evolution of learning

Many of us will remain interested in the abilities of other species, whether or not these abilities are of importance in the context of a specifically human psychology. But, on the basis of Darwinian evolution, it seems reasonable to assume that specifically human abilities are *not* entirely unrelated to those of our animal relatives, and of course there are many aspects of human behaviour that are by no means specifically human. When we are pricked we bleed, when we are hungry we want food, and when we are angry we are aggressive – in talking or thinking about these events we may enter into the realms of exclusively human cognition, but the processes which bring them about are not always so rarefied. Arguably, to fully understand human learning, if that is our goal, we must know exactly how and to what extent it differs from animal learning, and we must therefore examine animal learning as well.

2 Animal cognition

If it were true that, on the one hand, all animal behaviour was controlled like simple clockwork, and, on the other, that all human behaviour was controlled by biologically unique reasoning processes, then, although we would still want to know how the reasoning evolved from the clockwork, in practice there would be no overlap between human and animal psychology. However, from Freud to modern cognitive science (e.g. Johnson-Laird, 1983; Sulloway, 1979) there is agreement that the rationality of men and women is frail and suspect, and that various quite unconscious motivations and methods of inference underlie some of our simplest subjective impressions of reason. More recently, theories of animal learning have stressed that processes more complex than clockwork-like stimulus-response connections are implied by the results of laboratory experiments, and by natural patterns of foraging (Mackintosh, 1974, 1983; Dickinson, 1980; Hulse *et al.*, 1978; Spear and Miller, 1981; Griffin, 1984; Walker, 1983a; Kamil and Sargent, 1981; Roitblat *et al.* 1984). In particular, basic aspects of the perception, identification and recognition of objects, and coding, storage and retrieval of remembered events, are studied in animal experiments (see chapters 8 and 9). This strengthens considerably the argument above, that some of the elements of human cognitive abilities must be understood with reference to the much more general evolution of methods of information processing in animal species, some of which may be very widespread. The complete panoply of human psychology did not arise in splendid isolation from the biological world. Some parts of it undoubtedly did, and therefore the gains from the study of the basics may be rather fewer in psychology than they are in biochemistry and genetics, but there are many points of contact between theories of human and animal learning.

3   The importance of learning in human psychology

One of the main ways in which human learning differs from
animal learning is that there is simply more of it. Even
without taking the extreme empiricist view that everyone's
mind can be considered to be completely blank at birth,
waiting to be filled in with all the details of individual personality and temperament, as well as those of vocabulary, social
knowledge and higher education, it has always been obvious
that upbringing, training and apprenticeship and the informal
explorations of everyday life are aspects of personal experience
that mould and shape character and skill. Plato, who we
began with as the best example of someone who does not
believe in the theoretical basis of learning from experience,
was second to none in emphasizing the practical realities of
learning in upbringing and training. His recommendations
for a properly organized form of human society, in the
Republic, are usually criticized precisely because of the
extremes which Plato appeared to be willing to go to in order
to regulate individual experience. The recommendations
begin, for instance, with the necessity of abolishing all then-
current Greek myths and nursery rhymes, as told to children
by their nurses and mothers, and the issuing of specially
fabricated approved versions. Since the Greek myths, of which
the Oedipus legend is a fairly run-of-the-mill example, seem
frequently to involve violence and/or sex between parent and
child, of an explicitness well up to modern video-nasty standards, one can perhaps be sympathetic to this particular kind
of censorship, but Plato intended to be far more thorough-
going, since all literature and poetry, for all ages, was to be
inspected and bowdlerized, the originals being retained for
inspection by the rich on payment of a stiff fee. The same
was to apply to children's games, and all drama, painting and
music, since exposure to any of these could affect character
development. For instance, novel fashions in music would be
banned by Plato as dangerous to the whole fabric of society.
On a more positive note, high-minded civil servants would
have their noblest sentiments schooled by habit, since their
environment was to be carefully controlled from birth. They
were to be given rigorous physical training in late adolescence,

and a through academic education between the ages of 20 and 35, practical experience of life being gained between 35 and 50, at which age the best of them might be fit to divide their time between further study and high-level administration. As this suggests, the ancient Athenians were fanatical about education, physical training, and the practising of music and crafts of all kinds. The rare scepticism of the *Meno* (suggesting that there are some things which are inborn and which cannot be taught), which this chapter began with, was argued partly on the basis of Socrates' surprise and disappointment in the face of the fact that several famous and successful Greek leaders had had sons who had turned into bad characters, against the best intentions of their fathers. It is of course not very difficult to think of empiricist reasons as to why this might happen: in Plato's *Republic* the problem is solved at a stroke by the abolition of normal family life for the ruling classes.

Thus, although it is possible to find theorists who claim that, in principle, important aspects of human psychology are inborn and innate (with the linguist Chomsky (1957, 1980) being the modern equivalent of Plato in this respect), absolutely no one can deny that, in practice, culture, schooling, relations with parents and peers and, indeed, exposure to nursery rhymes and legends, or, in modern times, the impact of videos, advertising, and the myths of the media, are all the stuff and substance of real-life human psychology. And all involve the notion of learning, and the acquisition by the individual of knowledge from the environment. Therefore an adequate theory of learning should provide a scientific basis for empiricism, that is, it should help explain how human culture is biologically possible. The biological side of this will involve animal learning for the reasons given in the preceding two sections. In addition to these, a reason for animal experimentation is that it allows for the investigation of the effects of motivationally significant events on learning processes. Subjects in experiments on human cognition may vary in their interest, arousal and commitment, but rarely does their performance in the experiment represent a goal of an emotional intensity which is equivalent to that of even everyday interactions involving personal social interactions or personal life ambitions. By contrast, in experiments on animal learning such as those which will occupy most of the pages of the remaining chapters in this book, the experimenter is free to manipulate an animal's hunger or level of physical discomfort in ways which would be completely unacceptable if the subjects were people.[1]

Note

1 Voices are now often raised with the claim that anything unacceptable in the treatment of a person should be equally unacceptable in the treatment of any other species – striking examples, in their way, of belief in the relation of identity between human and animal psychology. A more considered view is usually taken by psychologists with specialized knowledge of the subject, and an example can be found in a report by a working party set up by the British Psychological Society (1979). Anyone conducting research with animals in English-speaking countries has both a moral and a legal responsibility to keep the animals involved in appropriate conditions and to minimize suffering and discomfort.

[handwritten notes:] Extensive disc of Plato Locke Hume etc. unusual in a learn text – perhaps overlong

Nice discussion of foragers & learn/instinct relation.

2 Habituation, sensitization and stimulus learning

'Habituation is an instance of the living system's power of establishing a conservative equilibrium to change of external conditions.'

The Nature of Learning (Humphrey, 1933, p. 133)

The phenomena of habituation should make an appropriate beginning for the experimental study of the learning process, since in many ways they are the simplest. However, the main lesson to be learned from the study of habituation – and this makes it an even more appropriate subject to start with – is that habituation is almost never as simple as it first seems.

Initial simplicity can be achieved by defining habituation as the reduction of response to a repeated stimulus (Humphrey, 1933; Harris, 1943; Thorpe, 1963; Hinde, 1970). Humphrey's experimental example was obtained by using a snail, crawling on a board. An electrical attachment meant that the board could be given a standardized jerk at regular intervals, usually of 2 seconds. At the first such jerk, a snail would usually draw in its horns, but as the jerks were repeated, the extent of the withdrawal would gradually decrease, until the snail crawled around without appearing to notice the movements of its wooden platform. A sudden increase in the intensity of the jerks might then bring back the withdrawal response, but with extended experience some animals became indifferent to all mechanical vibration, and were unperturbed by violent banging (Humphrey, 1933). This can serve as a paradigm for research into habituation, since a great deal of modern experimentation is performed on similar responses in another gastropod mollusc, the giant sea slug.

Habituation as a form of learning

Humphrey supposed that habituation was important as an example of learning – that is, being influenced by information received from the outside world – in the sense that his snail was learning not to respond to a stimulus that was not worth responding to, but there are difficulties in assuming that habituation is always a form of learning. There is often a close relation between the waning of response to repeated stimulation and fatigue – Sherrington (1906) referred to the fading of reflexes in spinal preparations as 'reflex fatigue', and one would wish to distinguish physical exhaustion, even of some temporary kind, from the retention of behavioural information. Thus although Thorpe (1963), Hinde (1970) and Gray (1975) have full discussions of habituation as a form of learning, in Hull (1943) and Mackintosh (1974), it is ignored. As far as the snail is concerned, any learning, even so far as it is distinguished from reflex fatigue, is clearly of a rather limited kind. The progress of learning is assessed by the absence of an in-built response, so there is no question of the organism learning any new motor organization, or dramatically increasing the frequency of certain motor performances, as happens in instrumental learning (see chapter 5; similarly, since the result of experience is that the animal ceases to respond to a stimulus which did elicit responding to start with, there is no increase in the range of stimuli responded to, as happens in the acquisition phase of classical conditioning: see chapter 3).

But suppose that a 5–month-old infant is shown a photograph of a particular human face, for 10 seconds, six times, and loses interest in it, but perks up when a different face is presented (Miranda and Fanz, 1974; Cornell, 1974) – surely the decline in response to the first face could be classed as habituation, according to our definition, and surely there is no doubt that external information about the visual pattern of the photograph has in some way been retained? For this reason alone, it would be unwise to exclude habituation from consideration as a form of learning. In addition, changes in responsiveness to repeated stimuli are often involved in the training procedures of operant and classical conditioning which are taken as the standard laboratory paradigms for learning.

Alternative mechanisms of habituation

Habituation, defined as the phenomenon of reduced response to repeated stimulation, can, according to Thorpe's review (1963), be found in flatworms and sea-anemones as well as snails and slugs. When comparing these results to those obtained with mammals, the first reaction must be agreement with Hinde's conclusion that descriptively similar phenomena 'may depend on mechanisms differing greatly in complexity' (Hinde, 1970, p. 579). This is amply confirmed by considering the two extremely different kinds of research and theory which are often conjoined in discussions of habituation (e.g. Tighe and Leaton, 1976; Peeke and Petrinovitch, 1984). The first theory (Groves and Thompson, 1970; Thompson and Spencer, 1966) is concerned to predict reactions obtained from isolated spinal cords; while the second (Sokolov, 1963, 1975) is based on experiments performed on normal human subjects. It is hardly surprising that these theories differ – but unfortunately there has been a tendency to see the theories as competitors, so that for instance Thon and Pauzie (1984) suggest that Sokolov's theory is wrong because it fails to explain some results obtained with the habituation of the cardiac response of the blowfly, while Thompson and Glanzman (1976) say that perhaps Sokolov's hypotheses can be interpreted as a special case of the spinal cord model. One of my themes in this and subsequent chapters will be support for the view, put forward by Thorpe (1963) and Hinde (1970) among others, that behavioural phenomena in different species, which may comply with the same descriptive definition, and possibly serve similar biological purposes, in the various species, may nevertheless be based on very different physiological and psychological mechanisms. As Tighe and Leaton (1976) emphasize in their comparison of habituation in human infants and simple animal models, this means that although there may be areas of behavioural similarity, if one looks for them it is easy enough to find ways in which one species may differ from another – for instance, a human infant will be sensitive to photographs of faces in ways that are neither desirable nor possible for a snail.

Before examining the claims of the two different theories (Groves and Thompson, 1970; Sokolov, 1963, 1975), consider certain obvious possible results of exposure to a repeated stimulus.

Results of exposure to stimuli

(i) Sensory fatigue

It is conceivable, though not very likely, that the snail's sense organs for detecting vibration become less sensitive with repeated use during a short time interval. When sniffing for the bouquet of a glass of wine, one should rely on the first few sniffs for this reason, and various tactile and other sense organs may respond mainly to changes in stimulation over time. Usually, response decrements which are attributable to this sort of sensory adaptation are not said to be habituation (Harris, 1943; Hinde, 1970). To show that sensory adaptation is *not* responsible for a reduced response, a number of tests can be made. For instance, the response decline may be shown to survive a change in sense organ – Dethier (1963) showed that reduced response in blowflies to a certain sugar solution detected by receptors on the left leg was retained when the solution was detected by the right leg.

(ii) Response fatigue

Similarly, fatigue in muscle systems could obviously cause reduced response to a repeated stimulus, without qualifying as a process of learning, and response fatigue is often distinguished from habituation. The experimental test to demonstrate that response fatigue is not responsible for a decline in response involves changing the stimulus – if a stronger (or in some cases just a weaker or different) stimulus brings back the response, then simple response fatigue cannot have been the cause of the response decline (Humphrey, 1930, 1933). This is called 'dishabituation'. Often giving a new stimulus will not only bring back response to the new stimulus, but will also mean that responses will start to be given again to the old stimulus. Thus Humphrey's snails, having habituated to a gentle jerk, would draw in their horns for a large bang, and also go back to drawing in their horns for the next few gentle jerks.

(iii) Habituation in the S-R connection

This is the standard kind of habituation in the 'synaptic theories of habituation' discussed by Groves and Thompson (1970). The idea is that a change is taking place not in the sensory input or in the motor output devices, as in (i) and (ii) above, but in the connection between the two. It is thus sometimes said to be more 'central' than the changes in the sensory and motor periphery. However, within the dissected out ganglia of the sea-slug, or the dissected out spinal cord of the frog, it has been possible to locate the S-R habituation process in individual synapses. In discussing both habituation and dishabituation of the gill withdrawal reflex of *Aplysia*, Castellucci and Kandel (1976) reported, 'These mechanisms share a common locus, the presynaptic terminals of the central neurons projecting on their central target cells. Habituation involves a homosynaptic depression of the terminal due to repeated activity of the sensory neurons' (p. 31). By recording the electrical activity in single neurons of the spinal cord taken from a frog and maintained in an oxygenated solution, Thompson and Glanzman (1976) discovered that 'this simplified monosynaptic system in the isolated frog spinal cord exhibits retention or "memory" of habituation, the critical parameter distinguishing habituation as a simple form of behavioural plasticity of learning from neuronal refractory phenomena' (p. 72). It is clear therefore that synapses between individual sensory and motor neurons can habituate, and it is likely that this mechanism controls a substantial fraction of the habituation seen in the total behavioural repertoire of sea-slugs. It does *not* therefore follow that this mechanism is the only one available to explain all reductions in response to repeated stimulation in all other animal species.

So neuronal habit not in all animals.

(iv) Sensitized states affecting the S-R connection

It is a matter of empirical fact that repeated stimulation sometimes has an effect which is the opposite of habituation – there is some kind of warm-up or sensitizing process so that later stimuli produce a bigger response than earlier ones. In Groves and Thompson's theory, it was proposed that sensitizing synapses were anatomically distinct from the S-R pathway, thus comprising an external state, whose increasing arousal with repeated stimulation would facilitate the S-R connection, and thus have behavioural effects in the opposite direction to the habituating synapses mentioned above (1970, pp. 433–4).

(v) Familiarity via formation of a memory of the stimulus

This brings the problems of perception and memory into theories of habituation, which is appropriate in discussing the reactions given to novel or familiar stimuli by intact mammals. The main theory is due to Sokolov (1963, 1975), who works in the Pavlovian tradition, and therefore usually uses the phrase 'extinction of the orienting reflex' to describe habituation, a practice which I shall not follow here. Another phrase of Sokolov's, which it is customary to retain, is 'the formation of a neuronal model of the stimulus' to describe the processes of categorization and memory which result from repeated experiences of an external event. The essentials of Sokolov's theory are given in Figure 2.1. The function of the neuronal model is to distinguish novel from familiar stimuli, and also unexpected and surprising from expected and therefore insignificant events (this being an extra function, since familiar or well-known stimuli may be surprising if they occur at an unexpected time or place). It is supposed in Sokolov's theory that there is an active process of comparison between an incoming stimulus and the established neuronal model: if

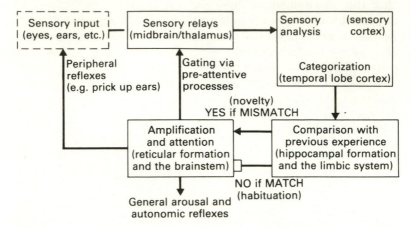

Figure 2.1   *Sokolov's theory of habituation.* After Sokolov (1963, 1975).

there is a match between the two, the incoming stimulus can be ignored.

(vi) Decreased attention to familiar stimuli

Given a comparator mechanism, any response orginally given to a stimulus, such as the drawing-in of a snail's horns, may be suspended when the stimulus has become familiar and matches expectations. However, in Sokolov's theory, emphasis is given to physiological reactions, measurable in human subjects, which are correlated to some degree with the attention and arousal generated by incoming stimuli. Such responses are selected partly for convenience, and partly because they appear to be useful indicators of stimulus novelty. They include, understandably, the turning of the head and eyes towards the source of a localized stimulus, and the desynchronization of the electroencephalograph (EEG) which is known to occur with subjective attention to external stimuli in normal human adults. Slightly less obviously, responses which are in practice correlated with stimulus novelty include dilation of blood vessels in the head, and the

'galvanic skin response' or 'GSR', which is a drop in the
electrical resistance of the skin, usually measured in the hand.
In the theory, these signs are taken to be indications of the
activity of the amplifying systems in Figure 2.1. For our
purposes it is convenient to refer to this as concerning attention – in intact vertebrates, and especially in birds and
mammals (Mackintosh, 1975) we assume that there is some
degree of gating for incoming stimuli, so that insignificant,
and habituated, stimuli are not processed in the same way as
novel or important ones (see chapter 8). Clearly this involves
multi-stage and hierarchically organized perceptual systems,
and we would not wish to invoke attention of this kind when
discussing the synapses or an individual neuron in the frog
spinal cord or in the abdominal ganglia of *Aplysia*, in (iii)
above. In mammals there is ample evidence that the anatomical basis of attention includes the reticular activating system
of the brain (Sokolov, 1963).

(vii) Increased capacities for discrimination and classification

Especially in the short term, increased familiarity with stimuli
means that they are ignored. However, exposure to the
stimulus in the first instance will have elicited increased attention to it, and according to (v) above, familiarity with a
stimulus implies that the perceiver possesses a neuronal
model, or memory of it, that 'registers not only the elementary, but also the complex properties of the signal' which
include temporal relationships (Sokolov, 1975, p. 218). Thus,
if an already familiar stimulus acquires new significance – for
instance, by a change in context, or by changes in internal
or external motivational factors – the existence of a pre-
formed neuronal model may improve perceptual performance.
This sort of effect was assumed in the theory of Hebb (1949)
and confirmed in the experiment of Gibson and Walk (1956),
in which rats reared in cages with bas-reliefs of circles and
triangles on the walls were able later to distinguish circles
from triangles in an experimental task which was failed by
others without this previous experience. This is called perceptual learning, or exposure learning (Hall, 1980; Bateson,

1973). Over shorter time intervals something similar may be called 'within-event learning' (Rescorla and Durlach, 1981), or 'latent learning' (Tolman, 1948). The point, perhaps, is that the biological function of sense organs and the perceptual apparatus of the nervous system is not to enable animals to become indifferent to events thereby perceived, it is to acquire useful information about the outside world. Habituation is in one sense a secondary phenomenon, in that it represents a lessening of response to consistent stimulation; making the appropriate response to a novel stimulus in the first place, and storing representations of familiar perceptions, are an at least equally important aspect of exposure to stimuli.

Habituation and sensitization in the spinal cord

Thompson and Spencer proposed in an influential theoretical paper in 1966 that the hindlimb flexion reflex of the acute spinal cat should be used 'as a model system for analysis of the neuronal mechanisms involved in habituation and sensitization'. Following on from the pioneering studies of Sherrington (1906) on spinal reflexes, the recommended object of study was the twitching of a muscle in the hindlimb of a decerebrate cat with a complete transection of the spinal cord at the 12th thoracic vertebra, in response to electric shocks delivered to the skin of the limb every 10 seconds. As no neural information could pass from the hindleg to the brain, and the cerebral hemispheres had in any case been removed in this preparation, it was possible to claim with confidence that any behavioural changes which took place were due to neuronal mechanisms in the spinal cord itself, and Thompson and Spencer provided a useful list of phenomena which they observed under these conditions.

(1) 'Given that a particular stimulus elicits a response, repeated applications of the stimulus result in decreased response.' This is of course the basic phenomenon of interest although by itself it is indistinguishable from stimulus or response fatigue.

(2) 'If the stimulus is withheld, the response tends to recover over time (spontaneous recovery).' This is more problem-

atical than it looks, since recovery time may vary from seconds to weeks. It is likely that different mechanisms are involved in habituation which lasts for seconds on the one hand and days or more on the other (e.g. Castellucci and Kandel, 1976).

(3) 'If repeated series of habituation training and spontaneous recovery are given, habituation becomes successively more rapid.' This also suggests a difference between short-term and long-term mechanisms.

(4) 'Other things being equal, the more rapid the frequency of stimulation, the more rapid and/or pronounced is habituation.'

(5) 'The weaker the stimulus, the more rapid and/or pronounced is habituation. Strong stimuli may yield no significant habituation.' This is why, in Sokolov's terms, habituation is confined to orienting responses – stronger stimuli giving rise to adaptive or defensive reflexes which do not habituate. Thus an animal may not habituate to the taste of its most valuable food, or the presence of its most dangerous predator.

(6) 'The effects of habituation training may proceed beyond the zero or asymptotic response level' This means that after an animal has stopped responding altogether, continued exposure to the stimulus will mean that when the series is ended, recovery of the response will be delayed.

(7) 'Habituation of response to a given stimulus exhibits stimulus generalization to other stimuli' (see chapter 8 for discussion of generalization).

(8) 'Presentation of another (usually strong) stimulus results in recovery of the habituation response (dishabituation).' This differentiates habituation proper from purely physical fatigue. For Sokolov, it provides evidence for the richness of the neuronal model, since slight changes in a complex stimulus may lead to dishabituation. This has also proved to be a convenient method for assessing the perceptual abilities of pre-verbal human infants (Olson, 1976).

(9) 'Upon repeated application of the dishabituatory stimulus, the amount of dishabituation produced habitu-

ates.' That is, the organism habituates to the dishabituatory stimulus as well.
(All the above points from Thompson and Spencer, 1966,
pp. 18–19.)

Having found all these phenomena mediated by the spinal
cord, Thompson and Spencer proposed that the lowering of
responsiveness in habituation was caused by one kind of
synaptic change, and that rapid dishabituation was caused by
a separate synaptic process of sensitization, which increases
responsiveness more generally (see (iv) above, p. 39) Groves
and Thompson (1970) went on to elaborate this 'dual process
theory' in a version which continues to receive support (Peeke,
1983; Thon and Pauzie, 1984; Peeke and Petrinovich, 1984).
The two processes are simply the decrememental one identified with habituation, and the incremental one identified
with sensitization, which are presumed to be to some extent
anatomically independent in the nervous system.

Application of the dual process theory to the startle response of the rat

Although the dual process theory of Groves and Thompson
(1970) arose from results obtained in spinal cats, in which
the sensitization process was prominent, it was applied with
some success to an experimental technique commonly used
with ordinary laboratory rats. In this the rat is placed in a
test chamber which allows for the measurement of overall
activity (for instance, by transducers which pick up forces
transmitted to the floor of the chamber) and a series of loud
tones is sounded. The first few of these induce a distinctive
jump from the animal, which gradually wanes in intensity as
the series proceeds. This is a standard form of habituation
(see point (1), page 42) but numerous other phenomena can
be observed, and the effects of ageing, drug treatment and so
on can be assessed. A most interesting result was obtained
by Davis and Wagner (1969) and termed the 'incremental
stimulus intensity effect' (see Figure 2.2). In their experiment
rats were divided into four groups matched for initial strength
of the startle response, and then given a session in which 750

tones were presented, 8 seconds apart. For one group, all the tones were 120 dB (which is very loud indeed) but over the session there was slow but steady habituation. Another group received tones of 100 dB, and this group showed a much larger reduction in the response to these, but, at the end of the session, when all groups were tested with 120 dB tones, as might be expected this group showed dishabituation (see point 8, page 43). A third group (labelled 'gradual' in Figure 2.2.) started off with 83 dB tones, and the loudness was increased in 2.5 dB steps after every 50 tones, the intensity thus ending up at 118 dB. The striking result was that not only did this gradual group show a low level of startle responses thoughout the session, but that this low level was retained to the end, even with the final test using a 120 dB tone. Thus the gradually increasing series appeared to have produced more effective habituation to 120 dB tones than continuous exposure to the 120 dB tones themselves. Clearly this would not follow directly from the 'neuronal model of the stimulus theory' of Sokolov (1963, 1975; see point (v), p. 39 above). It would be possible to claim that the fact of the gradual increase was itself incorporated into expectations of the animals, especially since a control group which received all the same stimuli as the gradual group but in a randomized order, gave very different results (this group is not shown on Figure 2.2, but the results for it were very similar to those for the 'constant 100' group).

However, since, as Figure 2.2. shows, Groves and Thompson were able to obtain roughly analogous results with the hindlimb flexion reflex of the spinal cat, it seems plausible that, as they suggest, an interaction between a sensitizing and an habituating process brought about the low level of responsiveness in the gradual group. Other results (e.g. Davis, 1972) support the idea that 100 or 120 dB tones, when presented repeatedly, have a generally arousing effect. The argument is along the lines that the gradually increasing intensity allows for very pronounced habituation at low intensities, before the sensitizing effects of the 100 dB and above tones make themselves felt, and that the systematic ordering of the increases allows for the maximum generalization of habituation.

(a)

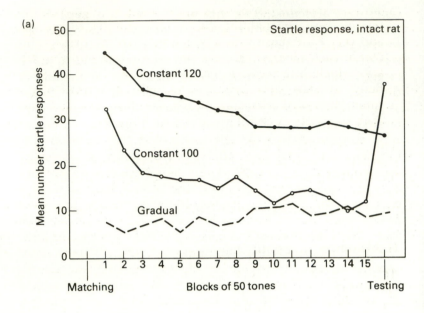

(b)

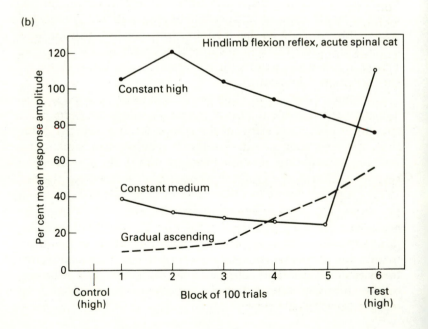

The incremental series of stimuli results in pronounced relative response habituation at low stimulus intensities, and very little sensitization which may decay considerably within each block of trials. Both habituation and sensitization (including decay of sensitization) generalize substantially to each new series of stimuli. The result is a summation of the habituation occurring within all blocks of trials. (Groves and Thompson, 1970, p. 442)

This is less than wholly convincing as a theory, but it is instructive that such complicated results can be obtained with the habituation of a spinal reflex. That this is so does not, however, require us to suppose that all other perceptual processes operate like spinal reflexes in intact animals.

Habituation in a giant sea-slug

Aplysia californica is a foot-long slug that grazes on seaweed and weighs several pounds (its English relatives are only a fraction of the size). Its popularity with experimental physiologists is due to the fact that its nerve cells are gigantic, some up to 1 mm across, and relatively few in number. The behavioural responses of its mantle-shelf, which contains gills and a siphon, are controlled by the abdominal ganglion which contains only about 2,000 neurons, several of which can be individually identified in every animal. This makes it an excellent subject for the plotting-out of which nerve cell does what, and the examination of how the electrical characteristics of neurons change as a function of experience (Kandel, 1976; Castellucci and Kandel, 1976). However, I do not think

Figure 2.2   *Habituation to gradual increases in (a) a rat and (b) a spinal cord.*
At a test with a stimulus of high intensity, on the far right of the figures, strength of response is least if the test has been preceded by a series of gradual increases in intensity, by comparison with a series of exactly similiar stimuli, or a series of medium intensity. This result has been obtained for (a) the startle reflex in rats and (b) for the spinal reflex of bending the leg in response to an electrical shock to its skin. After Groves and Thompson (1970).

I am alone in suspecting that its proponents may be over-rating its suitability for experiments on higher cognitive processes.

If *Aplysia californica* is kept in a tank of cooled and aerated seawater, its gill and siphon will normally be extended, but if various areas on the top of the animal, in its 'mantle-shelf' where these extensibles are located, are poked or brushed, or stimulated with a strong jet of water, the gill and siphon are temporarily withdrawn. This allows the performance of experiments on habituation of exactly the same kind as that of Humphrey (1930) on a terrestrial snail withdrawing its horns. Kandel (1976) and Castellucci and Kandel (1976) reviewed experiments on habituation in *Aplysia*. Pinsker *et al.* (1970) reported rapid habituation of the gill-withdrawal reflex over the first 10 elicitations by a jet of seawater, separated by 3–minute intervals. The reflex recovered after a rest of two hours, but could also be brought back without this long rest if a long and strong tactile stimulus was applied to the neck region. In that report Pinkser *et al.* note that six of Thompson and Spencer's nine characteristics of habituation (listed above, pp. 42–4) had been obtained in *Aplysia*, but that three others were absent: greater habituation with repeated periods of habituation and recovery(3); generalization of habituation to a stimulus in another part of the receptive field (7); and delayed recovery of the response when the habituation series is continued after the animal has stopped responding (6). Given the very specific nature of the neural circuits involved, and the limited body area which produces *Aplysia*'s withdrawal reflex, it seems inevitable that generalization will be limited: the other two missing characteristics suggest that habituation in *Aplysia* is only a short-term phenomenon, and does not include the longer-term mechanisms that obtain in even the spinal cords of vertebrates. However, Carew *et al.* (1972) and Carew and Kandel (1973) demonstrated that, with shorter inter-trial intervals, repeated periods of habituation and recovery do indeed produce faster habituation in the later blocks, in *Aplysia*, and that after this habituation is still very fast 24 hours later. Thus an appreciable range of behavioural phenomena characteristic of habituation is obtainable in *Aplysia*, and the essential features can be observed even when the abdominal ganglion is dissected out from the animal for greater ease of electrical recording.

It is almost tautologous that, if response output to a stimulus input is changing, then there must be changes in the activity of synapses between sensory and motor neurons, but it is of great scientific interest to observe the actual decrements in the excitatory post-synaptic potentials (EPSPs) in the motor neuron, and to discover that this arises because the pre-synaptic terminals of the sensory neuron release progressively less of their normal neurotransmitter substances, when the sensory neuron is repeatedly stimulated. It appears, then, that in *Aplysia*, synaptic habituation is a change in the sensory nerve – it is not that the motor nerve becomes less able to respond. Also, when there is dishabituation, or sensitization, this is because the synaptic activity of the sensory nerve is facilitated (Castellucci and Kandel, 1976, pp. 30–2).

There is no doubt that these are very important discoveries, and that *Aplysia californica*, and researchers dedicated to its use, may make further contributions of fundamental importance to the understanding of the neural basis of learning. But there are two notes of caution that need to be sounded. One is that there are general differences between invertebrate and vertebrate neurons, and therefore results obtained with *Aplysia* may not be completely representative of all animal synapses. (One difference is that invertebrate neurons are almost all unipolar, that is they do not have separate input and output lines, and therefore do not really have any dendrites: Bullock, 1974.) This is probably not so important in terms of psychological analysis as the fact that mechanisms of synaptic change, while being of the utmost interest physiologically, are simply on too small a scale to be of direct relevance in explaining the phenomena of perception, learning and memory in higher vertebrates or in any other animal (such as the distant relatives of *Aplysia*, the octopus and the squid) where the behavioural phenomena involve the activity of a whole brain with millions of neurons, rather than a small and very specialized circuit involving only dozens.

On these grounds we may wish to disagree with Castellucci and Kandel (1976, p. 43) when they say that investigations of the gill-withdrawal reflex 'could also be brought to bear on the analysis of several forms of complex learning'. Kandel (1976) went so far as to present a figure in which the top half is the reduction of a sea-slug's gill withdrawal reflex during five successive days of training, and the bottom half is the reduction in errors made by a human subject over five days of practice at the task of depressing a Morse key for exactly 0.7 seconds. Since in both cases scores reduce as the days go by, but tend to start off rather high at the beginning of a day's session, there are superficial similarities between the human and the slug data. But, with due respect to the value of physiological research, it is a form of behaviourist fallacy to believe that such similarities mean anything profound, or that because *Aplysia*'s habituation takes this form 'Studies along these lines could specify how long term memory is established and how it relates to the short term process' (Kandel, 1976).

Habituation in human infants and adults

John Locke (1689/1982) shared the view that the learning abilities of molluscs were in a fundamental sense equivalent to those of the human species, but suggested that the factor of perceptual complexity ought to be considered as supplying a measure of difference between mollusc and man (his examples were cockles and oysters – see p. 8 above). No evidence obtained in the last three centuries, concerning either snails and slugs or human subjects, suggests that Locke was wrong in this respect. One of the main reasons why theories of habituation based on experiments with human subjects incorporate a relatively elaborate form of stimulus memory, such as Sokolov's 'neuronal model', is that such experiments reveal a high degree of perceptual exactness. The typical form for these experiments is that a subject sits or lies quietly while a stimulus such as a tone of a certain pitch, loudness and duration is presented at regular intervals. Certain responses correlated with attention are measured, for instance the electroencephalogram or skin resistance (see p. 40 above), and these show a gradual decline over 10 to 20 presentations, after which the measurements give no sign that the subject has detected the stimulus. That the stimulus is indeed being detected, even if 'pre-attentively' (e.g. Deutsch and Deutsch, 1963) can be quickly shown by altering it. Even a very slight change in pitch, loudness (either up or down), or duration leads to an immediate recovery of the attentive responses, and in fact the thresholds of perceptual exactness obtained by this method are often lower than when a much more active process of recognition is required of the subjects (Sokolov, 1963; Gray, 1975).

Stimulus representation and the missing stimulus effect

It is because very small changes in the stimulus can be picked up in this way that it is necessary to assume that the internal representation or memory of the stimulus is relatively complete as to all perceivable details. This would appear to include not only the physical characteristics of the stimulus, such as pitch in the case of a tone, but also the context and in particular the temporal sequence in which stimuli are given. If compound stimuli of, say tones and lights, usually occur, then missing out one of the elements of the compound will reinstate attentive responses and, generally speaking, the amount of attention engaged will be proportional to the amount of change in the parameters of the complex stimulus (Sokolov, 1975, p. 218). A very direct way of demonstrating the incorporation of time values into the representation of the stimulus is simply to miss out a stimulus occasionally in a normally regular sequence. This often brings back attentive responses at a high level (Sokolov, 1963). It is arguable that any theory which succeeds in explaining this result, even if it is simpler than Sokolov's own theory, will nevertheless have to include devices of roughly similar power – for instance Horn's (1967) theoretical sketch includes 'extrapolatory' and 'comparator' neurons (Gray, 1975, pp. 20–1). Thus the results of experiments on habituation require us to adopt a position which ought to be agreeable for other reasons – that perception of stimuli by human subjects involves pre-attentive comparisons with stored representations derived and extrapolated from previous experience.

Habituation in human infants

This has proved in the first place to be an extremely useful technique for assessing the infant's perceptual abilities, but the theory of habituation is also relevant to accounts of the gradual development of the infant's perceptual competence (Olson, 1976). The usefulness of the techniques arises because, by presenting a standard stimulus repeatedly followed by an altered version of it, the infant's perceptual sensitivity to that particular form of alteration can be assessed (Jeffrey and Cohen, 1971). As the theory of human habituation demands the assumption that exposure to stimuli results in the building up of stored representations of the stimuli, it supplies a starting point for a general empiricist account of how the empty mind of the newborn gradually fills with knowledge derived from the outside world. This should not be lightly disregarded, even though, as Olson (1976, pp. 24–6) observes, the development of memory in human infants must quickly become elaborated in at least three other ways:

> (a) an increasingly fine-grained repertoire of mental features or categories with which an experience can be represented; (b) an increasingly sophisticated repertoire of encoding and retrieval strategies, largely involving language, to aid in recovering memories; and (c) increasingly accurate knowledge about the nature of one's own memory system, which in turn yields a more realistic selection of strategies and tasks.

Habituation, exploration and curiosity in animals

Such measures of human psychophysiology as the galvanic skin response and vasoconstriction of the limbs bear only a putative relation to the efficiency of perception; while another aspect of the human 'orienting reflex', the turning of the head towards a localized stimulus, has a very obvious functional role. In animals the functional aspects of orienting responses are often obvious, since the ears as well as the eyes may scan the environment, and sniffing in mammals is usually an active process. Frequently the whole posture of an animal betrays the detection of a novel stimulus, and many species have well-defined routines of 'inspective' or 'inquisitive' exploratory behaviour (Berlyne, 1960; Hinde, 1970; Erlich, 1970; Menzel and Juno, 1985). In these, the initial reactions to a novel stimulus and contrasting indifference given to familiar objects, both suggest that the process of habituation involves the use of stored representations or 'neuronal models' of perceived events, rather than merely the depression of activity at certain synapses. There has in fact been an enormous amount of physiological work on mammals such as the rabbit and the rat, not least that performed by Sokolov and his co-workers (Sokolov and Vinogradova 1975) designed to pinpoint the interactions between the sensory cortex and the limbic system, most significantly the hippocampus, which are presumed to provide an overall system for attention, memory and habituation, with quite different cognitive capacities from those exhibited by the spinal cord (see Gray 1982, 1984; O'Keefe and Nadel, 1978). This work will not be reviewed here, but it is pertinent to mention at every opportunity that behavioural similarities in habituation observed across disparate animal species, do not imply that identical physical mechanisms are at work in all cases, or that the summary of the phenomena that suffices for the simplest cases is all that it necessary to understand and account for all the others.

Also, the involvement of the limbic system of the brain in the development of stimulus knowledge and memory suggests that, in addition to the dimension of the perceptual complexity of habituation in intact higher animals, it is also necessary to discuss the motivational significance of the reactions to novel and familiar stimuli. In one sense the importance of habituation is that it refers to a category of experiences which are independent of the imperatives of pain and need – habituation occurs in the experimental context without the addition of the usual 'motivationally significant events' (Dickinson, 1980) of desired food objects or unwanted discomfort. On the other hand, a great deal of behavioural evidence (Berlyne, 1960; Hinde, 1970) suggests that stimulus novelty and familiarity should be regarded as a motivational system of its own, even if not unrelated to choice in foraging, or to wariness and fear. To some extent all these must interact in natural patterns of behaviour, and the concept of neophobia in feeding responses has been useful in descriptions of a number of aspects of food choice, especially in rats (Cowan, 1976; Rozin and Kalat, 1971) but in other species as well. As a species, rats are conservative about their food and prefer to eat what they are already used to, unless they are either (a) very hungry indeed, or (b) in poor health – in both cases a change in diet is advisable (Rozin and Kalat, 1971). Curiosity about novel but clearly inedible objects such as latches or manipulable puzzles is most marked in primates (e.g. Butler 1953; Harlow *et al.*, 1950) for reasons which are poorly understood. However many species show some kind of fear reaction to a stimulus that is intense and vivid and very novel – investigative reactions may follow when it becomes slightly less of a novelty. Very many other species also show some degree of social curiosity, whose expression depends of course on the instinctive social pattern of each. Search for additional physical or social stimulation as an apparent end in itself merges with the specialized subject of play (Smith, 1986) which is most common in the young of co-operative mammalian species including carnivores and primates.

In all these cases species-specific patterns of behaviour are dominant, but over and above these the most plausible generalization is that of Berlyne (1960) that an internal level of arousal, correlated with stimulus novelty, is responsible for some of the motivational impetus of play and exploration. Familiar stimuli are of course uninteresting and unarousing, and the essence of Berlyne's theory is that every individual has an optimal level of arousal. Therefore, for an underaroused or bored animal, novel stimuli may be rewarding, while once the optimal level has been exceeded, security and familiarity are sought. The alternation between these two states is sometimes directly visible in young primates (Harlow, 1962; Mason, 1967).

Conclusion: habituation is not always the simplest form of learning

The description of habituation – that we start off with one stimulus, which elicits one response, and then cease to do so as it is repeated – is certainly about as simple a description as one could give about a behavioural phenomenon which might qualify as learning from experience. Even the nine points listed by Thompson and Spencer (1966) to do with how much and when a response declines in habituation, and when it might recover, do not require a tremendously complex psychological theory for their explanation. That even the simplest of animals may exhibit responses which decline with repeated elicitation strongly suggests that relatively unelaborate biological solutions have been found to the problem of evolving a system which displays habituation, and the fact that all of the nine points can be obtained from vertebrate spinal cords, and most of them from the abdominal ganglion of a gastropod mollusc, is ample experimental confirmation that this is indeed the case. But, if we take exactly the same behavioural description, or set of behavioural descriptions, and apply it to the decline in attention which a human subject gives to a repeated stimulus of no great intrinsic interest, or even to the decline in exploratory behaviour elicited by a novel object placed in a rat's cage, we are under no obligation to begin with the assumption that the explanations which apply to the slug or spinal cord will continue to be appropriate. On the contrary, the results of such additional experiments, since they demonstrate the complexity of both the initial perceptions of novel stimuli and the comparisons with internal representations which change novel stimuli into familiar ones, mean that what is describable as a decline in responsiveness to a repeated stimulus in these cases requires an explanation of quite different order, involving both the perceptual and the motivational systems of the whole animal, rather than just a few synapses which intervene between stimulus and response. Similarity of behavioural description does *not* imply similarity of psychological explanation. I trust that the reader will become thoroughly bored and irritated by the repetition of this point during the next two chapters, since this will mean that he or she has begun to compare it with an internal representation which, while this may lower attentiveness to immediate repetitions, will also indicate the involvement of one of the highest and least reflexive forms of learning.

3 Pavlovian conditioning

'So infinitely complex, so continuously in flux, are the
conditions of the world around, that the complex animal
system which is itself in living flux, and that system only,
has a chance to establish dynamic equilibrium with the
environment. Thus we see that the most general function
of the hemispheres is that of reacting to signals presented
by innumerable stimuli of interchangeable signification'.
> The conclusion of Lecture 1, *Conditioned Reflexes*,
> Pavlov (1927)

Pavlov's theories

It is a great advantage to be able to discuss the phenomena
of habituation with a set of common descriptive terms – to
ask how fast the response decrement is, how long the recovery
takes, and which alternative stimuli result in dishabituation
– even though it is quite inescapable that the mechanisms
which cause the phenomena may be as different as the knee
jerk and visual pattern recognition. In the same way, it is
often useful to describe the phenomena of Pavlovian, or
classical, conditioning, as if they were the result of a single
set of processes. With the understanding that, since habituation to repeated stimuli may involve very complex cognitive
processes, we cannot fix habituation on the bottom rung of a
ladder of mechanisms of learning, it is possible to classify
Pavlovian conditioning as descriptively slightly more elaborate than habituation, since, at a minimum, it involves two
stimuli and one response, instead of only one stimulus and

one response. Much follows, however, from this difference between one and two. Adapting to environmental change by ceasing to respond to repeated events may be useful, but it involves a very limited form of behavioural change, no matter how elaborate the encoding of the information received about the events. If, because two different stimuli are associated in the environment, a response to one is given to the other, then, in the first place, the animal involved has increased rather than decreased its behavioural repertoire. And, theoretically, a device has been found which glues together any two sensory experiences, allowing in principle for the assembling of parts into wholes, for the detection of causal relationships, and for the reconstruction of indefinitely long sequences of mental representations.

At any rate, this was how Pavlov himself invariably presented his work on conditioned reflexes (1927, 1955). By the mechanisms studied as conditioning reflexes, 'groups of various agents or elements of nature, both simultaneous and consecutive, are synthesized by the animal into units. In this way *synthesis* is effected in general' (1955, p. 273). 'Thus, from the point of view of conditioned reflexes the cerebral hemispheres appear as a complex of analyzers, whose purpose is to decompose the complexity of the internal and external worlds into separate elements and moments and then to connect all these with the manifold activity of the organism, (1955, p. 300). The mechanism responsible for the conditioned reflex corresponds to what Helmholtz termed 'unconscious inference' (Pavlov, 1955, p. 215). What goes on the the brain of the dog is 'higher nervous activity' as opposed to the 'lower nervous activity' of the spinal cord, and thus:

> In the long run, the cerebral hemispheres of the dog constantly affect in the most varying degrees both the *analysis* and *synthesis* of stimuli coming to them, and this can and must be termed *elementary, concrete thinking.* And it follows that this thinking is responsible for the perfect adaptation of the organism, for its more delicate equilibration with the environment. (1955, p. 274 original italics)

As these quotations, especially the last one, show, from one point of view Pavlov had what would nowadays be called a very cognitive approach to the theory of conditioning. However, he did not neglect to mention the ecological func- tion of these processes. The point of the conditioning mech- anism was that it supplied 'a much more detailed and special- ized correlation between the animal and its environment than is afforded by the inborn reflexes alone' (1927, p. 16). The obvious examples of the evolutionary advantages of this were given by the ability of arbitrary and distant stimuli to evoke 'the reflex of seeking food', and also 'the reflex of self-defence', which arises because 'The strong carnivorous animal preys on weaker animals, and these if they waited to defend them- selves until the teeth of the foe were in their flesh would speedily be exterminated' (1927, p. 14).

Pavlov's treatment of conditioning was therefore spec- ifically cerebral rather than merely of the knee-jerk reflex kind, but his physiological terminology of conditioned reflexes, when taken up by Watson, Skinner and Hull, among others, was used in a much more mechanical way. As we shall see, evidence of classical conditioning can be obtained from a wide variety of animal species, and from several different kinds of human behaviour.

Pavlov's experiments

The essential features of Pavlov's experiments on conditioning in dogs are very well-known. The response measured was salivation, and the main experimental result was that dogs would salivate to a buzzer or bell which was given as a signal for a few seconds before food was presented. Given the very general theories which Pavlov put forward about animals adapting to their environment, as illustrated by the quotations above, the concentration on experiments where the main focus of interest was the activity of the salivary glands seems rather surprising, but it is completely explicable in terms of Pavlov's original interest, as a physiologist, in the process of digestion (see Boakes, 1984; Gray, 1979). In the lecture he gave in 1904 when he received the Nobel prize for his work on digestion, Pavlov said that it was quite unexpected that, in the course

Figure 3.1 *Pavlov's method.*
Pavlov's experiments were very carefully controlled. The dog was isolated from the experimenter, who delivered stimuli by means of automated devices, and recorded quantitative measures of response. After Asratyan (1953).

of his research, he discovered that psychological factors had such powerful effects:

> generally speaking, the outstanding role of psychological stimulation in the processing of food in the digestive canal has not met with proper acknowledgement. Our investigations forced us to bring these influences to the fore. Appetite, the craving for food, is a constant and powerful stimulus to the gastric glands. There is not a dog in which skilful teasing with food does not evoke a more or less considerable secretion of juice in the empty and hitherto inactive stomach. (1955, p. 141)

In order to study psychological effects on digestive secretions more thoroughly, it was enough to measure the effects of selected artificial stimuli on volume of salivation, and this could be accomplished by means of a minor operation to lead salivation out through a tube in the dog's cheek. The experimental methods adopted in Pavlov's laboratories were very systematic: the dog was usually separated from the experimenter, and from distracting outside noise, in a sound-proofed compartment, and pneumatic or electrical methods were used to control the delivery of the food and other stimuli (see Figure 3.1).

The acquisition of conditioned reflexes

A wide variety of experimental stimuli were used in Pavlov's experiments – bells, buzzers, pure tones, and the sounds of musical instruments, presentation of illuminated visual patterns, or the sight of gradually rotating objects. None of these artificial stimuli would normally induce a hungry dog to salivate, but if any of them were to be presented consistently for a few seconds before the dog was given food, then the 'conditioned stimulus' would by itself elicit copious salivation. But this is not a selective process confined to the salivary gland. As Pavlov put it, 'the motor component of the food reflex is also very apparent in experiments of this kind' (1927, p. 22). That is, the dog would turn and move towards the place where it normally got food, and lick its lips. Pavlov referred to the conditioned stimulus as a signal for food, and could be called a proponent of the 'stimulus-substitution' theory, since he emphasized that the signal had the same effects as the food – for instance if the beat of a metronome was the signal 'the animal reacts to the signal in the same way as if it were food; no distinction can be observed between the effects produced on the animal by the sounds of the beating metronome and showing it real food' (1927, p. 22). Pavlov's explanation for these new effects of artificial stimuli was in terms of the formation of new physiological paths or new connections within the brain. The analogy he used was the now familiar one of the telephone switchboard: he had a private line from his home to his laboratory – this is like a permanent, 'hard-wired' and readily available inborn connection. On the other hand he could call up the laboratory, or other numbers, through the central exchange, and in this case a special new path has to be provided at the switchboard (1927, p. 25). The formation of a new connection for a conditioned reflex could sometimes be done as quickly, after only a single combination of, say, an electric buzzer with food, but at other times, 10 or more combinations of the signal with food would be required before the artificial signal elicited salivation.

The inhibition and extinction of conditioned reflexes

The switchboard metaphor is limited, but is very straightforward. A much less direct explanation was given by Pavlov for cases where a conditioned reflex failed to occur when expected. Instead of being put down as a bad connection, such a case would be attributed to a special process of 'inhibition' – a much more specifically physiological theory. 'External inhibition' corresponds closely to distraction – if during an experiment a strange smell wafted into the laboratory, or there was an outside noise, or even if the sun went behind a cloud, the dog might prick up its ears, sniff the air, or gaze in the direction of the disturbance. This excitement of the investigatory reflex would have an inhibitory effect on the conditioned reflex – that is, the dog would not salivate as normal when the conditioned stimulus was presented (1927, p. 44). Very generally, Pavlov attributed the absence of behaviours to inhibitory brain processes, and the presence of any activity to 'excitatory' brain processes. The most influential case of this is the hypothesis of the internal inhibition of already formed conditioned reflexes, during experimental extinction.

Experimental extinction of conditioned reflexes

If a dog has been conditioned with the sound of a metronome preceding food, and then the metronome is sounded repeatedly without being followed by food, there are various reasons for expecting that salivation to the metronome should cease. Most generally, if conditioning is thought of in terms of the signalling or predictive function of the conditioned stimulus (CS), then disruption of the signalling relationship between the metronome and food ought to be indexed by salivary measurements. In terms of the telephone switchboard analogy, a temporary connection should now become unplugged. But neither of these interpretations was used by

Pavlov: instead, the cessation of salivation when a stimulus was no longer followed by food was attributed to a neural process of inhibition, which is assumed to have suppressive effects on response output, without changing the neural connection formed when the conditioned reflex was established. The main experimental result which supports this explanation is the phenomenon of 'spontaneous recovery'. In the demonstration quoted by Pavlov, a dog which salivates to a metronome is presented with the metronome for 30–second periods, at 2–minute intervals, seven times, no food being presented during this period, or at any other point in the demonstration. Though the first time it salivated within 3 seconds of the metronome starting, giving 10 drops altogether, by the seventh time it did not begin to salivate for 13 seconds, and then only produced 3 drops. This is a demonstration of 'experimental extinction'. (1927, p. 49). However, when, 23 minutes later, the metronome is turned on again, the dog salivates within 5 seconds and gets a score of 6 drops in the 30 seconds. This is a significant recovery, and because 'extinguished reflexes spontaneously regenerate in course of time', the initial extinction cannot have been due to 'disruption of the respective nervous connections' (1927, pp. 59–60).

Another result quoted by Pavlov is what he called 'secondary extinction'. It was common in his experiments to establish more than one conditioned stimulus at a time, partly since changes of this kind increased the alertness of the animals. Thus a dog might have dilute acid squirted into its mouth after the sound of a metronome, or after the sound of a buzzer, or after the tactile stimulus of a touch on the skin. Now if the metronome is given without the reinforcement, responses to the other two stimuli are extinguished as well (1927, p. 55). Pavlov found it profitable to discuss such cases of interactions between stimuli, as well as spontaneous changes over time, in terms of a labile and diffuse form in inhibitory brain activity. The concept of inhibition as a kind of brain function has proved to be long-lived (see Gray, 1979, 1982), and phrases such as 'inhibitory conditioning' are still in frequent use (e.g. Mackintosh, 1983).

Conditioned inhibition

A further kind of interaction between different conditioned stimuli is also consistent with the concept of a generally suppressive process. Suppose a metronome again normally signals food, but whenever a whistle is sounded along with the metronome, food is withheld. Accurate expectations would be aroused if the metronome alone was taken to be a positive signal, and the combination of whistle and metronome simply ignored. However, experiments in Pavlov's laboratory suggested that the whistle was not merely neutral, since its effects could immediately transfer to other combinations. In the case discussed (1927, p. 77), a dog given food after the metronome was also given acid (which also elicits salivation) after a tactile stimulus. When, after training when the addition of the whistle to the metronome signalled absence of food, the whistle was added to the tactile stimulus for the first time, salivation was almost completely suppressed. In all the experiments of this kind, it had to be shown first, of course, that the sounding of stimuli such as the whistle did not suppress salivation by distraction, but many examples confirmed that a stimulus which suppressed responding when combined with one positive signal tended to suppress salivation to any other signal. Thus Pavlov called additional stimuli of this kind 'conditioned inhibitors' (1927, p. 77). The procedure of assessing a stimulus with suspected inhibitory properties by adding it to another with known response-eliciting potential is still in use, and indeed Mackintosh (1983, p. 178) suggests that, under the soubriquet of 'the summation test', it is 'the single most useful measure of inhibitory conditioning'.

Synthesis and analysis in generalization and discrimination

Yet further areas of current research where Pavlov established the experimental procedures and some of the technical terms involve the effects of conditioning on perception. A separate chapter (chapter 8) will be devoted to modern research on these topics, but it is worth noting here some of Pavlov's assumptions which have been neglected, mainly the distinction between analysis and synthesis, and the corollary that perceptual complexity should be one of the dimensions which research can and should uncover. By 'analyzing mechanisms', Pavlov meant partly just what we would nowadays call the sensory systems, of vision, touch, hearing and so on, but also the involvement in these of attention, that is something 'which selects out of the whole complexity of the environment those units which are of significance' (1927, p. 110). Synthesis was the process 'by means of which individual units can be integrated into an excitatory complex', something which would more likely be referred to now as cross-modal perception, object perception, or the formation of schemata, representations, or internal descriptions (Walker, 1983a). Pavlov's constant reference to analysis and synthesis may merely be a consequence of the fact that as a young man his favourite author was Herbert Spencer, who also used these terms frequently, but the experimental facts of discrimination learning, no less now than then, require some roughly similar theoretical attempt to account for attention and pattern recognition (Sutherland and Mackintosh, 1971; Sutherland, 1960).

A more detailed account of Pavlov's experiments in these areas will be given in later chapters, with further discussion of this theoretical point, but for present purposes it is important to note that Pavlov carefully distinguished 'elementary' analysis and synthesis from 'higher' types: the former being associated with the capacities of the sense organs themselves, as with absolute thresholds for pitch or visual acuity, and the latter being what he took to be central perceptual processes – for instance the integration of information of both ears to compute localization of sound sources. It was very evident to Pavlov, though it has often been forgotten in subsequent discussions of Pavlovian conditioning, that 'only with the progressive development of the analyzing activity of the nervous system is the organism enabled to multiply the complexity of its contacts with the external world and to achieve a more and more varied and exact adaptation to external conditions' (1927, p. 111). That is, Pavlov believed that the scope and limits of perceptual functions would be different in different animal species, and indeed at different levels of the mammalian nervous system, and that these differences would be made clear by conditioning experiments (1927, p. 111).

Lesser systems

In 1931 Clark Hull, President of the American Psychological Association in 1936 and eventually to become one of the most famous stimulus-response theorists of all time, was co-author of two technical papers which described simple electrical circuits which displayed 'fairly accurately the behaviour of the mammalian conditioned reflex', it being made explicit that this was done since 'The conditioned reflex is the basic mechanism of more complex mammalian behavior' (Krueger and Hull, 1931, p. 266; Baernstein and Hull, 1931, p. 99). One of these circuits is shown in Figure 3.2.

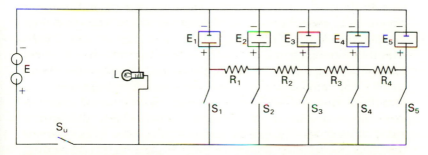

Figure 3.2   *The conditioned reflex modelled as a simple battery circuit.*
The large battery, E, on the left means that the switch Su can be regarded as an unconditioned stimulus turning on the lamp, L, as the unconditioned response. Small rechargeable batteries, E1 to E5, allow the switches S1 to S5 to act as conditioned stimuli. These will also turn on the lamp, L, but only if they have previously been turned on at the same time as the main switch, Su. The physical characteristics of this type of circuit can be chosen so that the effectiveness of any of the secondary switches will increase gradually with repeated 'conditioning' trials, decrease with 'extinction' trials, when they are used on their own; and exhibit 'generalization' due to leakage through the resistors R1 to R4 from adjacent batteries. After Krueger and Hull (1931).

Metaphorically, 'push buttons were the sense organs', the 'flashing on of a light the response', while 'copper wires serve as nerves'. In figure 3.2, the learning elements are storage cells or capacitors which are charged from the main battery when the push button switches of the unconditioned and conditioned stimuli are depressed simultaneously. With repeated conditionings of this kind, there is orderly generalization of the conditioned response through the resistors. Experimental extinction occurs if the conditioned stimulus switch is used often enough by itself, but, due to the characteristics of their storage batteries, Krueger and Hull were able to demonstrate a certain amount of 'spontaneous recovery' by giving the circuit a rest.

By comparison with modern electronics, this circuit is elementary in the extreme, but it serves all the better to make one of the points as originally intended – that several of the phenomena demonstrated by Pavlov with the salivary reflex of dogs require, *in their most basic form*, only the most rudimentary of physical mechanisms for their reproduction. In terms of behavioural evolution (see chapter 9), it is surely important to remember both that the neural control of some very adaptive behavioural processes need not be terribly complicated, and that if we describe 'classical conditioning' as a single behavioural process, it must be understood that the process includes both some very straightforward kinds of association and some very much more complex perceptual abilities, such as those demonstrated by Pavlov's dogs when they became conditioned to the sound of a particular musical instrument, a certain arpeggio played on any instrument, or the sound of their own name (see chapter 8). We should not expect any simple electrical circuit to do these more complicated things.

Neither should we expect very complicated perceptual processes from *Aplysia californica* – but we ought not to be surprised if, within a small range of stimuli and responses, it accomplishes the sort of conditioning that can be achieved by a row of batteries. This result has recently been reported by Carew *et al.* (1981, 1983). As is the case with most artificial systems, in *Aplysia* the conditioned stimulus tested already had a connection to the conditioned response wired in: the conditioned stimulus was a light tactile stimulation of the siphon of the animal (see chapter 2, pp. 47–8) which normally produces a weak withdrawal reflex of the siphon and gill. The unconditioned stimulus was an electric shock to the tail, of sufficient strength to produce a very vigorous withdrawal reflex including the siphon and gill. Thus, if the siphon is weakly stimulated just before the strong electric shock is applied, 15 times, at 5–minute intervals, then 30 minutes later a much longer than usual withdrawal response is given to the tactile stimulus to the siphon (delivered with a nylon brush) tested by itself. As this effect is less than compelling evidence for learned behavioural change, an important comparison is that there is no lengthening of response to siphon stimulation if this stimulus is given in the intervals between the strong electric shocks to the tail, these being signalled by a weak electric stimulus to the mantle-shelf. In this case it is the response to mantle-shelf stimulation which is lengthened. This comparison is at least metaphorically similar to the differential conditioning of a dog, to salivate to a buzzer but not to a bell. The crucial anatomical dissimilarity is that the two conditioning stimuli travel down different neurons in the *Aplysia* case, while the dog's brain has the task of distinguishing two stimuli which both arrive down the auditory nerve. A major reason for interest in the simpler task of the sea-slug is of course that the exact neural changes which take place during conditioning can be more readily studied. Hawkins *et al.* (1983) used rat-sized *Aplysia* preparations in which the nervous system was dissected free from the body but left attached to the tail. Direct stimulation of two individual sensory neurons for the siphon could then be used as conditioned stimuli, either paired or unpaired with electric shock to the tail, the conditioned response being assessed as the excitatory post-synaptic potential (EPSP) produced in a particular identified motor neuron for the siphon.

The model of conditioning in *Aplysia* suggested by the results of these experiments is rather different from the circuit presented by Krueger and Hull (1931), but quite similar in principle to the alternative circuit presented by Baernstein and Hull (1931), in which activity in the conditioned stimulus part (at the heater of a 'mercury-toluene thermoregulator') was necessary before the unconditioned stimulus could have an effect. (Hawkins *et al.* (1983) describe their model as 'activity-dependent amplification of pre-synaptic facilitation'. In this, the unconditioned stimulus not only produces the unconditioned response, but activates a 'facilitator neuron', which makes subsequent unconditioned responses more likely, even to unpaired conditioned stimuli (this is known as sensitization). However, if there is activity in a sensory neuron at the same time as the facilitator neuron is stimulated by the unconditioned stimulus, then the ability of that sensory neuron to produce a potential in the motor neuron, on the other side of a synapse, is selectively amplified. This model has yet to be confirmed, but its authors suggest that it could be very general, operating in vertebrate animals as well as in other parts of the nervous system of *Aplysia* (Hawkins *et al.*, 1983, p.404). The general thrust of their idea is conveyed in Figure 3.3. The crucial element is the facilitator neuron (F) which has the built-in capacity to greatly amplify the effect of any sensory neuron at the synapse with the motor neuron. There are cells in *Aplysia* denoted 'L29 cells' which are possible candidates, since they project very diffusely and are themselves excited by motivationally significant stimuli. In vertebrates there are diffusely projecting systems of neurons which might do a similar job, but this is purely speculative at present.

Eventually, the detailed theories of how Pavlovian conditioning is physiologically accomplished will presumably become much less speculative, but the work on *Aplysia* now stands as a *reductio ad absurdum* for the basic processes of association in classical conditioning of the same kind as the simplified electrical circuits discussed by Hull. That there are available neural circuits of the kind portrayed in Figure 3.3 is not in doubt. How such basic modules of association are assembled or utilized to produce central representations of complex perceptual and motor events, and mental associations between them, is of course a different kind of question, despite claims to the contrary (e.g. Hawkins and Kandel, 1984).

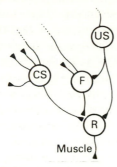

F = a facilitator nearon,
which makes the connection
between CS and R stronger

Figure 3.3   *The conditioned reflex modelled as a simple neural circuit.*
US is a neuron which is activated by the unconditioned stimulus, and is directly connected to the neuron R, which outputs the unconditioned response. CS is a neuron which has a connection to R, but which does not normally fire R. However, the CS becomes able to fire R if the CS output to R is accompanied by the output from the facilitator neuron, F. Thus the connection between CS and R is made stronger when CS and US are active at the same time. After Hawkins *et al.* (1983).

Spinal conditioning

If facilitatory circuits exist in the nervous system of the sea-slug, which enable the associative effects of stimulus pairings to be experimentally demonstrated, we have little reason to be sceptical of claims that the vertebrate spinal cord is also sensitive to temporal relationships between similar reflexes (though we have many reasons for being sceptical about whether the associative capacities of the spinal cord parallel in all respects those of the intact animal, *contra* Beggs *et al.*, 1983, p. 531). Shurrager and Culler in 1940 reported that the leg-flexion reflex in acute spinal dogs (anaesthetized dogs with severed spinal cords) could be transferred from the unconditioned stimulus of a shock to the hind paw to the conditioned stimulus of a weak shock delivered to the tail, by using this as a signal for the stronger shock. It should be noted that (a) perception of the stimuli was not in any sense a demanding task, and (b) the two stimuli were qualitatively similar, being both electric shocks: these two points also apply to other studies using spinal animals. Shurrager and Culler's experiments of 1940 were subsequently criticized by Kellogg (1947) and his colleagues, who failed to replicate them, on a number of technical grounds, and the results of conditioning experiments on spinal mammals have remained ambivalent (Patterson, 1976). Beggs *et al.* (1983) have presented rather more orderly data than usual, but with a highly specialized procedure: the conditioned stimulus was electrical stimulation of the sensory nerve for a particular muscle of the leg (the peroneal) and the conditioned response was electrical activity in the corresponding motor nerve, the unconditioned stimulus being strong electrical shock to the ankle skin of the same leg. (The animals were anaesthetized and also paralyzed by spinal cord transection). There appeared to be a gradual increase in the magnitude of the conditioned response over initial pairings, but there are several incongruities in the data. For instance, the magnitude of the response continued to increase if the conditioned stimulus was presented by itself at 10–minute intervals, though it decreased in groups where this was done at 1–minute intervals. Whether or not much weight is attached to such peculiarities in the results, it is obvious that increments in the response of a motor nerve to stimulation of its sensory partner is not what Pavlov had in mind when he spoke of the importance of conditioning lying in the function of 'reacting to signals presented by innumerable stimuli of interchangeable signification' (1927, p. 15). Spinal conditioning of this kind can only be a special case, which may be of value for several reasons, but which can tell us little about what Pavlov called the analyzing and synthesizing activities of 'the crowning achievement in the nervous development of the animal kingdom' – the cerebral hemispheres (1927, p. 1).

A curiosity of spinal conditioning is that some of the strongest data supporting the notion of associative connections in the spinal cord has been obtained from a human paraplegic patient. Ince *et al.* (1978) reported an experiment which was combined with an attempt to enable a patient to regain voluntary, though artificial, control of the bladder-emptying reflex. A self-administered strong electrical shock to the abdomen would elicit the emptying of the bladder, and the intention was to condition this reflex to the much less violent stimulus of a mild electrical shock to the thigh. It was first shown that this mild stimulus initially did not have any effect on bladder-emptying, even after experience of the stronger abdominal shock, thus ruling out sensitization. Then, during seven sessions, the conditioned stimulus was given for 3 seconds at a time, with the unconditioned stimulus, which elicited bladder emptying, always occupying the last 2.5 seconds of this interval. In this phase 54 pairings were given, and subsequently the conditioned stimulus by itself resulted in roughly the same amount of bladder emptying (77 ml. per session) as had the original strong shock used as the unconditioned stimulus. It is unlikely that associative processes of this kind, at the spinal level, are of any great importance in normal human behaviour, but the possibility of associations which, as in this instance, are divorced from the higher kinds of cognitive processing is useful to keep in mind for more intermediate phenomena, such as the metabolic responses discussed below (pp. 73–7)

Conditioning in decorticate mammals

Between 1901 and 1909, there was an intense controversy in physiological circles in St Petersburg between Pavlov and his associates on one side, and on the other workers in the laboratory of Bechterev, a very eminent neurologist (Babkin, 1949, pp. 89–94; see Boakes, 1984). The Bechterev side believed that there was a localized centre for salivation in the cerebral cortex, without which no conditioned salivary reflexes could be established, and this was contrary to several results obtained in Pavlov's laboratory. The conflict was resolved on a famous occasion on which Pavlov and his team went over to Bechterev's laboratories to observe two dogs with cortical lesions which, it was claimed, had thus lost all their salivary reflexes. The main demonstration apparently consisted of waving a glass jar containing sugar lumps in front of the animals, without eliciting salivation. Pavlov's reaction was to insist, against all protests, on performing a quick experiment of his own. He demanded a bottle of weak hydrochloric acid and a test tube, and poured acid from the bottle into the test tube, and then into the dogs' mouths, several times, and then waited for the salivation which this produced to stop. Now, pouring acid into the tube in front of the dogs consistently elicited more salivation, even though the acid itself was not transferred to their mouths.

This should have ended the controversy over the role of the cerebral cortex in conditioning: it is by no means essential for simple conditioned reflexes, but it is certainly necessary for the life of the normal animal, and for the full range of conditioning results. As Pavlov (1927) summarized it in the first chapter of his book, in a decorticate animal 'the number of stimuli evoking reflex reaction is considerably diminished; those remaining are of an elemental, generalized nature, and act at very short range . . . finely discriminating distance receptors lose their power' (p. 13). Subsequent research has amply confirmed both these points: conditioned reflexes may certainly be observed in decorticate mammals – but the range of possible stimuli is obviously drastically reduced, and various other abnormalities may appear. For instance, Oakley and Russell (1976) compared normal, decorticated and hemidecorticated rabbits in the conditioning of the eyeblink (nictitating membrane) response (hemidecorticates have the cerebral cortex removed from only one of the two hemispheres). A weak electric shock delivered to the skin near a rabbit's eye very reliably elicits the protective unconditioned response of closure of the nictitating membrane, or third eyelid. If a diffuse light is turned on half a second before each of a series of shocks, then there is gradual acquisition of the conditioned response of blinking immediately to the light. Oakley and Russell's procedure was slightly more elaborate, since sometimes a tone was sounded, without being followed by shock. For separate groups of animals, the tone was the signal for shock but the light was not. The results showed that even the totally decorticated animals were just as accurate as normals at blinking to whichever stimulus was the signal, but not to the other, even though they were slightly slow at acquiring the conditioned response. Thus, the differentiation between a visual and an auditory stimulus can be achieved by subcortical mechanisms. Pavlov's own results suggested that even the differentiation between two notes a semitone apart could be achieved in a dog lacking auditory cortex, although this dog showed no sign of differentiating between an ascending and a descending scale of the same notes, or of recognizing its own name (1927, p. 336).

Taking together these results from spinal or decortical mammals, and the conditioning phenomena observed in *Aplysia*, other gastropod molluscs, leeches, and various worms, and indeed taking into account the behaviour of simple electrical circuits, it is obvious that the bare bones of reflex association can be accomplished at relatively elementary levels of neural organization (Fantino and Logan, 1979; Sahley *et al.*, 1981).

Conditioning of metabolic responses

Continuing with the less cognitive aspects of conditioned associations, we return to various digestive or metabolic activities which are even more internal and less involved with purposive actions than salivation, like the gastric secretions first studied by Pavlov in dogs. Pavlov (1927) passed on the observations of a Dr Krylov of Tashkent, who had repeatedly injected dogs with morphine in the course of medical research. This initially produced a sequence of profuse salivation, and then vomiting, followed by sleep. But after five or six days of this, Krylov noticed that dogs would begin the phase of profuse salivation before he had actually given them the injection, and that they would also continue the sequence of vomiting and sleep without the drug itself. In the most striking cases the sequence began as soon as the dog saw the experimenter, whereas in other animals the effects were only observed if the complete normal procedure took place including wiping the dog's skin with alcohol, ending with the injection of saline solution (which without conditioning would have no effects). In Pavlov's own laboratory only mild symptoms of this kind were seen, but recent experiments on the phenomenon of taste-aversion learning (see pp. 232–42) confirm that, in coyotes and wolves, external stimuli which have been preliminaries to drug-induced nausea on only a few previous occasions will themselves induce vomiting (Garcia *et al.* 1977b).

Conditioned hypoglycemia

Another case where external stimuli appear to acquire the properties of injected drugs is where they precede repeated injections of large doses of insulin. These have the unconditioned effect of lowering blood sugar levels. The procedure to demonstrate conditioning (usually with rats as subjects) is to inject an animal several times, in distinctive circumstances: with the ringing of a bell, (Alvarez-Buylla and Alvarez-Buylla, 1975) or in the presence of a strong smell, such as mentholatum (Woods, 1976). Then the animal is injected with saline solution in the same circumstances and blood sugar level is measured and found to be lowered (see Woods and Kulkosky, 1976, for a review, and Figure 3.4).

Neural control of glandular responses and conditioned compensation

Conditioned nausea, and conditioned lowering of blood sugar, in some ways sound very straightforward. But the internal regulation of metabolic and hormonal processes is of course in most cases more involved. In a theoretical analysis of the conditioning of drug-induced physiological responses, Eikelboom and Stewart (1982) sensibly point out that what things actually function as conditioned and unconditioned stimuli and responses is not readily apparent, and suggest that it is inputs and outputs of the central nervous system parts of complex regulatory feedback systems which must be responsible for the observed peripheral effects, such as lowering of blood sugar levels. That the peripheral responses themselves may be symptoms rather than causes of conditioning effects is indicated by the experiment of Woods (1976), who included a group of rats which, during conditioning trials, was given a combined injection of insulin and glucose, with the net result that there was no change in peripheral blood sugar level during conditioning trials. This did not prevent the group showing a conditioned lowering of blood sugar when tested with saline solution (see Figure 3.4).

Thus insulin must have some direct action as a stimulus to neural control systems, which results in neural outputs

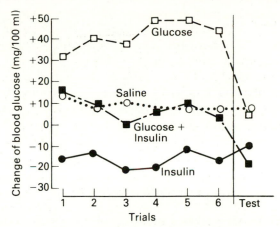

Figure 3.4 *Conditioned lowering of blood sugar level.*
Four groups of rats were given the test, at the right of the figure, of an
injection of a weak salt solution (saline), and their blood sugar level was
measured immediately afterwards. Groups with previous experience of
receiving injections of insulin, or insulin with glucose, showed a lowering
of blood glucose in response to the saline injection. Control groups with
previous injections of saline or glucose did not. After Woods (1976).

which reduce peripheral blood sugar, and these same outputs
apparently become conditioned to non-drug sensory stimuli.
That in itself would fit relatively easily into traditional stimu-
lus-substitutions theories of classical conditioning (Pavlov,
1927; Woods, 1976; Eikelboom and Stewart, 1982; Stewart *et
al.*, 1984). A complication of a more serious order arises
because in many cases conditioned effects of external stimuli
which precede drug injections are in the *opposite* direction to
the unconditioned effect of the drug injection itself. This is
true, for instance, of signals which precede low doses of insulin
– in this case the signals alone usually increase blood sugar
level (hyperglycemia) even though the insulin doses are
sufficient to lower it (hypoglycemia: Woods and Kulosky,
1976; Eikelboom and Stewart, 1982). There now appears to
be wide acceptance for theories which take the general form
of saying that the injection of the drug often produces antagonistic responses to the drug, and that under certain circum-

stance these antagonistic responses, as some of the body's main unconditioned responses to the drug, become conditioned to external sensory signals. This can be related to Solomon's 'opponent process' theory, which is designed to explain acquired motivational effects (Solomon, 1980; Solomon and Corbit, 1974), but was developed as a specific account of pharmacological tolerance to morphine by Siegel (1975, 1976, 1977; Siegel *et al.*, 1978) and is incorporated into the general account of conditioning of drug-induced metabolic responses given by Eikelboom and Stewart (1982).

Conditioning and morphine tolerance

The experimental evidence in favour of the conditioning factor in morphine tolerance is fairly straightforward, but the inferences from the evidence are slightly less direct than they are in the cases where external stimuli seem to exactly mimic a drug effect. The argument rests on the assumption that, when morphine is injected, there are bodily responses which antagonize the most obvious behavioural effects of the drug, and that it is these unspecified antagonistic responses which become conditioned to external stimuli. This would explain the essential feature of drug tolerance, which is that repeated doses of the same size produce less and less of the main drug effect. And clearly, the first test of this explanation is whether or not external conditions associated with drug administration make any difference to the degree of tolerance observed. Siegel (1975, 1976) assayed the degree of tolerance to morphine by a behavioural test of analgesia. If a rat is placed on a copper plate kept at exactly 54.2°C, it will lick one of its paws, because of the heat-induced discomfort, after about 10 seconds. However, rats given, for the first time, the standard injection of morphine used by Siegel, and placed on the same hotplate, do not lick a paw until they have been on it for approximately 50 seconds, and this is attributable to morphine's pain-killing effects. If they are given the same dose of morphine, and the same test, repeatedly, then their latency of paw-licking drops down to 10 seconds, indicating that this dose has ceased to have an analgesic effect, that is, to use the conventional term, tolerance has developed to the drug.

Now, of course this test by itself says nothing about how or why tolerance has developed. But if it could be shown that tolerance depends on an association between external circumstances and receipt of the drug, that would be evidence for the conditioning hypothesis. Several experiments, by Siegel and others, supply such evidence. Siegel (1976) gave the paw-lick test in distinctive circumstances in two different rooms. Rats were given a sequence of morphine doses in one of the rooms, and developed tolerance, but then when they were tested in the alternative room, tolerance disappeared (that is, the same dose had a full analgesic effect). Another result which suggests conditioning to external cues is that tolerance does not develop over three doses if these are all given in different environments, although it does if three doses are all given in the same environment (Siegel, 1975). If animals are made tolerant by repeated doses in the same environment, then several injections of saline, instead of morphine, in that environment, reduce the tolerance, which looks like an extinction of conditioning. In fact, the first time rats are given saline instead of morphine in the same room as usual, they appeal to be more sensitive to the heat stimulus than control animals, licking their paws sooner, and Siegel supposes that this is due to the conditioned physiological responses which are antagonistic to morphine producing the opposite effect to morphine, in this test hyperalgesia (Siegel, 1975, 1976).

Conditioning of emotions

It thus seems likely that a complex metabolic and hormonal balance can be influenced by conditioned physiological responses to external stimuli, which is of course consistent with the general assumption that all sorts of bodily conditions are affected by 'psychosomatic' factors. There is no reason to suppose that such conditioning effects are limited to drug injections. Cortico-steroid blood levels can be conditioned up to stimuli associated with a poison (Ader, 1976) and down to stimuli associated with daily feeding and drinking (Coover *et al.*, 1977), in rats, and are known to be influenced by experiential factors in human subjects. Therefore external stimuli associated with natural rather than experimental instances of disease and stress could very well have subsequent conditioned effects. (Russell *et al.*, 1984, report the conditioning of histamine release.) Most gastric secretion and internal biochemical change can take place with little direct psychological effect – we are not necessarily aware of salivation, let alone the detailed functioning of our livers. However, some definite fraction of our body chemistry is intimately connected to the subjective experience of emotion – the adrenal glands supplying the most obvious example, and even here the causal direction or directions of the connection is difficult to unravel (Schacter and Singer, 1962; Maslach 1979) – but clearly it would be surprising if physiological secretions could be conditioned, but subjective emotional changes could not. In most cases, in experiments on human psychophysiology, electrical measurements of bodily functions are used as indicators of more general emotional states. Many such experiments purport to demonstrate direct conditioning effects with human subjects. Increasingly it is being stressed that conditioned effects in people may be modulated by verbal instructions, attribution effects due to these and other variables, and cognitive expectations (Davey, 1983), but it is worth noting some examples where emotional changes observed in experiments with human subjects seem to follow the conditioning paradigm fairly closely. With animals, it is a very powerful theoretical assumption that central emotional or motivational states are influenced by classical conditioning (e.g. Rescorla and Solomon, 1967), but the examination of this assumption will be deferred until chapter 7.

Levey and Martin (1975) report what they describe as classical conditioning of an evaluative response, which is interesting here as an example of a human emotional judgment relatively far removed, one assumes, from glandular secretions. They first gave their volunteers 50 postcard reproductions of paintings and scenic photographs, and asked them to sort through these, rating the postcards as liked or disliked on a scale of −100 to +100. Then, for each subject in the experiment, the two most liked and the two most disliked postcards were paired with randomly selected neutral cards, in a tachistoscope, as if they were conditioned and unconditioned stimuli. Thus the subjects had the experience of looking at neutral cards either just before, or just after, they looked at highly preferred or highly disliked cards, with 20 presentations of each pairing. Subsequently they were asked to sort and rate these neutral cards again, with the finding that the ratings had shifted significantly in the direction of the more affecting scenes which they had been paired with. Thus neutral cards paired with disliked cards suffered a ratings drop of 30 points while those paired with liked cards increased their standing by 16 points. This looks like evaluation by association, which might be an affront to rational aesthetic judgment, but which is certainly not unknown in everyday life.

A rather more direct stimulus for eliciting human emotional change was used in the experiments reported by Ohman and his colleagues on conditioned reactions of another kind to pictures, since the volunteers in these had to submit to the UCS of an electric shock, which is usually confined to the animal laboratory. Shock was delivered to the third and fourth fingers, and skin conductance was measured from the first and second fingers, the unconditioned response being that skin conductance drops when shock is given, but the theoretical interest deriving from the fact that the shock is unpleasant, and may be assumed to induce negative affect beyond the third and fourth fingers. The conditioned stimuli were coloured slides, of either snakes or houses, which were shown to the student subjects for 8 seconds before shock deliveries. Although these produced no change in skin conductance in control conditions, after only one pairing with the electric shock, anticipatory skin conductance responses were given to the pictures. For pictures of houses, if one to five pairings with shock were given, then presenting the pictures after this by themselves quickly led to the disappearance of the conditioned response (extinction). But with the pictures of snakes (said to be 'potentially phobic'), the same amount of conditioning was followed by a continuation of conditioned responses when the pictures were given by themselves (high resistance to extinction: Ohman *et al.*, 1975b).

Varied effects of expectations derived from verbal instructions were illustrated in another experiment, using a similar conditioning procedure, in which for half the subjects, after they had received 10 shocks signalled by a picture of a certain type, the experimenter came into their cubicle, disconnected the shock leads (but not the skin resistance electrodes, which here were on a different hand) and told them that no more shocks were to be given. For the others, at the same point the experimenter merely checked the electrodes. Subjects told that there would be no more shocks showed lower skin conductance responses in extinction, as we might expect, but, with the pictures of snakes, even informed subjects continued to show the conditioned response at an appreciable level, after shocks had been discontinued, and they had experience of this fact as well as the experimenter's word for it (Ohman *et al.*, 1975a).

How far such artificial conjunctions of events in the laboratory correspond to normal or pathological emotional development in the life span of human individuals is uncertain, but few psychologists now share the view of Pavlov (1955, p. 273) and Watson (1931, p. 158) that direct conditioning is responsible for most or all of human emotional life (Eysenck, 1976; Gray, 1982; Rachman, 1977; Walker, 1984). None the less, it important for theoretical reasons to bear in mind the fact that direct conditioning of human emotions is occasionally possible, even if it is neither frequent nor in every sense fundamental. Experiments such as those described above demonstrate this under controlled conditions – real-life experience of random associations with strong emotions also suggests it, as in illness after certain foods, or when arbitrary geographical or social circumstances elicit distress after associations with rape, burglary or other personal disasters.

Conditioning and perception

Most examples of conditioning I have discussed so far have involved events of strong motivational significance, and this is probably not due merely to accidents of experimental convenience – it is reactions to emotionally loaded stimuli which are most likely always to be transferred to preceding signals. However, especially in treating relationships between classical conditioning and habituation, which is not tied to high emotion in the same way, it is necessary to consider whether pairings of complex events, or the constant repetition of stimuli in given sequences, may share in the associative mechanisms uncovered by more conventional experiments. The associationist tradition begun by Hume (see pp. 13–15) and continued by Hartley (1705–57) and J. S. Mill (1806–73: see Boakes, 1984) certainly requires that mental associations should be possible between sensations that do not necessarily impel flinching or salivation. According to this view, active exploration, or even passive experience of sequence, might be recorded as mental links between events or perceptions of them. For instance, associations between sight, sound, touch, smell and taste could be acquired in this way – a kitten learning by gradual experience that the sound of crumpling paper might be followed by the appearance of a white sphere of a certain size, which will smell not particularly interesting, but which will feel in such and such a way when patted or sensed with the whiskers. This will surely count as a set of associations, and was certainly what Pavlov meant when he talked of inquisitiveness as an investigatory reflex, which assists the animal to achieve equilibrium with the infinite complexities of the world around it; but nevertheless this sort of learning by perception seems a far cry from experiments revolving around reactions to food or shock.

Distinctions between different kinds of motivational system need to be retained, and ultimately it is a matter simply for experimental investigation how much ostensibly different types of learning from experience have in common. But one of the justifications for doing experiments on conditioning, or for developing theories about these, is that the phenomena mean something beyond the details of a single set of data. Therefore experiential effects of unconventional kinds deserve to be considered. It can and has been argued that *all* our perceptual experience derives from associations between sensations, but experimentally we can only point to oddities. Davis (1976) has reported what he describes as conditioned after-images, obtained by using a sound to signal the brief, bright illumination of a target such as a cross or triangle, observed by human subjects otherwise in total darkness. After about a week of this, at 10 trials a day, subjects report seeing quite vivid after-images if the tone is sounded without the real illumination. Perhaps this ought to be considered as another example when an 'opponent process' appears to be more sensitive to conditioning than the first or 'A' process (Solomon and Corbit, 1974; Solomon, 1980), since the subjects report the after-image rather than the normally illuminated figure. Another visual after-image, even more like an opponent-process in that it involves colours (and it is the theory of colour vision that first saw use of the term opponent process, e.g. by Hurvich and Jameson, 1974), is provided by the McCullough effect (McCullough, 1965). For this, the human observer stares at, say, a red vertical grating alter-nated with a green horizontal grating. Afterwards, if shown black and white gratings of a similar size and orientation, the observer will report that the vertical grating looks green and the horizontal one red. The complementary colour after-effects appear to have become linked to features of the shapes the original colours were experienced with (May and Matteson, 1976). It would seem likely that this is a peculiarity associated with neural adaptation very early on in the visual pathways, but what makes the phenomenon more like conditioning is that it is not necessarily temporary. Holding and Jones (1976) and Jones and Holding (1975) found that if, after the initial experience with coloured gratings, a period of four days intervened before subjects were shown mono-chrome gratings, the effect was still obtained, and indeed a discernible, though weakened, effect was obtainable even after three months. However, the experience of observing the black and white gratings, whenever it occurred, abolished the after-effect. This is superficially similar to the extinction of conditioned reflexes.

Clearly, on any theory of perception, after-effects are special cases, but they serve to draw attention to the extent of associ-ation, expectation and context in more ordinary experience, which is often so enormous that it is taken for granted. It is only by illusions and tricks that we are forced to confront the degree to which one sense modality is correlated with another (Day, 1972; Bruce and Green, 1985) in many cases because of habitual associations. If one experiences peculiar sensations of movement when sitting in a stationary train while a train alongside draws out, this is not because of a genetically programmed correlation between that sort of peripheral vision and that sort of movement, although it would not be surprising if peripheral vision in general was set up to associate self-produced movement with certain sorts of changes. All perceptual effects involved in movement on wheels, and there are many, from riding a bicycle to cornering with the seat of the pants at much higher speeds, are obviously the result of experienced associations between one set of stimuli and another, and cannot be assisted by specialized innate knowledge.

Classical conditioning in the laboratory rat and pigeon

Although the conditioning of salivation in dogs has a special place in the history of research on conditioning, this procedure is now very rarely used (see Ellison, 1964; Shapiro and Miller, 1965). With human subjects much data has been gathered with the technique of eyeblink conditioning (Gormezano, 1965), but, for convenience, a large fraction of all research on classical conditioning is performed with laboratory rats or pigeons, inside small chambers known as Skinner boxes. Some of the details of these procedures, and theoretical questions about them, will come up in the next three chapters, but it is necessary to give a brief account of them in the present context. I give the procedural details first, and then discuss the phenomena of backward and second-order conditioning.

Conditioned suppression of lever pressing in rats

This provides an indirect measure of conditioning, but is very reliable, and very frequently used. Rats are first trained to press a lever in a Skinner box, for intermittent food rewards (see chapter 5). Then, either while they are doing this, or ('off-baseline') when they are not, because the lever is withdrawn or they are in a separate apparatus, they experience widely spaced electric shocks, each signalled by a conditioned stimulus such as a tone or light, usually of relatively long duration, that is, the tone or light is turned on for 30 or 60 seconds say, and at the end of this a brief shock occurs. The assessment of the effects of this stimulus pairing must always occur while the rat is in the Skinner box, able to press the lever – most simply the stimulus pairings are delivered while the rat presses. What happens is that for unknown but not unexpected reasons, rats reduce the rate at which they press a lever for food reward while the signal for shock is present. The data is usually presented as a 'suppression ratio', that is, the number of lever presses made during the periods when the conditioned stimulus (CS) is present, divided by this number *plus* however many presses were made during an equivalent period of time without the CS. Thus if the CS has no effect the ratio is 0.5, and if it has maximum effect the ratio drops to 0.0. This means that graphs go down as learning proceeds, instead of up (e.g. see Fig. 4.1, p. 110, Hall and Pearce, 1979).

Taste-aversion learning in rats

This could be regarded as the conditioned suppression of eating or drinking. If rats are allowed to eat or drink some recognizable substance (e.g. saccharin-flavoured water) that has been poisoned, or a similar sequence of events occurs because they are made ill by an injection after eating or drinking, then they will consume very much less of that substance when allowed access to it on a future occasion (Garcia and Koelling, 1966). This is true even if they are made ill some hours after the taste experience (Andrews and Braveman, 1975). There has been some argument as to whether this is just another kind of classical conditioning, or a special learning process (it may be both: Garcia, 1981; Milgram *et al.*, 1977). Taste-aversion learning has in fact been studied in an impressive variety of animal species (Garcia *et al.*, 1977a; Sahley *et al.*, 1981).

Autoshaping in pigeons

As far as the stimulus pairings go, there is nothing to distinguish this from any other kind of classical conditioning

– the peculiar name for the procedure arose because the result of it is that pigeons appear to train themselves to peck an illuminated button. The birds are free to move about in the small box, and the illumination of the button, for some seconds (often 8 or 10) is the signal for the presentation of grain, for 2 or 3 seconds, in an illuminated hopper. Hungry pigeons need little training to peck at illuminated grain, and after a few dozen pairings in which the illumination of the button on the wall preceded the presentation of grain several inches below it, they will begin to peck at the button as well. There thus appears to be a transfer of the peck-eliciting attributes of the grain to the stimulus provided by the button. This may or may not be a pure form of classical conditioning (Brown and Jenkins, 1968; Williams and Williams, 1969; Terrace, 1981: see chapter 5) but it is a reliable and useful way of looking at the associative effects of stimulus pairings.

button?

Autoshaping and food signalling with rats

If a light bulb is placed inside a translucent lever for rats, or some other method is found of strongly drawing the rat's attention to something other than food, then autoshaping will occur with rats, that is, if the illumination of the lever signals that food (or water) will shortly become available, the conditioning of positive psychological affect to the lever will result in it being pressed (Boakes, 1977; Wasserman, 1981). This is not as effective a procedure with rats as it is with pigeons, no doubt partly because there is no obviously trans-ferable response pattern (see chapter 5). Using food signalling for rats rather more loosely has, however, proved to be valu-able. For instance Holland (1977) presented light or tone stimuli for 10 seconds before the delivery of food pellets to rats while he watched them, and recorded carefully what they did. As it happens the effect of this stimulus pairing was predominantly to cause rats to jerk their heads when they heard a tone which predicted food, but to rear up on their hind legs if they saw the light signal.

Second-order conditioning

This has been demonstrated using several different techniques (Rescorla, 1980). If, in using the conditioned suppression procedure, a light signals shock, responding to the light declines (see above). If, after this, rats receive no more shocks, but continue to receive 10–second presentations of the light, now preceded by the sounding of a tone for 30 seconds, then lever pressing in the presence of the tone drops rapidly over the first half-dozen of these pairings (Rizley and Rescorla, 1972).

Holland and Rescorla (1975) used the method of food-signalling with rats, taking a crude measure of general activity. This showed that if 10 seconds of diffuse light preceded the dropping of food pellets, activity in the light increased. Then, in the same experimental boxes, no more food pellets were dropped, but the 10–second sounding of a clicker preceded further presentations of the light, and activity to the clicker was substantially increased as a consequence. In both these experiments, behavioural effects accrued to an auditory stimulus, even though it had never been paired with a motivationally significant event, or rather, even though it had never been paired with a primary reinforcer, such as food or shock. The auditory stimulus in both cases *had* been paired with another event, the light, which control groups demon-strated would not otherwise have made any difference but which did make a difference because it itself had previously signalled the primary reinforcer. There would be grounds thus for supposing that the light had acquired secondary motivational significance, and could function as a secondary or conditioned reinforcer (Kelleher and Gollub, 1962) – at any rate, these experiments show that the light was able to serve as a bridge to establish what is known as second-order conditioning, in this case to a tone. Second-order conditioning from a tone to a light is equally possible, and conditioning from one light to another, or one tone to another, works even better, demonstrating that the traditional variable of similarity still facilitates the formation of associations (Rescorla, 1980).

A rather more complicated experiment makes use of the autoshaping technique to demonstrate second-order conditioning, and makes use of second-order conditioning to demonstrate the virtue of consistency in associative learning. Rescorla (1979) first trained pigeons with two alternative stimuli which equally often served as the signal for food. Before food was presented, the response button or key was either lit red on its left half, or lit yellow on its right half. This persuaded the birds to peck the key when it was illuminated in one of these ways, but not otherwise. They were then split into two groups, both of which now received second-order stimulus pairings, in which either horizontal or vertical black lines preceded either the yellow or the red stimulus. As a result, both groups began to peck at the line stimuli. This shows second-order conditioning with the technique of pigeon autoshaping. However, the finding of special interest was that the two groups differed. One of them received consistent pairings in which animals had always vertical then red or horizontal then yellow, or always the other way around, and in the other group all the birds experienced all four possibilities – vertical or horizontal followed by red or yellow. The group which received the more consistent and less variable set of stimulus pairings showed a much stronger second-order conditioning effect, since on the third day they pecked at the second-order line stimuli on 90 per cent of the opportunities, while the birds getting variable and inconsistent stimulus pairings pecked them on only about 50 per cent of their chances.

Backward conditioning

One of the rules of first-order conditioning which second-order conditioning appears to share is that backwards arrangements of stimulus pairings are usually ineffective (Rescorla, 1980, p. 9). If a buzzer is sounded just after food has been eaten, this does not lead to the buzzer acquiring the property of eliciting salivation when present on its own in the future, and, generally, behavioural attributes of the first event in a sequential pairing do not transfer themselves to the second very often. However, this is not an inviolable law of all associative learning, as has sometimes been suggested. Common human experience suggests that backwards associations between ideas are at least possible, although Aristotle suggested that it is always wisest, in trying to remember a sequence of things, to take the trouble to find some suitable starting point, and then work one's way forwards. Experimental studies of human verbal learning (e.g. Horowitz *et al.*, 1964) provide ample quantitative evidence that there are associations backwards in lists of words learned forwards, even though forwards may be better, and rote-learned lists such as the letters of the alphabet or Hamlet's soliloquies are not easily recited in reverse.

It is possible that backward conditioning is more likely at higher levels of stimulus representation than at lower ones, and that the emotional effects of aversive stimuli transfer more readily to following stimuli than do those of more attractive and appealing events, but no firm conclusions can be drawn at present except that backward conditioning is probably strongly influenced by mechanisms of attention. Using standard techniques, Heth and Rescorla (1973) and Heth (1976) have demonstrated that backward conditioning occurs in the conditioned suppression procedure (see p. 83), in the sense that when 4–second shocks were followed, half a second later, by a 2–second tone-and-light compound, then this stimulus substantially suppressed lever pressing after 10 or 20 pairings, although the effect appeared to dissipate as more and more pairings were given. Rather more dramatic evidence of backward conditioning has been obtained from rats when less conventional techniques of signalling aversive events have been used. Hudson (1939, 1950), as a student of Tolman's, put rats in a cage in which a striped pattern was mounted on an electrified food cup. After even only one shock from the food cup, his rats, when replaced in this cage a week later, would pile sawdust all over the pattern and withdraw to the other end of the cage, thus demonstrating a conditioned fear reaction (Pinel and Treit, 1978, 1979, and Terlecki *et al.*, 1979, have confirmed this result). What interested Hudson was that the rats appeared to him to look around *after* the shock, as it were 'to see what it was that had hit them' (Tolman, 1948). He then modified the apparatus so that, at the onset of shock, the lights went out briefly while the whole food cup and its distinctive striped pattern dropped out of sight, the rats then being tested for avoidance reactions with the food cup back in place at a later date, as before. Hudson's own conclusion from the data thus obtained was that:

> Learning what object to avoid . . . may occur exclusively during the period *after* the shock. For if the object from which the shock was actually received is removed at the moment of shock, a significant number of animals fail to learn to avoid it, some selecting other features of the environment for avoidance, and others avoiding nothing. (Tolman, 1948, p. 201)

Hudson also dropped a bundle of pipe cleaners into the cage after the shock had been delivered, finding that the rats then specifically avoided that object, and this aspect of his data was replicated by Keith-Lucas and Guttman (1975). Believing that visually complex 3–dimensional objects were more likely to attract conditioned associations than brief lights or tones, they used as their conditioned stimulus a red rubber toy hedgehog, which flew across the top of the experimental box (on wires) a certain number of seconds after a single shock had been received by several groups of rats, which differed according to this delay interval. Several quantitative measures of behaviour, made subsequently, indicated that if the slow flight of the hedgehog occurred within 10 seconds of the end of the shock, then the presence of the stationary hedgehog in the cage revealed conditioned avoidance.

Gray (1975) quotes a Russian experiment in which dogs got a puff of air in the eye, which elicited blinking, and also had their leg lifted, which meant they would then lift their own leg when it was touched. If these two stimuli were paired together in either order, dogs would afterwards always lift their leg and blink, when either touched or puffed alone, meaning that the response attributable initially to the first stimulus had become transferred to the second. It is conceivable that the relative perceptual vividness and motivational value of the two stimuli in a pairing is one of the variables which influences the greater ease of conditioning to prior, or signalling, stimuli, the lesser of the two being much more likely to command attention if it appears first rather than second. It is also possible that the factor of relevance to the more powerful event enters into this relationship, via varied attributional or weighting processes. Thus animals may be less likely to associate a subsequent signal with the delivery of food than with distressing experiences, because of the ecological importance of learning to avoid predators 'seen only after an abortive attack' (Mackintosh, 1983, p. 210).

Mental association and conditioning

For almost every aspect of modern life, from reading to voting, we can be satisfied that experience, and association in one form or another, are important causes of behaviour, by following more or less the same line of argument as that given by Locke. In many cases we might want to talk about purposive action and motor skills rather than pairings of perceived stimuli (see chapter 5), and for most things it would be appropriate to discuss human learning in terms of language and social structures rather than conditioning. But in considering the claims of learning theorists such as Pavlov and Watson, who argued that the conditioned reflex serves as some kind of model or module for more complex forms of experience, we need to say how far the rules which govern learning experiments can be applied to the rest of psychology. It is perhaps safe to say that there is more to human psychology than the rules of conditioning, but it is not clear that the principles of associative learning are therefore irrelevant to human psychology, if the question is put in terms of whether mental associations have anything at all to do with human cognition. Formal mnemonic systems (Yates, 1966; Eysenck, 1977) often use paired associations between numbers and letters or between ideas to be learned and an already known set of vivid images. Learning by rote is still technically possible, though not now in favour as an educational tool, and there are few better examples of the irrational workings of similarity and contiguity as principles of association than those which take place in the process of recollection of material with which to answer the questions set in a traditional 3–hour examination. However, the main connection that it is possible to make between human mental associations and work on Pavlovian conditioning is a purely theoretical one. As will be apparent in the next section and in subsequent chapters, the theory of classical conditioning as derived from experiments with laboratory mammals is now firmly mentalistic, in that the locus of associations is between central representations (Rescorla, 1978: Gray, 1979) which may indeed be formed into 'declarative representation' that one thing follows another (Dickinson, 1980) in the course of the animal's attempts to detect 'a true causal relation between the events to be associated' (Mackintosh, 1983, p. 222). In this sense it is now believed that, in the case of Pavlov's dogs at any rate, what was studied as a conditioned reflex in fact reflected a mental association: the dog salivates not as an isolated response, but because it has learned the relation between the events of the signalling buzzer and the subsequent food, and thus salivates when it hears the buzzer because the central representation of the buzzer elicits a mental expectancy of the food. Therefore, in so far as these theories are true and accurate, there is less difference than there was in the days of behaviourist stimulus-reponse postulates between the laboratory phenomena of conditioning and the laws of association which may apply to human thought.

[handwritten annotation:] More dumping on Aplysia — I propose — also dumping in special they might altho acknowledge be good for something —

4 Theories of classical conditioning and habituation

'It is evident from the description given in the present
lecture that we must distinguish in animals an
elementary, from a higher type of analysis and synthesis'
                                        Pavlov (1927; p. 148)

Having briefly introduced modern cognitive theories of
conditioning in the previous chapter, it is now possible to
point to their limitations. The main one is that these cognitive
theories, just as much as the theories which treat only with
reflexes, or even only with synapses, ignore the factor of
perceptual range, cognitive complexity, or whatever we wish
to call it that distinguishes the psychology of a ganglion which
once belonged to a slug from the capacities of the average
dog. In many cases the cognitive theories are testable by
reference to experiments with laboratory pigeons or rats, but
it is not part of the theory that the explanation for the behaviour of *Aplysia* should be in any way different from the explanation of the behaviour of higher vertebrates. In some cases
it is explicitly part of the theory that there is no important
difference (Fantino and Logan, 1979; Macphail, 1982; Hall,
1983), while in others the question is ignored (Mackintosh,
1983). Part of the reason for this is that the experimental data
indicate that there are a great many similarities in the overall
form of behaviour observed under conditioning procedures
with many different responses in widely varying species. This
could mean that it is in fact theoretically correct to give the
same explanation in all instances, but, alternatively, it

could mean that the superficially similar patterns of behaviour – that is, gradual acquisition of a conditioned response, extinction of it when reinforcement ceases, spontaneous recovery after a rest period, and so on – may be exhibited by biological systems of vastly different internal complexity and mode of operation. It is the latter view, the reader will have observed, which is taken in this text. This is not to deny the observed similarities in behaviour, but to argue for the possibility of different levels of association within and between the nervous systems of different grades of animal, which can be experimentally assessed provided differences in behaviour are counted up as well as similarities.

Levels of representation in habituation and classical conditioning

As a very similar point was made at the end of the chapter about habituation, it is perhaps better to discuss this issue in terms of the level of representation of stimuli, rather than the level of any association between them; it is not clear that any associations at all are necessarily involved in the habituation of response to a single stimulus. The term representation is now commonly used to refer to items of information that are involved in both human and animal learning, but without any clear agreed definition (e.g. Roitblat, 1982). I can offer no hard and fast definitions here, but the kinds of distinctions between levels of representation that could conceivably be supported by empirical evidence are illustrated, I hope, by Figure 4.1.

There should be little cause for confusion in saying that stimuli which are represented in the isolated spinal cord of a frog (Thompson and Glanzman, 1976), or the isolated abdominal ganglion of a slug (Carew and Kandel, 1973), are represented at a different level from stimuli which occupy the full attention of an intact and awake mammal. This would serve at least to differentiate level 1 from level 6 in Figure 4.1. All the other distinctions therein are problematical to some degree, since there may be considerable overlap between, for instance, emotional, subcortical and cognitive

Figure 4.1   *Levels of representation in habituation and classical conditioning*

Type of representation	Indicative phenomena in habituation	Indicative phenomena in classical conditioning
1 Synaptic stimulus-response connections	Spinal or ganglionic habituation (Thompson and Spencer, 1966; Kandel, 1976)	Anticipatory shift of spinal or ganglionic responses (Beggs *et al.*, 1983; Ince *et al.*, 1978; Carew *et al.*, 1981, 1983)
2 Autonomic nervous system and metabolic responses	Many forms of physiological adaptation and fatigue; also systemic tolerance to drugs (Eikelboom and Stewart, 1982)	Conditioned drug tolerance effects (Siegel, 1976; Stewart *et al.*, 1984)
3 Central emotional and motivational states	Habituation to emotionally significant stimuli (Berlyne, 1960; Eysenck, 1976)	Associative shifts of emotional response, forward and backward (Ohman *et al.*, 1975a; Miller, 1948; Keith-Lucas and Guttman, 1975)
4 Peripheral perceptual systems	Sensory adaptation (Hinde, 1970); some perceptual learning (e.g. Gibson and Walk, 1956)	Perceptual shifts between or within stimulus modalities due to contiguity (e.g. McCullough, 1965, see p. 82)
5 Central but sub-cortical mechanisms	Habituation in decorticate mammals and lower vertebrates (e.g. Thompson and Glanzman, 1976)	Classical conditioning in decorticate mammals with simple stimuli (Pavlov, 1927; Oakley, 1979b)
6 Central cognitive representations	Human perceptual habituation and similar results in vertebrates (Sokolov, 1963, 1975); some perceptual learning by exposure and exploration (e.g. Gibson and Walk, 1956)	Results with complex stimuli in intact mammals (Pavlov, 1927); similar results in people (Ohman *et al.*, 1975a; Levey and Martin, 1975); second-order conditioning and more elaborate results in higher vertebrates (e.g. Rescorla, 1978)

(*Note:* Types of representation are not mutually exclusive; thus, for instance, human emotional conditioning may link specific autonomic responses and more general emotional evaluations to complex perceptions – 1, 3 and 6.)

levels of representation, but on the other hand it would probably be difficult to obtain widespread consent for the position
that all the phenomena listed down the levels are identical.
The main point of adopting a classificatory scheme of the kind
shown in Figure 4.1, which is clearly extremely provisional, is
that it makes it easier to ask questions about any theoretical
analysis of classical conditioning that may be put forward. In
particular, of course, it prompts the general question of
whether a theory which is derived from experiments at one
level of representation of stimuli necessarily applies to all the
other levels. The usual assumption is that it does, because
some essential features of the behavioural phenomena of
Pavlovian conditioning, or habituation, must have been
observed for the level of representation to be in the table at
all. But this does not mean that there could not be extra
and additional behavioural tests which might allow us to
distinguish the functioning of one level of representation from
another. The main extra criterion of this kind is simply the
nature of the stimuli which the system can respond to, which taps both
perceptual complexity and the specializations or restrictions
imposed by species membership and/or neuroanatomical
factors.

If conditioning at one level of representation were only to
be observable if both conditioned and unconditioned stimuli
took the form of direct electrical stimulation of sensory nerves,
then this would provide a test of performance which would
distinguish this level from another at which, for instance, a
conditioned stimulus could be a particular human face.
Slightly more indirect and theoretical criteria which arise
from consideration of stimulus range concern the degree of
involvement of attentional and motivational mechanisms in
the conditioning process. A very rough-and-ready rule of
thumb would suggest that the lower the level of representation
of stimuli, the less attention and motivation need to be
considered. For instance, using standard procedures with
intact mammals, the parameters of conditioning will vary
with the motivational significance of the unconditioned
stimulus – in salivary conditioning performance will be
directly related to the animal's degree of hunger, and whether
it has any appetite or taste for the particular food signalled.

No doubt this is itself partly because of the effect of motivation on attention, but other attentional variables may also have a profound influence on conditioning – most crudely, it is necessary for the animal to be awake (with only very rare or physiologically abnormal exceptions: Weinberger *et al.*, 1984). However, there is no immediately obvious way in which wakefulness or emotional involvement can be attributed to the spinal cord, or to individual synapses. And this is not just a matter of all-or-none questions, which can be detached from the conditioning process itself, since overall vigilance in scanning the environment for remote stimuli, and very subtle differences in the amount of attention commanded by particular stimuli, are both likely to be involved in theories which apply to standard laboratory animals, and of course to human subjects. It is possible that, in the case of conditioning experiments with people (see Davey, 1986), Figure 4.1 ought really to have another, higher level added on, in which verbal reformulations of causal relationships between stimuli, and many other exclusively human attributional processes, are given more explicit acknowledgment; these may be considered to be subsumed in category 6.

Because of the normal influence of motivation on standard conditioning procedures, it is arguable that *all* conditioning must involve changes in motivational or emotional states, where these terms are applicable. There are a number of results, however, that suggest that while degree of motivation, or the motivational significance of the stimuli, are very important variables, it would be too restrictive to suppose that all associative learning required motivation significance as a necessary condition. The spinal level of representation would account for many of these, the human knee-jerk reflex being one of the earliest and most celebrated examples. In his pioneering study, Twitmeyer (1902/1974) noticed that one of the peculiarities of the conditioned knee-jerk response was that it appeared to be independent of motivation, since his subjects' voluntary attempts to inhibit their responses were wholly unsuccessful. The example serves also to illustrate, however, that there must be many cases where levels of stimulus representation and/or levels of association are mixed. Though the knee jerk may be regarded as a spinal reflex, and the unconditioned stimulus of a hammer blow to the patellar tendon would hardly qualify for a high score on a scale of perceptual complexity, the conditioned stimuli, at least as used by Twitmeyer, were not completely straightforward, since although a bell was sounded as a special signal, the operation of the special hammers almost certainly was also involved – on test trials the hammers swung as usual but were halted only just before contact with the knee was made. The conditioned knee jerks were observed after over 150 trials of conditioning in this apparatus, and this lengthy procedure suggests that familiarity with the whole context of the experiment may have been part of the learning process.

It is also possible to demonstrate conditioned associations which are relatively remote from stimuli of motivational significance within conventional paradigms in the animal laboratory. Rescorla and Durlach, (1981), for instance, suggest that rats allowed to drink sweet and quinine-flavoured water may associate the sweet and bitter flavours, even though these associations are not revealed in behaviour until more powerful motivating circumstances are imposed on the animals, in the taste-aversion procedure (see pp. 84 and 232). More generally, 'behaviourally silent' or 'latent' learning (Dickinson, 1980, see chapter 5), implies that associations may be formed in the absence of high levels of motivation, only to be revealed at a later date – motivation affects performance more strongly than it affects learning. Therefore although associations which are formed with emotionally arousing events are presumably of the greatest ecological significance, as well as being more likely to be amenable to laboratory study, it is necessary to allow for a category of relatively bloodless associations, as well as more highly charged 'hedonic shifts' in the value attached to real or experimental stimuli (Garcia *et al.*, 1977a).

The stimulus-response theory of classical conditioning

The stimulus-response theory of classical conditioning, as put forward by Hull (1943) and Spence (1956), was once widely held, but is now generally in disrepute (Mackintosh, 1974, 1983; Dickinson, 1980). It contains two parts. First is the assumption that the structure of the association in learning takes the form of a link between stimulus input and response output, and not for instance as a link between two stimuli, nor, in its strictest form, would a link between a stimulus and an inner emotional state be acceptable in stimulus-response theory. The second part of the stimulus-response theory of conditioning is the hypothesis that the crucial condition which leads to the formation of an association is the conjunction in time of the conditioned stimulus and the unconditioned response. This hypothesis may be readily disconfirmed at higher levels of stimulus representation. For example, with salivary conditioning in normal dogs, salivation may be blocked by use of the drug atropine, during pairings of a CS with acid – when tested with the CS alone when the drug has worn off the conditioned response is normal (Finch, 1938). Using pigeons in the autoshaping apparatus, the birds may be allowed simply to observe the sequence of the lighting-up of a key being followed by presentation of food, without being able to peck at the key, or actually get to the food, but after observing this conjunction of events without responding, they will peck at the key as soon as they have access to it (Browne, 1976). It would be possible for stimulus-response theorists to argue in these cases that the internal neural motor instructions for response output had been elicited, even if not implemented, making their theory less testable but more plausible. However, this modification does not help for the slightly less robust but nevertheless real phenomenon of sensory preconditioning (Mackintosh, 1974, 1983). An example of this was given above (p. 97) in the course of discussing conditioning without motivational significance – rats testing sweet and quinine-flavoured water (or almond- and banana-flavoured water) associate the two flavours together, before any definite 'unconditioned response' has been imposed on them – there can be no question of any small-scale version of the response, or motor instructions for it being performed, since the rats do not yet know what it is. Since the eventual motivationally significant event in this experimental procedure is intestinal distress, it is not clear that there is ever a specifiable unconditioned response. The traditional comeback for stimulus-response diehards in these cases is to argue that the fairly small effects measured should be interpreted as being due to unconditioned observing reactions, or something of that sort. Lip-smacking of some kind would have to be appealed to for associations between flavours – earlier experiments on sensory preconditioning which used the conventional tones and lights (Brogden, 1939; Rizley and Rescorla, 1972) had to be explained in terms of pricking up of ears and eye and head movements.

It is usually felt nowadays, however, that this type of sensory preconditioning experiment, along with others, negates the stimulus-response interpretation of classical conditioning in intact mammals and birds. However, it remains possible that some or other form of stimulus-response theory is applicable to classical conditioning when it is observed in the lesser systems discussed earlier, of mammalian spinal preparations or invertebrates. Certainly, when conditioning is attributed to synapses between particular identified sensory and motor neurons (Hawkins *et al.*, 1983; Hawkins and Kandel, 1984), it seems fair to invoke the first assumption of stimulus-response theory, that the nature of the association in this case is a link between stimulus and response. However, it is interesting to see that the theory put forward by Hawkins *et al.*, (1983) does not correspond to a cellular version of the second part of traditional stimulus-response theory. They do not say that the condition for learning is the conjunction of sensory input activity with motor nerve activity: instead they propose that it is the conjunction of CS input with the activity of a presynaptic facilitatory neuron. Thus their explanatory theory is of the stimulus pairing or 'S-S' form (see below), even though the result of this pairing can only be described as an increase in the ability of the CS neuron to fire the motor CR neuron. Nevertheless, this is still only a theory, and it is still only a theory about certain ganglia in *Aplysia californica*. It is not impossible that the animal world contains some neural systems or subsystems which correspond to what Hawkins *et al.*, (1983) refer to as the Hebb synapse, after Hebb (1949), in which the condition of modification is precisely that proposed in stimulus-response theory – the conjunction of some particular sensory input with a previously unconnected response motor output. Be that as it may, we already know that the animal world contains neural subsystems in which associations, however formed, are accurately described as stimulus-response connections, despite the fact that stimulus-response theory is inadequate when called upon to explain the majority of results describable as classical conditioning.

Stimulus-substitution theory of classical conditioning

Pavlov's own assumption about classical conditioning was that 'the neutral stimulus readily acquires the property of eliciting the same reaction in the animal as would food itself' (1927, p.26); workers directly in the Pavlovian tradition accepted and elaborated this view (Asratyan, 1965; Konorski, 1948, 1967), and various versions of the stimulus-substitution or 'S-S' theory have now replaced stimulus-response theory in the West (Jenkins and Moore, 1973; Boakes *et al.*, 1978; Mackintosh, 1974, 1983). As a generality, it is fairly accurate to say that, in classical conditioning, the conditioned stimulus becomes a substitute for the unconditioned stimulus, but, for particular cases, there is an almost infinite number of possibilities as to exactly what is substituted for exactly what. We may first get in our ritual celebration of the variousness of stimulus representations. When one stimulus is able to substitute for another, or acquires the properties of another, it is clearly not the stimuli outside that are changing but some internal representation of the stimulus inside the animal. At the lowest levels of representation which figures in Figure 4.1, the internal representation of an external event is simply activity in one particular sensory neuron in the spinal cord. Some physiological theorists (e.g. Barlow, 1972) might want to say that all other representations are activities in other individual neurons, at different places in the central nervous system, but by the criteria of range of stimuli and perceptual and psychological complexity, we are entitled to claim that some kinds of representation are richer and more elaborate than others.

Whether or not this claim is accepted, the behavioural results from many experiments make it clear that it is quite impossible to predict *all* the phenomena of conditioning by saying that the representation of the conditioned stimulus activates the representation of the unconditioned stimulus. In some cases, it is true, the behaviours elicited by the conditioned stimulus appear to be almost identical to the behaviours elicited by the UCS, thus tempting us to the conclusion that the animal is undergoing a complete hallucination of this particular unconditioned stimulus. Pavlov quoted the complex sequence of physiological reactions to morphine, all elicited by the sight of a syringe. A modern argument for stimulus substitution relies on evidence that, when a pigeon pecks at a key because this signals a reinforcer, slow-motion photographic analysis suggests that if the reinforcer is food they peck at the key as if they were pecking at grain, but if it is water that is signalled they peck at the signal as if it were water (Jenkins and Moore, 1973). But in other cases there are very large differences between the set of responses elicited by the conditioned stimulus and that normally given to the reinforcer.

Although Pavlov pointed to the principle of stimulus substitution for physiological responses, he also took a very broad view of the natural function of conditioning as a signalling process, and suggested that great adaptive importance attached to the way in which auditory and visual signals for food elicited the response of seeking for the food (1927, p. 14). Similarly, there are behaviours aroused by conditioned stimuli which can be put under the heading of investigation, or exploration. Pavlov called this the 'what is it?' reflex, and said that its biological significance was obvious (1927, p. 12). Specific searches for food, or more general investigation and inquisitiveness, are in some ways the opposite of the responses elicited by food itself, and therefore are at variance with the stimulus substitution idea. Fortunately Mackintosh (1983, pp. 56–7), has recently restored order to the confused ranks of stimulus-substitution theorists by arguing that the unconditioned stimulus, or reinforcer, should not be taken as a single unit, to be substituted or not, but as a large collection of *attributes*, any sample of which may or may not be transferred to the conditioned stimulus or signal. The attributes are not a random and unorganized collection, and Mackintosh (1983) emphasizes that a broad distinction can be drawn between the emotional and the sensory attributes of any reinforcing event, and also between 'preparatory conditioning' which may be diffuse emotional restlessness or excitement, and 'consummatory conditioning', which involves the transfer of more precisely definable responses, normally elicited by the reinforcer, such as salivation or blinking, to its signal. The later distinction, between preparatory and consummatory conditioning, was also made earlier by Konorski (1967). Further, for both emotional and hedonic, and more specific sensory and physiological, responses to a signalled event, there may be contrasting reactions, the 'opponent processes' of Solomon and Corbit (1974), with an initial process (the 'a-process') which is the first reaction, and then a compensatory or antagonistic process (the 'b-process') which has behavioural effects in the opposite direction.

This is a very much richer and more complete version of the stimulus-substitution theory than the usual straw man, and it can account for the varying results listed under different levels of representation in Figure 4.1. Thus emotional state conditioning would be distinguished from purely sensory or perceptual effects (levels 3 and 4) and the conditioning of compensatory reactions or opponent processes in the cases of morphine tolerance (level 2) or colour after effects (level 4) is taken into account. But all these cases are based on separating out attributes of the signalled event (or unconditioned stimulus). A further modification to stimulus-substitution theory, included by Mackintosh (1983) and stressed by others such as Boakes (1977), is that the behavioural effects of stimulus pairings will also depend on the attributes of the first event, the conditioned stimulus, which does the signalling. In many cases this is obviously bound up with attentional processes or orienting reflexes specific to a stimulus modality – animals may prick up their ears to an auditory but not to a visual signalling event. Holland (1977), in a very systematic study, found that rats given the stimulus of a light to signal the impending arrival of food pellets in a magazine reacted to the light predominantly by rearing up on their hind legs. This behaviour was more frequent than the next most popular, and readily explicable, response of standing motionless in front of the food magazine with the nose positioned at the spot where food pellets would shortly fall. His rats that

were given the signal of a tone instead of a light made anticipatory responses of this kind, but never reared up, as the
light signal animals did, but instead gave a snap of the head
or a jerk of the hind quarters, suggesting components of the
startle response given to much louder non-signalling noises.

Although Mackintosh (1983) himself resists it, it would
seem natural to blend the instinctive investigatory reactions
of animals to the sensory attributes of signalling events into
more complex reactions to these conditioned stimuli. For
instance, if, in an experimental procedure very like that used
by Holland (1977), the signalling event is not the presence of
a light or tone but rather the presence of another rat, dropped
into the experimental cage, reactions to the new and social
stimulus reflect its food signalling properties, but only in
social ways. Another rat dropped into the cage as a signal for
food is greeted more enthusiastically, by pawing and
grooming of the normal rat kind, than a conspecific similarly
dropped but without a history of bearing gifts (Timberlake
and Grant, 1975).

With dogs, explicitly social reactions are observed even
when the conditioned stimulus itself supplies no social
prompt. Jenkins *et al.*, (1978) used a speaker above a
protruding lamp to provide a localized compound signal for
10 seconds before small pieces of hot-dog were dropped into
a tray a metre or so away. The enthusiastic anticipation of
these titbits by the dogs was indicated not merely by alertness
or salivation, but by the fact that they approached the signal
source and showed individual patterns of social behaviour.
Some dogs devoted the time when the signal was on to
prancing in front of the food tray, but others nuzzled or
stood by the signal, and wagged their tails. This can all be
incorporated into the modified stimulus-substitution theory
advanced by Mackintosh (1983), as it is clearly the shift of
emotional associations of hot-dogs to the signal source which
arouses tail-wagging directed at it. However, when the attributes of the signalling event elicits social behaviour, as with
Timberlake and Grant's experiment above, or if, as we may
imagine, smells or sounds remotely associated with game elicit
tracking or co-operative hunting in canines, then the release
of instinctive behaviours characteristic of particular species

will have been subsumed in a large measure under the stimulus-substitution heading (Pavlov, 1927, p. 14).

Modified stimulus-substitution theory – conclusion

That psychological effects due to one stimulus come to be elicited by another is the essence of Pavlovian conditioning, and putting this in terms of the substitution of the signalling for the signalled event is usually satisfactory. It is clear, however, that the real meat of the experimental data, if one can put it that way, is not in this truism, but in the great variety of psychological effects to which it applies. If Pavlovian conditioning applied only to salivation, then not even Pavlov could have made very much of it. It is only because results obtained with salivation could be put in the contexts of general theories about signalling stimuli, and the action of the cerebral hemispheres, that the results acquired theoretical importance. Thus the question within stimulus-substitution theory is now not whether it is happening, but exactly what is being substituted for what. Is it a diffuse emotional substitution or a precise perceptual one? And is the psychological or physiological effect which is transferred to a signalling stimulus an instinctive general preparation, a premature jumping of the gun with a precise response characteristic of those given to the goal, or actually a conditioning of internal responses which will resist and oppose the final event? The variety of results discussed above demonstrates that these do not always boil down to the same thing. In any case stimulus-substitution is not really a theory at all, but a glorified description – it does not say why or how the changes take place or what other neural or psychological mechanisms are at work. The detailed explanations of why stimulus-substitution appears to take place will almost certainly depend on which attributes of the signalled event are involved, and on what I have called the level of representation of the stimuli – whether the behaviour concerns only spinal reflexes, metabolic reactions to injected drugs, or the attentive perceptual and motivational resources of the whole animal.

Discrepancy and expectancy theories of stimulus repetition and stimulus pairing

The most active area of theoretical development in the study of classical conditioning for more than the last decade has been in the test of assumptions originally put forward by Rescorla and Wagner (1972). One of the reasons for the fertility of these ideas is that they are capable of precise mathematical expression, but this means that the ideas may not be very accessible to an audience who are not specialists in the area. Therefore I shall attempt here to discuss the theoretical questions with a minimum of mathematical exactness. Readers who wish to follow up the original references might consult also Wagner (1976, 1978, 1979, 1981), Mackintosh (1975), Pearce and Hall (1980) and Grossberg (1982), but excellent detailed accounts of this work are also given in Dickinson (1980) and Mackintosh (1983). Despite the great fertility of this area, one of the difficulties of relating it to the present context is that the mathematical assumptions are not usually clearly tied down to biological and physiological realities. In fact, most of the testing of the theories takes place with the standard laboratory procedures discussed on pp. 83–90, which use intact mammals, and therefore I shall interpret the theories in terms of the perceptual and attentional capacities that might be expected to be present in these instances. The usefulness of the mathematical equations lies partly in the fact that they might apply equally well to the behaviour of very different systems, in some cases to the synaptic and stimulus-response level of stimulus representation (Sahley *et al.*, 1981), but the biological mechanisms responsible for the success of the equations might presumably be different in different systems.

The basic idea put forward by Rescorla and Wagner (1972) may be interpreted in terms of the discrepancy between actual and expected events in conditioning procedures. Their assumption was that a change in the properties of a conditioned stimulus only occurs when something happens which is surprising or unexpected. Thus a dog receiving food for the first time after hearing a buzzer will be pleasantly surprised, and a large increase in the conditioned effects of the buzzer should therefore take place. However, on receiving food after the buzzer for the umpteenth time, there is no surprise or unexpectedness, and therefore little change should accrue to the properties of the conditioning stimulus. This can be and was put in terms of attentiveness and expectations; and is experimentally testable in the phenomena of blocking in classical conditioning. If the dog is already conditioned to salivate to the buzzer, and a light is then added to the buzzer as a signal, subsequent testing reveals little salivation to the light (Pavlov, 1927; see Kamin, 1969), even though if the light had been used by itself to start with for the same number of trials, it might have been a most effective conditioned stimulus. This result of blocking of attention to the light is readily explained by saying that signalled events which are already expected contribute little to further conditioning. The more mathematically precise way of expressing this was in the equation below:

$$\Delta V_A = \alpha_A \cdot \beta_R \, (\lambda_R - \bar{V})$$

This refers to a conditioned stimulus A which precedes a reinforcer or unconditioned stimulus R. ΔV_A is the increment to the conditioned properties of A. This depends on two constants, one of which is α_A, the salience or associability of A, which has recently been a point of theoretical controversy, the other, β_R, the intensity or emotional significance of the reinforcer, being of unquestioned but little investigated practical importance. The originally vital part of the equation is $(\lambda_R - \bar{V})$, which represents the upper limit of all conditioned properties for the reinforcer R, minus the overall value of conditioned properties that are already present on a given trial covered by the equation. The equation would work perfectly well whatever these conditioned properties happened to be, and in terms of gradual acquisition of a conditioned response, as its strength approaches an upper limit, it would apply to the spinal leg flexions of Beggs *et al.*, (1983), and for the reduced response to a second conditioned stimulus which is added to one which is already functioning, it would apply to the behaviour of the terrestrial slug (Sahley *et al.*, 1981). It is conventional to interpret the equation, and others of the same form, in terms of expectations and representations of the conditioned and unconditioned stimuli, but it should be borne in mind that in some cases the internal representation of outer events will be accomplished by the activity of very rudimentary neural systems.

Following the convention, and ignoring the degree of significance of the signalled event, the equation can be interpreted as follows: the increase in the predictive value of a signal is proportional to a measure of its associability times the discrepancy between the obtained experience of the unconditioned stimulus and the overall level of expectation. In Rescorla and Wagner's treatment, the associability of the signal was a fixed property to do with physical things such as the intensity of a tone, and thus the explanation of conditioning phenomena rested entirely on reactions to the reinforcer. If the reinforcer was surprising, then extra conditioning could happen, but if the reinforcer was already expected, no further changes were necessary. What is missed out here, both in the equation and informally, is any other way of representing the attention given to signals.

Only expectations of the reinforcer change in the original Rescorla and Wagner (1972) theory, but a brief look at chapter 2 would be sufficient to indicate that the idea of expectations which change with repeated experience was used by Sokolov (1963) as a theory of response to stimuli which are repeated by themselves, without signalling anything of powerful motivational significance. Thus, if a stimulus is presented on its own repeatedly, a theory of habituation supposes that certain important things happen: in Sokolov's theory, it will be recalled, attention to that stimulus declines as knowledge of the stimulus, embodied in a neuronal model, increases. What, then, would Sokolov (or Pavlov) predict if a stimulus is first thoroughly habituated, and then used as a signal for food, or some other standard unconditioned stimulus? For two separate reasons, it could be predicted that subsequent conditioning will be somewhat delayed. First, the initial attention given to an habituated stimulus is reduced (the 'orienting reflex' has extinguished); and second, if the neuronal model of the repeated stimulus is as comprehensive in terms of temporal relationships as Sokolov (1963, 1975) supposed, then the neuronal model will include the fact that nothing else normally happens at the end of the signal stimulus, and it may take some time to overlay this bias with the new knowledge that the habituated stimulus now usually precedes a more powerfully motivating stimulus.

For whatever reason, it is a well-established experimental phenomenon that prior habituation of a stimulus to be used as a signal in Pavlovian conditioning will delay the process (Baker and Mackintosh, 1977; see Mackintosh, 1983). Frequently this phenomenon is referred to as 'latent inhibition', on the assumption that some inhibitory process is building up during habituation, but habituation does not necessarily involve the inhibitory processes which are appealed to to account for the suppression of responding by non-reinforcement (Mackintosh, 1983). There are both theoretical and factual reasons therefore to elaborate the theory of Rescorla and Wagner (1972) to incorporate habituation, and more generally the amount of attention devoted to conditioned stimuli, usually discussed in terms of the associability of those stimuli with subsequent signalled events. There is not yet complete agreement about the exact form such an elaboration should take. Pearce and Hall (1980) give a very thorough and formal account of the complexities and subtleties of the theoretical problems, but supply some ideas which may be usefully paraphrased, and link most directly with Sokolov's theory of habituation. They retain the central hypothesis of Rescorla and Wagner that the essence of conditioning is surprise, and that equations must therefore incorporate expressions which compare obtained experience with expectations. But instead of assuming that the unconditioned stimulus (US) loses effectiveness, they propose that the factor of associability of the conditioned stimulus, a separate entry in the equation, will depend on the confirmation of expectations, since they argue that any conditioned stimulus loses associability when its consequences are accurately predicted. Metaphorically, at least, they suggest that this is equivalent to the shift from controlled to automatic processing observed by Schneider and Shiffrin (1977) in studies of vigilance in human subjects. If we were to suppose that the sequence of conditioned stimulus followed by unconditioned stimulus was a complex single whole in Sokolov's model, we should similarly expect that a very often repeated sequence would lead to some reduction in attention and activation (see Figure 2.1). In Pavlov's laboratories, dogs were very often given several different positive conditioned stimuli, simply because some of them became so inattentive of repeated sequences that they were overcome by sleep. On grounds of general plausibility therefore, the familiarity of a signalling sequence of stimuli might be thought to result in some change in processing. Several particular experimental results also support the theory put forward by Pearce and Hall (1980). Most directly, Hall and Pearce (1979) used a tone as a signal for a weak shock, in a conditioned suppression procedure, (see pp. 83–4). Then this tone was used as a signal for a stronger shock, and the rapidity of the behavioural effects of this compared in control groups which had previously received the tone with no shock at all, or the weak shock signalled by a light. The results (see Figure 4.1) showed that having experienced the tone-weak shock sequence appeared to delay the effects of the tone-strong shock procedure. This is evidence against the idea that the initial pairing of the tone with weak shock should enhance subsequent conditioning using very similar stimuli. However it is not clear from this data whether the previous tone-shock experience had reduced attention to the tone, or built up a tone-weak shock association which delayed the tone-strong shock learning by a process analogous to proactive interference.

The simplest encapsulation of the Pearce-Hall (1980) theory is that a stimulus is more actively processed if there is uncertainty about its consequences (Mackintosh, 1983, p. 231). This certainly covers ordinary habituation, since there is little scope for uncertainty in the sense that there are no consequences, or, in Sokolov's model, the consequences are built into the model in terms of the temporal relationships between succesive single stimuli.

An elaboration of the Rescorla-Wagner theory which at first sight is in conflict with the Hall-Pearce model is that presented by Mackintosh in 1975, in which he suggested that stimuli which are already good predictors of other events will

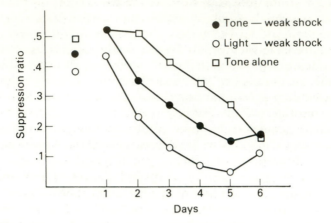

Figure 4.2   *An experiment on stimulus familiarity using tones and lights.*
The effects of pairing the same tone with a strong shock, for 3 groups of rats with varying experience of the tone. The lower a point on the graphs, the stronger the effects of the pairing. Thus the group with no previous experience of the tone but with experience of a light signalling a weak shock showed the fastest conditioned suppression and the group which had experienced the tone but no previous shocks showed the slowest effect of the pairing. In between was a group which had previously experienced the same tone signalling a weaker shock. After Hall and Pearce (1979).

be more actively attended to, and therefore more readily associable with a new unconditioned stimulus. There is ample evidence in favour of this view from rather different experimental procedures, which will be discussed in chapter 8. Most obviously, if an animal merely hears a pure tone, uncorrelated with motivating events, it is unlikely to continue to attend to it for very long; but if the same tone is a signal for food or shock, then attention to the tone will be increased. This is confirmed by the comparison in the experiment of Hall and Pearce (1979: see Fig. 4.1). One resolution of this conflict would be to assume that the loss of associability indicated by the comparison between the tone-shock and light-shock groups in that experiment was not due to lack of attention to the tone, but because attention given to the tone was combined with an expectation of weak shock, which expectation had to be altered. In general it is very difficult to be sure from such experiments exactly what form changes in 'associability' might be taking. However, it is possible to include, in the notion that uncertainty increases processing, the possibility that in the early stages of conditioning attention to a stimulus will be increased, only to wane again when the whole procedure becomes routine. This again is roughly similar to what happens in the development of habituation to novel stimuli.

Finally, Wagner himself has proposed a number of elaborations to the Rescorla and Wagner (1972) theory, which are explicitly intended to apply to habituation (Wagner, 1976), which make use of the previous theories of both Sokolov (1963) and Konorski (1967), and which are extended to link the phenomena of classical conditioning with some aspects of automatic processing in human memory (Wagner, 1981). Animals are assumed to represent stimuli in both short-term and long-term stores (see Figure 4.2 from Wagner, 1978). If such representations are already primed, either by recent presentation of the stimulus itself (in habituation) or by presentation of another signal previously associated with the stimulus (in classical conditioning), then response decrements of some kind are theoretically predicted (Wagner, 1976, p. 124). The former process (in habituation) is referred to as 'self-generated priming', and the later (in classical conditioning) as 'retrieval-generated priming' (ibid., p. 124). The storage of information in classical conditioning can be regarded as the 'course of activity in an individual memorial node under different circumstances of stimulation' (Wagner, 1981, p. 17), and equations specifying in detail such changes can be mapped on to precise experimental data. The most relevant data are of course those from experiments on habituation before conditioning, or latent inhibition. An important contribution of Wagner's theory (1976, 1981) is the suggestion that habituation to repeated stimuli should be *context-specific* (1976, p. 120). Just as it is possible to view repeated stimulus pairings as requiring some degree of habituation to the pairing interpreted as a single complex stimulus, so it is possible to

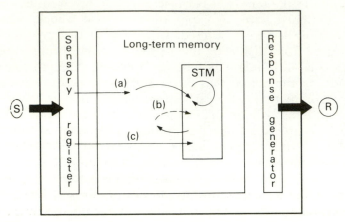

Figure 4.3   *Habituation as a form of priming.*
A theory of stimulus-response habituation in terms of short-term and long-term memory stores. It is assumed that, if a representation of a stimulus is already primed in the short-term store (STM) when the stimulus arrives at the sensory register, then response output is reduced. At (a) the receipt of a stimulus leads to a representation of the stimulus being moved from long-term to short-term memory, where it may be maintained by the loop ('rehearsal'). At (b) a representation may be retrieved without the stimulus itself being present, as in classical conditioning. At (c) the external stimulus directly accesses its already present representation in STM. After Wagner (1978).

think of a simple habituation experiment as the formation of an association between the *context* in which an experimental stimulus is presented and the stimulus itself. If a human subject listens to repetitions of a tone in a given room then habituation to the tone will probably involve associations between that tone and that room. Detailed studies of habituation and conditioning in animal experiments suggest that habituation (tested as the latent inhibition phenomenon of delayed subsequent conditioning) is certainly context-specific in this way, though a particular CS-US association is much less influenced by such contextual cues as background odours (Lovibond *et al.*, 1984). Clearly one would not want an infinite regress of all stimuli being regarded as forming associations with prior contexts, but the notion that repetitions of a stimulus will be coded in terms of surrounding cues is certainly consistent with Sokolov's treatment of the 'neuronal model', and with the common experimental result of dishabituation when background cues are changed. Wagner's theories should therefore be regarded as strong support for the strategy of treating habituation and classical conditioning as alternative experimental procedures applied to the same subjects and therefore as requiring theories about the general nature of information processing in those subjects.

Levels of representation in discrepancy theories of conditioning

As yet, it is a feature of the expectancy and discrepancy theories of classical conditioning and habituation that few predictions can be made from them about the phenomena to be expected at the different levels of stimulus representation shown in Figure 4.1 and discussed earlier in this chapter. It may be that analogous neural mechanisms in very different biological systems mean that no difference in predictions is necessary. For instance, the 'Standard Operating Procedures' of automatic memory processing which are discussed at length by Wagner (1981) are mainly based on the experimental phenomenon of 'conditioned diminution of the UR' in the nictitating membrane response of restrained rabbits, where the main stimulus is electric shock to the eye region. When the shock is applied, there is normally an eyeblink whose amplitude can be measured, and 'gross body movements' which similarly may be quantified. If a signal of a 1–second tone is given before all shocks, then some blinking and movement occurs to the signal, but also, the blinking and movement then given to the shocks themselves are reduced (Wagner, 1981, p. 27). The theory of retrieval-generated priming, by the signal, of a representation of the unconditioned stimulus may be the best way to account for this result, but it is easy to see that not wholly dissimilar data might be obtained, possibly from decorticate rabbits (Oakley and Russel, 1976, see pp. 72–3) or possible from conditioning with *Aplysia* (e.g. Carew *et al.*, 1983; Hawkins and Kandel,

1984), in which the reduction in response to the unconditioned stimulus was a result of relatively straightforward
short-term fatigue in the appropriate muscle systems.

Therefore it is not necessary to assume that short-term and
long-term memory stores, and processes of exchange between
them, always take precisely the same form at all levels of
stimulus representation. In particular, it would be expected
that active processes of attention, which are to be increased
when certain stimuli are recognized as good predictors, as
proposed by Mackintosh (1975), should not be as obvious at
lower levels of representation and/or in simpler neural
systems. Mackintosh himself has proposed that this may be
one of the dimensions of the difference between the behavioural capacities of the various species of vertebrate animals,
from fish to mammal (Mackintosh, 1969).

Habituation and conditioning – conclusions

In the first few years of this century, it was a view held by
some that the conditioning of the response of salivation to a
signal, as was then being studied by Pavlov, could not occur
in dogs with certain parts of the cortex of their cerebral
hemispheres removed. Pavlov himself demolished this
hypothesis by sitting in front of two such dogs, in someone
else's laboratory, and demonstrating the conditioning of the
salivary reflex on the spot. A main trend in the study of
conditioning ever since has been the discovery of anticipatory
shifts of simple reflexes to new signals in neural systems
progressively further removed from that possessed by a fully
equipped dog, culminating most recently with some physiologically important work on the gastropod mollusc *Aplysia
californica*. It was certainly not Pavlov's point that the cerebral
cortex was irrelevant for classical conditioning; on the
contrary he felt, erroneously as it turns out, that conditioned
reflex techniques would provide the key to uncovering its
mysteries. There are signs, however, that the more complex
and cognitive aspects of associative learning in higher organisms, as well as the physiogical basis of reflex connections in
lower ones, are becoming better understood. In new versions
of the stimulus-substitution theory, it is fully recognized that

a signalled event may be made up of a multiplicity of attributes, some in the form of internal perceptual representations
of various degrees of elaboration, some in the form of
emotional states, others being best seen as a delicate balance
between opposed metabolic processes (Mackintosh, 1983). In
conditioning, some sample of these attributes is transferred
to a signalling event, the mere size of the sample, but also in
particular the degree of elaboration of the perceptual
representations transferred, providing some measure of the
complexity of the associative processes involved. Theories of
precisely how these associative processes operate now cluster
around the notion of the ability to detect a discrepancy
between expected and observed events. (Rescorla and
Wagner, 1972; Rescorla, 1978; Wagner, 1976, 1981; Pearce
and Hall, 1980). This provides a useful bridge to the theory
of habituation (Sokolov, 1963, 1975). Animals may be viewed
as engaged in a continuous process of updating an internal
model of how external reality should be. Anticipation is an
adaptive virtue, and the functional end of both habituation
and classical conditioning is that there are no surprises: when
a surprising event occurs the animal system changes so as to
predict it in the future on the basis of time, place, or cause.

Detailed experimental results along these lines can be
obtained with laboratory mammals and birds, which allow
the testing of some precisely formulated theories, but the
essential feature of anticipatory reflexes, if not the mechanisms for cognitive expectation, can be studied in simpler preparations. Here again it would appear that internal organization reflects the procedural commonalities of the repetition
of a single stimulus (habituation) or of a stimulus pairing in
classical conditioning, since changes in the responsiveness of
simple neural systems to either procedure is thought to be
based on some or other kind of pre-synaptic facilitation, that
is, changes in the interactions of sensory neurons which are
independent of the characteristics of the motor or output
neuron (Thompson and Glanzman, 1976; Kandel, 1976;
Hawkins *et al*, 1983). This might be regarded as a form of
prediction for the future at the simplest possible level of
sensory representation of external events. Be that as it may,
the descriptive features of classical conditioning, as the

transfer of psychological effects from one stimulus to another, are common to very many kinds of learning from experience, and several different theoretical issues. Therefore the phenomena of classical conditioning, and the various attempts to explain them, will come up frequently in subsequent chapters.

5 Instrumental learning

'The things which move the animal are intellect,
imagination, purpose, wish and appetite.'
                    Aristotle, *De Motu Animalium*, 700b.

Although any mechanism which reduces responsiveness to a
repetitive and insignificant series of events may have biologically useful functions, if only in energy-saving, and any mechanism which produces anticipatory reactions to the precursors
of pain and pleasure has rather more obvious utilitarian possibilities, in neither of these cases is any account taken of on-
the-spot cost-benefit analyses, which might lead to either
active seeking of goals or more passive abstention from possible courses of action, according to evaluations of the pay-
offs, positive or negative, thereby obtainable. The basics of
habituation and classical conditioning do not therefore entail
a truly purposive form of goal-oriented behaviour, even
though Pavlov suggested that the arousal of food-seeking
intincts by remote signs of the presence of food was part of
the utility of the Pavlovian conditioning process. Thus, after
considering theories which confine themselves to the effects
of repeated stimuli, or of repeated stimulus pairings, we are
entitled to ask whether a new theory is needed to encompass
the learning of motor activities, especially those which are
associated with wish and appetite. Various detailed ways
in which the phenomena of classical conditioning may be
contrasted with those of active and purposive, or, more
conventionally, 'instrumental' learning, are discussed in

117

chapter 6, but clearly the question of motivation, in the form of drives, goals and incentives, is an initial reason for wanting to add something to theories of classical conditioning pure and simple.

A second obvious reason why one would want to add something to theories of learning concerned only with habituation and classical conditioning is that they say almost nothing about the learning of new response strategies or skills. Typically, in habituation an instinctive response disappears, and in classical conditioning an already present instinctive response is seen on new occasions, and thus there is no direct allowance for large increases in the repertoire of available behaviours. It is possible, though far-fetched, to propose that anticipatory changes due to classical conditioning underlie new response patterns and skills (Watson, 1914/1967; Spence, 1956; Bindra, 1968, 1976). In a sense, all any of us can ever do is contract the muscles we were born with in different sequences and degrees of intensity, but the setting up of new sequences, whether in the human skills of carpentry and carpet-weaving or in the more limited performances of circus and laboratory animals, surely requires principles of response organization which could never be made obvious from the study of salivation or withdrawal reflexes.

Thorndike's stimulus-response connections and the Law of Effect

A very ancient and very general principle of behavioural organization is that of reward and punishment – responses are directed so that the unpleasant is avoided and the pleasant pursued. However, there are many and various possible internal mechanisms which could produce behaviour which corresponds to this vague descriptive generalization. Thorndike (1898, 1901) provided, at the same time as Pavlov's discoveries in stimulus-pairing experiments, both a more specific descriptive law and a theory of the mechanism of response selection, both of which were extremely influential. At the descriptive level, filtering out as much as possible of Thorndike's hypothetical mechanisms, his 'Law of Effect' says that individual responses are initially made at random, but are selected according to their effects, that is according to their consequences for the responding animal. This is 'the method of trial and error with accumulated success' (Thorndike, 1898, p.105), which has something in common with Darwinian natural selection, since particular behaviours which turn out to be advantageous to the animal are retained from a range of unorganized variation.

In the experiments which Thorndike performed, the change from variable reactions in the 'trial and error' phase to a single advantageous response was easily observed, and in some cases very gradual. The main experiments were performed by putting hungry cats inside small crates or 'problem boxes' (see Figure 5.1) from which they could escape: there were 15 boxes, each with a different mechanical system – a loop of string to be pulled, or a lever to be pressed, for instance – which allowed a cat to open a door if an appropriate response was made. A piece of fish was available outside the boxes, which a cat could eat if it got out, but the initial reactions of most of the cats he tested appeared to Thorndike to be directed at getting out of the box rather than reaching the food. In all the boxes these initial reactions were very similar in 11 of the 13 cats Thorndike tested (the other two being more sluggish). 'When put into the box the cat

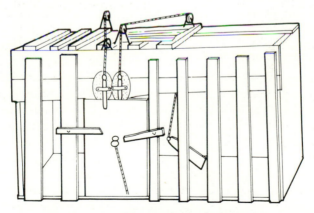

Figure 5.1 *Thorndike's problem box.*
See text. After Thorndike (1898).

would show evident signs of discomfort and of an impulse to escape from confinement. It tries to squeeze through any opening; it claws and bites at the bars or wire; it thrusts its paws through any opening and claws at everything it reaches; it continues its efforts when it strikes anything loose and shaky; it may claw at things within the box' (Thorndike, 1898, p. 13). These various behaviours were counted by Thorndike as relatively undirected trial and error. But, in the course of these 'impulsive struggles' it was likely that the cat would, eventually and by accident, make the response which opened the door to the box it was confined in. For example, in the simplest box, Box A, there was a large wire loop hung 6 inches above the floor in the centre, in front of the door, which opened the box if pulled, and on the first occasion on which the cats were put in this, most of them had accidentally opened the door within three minutes. But of course the important experimental result is that all the animals learned to do better than this, and escaped in less than a minute on the third and subsequent tests, on average, and in less than 10 seconds by the twentieth trial (see Figure 5.2). This is the experimental demonstration of the Law of Effect – the effects or consequences of a response change the probability that it will be performed in the future. Learning curves such as that in Figure 5.2 assess this in terms of the time taken to perform the response, or its latency, but the topography of the movements involved change as well, so that a well-trained cat,

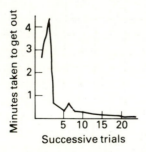

Figure 5.2   *Thorndike's results.*
See text. After Thorndike (1898).

instead of struggling wildly, will, as soon as it is confined 'immediately claw the button or loop in a definite way' (Thorndike, 1898, p. 13).

However, it was the theory which Thorndike used to explain the result, as much as the result itself, which attracted comment. Applying the rule of parsimony in explanation advocated in Lloyd Morgan's Canon (Morgan, 1894), Thorndike attacked Lloyd Morgan's own view that animal learning of this kind was an example of the association of ideas, that is, that the cats should be assumed to have associated the response of pulling a loop of wire and the outcome of getting out of the box and eating fish (Thorndike, 1898, p.66). As an alternative, Thorndike proposed that learned associations took a much simpler form, being always between the sense-impression of an external stimulus situation and a direct impulse to act. The consequences of actions, in terms of perceived pleasure or pain, or in terms of 'satisfying' or 'annoying' states of affairs, were important in Thorndike's theory only because pleasurable results 'stamped-in' or burned in the situation-response connection which led to them, while, at least in the early versions of his theory (see chapter 7), annoying results of an action stamped such connections out again. 'The impulse is the *sine qua non* of the association', and thus animals must have the impulse to act, and perform an act, before any associations are formed, and animals must always learn by doing and by actual experience of actions followed by reward. Thus Thorndike did not expect, nor did he find, learning taking place by one animal imitating what another animal did, even in his experiments on cebus monkeys (1901). For monkeys and other primates, and even eventually for people (Thorndike, 1931), Thorndike proposed that situation-response, or stimulus-response, connections were the basis of all learning. This proposal clearly bears some resemblance to Pavlov's idea of the formation of temporary connections in the nervous system (pp. 60–2), but the crucial addition made by Thorndike was immediate effect of reward and punishment in stamping-in or stamping-out connections between quite arbitrary preceding responses and their eliciting stimuli (see chapter 6).

As we shall see, the basic results of Thorndike's experiments with cats, even though he replicated them with dogs, chicks and monkeys, are not sufficient to establish his theory that all the effects of reward and punishment take place via the formation of stimulus-response connections. It is therefore worth noting briefly some further details reported by Thorndike which, he admitted, did not seem consistent with the most extreme position which he considered – the possibility 'that animals may have *no images or memories at all, no ideas to associate*' (1898, p. 73, original italics). One such detail is the fact that cats were very slow to learn to lick or scratch themselves if these responses were rewarded by the opening of the door (by Thorndike). This would not be expected if the only principle at work was a mechanical tendency to repeated any rewarded act, but various additional explanations can be offered, such as 'an absence of preparation in the nervous system for connections between these particular acts and sense-impressions' (Thorndike, 1898, p. 76; see Seligman, 1970). The more elaborate alternative is to suppose that the idea of clawing a loop to get out is more readily formed than the idea of licking oneself to get out. Indeed, a general feature of Thorndike's discussion of his results is an appeal to the process of attention. A particular response such as pushing a lever was more likely to be learned if the animal 'pays attention to what it is doing' (1898, p. 27). This factor is also appealed to to explain why it is that individual cats learned more and more quickly as they had experience of more and more difficult problem boxes. Part of Thorndike's explanation for this was that 'the cat's general tendency to claw at loose objects within the box is strengthened, and its tendency to squeeze through holes and bite bars is weakened', but in addition he noted that 'its tendency to pay attention to what it is doing gets strengthened, and this is something which may properly be called a change in degree of intelligence' (1898, p. 28).

Finally, in ignorance of Pavlov's work, Thorndike performed a stimulus-pairing experiment, which led him to the view that his cats formed representations of sense-impressions (1898, pp. 75–6). A hungry cat was kept in a large enclosure with a side of wire netting. Outside this Thorndike practised a routine of clapping his hands (and saying out loud, 'I must feed those cats'), ten seconds before going over and holding a piece of fish through the netting, 3 feet up from the floor. It will surprise few readers to learn that, after this had taken place 30 times, the cat climbed 3 feet up the wire netting immediately Thorndike clapped his hands, without waiting for the actual sight of the fish. Thorndike tentatively took the view that this was because the cat had some anticipatory idea or representation of the fish being presented in this case, without, however, acknowledging any anticipation of getting out and eating fish as a necessary factor in the string-pulling and lever-pressing experiments.

Hull's stimulus-response principles and reward by drive reduction

It can be seen from the example above that Thorndike was less than completely rigorous in his application of the principle that learning takes place when motivationally significant events stamp in connections between sense-impressions and arbitrary impulses to action. His account of learning relies to a large extent on subjective factors, even though he minimized the importance of inference and reasoning in animal experiments, since the learned connections were supposedly between the internal perception of external stimuli, which could be significantly modified by attentional processes, and a subjective compulsion to perform a given response. Equally obvious is the fact that the 'satisfaction' or 'pleasure', which is responsible for burning in preceding stimulus-response connections, is a hypothetical mental state of the subject, albeit one that can be inferred on the basis of behavioural evidence. Hull (1937, 1943, 1952) attempted to provide a far more rigorous and systematic theory of learning based on the principle of automatic stimulus-response connections, which had a far-reaching influence on many areas of both academic and applied psychology, but which stands today mainly as a monument to the limitations of this approach.

Hull attempted to strip away from Thorndike's Law of Effect all the more mentalistic or psychological extra processes involved in the perception of the environment, the organization of response output, and the emotional assessment of reward and punishment. Learned connections were no longer between sense-impressions of what the animal was attending to and its impulse to perform a particular act, but directly between the neural impulses from activated sensory receptors and certain muscular reactions – the term Hull used was 'receptor-effector connections'. The complexities of attention and perception were thus (temporally) side-stepped. Although this approach was initially plausible in terms of biological function, Hull also attempted what turned out to be an even more dangerous simplification by tying all motivation to states of physiological need, avoiding any reference to subjective states of pleasure or satisfaction. Animals have a biological need for food; lack of food was thus supposed to produce internal physiological stimuli described as the 'drive' of hunger. This would serve two purposes: the drive would in the first place be expected to activate and energize behaviours, but it also had an essential place in Hull's theory of reward, since eating food was supposed to affect the animal only in so far as it *reduced* the drive of hunger or the physiological deficit in nutrition.

Hull adopted Pavlov's (and Skinner's) term of 'reinforcement', for the event which strengthened stimulus-response connections, and thus Thorndike's Law of Effect became the *Law of primary reinforcement*, stated as follows:

> Whenever an effector activity occurs in temporal contiguity with the afferent impulse, or the perseverative trace of such an impulse, resulting from the impact of stimulus energy upon a receptor, and this conjunction is closely associated in time with the diminution in the receptor discharge characteristic of a need, there will result an increment to the tendency for that stimulus on subsequent occasions to evoke that reaction. (Hull, 1943, p. 80)

It was clear even to Hull that there might be a digestive delay before eating food actually changed physiological need states, and therefore he proposed that, normally, eating food reinforced preceding stimulus-response connections not by the 'primary reinforcement' of reducing the state of need, but by 'secondary reinforcement' caused because the stimuli involved in eating will have been 'closely and consistently associated' with eventual need satisfaction (Hull, 1943, p. 98). There is no doubt that particular experiences of eating do indeed acquire motivational significance partly because of subsequent metabolic changes (see for instance pp. 232ff on taste-aversion learning, and Rozin and Kalat, 1971), and the appeal to drive reduction has the advantage of being directly applicable to the learning of responses which allow escape from external imposed aversive states (see chapter 7). However, the notion that the reduction of needs or drives is in any sense a *necessary* condition for learning has been almost universally abandoned (although see Hall, 1983, pp. 206–13). The most important reason for this is that the learning which occurs in the course of habituation, more active exploration of the environment (see discussion of latent learning, pp. 150–2) and in several forms of Pavlovian conditioning, all lack the support of any physiological imbalance as obvious as those involved in hunger or lack of food. Further, learning under the influence of general social motivation (Thorndike rewarded chicks by allowing them access to the company of their fellows: see discussion of imprinting, pp. 23–4), or that rewarded by specific sexual stimuli (Sheffield, *et al.*, 1951 showed that proximity to a female rat, even without completed sexual activities, was rewarding to males of the species) appears to be governed more by the properties of external events than by hypothetical internal needs (Hinde, 1960, 1970). But, even in the prototypical case of the reduction of hunger by eating, motivational effects are considerably more complex than originally suggested by Hull. The tendency of human beings to eat things which are not medically good for them (for instance, large amounts of sweetened saturated fat in the form of chocolate or ice cream) itself suggests that an abstract conception of biological need is not an adequate guide to motivational significance. A general alternative to drive reduction, indicated for instance by the apparent equivalence of low-calorie and high-calorie sweeteners as reinforcers for rats (Sheffield and Roby, 1950), is that the stimulus properties of food substance when ingested, as well as their post-ingestional consequences, may have built-in rewarding effects.

However, the experimental results which led Hull to modify

his theory (though not to abandon drive reduction altogether) suggested that even the physical properties of reinforcing agents themselves do not adequately predict their behavioural effects, but rather, an internal evaluation of a given reward determines its effects on the learned performance of hungry rats. Crespi (1942) compared the performance of rats trained to run down an alley for food rewards of just less than a third of a gram with that of groups trained first with larger or smaller rewards, and then shifted to this reward amount. Figure 5.3 illustrates the case of rats which first experienced

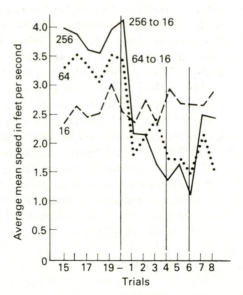

Figure 5.3   *The emotional effects of rapid incentive learning.*
Results of an experiment in which the amount of food obtained as reward by rats for running to the end of a straight alley was varied, using units of a 50th of a gram. Rats trained with larger rewards ran faster than rats trained with a small reward, but when all then received that small reward, a rapid reduction in speed of running took place in those rats which had formerly been given large rewards, so that they ran more slowly than rats already accustomed to receiving small rewards. After Crespi (1942).

5–gram rewards, and were then given a fraction of that amount for the same response, showing that their speed of running dropped sharply, and to a level well below that of animals' which had received the smaller reward consistently. Crespi's own interpretation of this was that the reduction in reward size engendered an emotional depression in the animals. Hull (1952, p. 142) retained the notion of a temporary emotional effect caused by reward reduction to account for the drop in response speed below the normal level, but also added a special process of 'incentive learning', detached from both drive reduction and the formation of stimulus-response connections, which he used to explain both the rapid change in performance in this experiment, and the immediate improvement in accuracy of maze-running when rewards are introduced following a period of unrewarded exploration ('latent learning' – see pp. 150–2). There are a number of other results from standard laboratory experiments, under the heading of 'contrast effects' (Dunham, 1968; Mackintosh, 1974, pp. 213–6) or 'post-conditioning changes in the value of the instrumental reinforcer' (Mackintosh, 1983, pp. 80–6) which seem to indicate that a re-assessment of the emotional value to be put on a given reward can take place in separation from the response-learning process, and some of these will be discussed in a later section (pp. 137–7). It is usual now to conclude that 'instrumental learning cannot be reduced to an S-R association' (Mackintosh, 1983, p. 86), and since the drive reduction factor in the reward process tends also to be discounted, Hull's reformulation of the Law of Effect has lost both its mainstays.

Skinnerian pragmatics

The best-known modern protagonist of the Law of Effect is B. F. Skinner, who has gradually abandoned almost all theoretical speculation as to the role of drive, stimulus-response connections, or any other internal mechanism or process which might explain how or why learning takes place, in favour of empirical demonstration of the practical power of reward procedures in the animal laboratory, and rhetorical assertions about the ubiquity of strictly analogous effects in

128 Instrumental learning

human life. I shall for the present confine myself to a discussion of the former, and ignore the latter (see Walker, 1984, chapter 10).

Thorndike's technique for studying learning in cats and dogs required him to replace the animal inside a box each time it made the successful response of getting out. In his experiments on cebus monkeys however, Thorndike found it expedient to change this procedure so that the animal remained inside an experimental enclosure, a piece of banana being dropped to it down a chute whenever it depressed a lever. Skinner (1938) used a similar set-up for laboratory rats, with automated devices for recording lever presses and delivering food pellets, and later developed a version which was used in very extensive experiments on pigeons (Ferster and Skinner, 1957) thus inventing what is now a very widely used piece of apparatus in animal laboratories, known as the Skinner box. The isolation of the animal subject, and the automatization of the experimental procedures, may be partly responsible for the fact that a wide variety of extremely reliable (and replicable) behavioural results can be obtained by this method, and it is of course extensively used today by researchers with no commitment to Skinner's theoretical views. In fact, Skinnerian apparatus and behavioural techniques are used in so many theoretical contexts that it is quite inappropriate to gather together all the obtainable results here, but the basic phenomena associated with 'schedules of reinforcement' can usefully be reviewed at this point.

Schedules and contingencies of reinforcement

There is a good deal in common between certain kinds of Skinnerian reinforcement theory and general principles of economics (see, e.g., Lea, 1978, 1981; Rachlin *et al.*, 1981). It is assumed in economics that certain global aspects of human business – savings, investment, employment and so on – may be ultimately determined by certain quantifiable variables – money supply or interest rates for instance, without too much detailed attention being given to the actual psychology of individual decision-making or the gradual change or growth of business enterprises. The success (or failure) of such assumptions rests partly on the degree to which people or companies do indeed act predictably in always acting to maximize their own economic advantage. In the same way it is a central assumption of reinforcement theory that animals will learn anything and everything which maximizes their receipt of food rewards, with many subtle and global aspects of learned behaviour thus being ultimately determined by quantifiable variables concerned with the conditions of availability of food rewards (or 'contingencies of reinforcement'). The end relationship between the scheduling of food rewards and the exact patterns of behaviour which are eventually determined by various conditions of reward can be and often is discussed without too much attention being given to gradual learned changes in behaviour (and the mechanisms which might be responsible for these). However, there can only be fixed relationships between contingencies of reinforcement and patterns of behaviour engendered by them if animals act predictably in accordance with the Law of Effect, and at the descriptive level always select behaviour which has beneficial consequences. This is not always the case – individual species are influenced by particular reinforcers in ways which reflect instinctive processes that are relatively immune from experienced pay-offs (Roper *et al.*, 1983; Breland and Breland, 1961; see chapter 6) – but with the now standard laboratory procedures first used by Skinner, the predictability of relationships between contingencies of reinforcement and behaviours learned thereby is surprisingly high.

Continuous and ratio reinforcement

The simplest possible Skinner-box experiment, analogous to the Pavlovian case where a buzzer always signals food, is performed when an animal is able to deliver to itself a small amount of food each time it performs a single response such as pressing a lever or pushing a button. Left to itself, an individual of any common laboratory species will eventually discover this by trial and error, if the response is such as is made occasionally by accident; but it is usual to give prior adaption to the working of the food delivery mechanism, and there are other methods of training, such as autoshaping (see pp. 84–5 and chapter 6), or 'shaping' the response by carefully watching the animal and delivering reward for successive approximations to the required behaviour (e.g. delivering rewards initially when a rat sniffs at a lever, then only when it touches it, then only when it presses the lever down). Once such a response has been learned, then if the animal is already hungry when it is placed in its experimental box, it will press the lever at regular intervals, gradually slowing down if it is allowed to become satiated. After such training, an additional learning process can be observed by disconnecting the food mechanism, since a hungry animal will at first continue vainly to make the response but will gradually cease to do so – the process of response extinction. Little can be concluded from this simple confirmation of trial and error learning, but the nature of the procedure allows for many extensions of the basic task. For instance, the animal may be required to make a fixed number of responses for each reward – a fixed-ratio schedule. This involves gradual learning, especially if the fixed number is large. Clearly the animal is not able to obtain rewards as frequently if it has to make 100 responses before each one, but additional standard results are that there is a pause in responding after each reward, roughly proportional to the size of the ratio, and that a run of responses is then made at a fast and gradually increasing rate (Ferster and Skinner, 1957). Obviously, the higher the ratio the higher in some sense is the cost in time and effort of obtaining rewards, and this is reflected in the variation both in vigour of performance and the size of the highest ratios that animals will continue to perform, which are systematically related to motivational factors such as degree of prior deprivation and the size and palatability of the rewards used (Hodos, 1961; Hodos and Kalman, 1963; Powell, 1979). Ecologically speaking, the relationships between effort and food reward would be expected to be vastly different between species, depending on niche. For instance, herbivorous browsers, need to feed for long periods but carnivores (especially cold-blooded ones), eat relatively infrequently and difficult-to-obtain but richer meals. However, it appears that rats, being omnivorous, are extremely flexible in this respect, when they are left permanently in a Skinner box with various ratios of lever-pressing necessary to obtain food rewards (Collier *et al.*, 1972). If allowed one small pellet for every press, then about once every hour they would go and press 20 times in succession, eating 20 pellets in less than 10 minutes. When required to make 160 presses for each pellet, they were able to obtain almost as much food as before, by spending 14 hours a day making the necessary 70,000 responses. Even more flexibility was shown if the unusual procedure was used of rewarding rats by allowing them to enter a tunnel and eat for as long as they liked – but with the constraint that if they left the tunnel for more than 10 minutes then a fixed ratio of lever presses was necessary to make food available again. In this case rats required to make only one response to produce free access to food ate 10 separate meals a day, but if the ratio was increased they chose, reasonably enough, to eat fewer but longer meals, eating only five times a day when 40 responses were necessary to gain access to food, and eating only one large meal per day when just over 5,000 lever presses were required to gain access to food. In this experiment (Collier *et al.*, 1972) water was always available, but exactly analogous results were obtained when fixed ratios of responses were necessary to obtain water, with food always available, except that with indefinitely long access to water as the reward, a ratio of only 300 bar presses was required to persuade the rats to take just one (long) drink of water per day (Marwine and Collier, 1979). This strongly suggests that frequent access to food is rather more rewarding for individual rats than frequent access to water. Lore and Flannelly (1978) deduced that access to water is ecologically important from their naturalistic study of the location of the burrows of wild rats on a large landfill, since these tended to be located within 50 metres of a stream but only within 100 metres of the food source, (a mound of refuse). Clearly many factors, notably in this case an obvious preference for sloping ground, may determine burrow location.

The general descriptive conclusion from experiments on fixed ratio schedules is simply that the size of the ratio significantly affects the pattern of responding for a given reward.

The theoretical implications of this are not always clear, but several experiments suggest that laboratory animals are capable of learning some representation of the size of the fixed ratio (Adams and Walker, 1972; Mechner, 1958; Rilling and McDiarmid, 1965). That this is not strictly necessary for performance on ratio schedules is shown by the possiblity of variable ratio schedules, in which a probabilistic device such as random number generator ensures that the exact point at which reward is given is always unpredictable, even though the average value of the ratio can be specified. Only a limited amount of evidence about the effects of this is available, but some rather complicated comparisons suggest that a variable ratio schedule produces somewhat faster responding than a fixed ratio of the same average value, with shorter pauses after reward is received, due to the effects of the occasional reinforcement of a single response or a very short run of responses. Given the choice, pigeons appear to prefer to work on the uncertain variable ratio than on a fixed ratio of equivalent average value (Ferster and Skinner, 1957; Fantino, 1967; Sherman and Thomas, 1968).

Interval schedules of reinforcement

It also appears to be the case that variable ratio scheduling of reinforcements produces a higher rate of response than the same number of reinforcements (that is the equivalent frequency over time, and thus the same rate of gain of food) which are made available according to a different rule, based on the minimum interval of time between one reward and the next. For a variable interval schedule of reinforcement, a certain period of time, random about some mean, must elapse after one reward has been given before a *single* response produces the next. Since only one response per reward is necessary, it is not surprising that fewer are made than when multiple responses are mandatory on variable ratio schedules (Ferster and Skinner, 1957; Thomas and Switalski, 1966; Peele *et al.*, 1984; Zurif, 1970). Variable interval schedules are very widely used because they produce a very consistent and steady rate of responding, which accelerates only slightly as time without a reward passes (Ferster and Skinner, 1957: Catania and

Reynolds, 1970). For instance, if hungry pigeons can obtain reward for a single key peck on a variable interval of 1 minute, they typically begin pecking the key again within a few seconds of receiving food. Very occasionally they are rewarded at this point, but at other times they may continue to peck regularly, without anything else happening, for 4 or 5 minutes, until the next reward finally becomes available.

The theoretical analysis of performance on interval schedules is easier in the alternative case of a fixed interval, where the minimum period between successive rewards is always the same. Here the typical performance in a rat or pigeon, depending on the length of the interval, is that there is a distinct pause after a reinforcement has been received (as with fixed ratios) followed by a gradual increase in the rate of responding, such that the highest rates of response occur just before the next reinforcement becomes due. This increase in response rate with time, along with other measurements, has been used to deduce that laboratory animals make use of an 'internal clock', which can be accurate to within a few seconds, to govern responses (Dews, 1962, 1970; Roberts and Church, 1978; Roberts, 1981; Meck and Church, 1984; Gibbon, 1977). According to Roberts (1981), this clock is a linear measure of time, which can be reset by food rewards, stopped at a given point by appropriate external signals, and used to time intervals of several different lengths concurrently. This is rather hypothetical, but it is clear that one of the factors that may be involved in performance on interval schedules is the engagement of some sort of representation of the passage of time. Whether the internal clock is associated with expectancies of reward, or serves rather as a stimulus for more mechanical habits of response, is not usually obvious.

Choice in reinforcement schedules

The reinforcement schedules described so far have all concerned the relationship between a single response and the availability of reward. A strikingly more complex state of affairs arises if an animal is confronted with two available responses, each assigned its own schedule of reinforcement. A degree of orderliness prevails, however, if both available responses are rewarded on variable interval schedules. Suppose a pigeon is allowed for one hour every day to obtain grain in a box where pecking the left key is rewarded on average every 3 minutes (VI3min) and pecking the right key is rewarded on average every 6 minutes (VI6min). What is the optimal way for it behave? The answer, of course, depends on what one means by 'optimal'. To gain the most food with the least amount of effort, physical or intellectual, it would be sufficient for the bird to peck the keys alternately, about once every 10 seconds. In fact, with the schedule as described, and a not-very-hungry pigeon, this is exactly what happens – the bird pecks at roughly the same rate on both keys, even though it gets 20 rewards per hour from the left key but only 10 from the right. The nature of the variable interval schedules means that the distribution and rate of responding has very little effect on the distribution of rewards, provided that both responses are made occasionally. But, by increasing the psychological separation between the two responses, the effects of rewarding one twice as often as the other can soon be observed: the standard procedure is to ensure that a left response is not rewarded if it is made just after a right response, or vice versa (a 'change-over delay', Herrnstein, 1961; Silberberg and Fantino, 1970).

Once this is done, data of impressive regularity may be obtained, since the procedure of giving twice as many rewards for left pecks as for right pecks then means that pigeons peck left twice as often as they peck right (Herrnstein, 1961, 1970). The interpretation of this unsurprising result has, however, proved to be difficult, and theories of increasing mathematical complexity are now proposed to account for it (Herrnstein, 1970; Baum, 1974; Rachlin *et al.*, 1981; Prelec, 1982, 1984; Shimp, 1969; de Villiers and Herrnstein, 1976). For present purposes it is sufficient merely to stress that the regularity does not arise only because a response is strengthened in proportion to the exact number of times it is rewarded.

There is a descriptive generality, called the 'matching law', which can be given either as

$$\frac{B_1}{B_1 + B_2} = \frac{R_1}{R_1 + R_2} \qquad (1)$$

or as

$$\frac{B_1}{B_2} = \frac{R_1}{R_2} \qquad (2)$$

where B_1 and B_2 are the absolute frequencies of two behaviours, and R_1 and R_2 are the absolute numbers of rewards each receives per hour. There are two general kinds of explanation for why this equation satisfactorily predicts behaviour, and therefore predicts in some sense the choice that a pigeon makes between two responses. The first kind says that the matching law arises because in some way or other animals are sensitive to the ratio of reinforcements for two responses and adjust their response choices accordingly. The second supposes that the matching relationship arises because the animals are attempting to respond optimally and that the observed allocation of responses results from their 'maximizing' their momentary chances of reward. Although these theories sound very different, as it happens close examination of what the two theories predict about experimental results suggests that they are 'empirically indistinguishable' (Ziriax and Silberberg, 1984; see Mackintosh, 1983, p. 258).

Relative reward value

There is, however, an extremely unambiguous empirical distinction between two possible rules which would both produce the matching law in practice. One rule implies that any response is performed according to the reinforcements it itself receives; the other says that a response is performed according to the *relative* value of the reinforcements it receives – most directly according to the proportion of the total rewards that are assigned to it in circumstances of choice. Thus

$$B_1 = kR_1 \qquad (3)$$

is the first case and

$$B_1 = \frac{kR_1}{R_1 + R_2} \qquad (4)$$

is the second. Either equation (3) or equation (4) would

produce equations (1) and (2). But, 'the data unequivocally support' equation (4): (Herrnstein, 1970). This is because there is a very simple experimental test: a pigeon is rewarded at a standard level – say 20 times per hour, for pecks on the left key; while over a period of days or weeks, the frequency of rewards for right key pecks is varied between zero and 40 per hour. Even though the left key pecks are being rewarded at the same level, the rate of left-key pecking varies systematically, roughly in line with equation (4), although the fit of the data is even better when the total frequency of rewards in the denominator is raised to a fractional power (Catania, 1963). As with the matching law itself, the reason why equation (4) works is more obscure than might be expected. We can rule out the argument that left-key pecks are made less often if right-key pecks are rewarded a lot, because the animal is then too busy making right-key pecks, since it can be arranged, by giving a visual signal for exactly when they will be rewarded, that it gets many rewards for right-key pecks without having to spend much time on that behaviour (Catania, 1963).

The descriptive alternative is that the effectiveness of a certain level of reward on the left key declines when an alternative source of reward is available. It is likely that this sometimes involves perceptual or emotional contrast effects between two levels of incentive experienced by the same animal, but a simpler possiblity is that the satisfying or even satiating effects of one reward alternative detract from overall drive in general, or from the incentive properties of all alternatives. (Crespi, 1942; Walker *et al.*, 1970; de Villiers and Herrnstein 1976). Hull (1952) found it necessary to distinguish between the drive-reducing and the incentive effects of rewards, and (at least) these two factors probably have to be taken into account. The satiating effect of rewards seems obvious, for instance, in the experiment of Rachlin and Baum (1969), in which pigeons received 20 rewards per hour (VI3 min) and 4 seconds access to grain, for pecks on their right key, while the same number of signalled rewards on the left key varied in duration from 1 to 16 seconds. When this alternative was 16 seconds, the birds gained 10 grams more weight in the experimental hour than when it was 1 second, and this would be sufficient to account for the fact that the rate of response for the standard reward was slower in the first case.

However, a fairly general finding is that the duration or magnitude of rewards given in concurrent schedules has much less effect on behaviour, and produces much less close matching of behaviour to relative reward properties, than does the variable of frequency of reinforcement (Walker *et al.*, 1970, Walker and Hurwitz 1970; Schneider, 1973; Todorov *et al.*, 1984). In other words, animals are much more likely to notice that they get an extra small reward from an alternative source, than that they get a reward which is twice as big. Frequent access to small amounts of food is generally much preferred to infrequent access to large amounts (see Collier *et al.*, 1972, p. 131), and thus it is the details of the distribution of rewards over time, rather than the gross total of consumption, that has the strongest psychological effect in the experiments.

Skilled performance and the form of a response

In the use of Skinnerian techniques for detailed laboratory work on 'the experimental analysis of behaviour', the emphasis is very often on the rate at which a given response is performed, with little attention given to the initial learning which determined its qualitative form. But reward procedures have just as much of an effect on 'how' as they do on 'how often' a response is performed. Skinner (1938) described the training of rats to press a lever with a certain force, or to press it down for a certain length of time. As a general rule, he found that 'Rats tend to adjust to a force which secures only slightly above the reinforcement of every other response' (1938, p. 317). Thus, if a lever needs to be pressed with a force equivalent to a dead weight of 20 grams, even experienced animals will make up to 40 per cent of their attempts at pushing it down with insufficient effort. They are strong enough to do better than this, since if the criterion is shifted, and a mechanical adjustment made so that a press of 60 grams or more is needed, then the animals quickly learn to make harder presses, but still make a third or more partial presses of less than 60 grams in force. Skinner found that one animal which weighed less than 200 grams itself could sustain presses averaging over 100 grams each, but even at much lower force requirements there seemed to be a principle of least effort bringing responses down below the minimum force necessary.

Normally for food rewards rats press a lever for only a fraction of a second. However, they may be gradually trained to hold it pressed down for 20 or 30 seconds at a time (Skinner, 1938), and various more complex techniques can be used to assess the accuracy of such timing, when there is no external feedback to signal when the lever has been pressed long enough. A further possible variation in the topography of a rat's lever-pressing is the amount of angular movement: Herrick (1964) succeeding in training his animals to depress a lever through an angular displacement of at least 20.35 degrees, but not more than 25.50 degrees. Rewards were delivered only when the lever returned to its home position after excursions which met this criterion, and therefore the judgment of a correct lever press required some muscular finesse on the part of the rats (and some technical ingenuity in the design of the apparatus). However Herrick's rats satisfied Skinner's expectation that they should adjust their behaviour so that at least every other response gained reward.

Although the acquisition of motor skills in animal learning is sometimes overlooked, it is clear that laboratory animals, starting with Thorndike's cats, are able to learn to operate with considerable accuracy mechanical apparatus that is quite different from anything members of the same species would ever encounter in a natural environment. Often natural and instinctive behaviour patterns are also elicited (see chapter 6), but it is undeniable that new muscular patterns of some skill emerge under the influence of artificial training procedures.

Creativity in response selection

It is a Skinnerian dogma that changes in the form of a response always reflect the shaping effect of contingencies of reinforcement in the environment on a passive subject. This probably overstates the case even for laboratory rats and pigeons, but an explicit counter-example is available from systematic experiment on two rough-toothed porpoises, members of the only mammalian group, the whales, better endowed with brain tissue than the primates. Pryor *et al.* (1969) were initially attempting to demonstrate only the power of the Law of Effect in the shaping of new behaviours by reward. For five days a porpoise was, in the course of public performance at a sea life park in Hawaii, rewarded for a different particular behaviour each day, but the procedure had to be aborted because the animal began to perform a large number of response sequences which not only had not been specifically trained, but which had not previously been observed by the experimenters. These included various aerial flips and swimming with the tail out of the water. Pryor *et al.* assumed that 'novelty was an intrinsic factor' in the origin of the new responses, and that what had happened was that the procedure of giving rewards for something different each day had inadvertently rewarded novelty as a category of response. A second and more docile animal was therefore tested with a similar procedure with two observers and systematic recording of data. For the first seven days only breaching, beaching, porpoising and swimming upside down were observed and the animal tended to adopt a rigid pattern of these previously reinforced tricks. After a further seven sessions of training with particular new tricks, this second animal began to display the same varied behaviour as the first, emitting eight different kinds of behaviour in the sixteenth session, including a spin, a flip, an aerial spin, an upside-down tailslap, and a tail side-swipe, which were all seen for the first time. These were then rewarded one by one until, in five final sessions (28–33), the animal had to come up with a new response each time to obtain its fish rewards. On session 30, it performed 60 different patterns of movement, but all had been seen before, and thus it got no fish. On the next three sessions however, it managed to come up with a backwards flip, an upside-down porpoise, and finally the response of standing on its tail and spitting water at the trainer. It may be stretching a point to refer to this as 'creativity', but clearly, the cumulative effects of the training procedure resulted in the animal learning something other than merely the mechanical repetition of stereotyped and unchanging patterns of response.

Spatial learning and 'cognitive maps'

The conclusion that instrumental conditioning typically consists of something more than the repetition of particular stamped-in stimulus-response connections was of course reached earlier by Tolman (1932, 1948) on the basis of rather different evidence, namely, the behaviour of rats in mazes. Hardly anything about the behaviour of rats in mazes supports the existence of specific stimulus-response connections, since, in the first place, it is impossible to identify a specific stimulus, or a specific response. Small (1901) trained rats to follow the correct path to food in a modified form (suitably scaled down) of the maze built for human amusement at Hampton Court Palace (see Figure 5.4). Yew hedges are replaced by high sided boards, which the animals cannot see over, and they must thus move in enclosed alleys. Clearly in this type of maze, detailed visual cues will be likely to be less important than they are in the other main type, the 'elevated maze', where the rats run on planks without sides

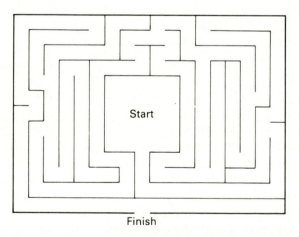

Figure 5.4   *The Hampton Court Maze for rats.*
See text. After Small (1901).

fixed several feet above the ground. Both Small (1901) and later Watson (1907) who used the same maze with rats variously handicapped by blindness, deafness or lack of the sense of smell, speculated that the learning of the maze was accomplished as a motor pattern – by associations of 'motor images of turning', for Small, and 'a serially chained kinesthetic reflex-arc system' for Watson. An enormous amount of evidence (summarized by Munn, 1950) suggests that associations between successive movements are rarely important in maze-learning. MacFarlane (1930) and Evans (1936) by flooding enclosed alley mazes with water, showed that rats which had learned a maze by swimming, running or wading could follow the correct path by an alternative form of locomotion, that is using very different kinesthetic cues. More drastically, Lashley and Ball (1929) and Ingebritsen (1932) lesioned ascending propioceptive nerve tracts in the spinal cord, producing in many cases aberrant posture or patterns of movement, but with relatively little effect on the rats' ability to learn or retain the correct pattern of turns in a maze. Since direct associations of series of movements does not thus seem important, and since also no individual sense modality appears crucial to maze-learning (Watson, 1907; Honzik, 1933, 1936), the alternative theory is that maze performance has to be under the control of multiple stimuli, and feasible with multiple responses (Hunter, 1930) or, in what may be another way of saying the same thing, controlled by 'central' or 'symbolic' factors (Lashley, 1929).

Tolman's contribution can be summarized as the designing of elegant behavioural experiments to demonstrate that rats use various cues to achieve a sense of geographic place, and as the providing of the long-lived term 'cognitive map' as part of his theory of 'purposive behaviourism'. The best examples of experiments used by Tolman to support his theory are thus those on the phenomenon of 'place learning'. The normal laboratory rat will give every appearance of expecting food at a particular familiar place in a maze it has learned: it will sniff and search for the food if it is absent, and attempt to burrow under or climb over obstacles placed in its normal path. Alternative routes to the same food may be used if several of equivalent length are available (Dashiell, 1930).

There are many anecdotal reports of rats finding short cuts (e.g. Helson, 1927). Tolman *et al.* (1946) attempted a systematic study of this, by first training animals to take a right-angled dog's leg path to a goal box which was situated in a direction of 60 degrees from the starting point, and then providing them with 18 paths at 10–degree intervals. More than a third of Tolman's rats did indeed take the sixth path, going directly towards the site of the goal box, but another 17 per cent took the first path on the right, and other experimenters trying to replicate the result found rats apparently trying to retrace the dog's leg. However, a simpler experiment, which opposes turns in a particular direction against movement towards a particular place, produces easily replicable results. The procedure is to start rats from different sides of a cross-maze (see Figure 5.5), and to compare animals always rewarded for turning in the same direction (and therefore rewarded in different places) with others always rewarded in the same place (and therefore rewarded after both left– and right-turns). Tolman *et al.* (1946, 1947) found that their animals were much better at always going to the same place, using an elevated maze with asymmetrical lighting and other obvious possible landmarks. It is not now doubted that this sort of place-learning comes relatively easily to rats, but, if a similar experiment is run in the dark, or under a homogeneous white dome, then, not surprisingly, it is easier for the animals to learn a consistent turning response (e.g. Blodgett and McCutchan, 1948).

Several more kinds of experiment have more recently confirmed the complicated nature of place learning. O'Keefe has identified not only particular external landmarks used by his rats (coatracks, etc., which when moved produced errors in a predictable direction), but also particular brain cells (in the hippocampus) which, among a large population, fire whenever the rat goes to a certain place in its apparatus (O'Keefe and Nadel, 1978; O'Keefe, 1979). The prize for the most Tolmanian experiment of the 1980s will probably go to R. G. M. Morris (1981), since he combined the swimming which was used in Tolman's laboratory by MacFarlane (1930) with an appeal to remote landmarks. Rats were put in a large circular tank of water made opaque by the addition

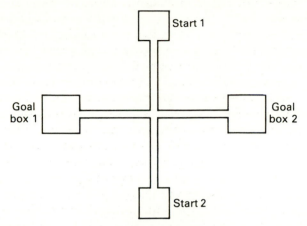

Figure 5.5   *Place versus response learning.*
A maze in which rats may be trained to always make the same turn, to different places, or to turn either left or right, in order to get to the same place. See text.

of milk (mud would have been more naturalistic). At a certain point in the tank was a cylinder with its top 1 centimetre below the surface – as soon as they found this rats would climb up on to it, and the test of learning was that, with experience, they would swim eventually to the invisible submerged platform from any point in the tank, thus demonstrating their degree of knowledge of its location.

However, the most widely used spatial learning technique in modern animal laboratories is undoubtedly the radial maze, introduced by Olton and Samuelson (1976). In this several arms (initially eight elevated planks of different widths) radiate out from a central point, where a hungry rat is placed to start with, and a single pellet of food is put, out of sight, at the end of some or all of these arms (see Figure 5.6). If, as in the original experiment, all the arms are baited with food, then the rats' best strategy is to run down each arm only once, on a given daily test. After several days' training, rats on average choose about 7.5 novel arms in their first eight choices. Control experiments show that this statistically significant result is still obtained if odour cues

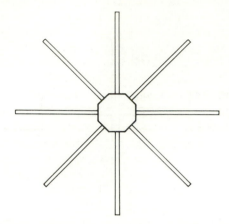

Figure 5.6   *The radial maze.*
If rats are placed on the central platform of a maze with a plan such as
this, food rewards being available but out of sight at the end of each
arm, experienced animals will visit each arm only once, thus
demonstrating some form of memory for their activities in the recent
past.

are eliminated either by the crude method of drenching the
apparatus with Old Spice aftershave, or by the more revealing
technique of confining the rat in the central area between
choices, and surreptitiously exchanging an arm which had
already been run down with another, or by rotating all the
arms to different positions (Olton *et al.*, 1977; Olton *et
al.*,1979). Thus on any given day, the rats' cognitive map and
associated memory is sufficiently detailed to record which
seven places the animal has already been to; and even with
a 17–arm maze, an average of 14 different arms were chosen
in the first 17 choices, (Olton *et al.*, 1977). This is a matter
of recent memory, since the procedure works without the
animals having to visit arms in any fixed order, and therefore
it works when the memory is of exactly what has happened
on a particular day (see chapter 10). A more traditional form
of spatial learning is obtained if the radial maze is used with
only the same one or two (or four) arms baited each day, so
that the animal has to remember that food is always in some

places but not in others (Olton, 1979; Olton and Papas, 1979).

Multiple levels of representation in instrumental conditioning

Tradition in the theoretical analysis of instrumental conditioning requires that we ask the questions of 'what is learned?' and 'what is the necessary and sufficient condition for learning?'. Modern research suggests the answers that there is no single kind of thing invariably learned in all cases of instrumental (or operant) conditioning; that there is no obvious essential ingredient; and that there are several limiting cases which are just sufficient to demonstrate one of the many phenomena which instrumental conditioning involves. However, in general the answers previously given to the questions of what is learned, and in what way, are not irrelevant to modern concerns, since it may be argued that almost every proposed theoretical form of association should be retained as one of several possibilities, and almost every supposedly critical condition is a variable which may affect the course of learning, even if it is not critical.

Although the views of earlier theorists such as Thorndike and Hull should thus not be dismissed out of hand, it is undeniable that there has been a general shift of opinion away from the theory of learning-as-doing towards more cognitive theories of learning-as-knowing, even for laboratory animals. Part of this distinction corresponds in fact to a difference between two kinds of knowing, 'knowing how' and 'knowing that', which Dickinson (1980) has imported into learning theory from cognitive science as the contrast between 'procedural' and 'declarative' representations. It is important that neither kind of representation necessarily has to be in verbal form; but the distinction can be illustrated by the example that an instruction in the form 'pull the gear lever back when the engine makes a loud high-pitched noise' is procedural; while instructions which are more explanatory, such as 'moving the lever changes the gear'; 'higher gears are used when the car goes faster', or 'the positions of the gears are as follows', are initially only declarative, but are well

suited to the deriving of a wide range of procedural instructions, by processes of inference and integration (see Dickinson, 1980, p. 23). In human practice, the distinction
between procedural and declarative representations usually
maps onto the difference between automatic habits and more
considered and controlled reflections (cf Shiffrin and Schneider, 1984). This is the case in most people's experience of
learning to change gear, along with other aspects of learning
to drive. First attempts, and the early stages of learning,
require a surprising amount of concentration and effort for
activities which later on become second nature. When this
has happened, the declarative aspects of early learning may
become irrelevant, with eventual skills including some
accomplished but fairly isolated habits. I hope I am not the
only driver to have had the experience of hiring a car on the
Continent, and on the first occasions of reaching a suitable
speed in first gear, putting in the clutch and making sweeping
movements with my left hand, where the gear lever normally
is (and, even more embarrassing, doing the same thing the
opposite way around when first driving my own car on
returning home). There is a wealth of anecdotal evidence,
first emphasized by James (1890/1983) that well-learned
human skills produce automatic habits, which are independent of rational purpose; Reason and Mycielska (1982) have
examined the degree to which this contributes to 'action slips'
of mixing up habits (pouring the water from the kettle into
the tea caddy and so on).

In the context of learning theory, the contrast is between
automatic habits and planned actions, but also between the
level of representation, whether procedural or declarative. By
and large, more habitual processes apply to muscle or limb
movements, while purposive actions are coded in terms of
goals, or sub-goals, but it is possible to speak of mental habits,
and emotional reflexes, and relatively goal-directed muscle-
twitches. As previously discussed (pp. 118–22), Thorndike's
(1898) answer to the question of what is learned was very
procedural, since it corresponded to the instruction 'when in
the box, press the lever', but it was not at the lowest level of
representation of the stimuli and responses involved, since it
concerned learned connections between the sense-impression

of being in the box, and an impulse to make a response, directed at a controlling feature of the environment, such as a lever or a loop of wire. By comparison, Hull's refinement of Thorndike's Law of Effect was equally procedural, but at a lower level of representation, since the learned connections were proposed to be directly between stimulus receptors and muscle movements. Schematic versions of both these theories are given in Figure 5.7.

Opinion has decisively swung against them, and there is now much support for the Tolmanian alternative answer to the question of what is learned in instrumental conditioning, sketched at the bottom of Figure 5.7. It should be noted that the Tolmanian version differs from the others in at least two respects. First, it is at a higher level of stimulus and response representation than Hullian theory; it assumes internal ideas or representations of wanted or expected rewards, and coherent impulses for actions rather than direct conditioning of muscle movements.

Second, it does not include a direct link between environmental input and response output at any level of representation: in Tolman's terms, what is learned is a 'means-end readiness', or a 'sign-Gestalt-expectation'. In the sketch in Figure 5.7, the sequence is that an animal first wants food, then searches for an action which, if performed, will produce the wanted food. The main learning in instrumental conditioning is thus the learning of what response is necessary to gain desired consequences, or, in its simplest form, an association between a response and the reward which follows it (Mackintosh, 1983; Adams and Dickinson, 1981b; Dickinson, 1980). In freer language, it is now said that in instrumental conditioning an animal is required to 'reach certain conclusions' about what its behaviour should be, or to 'track causal relationships' between its behaviour and reward (Mackintosh, 1983, p. 112; Dickinson, 1980, p. 143). This kind of theory, that is (c) in Figure 5.7, is certainly considerably more complicated than the other two which it has supplanted, and we should thus briefly review the evidence in its favour.

The evidence in favour of the Tolmanian two-stage theory of instrumental learning, in which responses are selected according to whether they are associated with a desired goal,

(a) *Thorndike : impression-impulse associations*

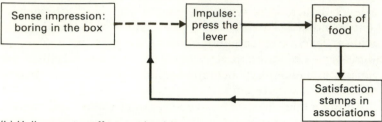

(b) *Hull : receptor-effect or stimulus response connections*

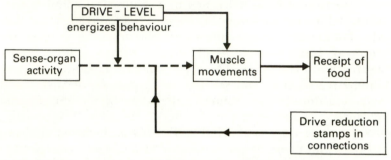

(c) *Pavlov/Tolman: stimulus-reward and response-reward associations*

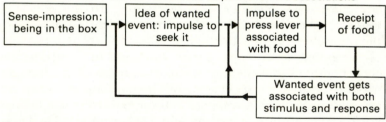

Figure 5.7   *Theories of instrumental learning.*
See text.

is in part indirect, in the form of evidence *against* stimulus-response principles, and in part more positive, in the form of evidence that an evaluation of goals determines instrumental performance and that responses become associated with consequent rewards.

Spatial learning as opposed to stimulus-response connections

The difficulty of accounting for an animal's learned movements in space in terms of specific stimulus-response connections was a niggling problem for S-R theory of the Watsonian type from its inception, and Tolman's criticisms of S-R theory, with recent developments, are discussed above, (pp. 141–2). Only two further points need be added. First, the recent use of the radial maze, and similar techniques in which animals learn *not* to return to a depleted food source, emphasizes the failings of the Thorndike principle that rewards stamp in only immediately preceding behaviours. Theories about cognitive maps, or working memory, are vague, but the vagueness is necessary to account for the behavioural results. As a second point, we may resurrect an old anecdotal result which may have considerable ecological validity. Helson (1927) argued against stimulus-response theories on the grounds that reward procedures could induce relatively novel behaviours. He had attempted to train rats to distinguish between two shades of grey card that indicated which of two parallel routes they should take over a raised barrier which was placed across the end of a long deep box, with a partition down the middle dividing these routes and two food compartments on the other side of the barrier. The barrier was covered with wires, the side with the incorrect card being electrified. The animals showed no sign of detecting the difference between shades of grey. However they quickly acquired a distaste for wires which delivered shock. One small rat of the four tested refused to climb over either barrier, while two others circumvented the barriers by climbing up the wall of the experimental enclosure, and walking round on top of it to the food boxes. Helson argued that this was not an accidental response which was stamped in. There is very little doubt that laboratory rats, and most wild animals, will attempt alternative methods of locomotion, via alternative routes, to get to a desired location, if this becomes necessary. A strict interpretation of the Law of Effect would require that animals be permanently halted if a tree falls across their accustomed route to a water hole. Stimulus-response theorists have always made attempts to account for the emergence of relatively novel goal-directed behaviour, in terms of generalization of previously acquired reponses, 'habit-family hierarchies (Hull, 1934, 1952) and the like. These attempts have never been particularly convincing, but are now less often attempted because of an accumulation of other evidence against stimulus-response theory, and against the explanatory version of the Law of Effect.

Re-evaluation of goals and response consequences

When 'stimulus-response connections' was the answer to the question of 'what is learned?', 'reward' or 'drive reduction' was the force which made the connections, and hence was once regarded as a necessary condition for all learning. This view can also now be speedily dismissed, and has already been bypassed by the previous chapters in which learning is presumed to take place in the course of habituation and classical conditioning, without the operation of a reward mechanism being necessary. Recent evidence has however been directed at the proposition that expectations of a goal or specific reward is one of the mechanisms responsible for the results of instrumental conditioning procedures.

Latent learning

A phenomenon which weakened the assumption that drive reduction was necessary for learning, and which suggests that performance in mazes is influenced by expectancies of rewards, was investigated in Tolman's laboratory by Blodgett (1929) and Tolman and Honzik (1930b). Rats allowed to find food in the goal box of fairly complicated mazes (e.g. 14 T-sections in succession) gradually improve their speed of getting through, and gradually make fewer errors, over a matter of weeks (that is 10 or more daily trials). This could be interpreted, albeit implausibly in view of the number of possible wrong alternatives, as the gradual strengthening of accidental correct responses, by the experience of reward. However, if other animals are allowed an equivalent amount of experience of wandering about the maze without getting food at the end, and therefore without very much change in behaviour, it can be shown that a form of 'behaviourally silent' learning has taken place, since the sudden introduction of reward in the goal box leads to a sudden change in performance, animals with unrewarded experience immediately catching up with those always rewarded after their first reward in the experiment of Tolman and Honzik (1930b). Rats allowed to explore a maze thoroughly will return efficiently on the next opportunity to any point in the maze where food is first given (Herb, 1940) and thus the evidence is very strong that geographical information is learned for its own sake.

The independence of expectations with regard to goals, and methods of response which achieve goals, is best illustrated by experiments in which these two factors are separately manipulated. With monkeys or chimpanzees, showing an animal where food is being hidden will induce strategies of response designed to retrieve it, and there is little argument about the role of internal representations of the hidden food in these cases (see chapter 10). With laboratory rats, it appears to be possible to change expectations of what will be found in the goal box of a maze simply by placing the rat in the goal box, and thus 'placement studies' supply evidence that expectations can in some circumstances dictate choice and intensity of response. For instance Seward (1949) allowed 64 rats to explore a simple T-maze with goal boxes of differing texture and colour, these differences not being visible from the choice point. He then placed the rats in one of the goal boxes by hand, where they were allowed to eat. When they were next put in the start box of the T-maze, 54 of them turned towards the goal box in which they had been previously fed. Since they had not made the turning response before being fed, the assumption must be that they had previously learned that turning in a given direction brought them to a given goal box, and that when a particular goal box was made attractive by an association with feeding, this new evaluation of the goal could be applied to the old spatial knowledge. Similarly, if rats have already learned to go in a particular direction to food in a T-maze, then if they are placed in the usually correct goal box with no food present, this is sufficient to increase subsequent turns in the opposite direction ('latent extinction': Deese, 1951). A slightly different form of latent learning occurs if changes in motivational states occur after an explanatory phase. Rats may remember where food was in a maze when they are made hungry, even if they were not hungry at the time when they saw it (Bendig, 1952). Rats allowed to drink salty water for lever-pressing when just thirsty, will press that lever, but not one which has been previously rewarded with plain water, if they become seriously salt-deficient (Kriekhaus and Wolf, 1968). 'Latent extinction' of a food-rewarded lever-pressing response is obtained if the animals are pre-exposed to the functioning of the reward-delivery mechanism without the usual rewards (Hurwitz, 1955).

De-valuation of reward

In all the above cases, learning about the consequences of a response took place without performance of the response itself, and subsequent effects on behaviour are therefore probably attributable to the prior association between the response and its consequences. In latent learning, it can be said that expectations as to the value of responding in a certain way are increased, while in latent extinction, expectations with regard to the value of responding are lowered. A further example of changes in the value of a goal is provided by the taste-aversion technique (Holman, 1975; Chen and Amsel, 1980; Dickinson, 1986; Adams, 1982; Dickinson *et al.*, 1983). Animals poisoned after eating food of a certain flavour or smell eat very much less of that particular food subsequently (Garcia *et al.*, 1977a, see pages 232–42). Under certain circumstances, rats poisoned after eating the particular flavour of food which they have previously received as rewards for bar-pressing in a Skinner box will thereafter show a greatly reduced tendency to perform this response (Adams and Dickinson, 1981a, 1981b). In these circumstances, it is arguable that the lever-pressing should have the status of 'a true action that is under the control of the current value of the reinforcer or goal' (Adams and Dickinson, 1981b, p. 163).

Specific associations between responses and rewards

In the ideal form of the expectancy theory of instrumental learning (Figure 5.7(c)), all responses are made for specific consequences. If a rat knows that food is available at one end of its cage but water at the other, it will go to the appropriate place when hungry or thirsty, and sometimes similar behaviour can be demonstrated in less familiar T-mazes, with water on one side and food on the other (Thistlethwaite, 1951). It is unlikely, however, that an exact representation of reward is necessary, in all cases of instrumental conditioning. For instance, rats rewarded unpredictably with 10 or zero units of food, or with 8 or 2, learn to run up an alley more vigorously, if anything, than rats always rewarded with 5 units (e.g. Yamaguchi, 1961). Though not strictly necessary, it has always been suspected that very specific expectancies of reward are sometimes formed in experiments with animal subjects. The best-known study was performed with rhesus monkeys by Tinkelpaugh (1928), under Tolman's supervision. The main purpose was to demonstrate what would now be termed 'representational' factors (Tinkelpaugh called them 'representative') in monkeys by allowing them to watch items of food being put in particular places or containers at some time before they were permitted to retrieve the food for themselves. Overnight delays of up to 20 hours proved to be possible (see chapter 10). However, the study is now remembered for the checks made on memory for the identity as well as the location of hidden food. Films were taken of the animals' facial expressions and searching activities aroused when a piece of banana had been hidden, but a piece of lettuce (which the animals liked much less than banana) substituted during the delay interval. Reactions to lettuce were sufficiently pronounced to convince Tinkelpaugh that the monkey had specific expectations of finding 'banana', rather than 'some food object', in the container, although an expectation of 'highly desired food object' would account for the results. It is difficult to obtain any more direct evidence of the specificity of representations of the reinforcer in instrumental conditioning.

Lorge and Sells (1936) claimed to have repeated Tinklepaugh's finding when rats were trained in Thorndikean problem boxes. Nine rats had already been trained with two trials per day in each of three different boxes. The responses required for escape were designated as 'face-washing', 'stand-up' and 'begging' which after training were essentially three different stereotyped postural responses. Throughout training adoption of the correct posture for a particular box resulted in a door being opened so that the animals could exit from the box to a small cup containing bread and milk. To examine 'representative factors' the nine well-trained rats were simply run as usual, but with sunflower seeds in the reward cup instead of the bread and milk. Although rats' facial expressions are not as revealing as those of monkeys, their general behaviour was changed considerably by the substi-tution of sunflower seeds. For the two days that they were observed, all rats on all occasions, on making the appropriate response and getting to the food cup, picked up one of the seeds, threw it aside, then ran back into the box and repeated the response. Although the animals had previously eaten sunflower seeds, this experiment would have been better controlled if some of the animals had received sunflower seeds throughout the experiment. However, precisely this comparison was possible in the earlier experiment of Elliot (1928), who trained rats on a multi-unit maze for either sunflower seed or branmash as reward, and found that animals switched from mash to seeds began to make many errors, whereas animals always rewarded with seeds performed accurately.

Although there is very little doubt that chimpanzees may form specific expectancies about particular food stuffs, which then determine both direct goal-seeking and other forms of behaviour which make the expectancies obvious to an observer (Savage-Rumbaugh *et al.*, 1983; see chapter 10), evidence supporting a role for specific expectancies of reward in instrumental learning by laboratory rats and pigeons is understandably less strong. The experiments in which rewards are changed, such as those of Elliot (1928), just mentioned, and Crespi (1942, see pp. 126–7) can be inter-preted as indicating an overall motivational value of reward associated with instrumental behaviour, with reductions in motivational value having various emotional effects (including 'frustration' in the theory of Amsel, 1962; see Capaldi *et al.*, 1984). However, a different kind of experiment, first suggested by Trapold (1970), provides an additional source of evidence for the theory that the qualitative nature of rewarding events, other than just their degree of goodness or badness, is usually noticed by rats and pigeons, and occasionally assists in the selection of appropriate responses. In Trapold's experiment the task for rats was to press one lever, on the left, when a clicker was sounding, but another lever, on the right, when they heard a tone. Providing the two stimuli, and the two separate responses to be made to them, are easily distinguishable, rats are perfectly capable of learning such tasks, by trial and error, although they may need thousands of trials to get things completely right (that is, to be right 9 times out of 10). Trapold's finding was that the task was made much easier if two different rewards were used, food pellets for the left lever and sugar solution for the right, even if both rewards were presented at the same place. Furthermore, in a separate experiment, he showed that associating particular rewards with the clicker and tone signals, before these were used as cues for the bar-pressing task, also made the eventual learning of the task faster if the rewards were kept the same way around, but slower if they were reversed. This supports the expectancy theory of instrumental learning illustrated in Figure 5.7(c), in which the animal is supposed to think of the reward first, and then decide which response must be made to obtain the reward. Clearly this decision should be easier if separate rewards need separate responses.

Various elaborations of this type of experiment have confirmed that what is known as the 'differential outcome procedure' (Peterson, 1984) usually enhances learning or has other effects predictable in terms of differential expectancies of specific rewards, with both rats (Carlson and Wielkiewicz, 1976; Kruse *et al.*, 1983) and pigeons (Peterson, 1984; Delong and Wasserman, 1981). For pigeons a rather more difficult task has been used, in which one signal, which may be either green or red, say, determines which of two stimuli, say black or white lines, should be chosen next. If the first green signal means that the bird should now choose black to get a reward of food, but a red signal means it should choose white, to get a reward of water, then learning is quicker, and performance more accurate, than when all correct choices are reinforced by either food or water at random (Peterson *et al.*,, 1978). With this procedure, if the task is made even more difficult by a delay between the red/green signal and the opportunity to make the next choice, between horizontal or vertical lines, then differential reward outcomes of food and water for the two correct choices allowed 95 per cent correct performance with a 10–second delay, while the use of only a single reward reduced accuracy to chance levels. It was thus argued that it was the expectancy of a particular reward, retained over the delay interval, which was responsible for directing the eventual choice (Peterson *et al.*, 1978; Peterson, 1984). If green and vertical are two visual stimuli both associated with food, and red and horizontal both associated with water, then representations of food or water (or peripheral responses specific to these) will be sufficient to bridge the delay, and that should certainly make the task easier by comparison with that of remembering whether the first signal has just been green or red, and knowing that green means horizontal and red means vertical.

Various alternative sorts of instrumental learning

The evidence in the section above might tempt one to conclude that the Tolmanian explanation for what is learned is right, whereas Hull's and Thorndike's ideas were wrong (see Figure 5.7). But not only are there some reasons for hesitation in interpreting this favourable evidence, there are also many results which argue quite unequivocally against specific expectations of rewards being always a necessary factor in instrumental learning. For instance, some attempts to demonstrate latent learning fail (Thistlethwaite, 1951; e.g. rats which find food in a T-maze when thirsty but not hungry do not go to it when they are hungry, Spence and Lippit, 1946). More important, there are many cases where laboratory animals appear to learn rigid and mechanical automatic habits which become more or less completely independent of the desirability of the goals used to establish the habits. For instance Holman (1975) trained rats to press a lever for a reward of saccharin solution, and then made the rats averse to saccharin by injections of lithium cholide. This stopped the rats drinking saccharin solution, but had no effect on their habit of pressing the lever. Adams (1982) and Dickinson *et al.* (1983), having previously shown that in some circumstances a conditioned aversion to previous rewards will immediately reduce the strength of habits they reinforced, agree that with long-established habits, especially those conditioned on fixed interval schedules of reinforcement, the learned performance is very little affected, if at all, by manifest devaluation of the ostensible goals.

The relative independence of habits from goals was stressed theoretically by Thorndike (1898) but with the empirical support of the fact that cats which had learned to press a latch to get out of a box often (but not always) continued to do so when he cut a hole in the roof. More dramatic apparent obliviousness to the final purpose of their activities is easy to demonstrate in rats, which, after being thoroughly trained to run down an alley for food pellets, may then run quickly over identical food pellets strewn in their path. Similarly, it is a reliable result that rats trained in Skinner boxes to press a lever for food pellets may ignore similar rewards presented in a bowl, preferring to obtain the same objects in the more usual way (Neuringer, 1969; see Morgan, 1974, 1979 for reviews). This is partly a trade-off between accustomed habits and degree of effort, since, understandably, rats required to press many times for a single food pellet are relatively eager to accept free pellets from a new place. However, there is sufficient rigidity in rats' learned behaviour to support a good measure of Thorndikean or Hullian habits – it must be remembered that human behaviour, and not only that classed as neurotic or abnormal, is composed of established routines performed unthinkingly, as much as of rational purposes.

There is thus good reason to believe that rats and people, though occasionally and fleetingly directing their behaviour towards expected goals, make extensive use of the less taxing mechanism of automatic habit for behaviours which are often repeated. Morgan (1894), just before Thorndike, had clearly stated the proposition that goal-seeking is always responsible for the early stages of learning, and for dealing with new problems, but that there is rapid drift to the habit mechanism whenever possible. There is no reason to assume that a goal-seeking phase is always necessary. There is something to be said for the position that even human learning may on occasion occur in a Thorndikean or Skinnerian fashion. This certainly goes for muscle co-ordination in complex skills, but there is experimental evidence that mannerisms, habits of speech, and social skills are sometimes unknowingly stamped in (Rosenfeld and Baer, 1969). However, for the general theory of learning, the more important cases are those at the opposite end of the scale of intellectual capacity (or, if you prefer, at some other corner of a diffuse array of psychological abilities). Although claims for instrumental learning in *Aplysia* are at present muted (Hawkins and Kandel, 1984; see chapter 4), the basic feature of a tendency to repeat rewarded acts is claimed for creatures as diverse as earthworms and flatworms (Fantino and Logan, 1979) and not only for advanced anthropods like honey-bees (Couvillon and Bitterman, 1982, 1984) but also for less advanced insects like cockroaches, and even for the decapitated cockroach, and legs of cockroaches detached from the rest of the body (Horridge, 1962; Distenhoff *et al.*, 1971). There are ample physiological reasons for doubting whether these neural systems are capable of sustaining, for instance, specific expectations of reinforcers which are as rich in information as those claimed for rats and pigeons (Peterson, 1984). Further, for rats and pigeons, and other laboratory animals; it is possible to demonstrate forms of instrumental conditioning after radical interference with normal brain functions such as complete removal of the neocortex of the cerebral hemispheres (decortication) or removal of most of the hemispheres themselves (decerebration; e.g. Heaton *et al.*, 1981). Oakley (1979b; 1983) has reviewed such results, obtained by himself and others. Decorticate rabbits will eventually, after slightly slower learning, press levers for food in Skinner boxes, on basic fixed interval and fixed ratio schedules (Oakley, 1979b). There must therefore exist subcortical mechanisms which are sufficient for the demonstration of instrumental learning. This raises the possibility, at least, that there are subcortical methods of stimulus-response association, which differ in some way from the full range of psychological processes available to the normal animal.

Evidence from common laboratory animals, from cross-species comparisons and from physiological investigations, all suggests that there may be more than one answer to the question of what is learned. As a general rule of thumb, any mechanism proposed in the last 100 years as *the* universal principle of learning may be accepted as *a* form of learning in some or other species or preparation. Instead of choosing between the alternatives presented in Figure 5.7, a more accurate and comprehensive answer to 'what is learned?' is obtained by combining all three processes illustrated in Figure 5.7, with some additions suggested by the results discussed above, to give a diagram such as that shown in Figure 5.8. The purpose of this is to show that more than one process may be involved in instrumental learning, and there are many more possibilities than can conveniently be drawn in. For instance, the example chosen is the pressing of a lever for food rewards by a hungry animal in a Skinner box. Instrumental learning to escape from dangerous or unpleasant external stimuli has not yet been considered, and would require some changes, though not wholesale ones (see chapter 7). Also not immediately obvious is the fact that learning of some kinds is possible without any strong motivational events occurring; latent learning of the kind which commonly takes place when rats explore mazes is subsumed along with much else in the box which refers to responses which are 'appropriately associated with the wanted event'. Although this covers a multitude of possible forms of association, including any method of getting to the known location of a wanted event, it does not seem unreasonable to assume that getting a food reward after a particular response may contribute to the association between the reward and that response. This may work in both directions, so that wanting a reward will in future produce an impulse for that response (1), and when the response is made, a firmer expectation of specific impending reward might very well be justified (2). In the situation in which rewards are regularly obtained, it is assumed that some

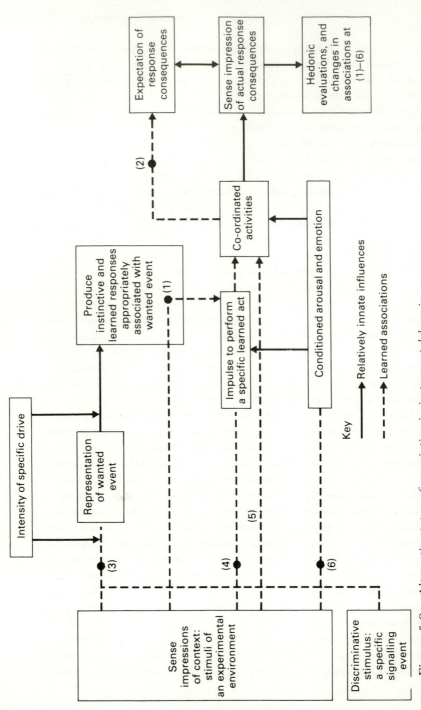

Figure 5.8 *Alternative types of association in instrumental learning.*
Points (1) to (6) indicate various different kinds of association, each or all of which might be strengthened during goal-

representation of these goals is conditioned to the context (3); but this needs to be modifiable by the effects of specific signals, which often have stronger conditioned effect than background or contextual stimuli (Wagner, 1976; Lovibond *et al.*, 1984). Clearly, ordinary classical conditioning should provide representation of the reinforcer associated with particular signals, as at (3), and similar effects are frequently now supposed to play a role in instrumental conditioning (Rescorla and Solomon, 1967; Kruse *et al.*, 1983). But as Jenkins (1977) pointed out, and as Mackintosh (1983) has cogently emphasized, this cannot be the only role for what is known as a discriminative stimulus in operant conditioning for, to put it loosely, this does not merely inform the animal that rewards may be forthcoming (as in classical conditioning); it also instructs the animal that if it wants a reward, then a particular response is necessary. Thus, laboratory animals learn easily, if they have to, that rewards are sometimes delivered free but that when a signal is on they must work for them (Weiss, 1971; Jenkins, 1977). The signal in this case does not indicate any increase in expectations of rewards, but rather that a given response is now appropriately associated with reward, and thus there is an input from the discriminative stimulus at (1).

Now, in order to accommodate the evidence for Thorndikean habits, we can further assume that the pure frequency of occurrence (not illustrated), or the effects of reward (4), will increase an automatic impulse to make the behavioural act normally rewarded, either in response to the background cues, as in Thorndike's original experiment, or connected with specific experimental signals (or discriminative stimuli). This is a fairly high level of representation of the response, since a variety of muscular co-ordinations, some undoubtedly unlearned, will be necessary to actually do something. However, both in animals lacking that level of representation of the response and for detailed stimulus-response co-ordination, such as is involved in gear-changing in higher animals, then the muscular co-ordinations themselves will be one of the things learned in instrumental conditioning procedures (5). We might expect that these will be mainly internal (some kinesthetic) associations (Watson, 1914/1967) and less tied either to the external cues or to the motivating effects of reward, but we have Locke's example of dance steps learned in a particular room to remind us that skills may sometimes need familiar external conditions, and the rewards are likely to be involved both as feedback to confirm correctness and in various kinds of motivation (Barber and Legge, 1986).

Finally, although considerable attention is currently given to expectations of reward, representations of the reinforcer and such like, concern with the 'wanted' character of reward representation (Tolman, 1959) and the role of specific drive states (Hull, 1952) is probably due for a comeback. Drive states such as hunger, thirst or salt deficiency presumably have an innate multiplying effect on internal representations of food, water and salt: there may be many other in-built drive states, and there can certainly be alterations of these by which cravings for cigarettes, chocolates, morphine and numerous other ingestible substances are controlled metabolically (see pp. 73–7, under classical conditioning). Therefore the level of specific drive is shown as modulating the degree to which external cues arouse ideas of reward and the intensity with which any such ideas are followed by the various response-producing processes encompassed by the 'perform response' box (top of Figure 5.8). In the variation of Hullian theory adopted by Spence (1956) and perpetuated by Bindra (1968, 1976) and others, the effect of rewards was interpreted as 'incentive motivation', which appeared to consist in part of general activation and energy available, with which to perform conditioned responses. Whether or not such a process is of any great importance in conditioning experiments has been disputed (Mackintosh 1974) but, depending on the exact reward (Roper *et al.*, 1983; Peterson, 1984), it is possible that some or other form of arousal or emotion can become conditioned to external cues (6). The restlessness exhibited by caged animals in anticipation of regular feeding times would seem to be partly attributable to general arousal, and since a similar effect is observed in general movements of decorticated rabbits, and in measures of heartbeat in goldfish (Oakley 1979a; Savage, 1980), it seems wisest to allow associations of arousal with external cues which are separable from those of more concrete and informative expectations. However, the distinction is not intended as a hard and fast one: some kinds of conditioned arousal may be reward-specific – possibly including sali-vation, licking of lips and so on in the case of food, and hormonal and autonomic changes in anticipation of sexual contacts – while what are regarded as more cognitive expect-ancies, as of a goal in a lucky dip, or a prize behind the curtain, may have general motivating effects, while being altogether vague, nebulous, or mistaken.

Instrumental conditioning – conclusion

The extent to which instrumental conditioning differs from classical conditioning and habituation, the degree to which it reflects the biological adaptations of particular species, and varied requirements it may place on brain capacities – these are all topics left to the next chapter. The present conclusions might be given by saying that everyone is right about instru-mental learning. The achievement of goals, the fulfillment of needs and the enactment of inner purposes are of fundamental biological importance, as both Aristotle and Hull suggested. Both in descriptive terms for most animals, and in mechanical process for some of them, these biological functions are served by the establishment of connections between external circumstances and response output, reinforced by practice and by successful outcomes in a relatively direct fashion, as proposed at the end of the last century by Thorndike. Descriptively also, the experimental control of the delivery of food rewards to hungry animals has the power and reliability in its effects on behaviour that was claimed for it by Skinner. However, the tide of theory at present flows in favour of more cognitive interpretations of the descriptive Law of Effect, which is the principle of Skinner's operant conditioning tech-niques, and it is now commonly supposed that responses learned by reward are guided by specific expectancies of achievable goals, thus supporting the role of purpose in instru-mental behaviour, more or less according to the views of Tolman. But instrumental learning is a chapter heading, not a psychological unity with a single explanation. The internal psychological effects of reward procedures encompass, at the very least the mechanisms of association both between stimulus and response, *and* between response and expected reward, which have been previously presented as mutually exclusive possibilities.

6 Biological bases of classical and instrumental conditioning

'Trial-and-error learning, of which instrumental conditioning is the core, is a different matter from the classical conditioned reflex in a number of important respects.'

Thorpe (1963, p. 85)

General process learning theory

The comparison of classical and instrumental conditioning, with a listing of similarities and differences, is a fairly congenial activity for learning theorists, since for those desirous of parsimony the worst outcome is only two separate processes, each, in the traditional view, subject to a limited set of principles of operation. I have already suggested in the previous chapters that each behaviourally defined version of conditioning will have to be given its own separate explanation, according to whether it is working on spinal reflexes or on the cognitive processes of the whole animal. This violates a strict version of parsimony, but means that no further losses of simplicity are likely to come from comparisons across the procedural boundaries of stimulus-pairing and response-rewarding techniques. However, the discussion of the biological bases of either kind of learning threatens general process learning theories, because it raises the spectre of species differences. As Seligman (1970) pointed out, general process theorists such as Pavlov and Skinner not only assumed that they could apply to other species results obtained from a small number of domesticated dogs, or rats or pigeons, but chose very narrow samples of the behaviour of the animals so favoured. Thus, 'It is obvious that the reflex activity of any effector organ can be chosen for the purpose of this investigation, since signalling stimuli can get linked up with any of the inborn reflexes' (Pavlov, 1927, p. 17), and, 'The general topography of operant behaviour is not important, because most if not all specific operants are conditioned. I suggest that the dynamic properties of operant behaviour may be studied with a single reflex' (Skinner, 1938, p. 45).

It would be foolish to deny that the research strategies adopted by Pavlov and Skinner led to striking achievements: nevertheless it is difficult to sustain the view that all remaining questions about learning will eventually be answered by further experiments on dogs in conditioning stands and pigeons and rats in Skinner boxes. The points made under the heading of 'constraints on learning' or 'biological boundaries of conditioning' (see for instance Hinde and Stevenson-Hinde, 1973; Seligman and Hager 1972) have by now been acknowledged in almost all quarters, and there is no reason to resist the argument that species may differ in motives, in sensory, motor and cognitive capacities, and certainly in the degree to which their natural style of life depends on individually acquired information. This last difference is perhaps the most fundamental, and theories about the evolution of the capacity to learn, such as that put forward by Plotkin and Odling-Smee (1981), are covered in the final chapter of this book. For the present it is enough to acknowledge first that we should not expect the psychology of a tick, which can probably succeed admirably in its chosen psychological niche without learning anything at all, to overlap a great deal with the psychology of a chimpanzee, which must learn about the territory it lives in and the food to be found there, and, probably most crucially, about the exact ways it should interact with the other individuals with whom it shares its long life. As Darwin would have said, the difference in the importance of learning in chimpanzee and human societies, though immense, should be compared with the difference in the importance of learning for the chimpanzee and the tick. But second, we must also take heed of the warnings of Hodos and Campbell (1969) that we cannot simply string out all animal life between the tick and the chimpanzee on any kind of single scale. In fact ticks are related to spiders, and there are blood-sucking degenerate flies with similar habits, and neither spiders nor flies should be close to the bottom of the scale. More important is the point that for any class or family of animal species, small changes in ecological niche may lead to large changes in psychology – it is very difficult to predict, for instance, which song-bird species should learn their songs from scratch and which should inherit each note (Marler, 1970; Green and Marler, 1979).

Thus, we must agree to be cautious about any generalization from one species to another, and generalizations which apply to all species, though usually vague enough to be less dangerous, must always allow for exceptions. Is it therefore possible to make any meaningful comparisons at all, between categories of learning as global as classical conditioning by stimulus-pairing, and instrumental conditioning by response-reward-pairing? Is not each category made up of several different kinds of association, or levels of neural representation, of the relevant stimuli and responses? And would we not be better off instead if we looked at naturalistic categories of learning, such as social imprinting in ducks and geese, vocal learning in canaries and parrots, co-operative hunting in wolves and lions, foraging strategies in insectivores versus herbivores, language-learning in human infants, or second language-learning in immigrant adults – all of which, we might suppose, are governed by their own peculiar and specialized principles and laws? Maybe so. All those areas repay specific investigation for their own sake. But we cannot tell until we've tried it whether or not there are principles of learning theory, or at least types of question in learning theory, which apply to or can be asked about all the more lifelike categories. Some phenomena which look specialized at first sight turn out to be a new form of old general principles, and thus an accommodation can be reached between naturalistic explanations and laboratory testing. This appears to be so for the two phenomena, taste aversion learning and autoshaping, which led Seligman (1970) and others to call for the abandoning of general discussions of learning. I shall come to these two cases later in the chapter, in the context of more general questions about classical and instrumental conditioning.

The comparison of classical and instrumental conditioning

The most interesting point of general comparison between Pavlovian conditioning and goal-directed learning is that one is voluntary and the other is not. This of course is extremely difficult to pin down in anything but a purely subjective sense, but one of the reasons for examining closely the classical-instrumental distinction is that it might supply some clues about where our subjective sense of the voluntary comes from. Clearly part, perhaps a major part, of a human act of will arises from the possibility of *saying* (out loud or to oneself) 'I am voluntarily going to get up and open the door', before doing it, and the analysis of this is a philosophical or even a legal exercise, rather than a problem for the experimental laboratory. But we do not always have to verbally justify voluntary actions – we cannot very well do this for voluntary verbalizations themselves in any case, and the separate volition of the right hemisphere, which lacks (relatively) the necessary verbal skills, in split-brained human patients, has been a major source of recent philosophical puzzles. Therefore, the question is not just a matter of verbal determination, and biologically more general issues of purpose and goal direction have to be addressed. Slightly simpler questions concern types of response and degrees of response change. Why is it hard to voluntarily control perspiration or (usually) ear wiggling, but easy to successfully raise an arm? Almost everyone can voluntarily raise an arm, but no one can play the violin, or copy John McEnroe's serve, just by wanting to.

Different types of response in conditioning

Aristotle (*Movement of Animals*, 703b) supposed that all geographical movements of all animal species are voluntary, but that certain bodily organs, most noticeably the heart and the penis, undergo involuntary movements, since they are not at our bidding, but appear to have their own reasons for moving, when certain stimuli present themselves. This corresponds roughly to the physiological distinction between the autonomic and the skeletal nervous system, the former being responsible generally for the internal organs of the body (digestion, regulation of blood supply, glandular secretions and so on), but the latter controlling the muscles which move the body about. This distinction is anatomically and biochemically fairly clear-cut, at least in vertebrates, though for medical reasons most is known about mammals. One can take pills which affect one system more than the other (or affect mainly one part of the autonomic nervous system). The most obvious exception is breathing, which is normally autonomic, that is, literally, self-governing, but can also be changed at will, since the relevant muscles are fed from both parts of the nervous system.

It is thus possible to follow Aristotle in this instance, since he put breathing in a separate category, along with sleeping and waking, of activities which are not normally the product of purpose and rationality, but which are not as resistant to voluntary control as movements of the heart or penis. Since Pavlovian conditioning was initially studied with salivation and other digestive secretions, and is frequently measured in terms of other autonomic responses such as heart rate or electrical resistance of the skin, it is understandable that several theorists have wondered whether the difference between classical and instrumental conditioning, and/or the difference between voluntary and involuntary responding, can be explained entirely on neuropsychological grounds: classical conditioning applying exclusively to the autonomic nervous system, and instrumental or operant learning being possible only in the brain systems that control the skeletal musculature (Konorski and Miller, 1937; Skinner, 1938; Mowrer, 1947). It turns out that very much more needs to be said than just this (e.g. Mackintosh, 1974, 1983), but it is nevertheless important in the context of biological constraints on learning to acknowledge that some response systems are more conditionable than others (with a given set of procedures) and that the autonomic nervous system is extremely sensitive to stimulus-pairing procedures, as Pavlov's work on digestion first showed (see chapter 3, pp. 58–63), and barely (if at all) influenced by the Law of Effect. The justification for saying this has to be given by the rest of this chapter, but to begin with it is essential to stress that only the autonomic nervous system is restricted, according to this hypothesis. The skeletal muscles are certainly used in the standard instrumental learning test of maze-learning or Skinner-box-responding, but they are also involved in obviously classically conditioned responses, such as the human knee jerk, or eyeblink, or the conditioned flexing of the leg of a dog in a conditioning stand. The motor system as such can perform both classically and instrumentally conditioned responses. But there may be other constraints or restrictions, in so far as certain instinctive motor patterns in animals, such as face-washing or scratching in rats or cats, are relatively resistant to food rewards. It is now generally accepted that a given species will be biologically 'prepared' to do certain kinds of things to achieve certain kinds of goals (Seligman, 1970; Breland and Breland, 1961). Thus cats are naturally prepared to stalk and crouch and spring at bird-like or mouse-like prey, and to snarl and arch their back when threatened or afraid – it would be easy to train cats to stalk artificial moving objects for food reward, or to arch their back to make an artificially threatening object disappear – but not vice versa. Similarly it is very easy to train pigeons to peck at buttons for food rewards (see 'autoshaping', below) but very difficult indeed to train them to peck a similar key to escape from electric shocks (see chapter 7). This now seems so obvious that one wonders why any fuss needed to be made about it. The answer, regrettably, is that the fuss had to be made because influential theorists resisted the implication that different species might more easily learn different kinds of behaviours for biologically appropriate rewards. Skinner (1977), for instance, while freely admitting the importance of evolutionary factors in determining instinctive behaviour, wishes to still keep instinctive behaviour in a different category from learned behaviour, and is thus led to the absurd and unsupported claim that, with the right contingencies of reinforcement, a cow could be trained to stalk and pounce on 'an animated bundle of corn' (Skinner, 1977, p. 1011). Skinner also refuses to accept Herrnstein's

(1977) suggestion that one of the differences between cows and cats is that cats innately enjoy stalking and chasing suitably sized objects. It is true that one cannot observe the enjoyment directly, but as many animals can be trained to press levers to gain the opportunity of engaging in instinctive behaviours (e.g. mice pressing levers to obtain lengths of paper which they then make into nests), there is behavioural data to support the conclusion that instinctive behaviours are 'self-reinforcing' (Herrnstein, 1977).

There are various theories of why some motor responses are more easily learned than others, under the influence of reward and punishment, but not all these are directly relevant to the question of differences between classical and instrumental conditioning as psychological processes. The more serious claim in this context is that the autonomic nervous system is readily amenable to the classical conditioning process, but not directly susceptible to instrumental conditioning. In practice, of course, many autonomic responses may be determined by prior acts of will – in a sense one can voluntarily raise one's heart rate by running on the spot, lower it by certain techniques of relaxation, or by taking a suitable pill, and deliberately change many other internal secretions by muscular or mental exertions. There is an enormous amount of medical and applied work done on techniques of 'biofeedback' because of the potential benefits of having indirect voluntary control of one's viscera, without recourse to drugs, although the benefits have not yet been fully realized (Yates, 1980). The first point is that special techniques of biofeedback were devised precisely because autonomic responses are not normally under voluntary control, and do not respond readily to reward contingencies. It is easy enough to condition someone's skin resistance by pairing a visual stimulus with an electrical shock (Ohman *et al.*, 1975a, see pp. 79–80), in a matter of minutes, but training the same response by using rewarding consequences is difficult, and, by comparison, involves much more by way of special mental and physical strategies. Thus the second point is that, to the degree that practical biofeedback techniques work at all, there is still no reason to suppose that any visceral responses can be directly conditioned in the same way that some motor responses can. A considerable amount of confusion still surrounds this point because reports by Miller and his associates (Miller and Dicara, 1967; Miller, 1969) once suggested that instrumental conditioning of autonomic response such as increases and decreases in heart rate could be obtained by using rewarding brain stimulation or electric shock punishment on rats whose entire skeletal musculature was paralysed by a curare-like drug. The theoretical reason for performing these experiments was to demonstrate that the autonomic nervous system *could* respond to reward and punishment directly, even if the motor system was inactive. This idea is suspect, because paralysis of the peripheral muscles would not necessarily preclude the conditioning of central motor instructions, which might have effects on the heart, but in any case it now appears that the original results were unreliable since they have not proved to be capable of replication. Miller himself therefore came to the conclusion that 'it is not prudent to rely on any of the experiments on curarized animals for evidence on the instrumental learning of visceral responses' (Miller, 1978, p. 376; Dworkin and Miller, 1986).

In the absence of the evidence from these experiments, we may retain the conclusion that one of the differences between classical and instrumental conditioning is that classical conditioning effects may indubitably be obtained both from motor responses and from the autonomic systems involved in the various emotional and metabolic phenomena previously listed (chapter 3), whereas the procedures of instrumental conditioning have strong and obvious direct effects on many (though not all) motor actions, but are relatively ineffective for producing learned changes in the glandular and other visceral activities controlled by the autonomic division of the central nervous system.

Degrees of response change in conditioning

Since one kind of conditioning, called instrumental or operant, appears to have differential effects on the motor and autonomic control mechanisms of the brain, but the other kind, called classical, does not, it would seem there is adequate justification for saying that the two kinds of procedure engage two different kinds of psychological process. But there are many complications. As we shall see, there are sound reasons for believing that the classical kind of process is engaged by many if not all forms of instrumental training, and therefore some have thought that there is really only one process – a classical process depending upon stimulus pairings – which in some way applies in a more elaborate form when rewards and punishments are applied to motor behaviour (e.g. Pavlov, 1927; Spence, 1956; Moore, 1973; Dickinson, 1980). For very much less sound reasons, other theorists have ignored the implication of the last section, and proposed that there is a single process, which is an instrumental mechanism related to drive reduction, that is responsible for the phenomena observed with both stimulus-pairing and response-reward procedures (Hull, 1943, 1952; Perkins, 1968; Miller and Balaz, 1981).

The conclusion I shall attempt to support here is that there are two distinct kinds of psychological process, even though both kinds of process – one of stimulus-associations and the other the linking of responses to pay-offs – may both be engaged by the same training procedures. This is a 'two-factor' or 'two-process' theory, as originally put forward by Kornorski and Miller (1937) and Skinner (1938) and revived with some modifications by Gray (1975) and Mackintosh (1974, 1983). Before getting on to the theoretical complexities of two-factor theories, it may be helpful to draw attention to a relatively straightforward category of evidence which on the face of it provides direct support for the two-factor view. This is simply the magnitude of behavioural effect, in terms of changes in response repertoire that can be brought about by the two processes. Even the modified stimulus-substitution theory of the classical conditioning process provides no obvious mechanism for the learning of skills such as riding a bicycle or for the other performances of circus animals. If human manual skills are interpreted as examples of instrumental learning (e.g. Mackintosh, 1983, p. 43), it becomes even more odd that anyone should try to explain all instrumental learning as due to the process responsible for salivary conditioning. The essential feature of both the procedure and the theoretical process of Pavlovian conditioning is that some portion of the already present response given to a significant stimulus becomes transferred to an associated but hitherto insignificant signal. The most that can happen directly in terms of originality and novelty of response is that a known behaviour occurs more often, or at different times.

By contrast, according to both the theory and practice of trial-and-error learning and the Law of Effect, random variations in behaviour can be permanently acquired, and thus, by degrees, if not occasionally faster (see pp. 138–9 on porpoise learning), radically new skilled forms of responding can be acquired. There may certainly be limits to this, set by any species' natural propensities and capacities, but there is no shortage of examples, from cows opening gates (Romanes, 1883) to monkeys and chimpanzees learning to use wrenches or turn keys in locks (Savage-Rumbaugh *et al.*, 1978b) which demonstrate the acquisition by individuals of qualitatively new kinds of behaviour. Thus, at any rate at the procedural level, we can say that instrumental training techniques produce a wide range of learned behaviours, while the signalling of one stimulus by another, which is the defining feature of the Pavlovian conditioning procedure, should only produce minor alterations in already present responses. This strongly suggests that there is a difference in processes which accounts for the different effects of the two procedures.

Pay-offs versus classically conditioned effects in instrumental procedures

The reason why it has been possible to argue against this strong suggestion, on theoretical grounds, can be gathered from close inspection of Figure 5.8 in the chapter on instrumental conditioning (p. 160). This sketch assumes that food rewards are obtained in the presence of a discriminative stimulus. At (3) it is assumed that the stimulus thus elicits a representation of the reward. This would appear to be little different from the assumption that the buzzer in a Pavlovian procedure elicits a representation of the signalled reward, and indeed in this diagram (3) can be regarded as a classical conditioning process. Similarly, the learned connection at (6) between the stimulus and emotional arousal can be taken as an example of classical conditioning of a central motivational state (Rescorla and Solomon, 1967, see pp. 77–80). For some activities, in particular that of a rat running down an alley towards food, the argument can be made that only these two classical conditioning processes are needed to explain instrumentally rewarded performance. Spence (1951, 1956), used the Hullian theoretical elaboration of an 'anticipatory goal response' (or r_g-s_g) to serve as what in Figure 5.8 is listed at (3) as a representation of the wanted reward. He also used the concept of conditioned incentive motivation, which would correspond to the conditioned emotional effect of rewards (6) except that for Spence the amount of incentive motivation depended upon the anticipatory goal response mechanism. Spence thus provides an example of the view that 'classical conditioning is really an inherent part of instrumental conditioning' (1956, p. 49). Additional explanation is required for why the rat actually runs down the alley. Spence (1951, 1956) appealed mainly to contiguity – that is because the rat runs at all in the presence of the external stimuli of the alley, it is more likely to do so again, and the degree of enthusiasm with which it does so is a function of classically conditioned emotional arousal, or incentive. A further and plausible suggestion is that animals have a built-in tendency to approach wanted rewards. Less plausible is the deduction that the classical conditioning of approach responses is all that is required to explain the behaviour of rats in mazes, but this has been attempted (Deutsch, 1960; Mackintosh, 1983, p. 39). Generally speaking, the appeal to classical conditioning depends on the similarity between what the animal is trained to do, and what its instinctive response to the reward is. If 'run towards the food' is regarded as already associated with any representation of food in Figure 5.8, then only the classi- cally conditioned connection at (3) would be needed to cause the rats' behaviour of running down a plank towards food they have previously experienced at the end of it. *But*, and this is a large but, this is hardly enough to explain the skills of circus animals, or even the various different escape responses performed by Thorndike's cats.

As a simpler and more tractable example, consider the experiment already discussed in which rats learn to press one lever for food rewards when a clicker is on, and another for sugar rewards when a tone sounds. How could this be explained using only the classical conditioning process? Well, this experiment was first performed (Trapold, 1970; see pp. 155–6) with Spence's 'anticipatory goal responses' in mind as providing two different representations of reward, conditioned to the clicker and the tone respectively. Thus, in the course of successful learning, we can assume that the clicker elicits an expectancy of dry food, and the tone an expectancy of sugar solution, by a process of stimulus-associations. But how does the rat achieve successful learning – that is, how does it know which lever to press when? There are several possibilities but most require that reinforcement selectively strengthens an arbitrary response which happens to precede it, which is a different process from the stimulus-substitution possibilities of purely Pavlovian conditioning. Trapold (1970) was content with a Hullian stamping-in of responses which happened to precede reward, which is more effective when there are differential response outcomes because the clicker and tone are thus made more distinctive stimuli. This is one of a number of possibilities arbitrarily excluded from Figure 5.8. The alternative is that at (1), it is assumed that the representation of a particular wanted event will elicit an impulse to perform the response associated with getting that event, and thus left lever response (if that is correct) is directly associated with the reward it obtains.

There is a fair measure of consensus that *either* rewards stamp in arbitary responses, by the Law of Effect, which is a different process from stimulus-substitution in classical conditioning, *or* that particular responses become themselves associated with rewards, so that there are processes of both response-reinforcer associations and stimulus-reinforcer associations (Dickinson, 1980; Mackintosh, 1983). Dissidents may continue to insist that both response-reinforcer and stimulus-reinforcer association are forms of classical conditioning, but these forms eventually become stretched rather far apart. Initially, it looks possible to say for the Trapold (1970) experiment that a stimulus of the sight of the left lever, or the kinesthetic sensation of pressing down on the left lever, becomes a signal for reward, and that these Pavlo-

vian processes account for the selective effect of rewards on
this arbitrarily correct response. There are, however,
numerous indications that kinesthetic feedback is not an
essential part of instrumental learning, although it must have
its uses. The early investigation of maze-learning, for instance,
suggests no kinesthetic specificity is necessary (see p. 141),
and the experiment of Taub *et al.* (1965) is often quoted as
an example of lever-pressing learned without kinesthetic or
proprioceptive feedback, which was surgically eliminated.
(Polit and Bizzi, 1978, confirmed this finding.) Mackintosh
(1983, p. 40) points out that although dogs learn to flex their
leg away from a shock to the paw, which may be a classical
conditioned reflex, the fact that they readily learn to flex a
leg to avoid a puff of air to the ear is less easily attributed to
stimulus-substitution. Even decerebrate duck embryos can
learn something similar, since they will learn to flex their foot
in order to terminate an electric shock applied to the wing
(Heaton *et al.*, 1981). For the dogs, it might seem worthwhile
to speculate along the lines that a straight leg becomes associated with unpleasant air puffs, but a flexed leg becomes a
Pavlovian signal for no puffs. Then an account of the selection
of the response with the desired associations is still required.
For the duck embryos it makes more sense, surely, to include
some other lower-level mechanism for the selection of
muscular activities which terminate intense stimulation.

This brings us to the essence of the theoretical difference
between the processes of stimulus-substitution (classical
conditioning) and response selection (instrumental conditioning), which is that evaluated pay-offs are the critical
element of response-selection but not of the stimulus-substitution process. For response-selection to work, there has to be
a system which performs the function of measuring immediate
advantage and disadvantage, and selecting responses accordingly. It is usually part of the background to classical
conditioning theories that the process should be useful in the
evolutionary sense, but the stimulus substitution mechanism
can in principle be built in without any hedonic (pleasure/
pain) system, or anything corresponding to it. This is not
to imply that there is no motivational angle to stimulus-
substitution – on the contrary, the classical conditioning

process in two-factor theory is often held to be responsible for changing motivation, via conditioned emotional effects. But stimulus-substitution is the agent for changing emotions rather than their product. In salivary conditioning, either food (good) or acid (bad) can be put in the dog's mouth after a buzzer sounds, to induce salivation to the buzzer. The point of the stimulus-substitution theory is that both have conditioned effects, irrespective of their goodness or badness. But if the dog receives food for turning its head to the left but acid for turning its head to the right (or vice versa), then it will very quickly learn to move its head to the left rather than to the right (or vice versa) because of the goodness or badness of the stimulus experiences. The food is a wanted event, and this will determine the quality of the emotion conditioned to a signal for it, but the argument is that the motor-control system has evolved in ways such that efforts are made to make wanted stimuli happen (and unwanted stimuli not happen).

It is hardly necessary to enquire very deeply into the question of why the motor system should have evolved this property rather than the autonomic nervous system, or indeed the sensory parts of the nervous system. It is the job of the sensory system to detect whether something wanted *has* happened or not, or to detect other useful signals, and it is the job of the autonomic nervous system to adjust the internal environment in accordance with many in-built checks and balances, for which anticipatory reflexes, via stimulus substitution, may often be helpful (e.g. release of digestive and other juices in good time). The motor system must also accomplish a great many reflexive adjustments (blinking, flinching, fight and flight) which can usefully be shifted to anticipatory signals, but, in addition, there are obvious long-term evolutionary advantages in some niches if there is flexibility in behavioural efforts modulated by on-the-spot cost-benefit analyses conducted by some or other version of the pleasure/pain principle in an individual animal. Thus it was assumed in Figure 5.8 that an essential feature of instrumental learning is that representations of wanted events should be intrinsically linked to the performance of motor responses associated with making the wanted event happen. Many of these responses may themselves already be built in, but in species which display trial-and-error learning, the assumption is that relatively arbitrary actions, such as pulling loops of string or pressing levers, can, through experience, be included in the 'making it happen' system, either because they become associated with the wanted event or because some simpler mechanism stamps in arbitrary responses to arbitrary stimuli.

That, I hope, makes some sense as an abstract theory, but the previous sections of this chapter will have shown that there are many competing theories. There are two sources of behavioural evidence in favour of a special pay-off principle acting on response selection, that is, in addition to the circumstantial evidence based on the difference between motor and visceral control in the nervous system, and the plain fact of response flexibility in trial-and-error learning. Several standard laboratory responses, such as maze-running and lever-pressing in rats and key-pecking in pigeons, are sufficiently close to reflexive motor patterns in the relevant species to require close investigation. Two experimental procedures have theoretical importance: *omission schedules* and *intermittent reinforcement* as in Skinnerian schedules of reinforcement.

Omission schedules

This term often appears to cause confusion, possibly because of the uncertainty of its relationship to 'schedules of reinforcement'. Although the experimental set-up requires some attention to detail, the theoretical meaning of an omission schedule is simply that of 'no pay-offs for responding'. The original purpose of these arrangements was to demonstrate that classically conditioned responses such as salivation in dogs were not due to a pay-off principle (Sheffield, 1965), but they may in other circumstances provide evidence that instrumental responses *are* influenced by their consequences. Hull (1943) had assumed that all conditioning involved some form of pay-off, ultimately via drive reduction. Thus it could be argued that the reason why Pavlov's dogs salivated is that by accident salivation preceded drive reduction, or that prior salivation had the advantage of making food taste better, and acid taste not so bad (e.g. Perkins, 1968). Now, suppose that we conduct the standard Pavlovian experiment, in which a buzzer signals the imminence of food to a dog, but with an 'omission contingency' which makes it greatly to the advantage of the dog that it should *not* salivate, because if it does, we do not give it any food, but if it can manage to sit through the buzzer signal without salivating, we do. If Perkins's hypothesis was correct, that all classically conditioned responses occur because they make life more attractive for the animal concerned (1968, pp. 163–5), then it is quite clear that the dog should never salivate to the buzzer in this experiment, since if ever it does, it gets no food, while there is every reason in terms of the pay-off of food to delay salivation until food is actually presented. But Sheffield's experiments (1965) with dogs along these lines suggested that the reward factor has very little influence on salivation. Some dogs do indeed wait to salivate until food is actually presented, as Pavlov (1927) suggested, but this is based on temporal discrimination. There is good reason to believe that salivation is an involuntary response, because in some cases dogs continue to salivate frequently to the sound of the buzzer, even though this prevents them getting food, because of the omission procedure (Sheffield, 1965). A rough analogy is asking someone who is very hungry to choose something from an attractive menu, with the catch that if they salivate while making the choice, they get nothing. Not everyone salivates the same amount while reading a menu, but those who salivate a lot would not find it easy to inhibit salivation as a voluntary decision.

Motor movements can also be involuntary, and the omission schedule provided an important test of the hypothesis that the pigeon's key peck in a standard Skinner box, far from being a pure example of operant or instrumental learning, is influenced by stimulus-pairings with no pay-offs almost as much as salivation. The experimental procedure here is to present hungry pigeons with food (from an illuminated grain hopper) for brief periods – say for 3 seconds once a minute on average. The pigeon key (a round disc a few inches above the grain hopper) is lit for 10 seconds before food presentations. If the bird never pecks the key, food will continue to be presented after the signal, at irregular intervals. If the bird ever pecks the key when the light is on, the light goes out, and it misses the food it would otherwise have had. There is thus no conceivable advantage to the bird, in terms of the frequency of food presentations, or overall amount of food obtained, in key-pecking behaviours. Notwithstanding this lack of favourable outcomes for responding, pigeons very reliably develop and maintain the habit of pecking at the illuminated key, to the extent that they miss about half the food available (Williams and Williams, 1969; review by Williams, 1981). This is hardly optimal foraging, or optimal anything else, in the microsm of the autoshaping procedure. It is much more like a reflexive or knee-jerk-like involuntary response, which pigeons find as difficult to inhibit as dogs do salivation. The key pecks show other reflexive properties, since when food is the reinforcer pecks look like pecks at grain (beak open), but when the reinforcer is water, pecks are slower, and look as if the bird is attempting to drink (beak closed) and thus it has been proposed that this behaviour is just a classically conditioned motor response and nothing else (Moore, 1973; Jenkins and Moore, 1973) and that possibly pigeons can *only* learn by classical conditioning (Gray, 1975) or that *all* instrumental learning is mainly classical conditioning (Bindra, 1968; Spence, 1956).

All these proposals are misguided and mistaken. The omission procedure itself can be used to show that other responses, unlike the key peck or salivation, are extremely sensitive to their consequences. For instance, the other Skinner-box standard, lever-pressing by rats, is effectively demolished if rats lose rather than gain food by its performance (Zeiler, 1971; Locurto *et al.*, 1976). This is such a strong result, and one potentially obtainable with many responses in many species, that discussion of it tends to go by default. But if the omission schedule can be used as evidence that some behaviours are insensitive to their consequences, and therefore should be regarded as a product of classical rather than instrumental learning (Sheffield, 1965; Mackintosh, 1974, 1983), then equal weight ought to be given to all the behaviours which would immediately cease if they produced outcomes as unfavourable to the individual animal as that provided by an omission schedule. Moreover, it is not simply that there are other cases, or other species. Many other response patterns in the pigeon, which are less intrinsically related to food-getting than a directed peck of the beak, can be shaped by food rewards and are sensitive to the omission of reward (e.g. the raising of the head, as studied by Skinner as superstition, and closely examined in an omission schedule by Jenkins, 1977). And the pigeon's key peck itself, which has been the focus of a good deal of scepticism about the Law of Effect (Seligman, 1970; Herrnstein, 1977) is, surprising as this may seem, influenced *both* by the food-signalling stimulus-pairing operation which produces reflexive autoshaping *and* by a host of other procedures which indicate choice and response selection according to pay-offs. Using an ingenious inversion of the usual 'autoshaping' procedure, Jenkins (1977) measured the key-pecking of pigeons when their key was lit for 8 seconds as a signal twice a minute on average, but the meaning of the signal was that food would only be delivered if the pigeons did peck the key, with the crucial elaboration that food was presented anyway, with an equal probability in the periods without the signal, whatever the pigeons did. Thus, colloquially, the only message in the signal was 'Now you must earn the food you otherwise get freely' (Jenkins, 1977, p.54). It was not a signal for food, only a signal that the response was necessary for food. The birds learned to peck when the signal was on, and not to peck when it wasn't, thus demonstrating a grasp of the instrumental necessities of the procedure which goes beyond merely a conditioned anticipation of food (suggesting an association at (1) in Figure 5.8 rather that at (3)).

Choice and effort on intermittent schedules of reinforcement

The causes of behaviour observed under Skinnerian schedules of reinforcement (see pp. 128–37) are not always easy to establish, partly because of the complexity of the procedures, but partly also because the evidence suggests that several alternative psychological processes, notably automatic habits and more goal-sensitive responding, may have roughly equivalent effects on observed behaviour (see pp. 156–63). Several standard results, such as reactions to a discriminative stimulus which signals that otherwise unavailable rewards may be procured by responding, can be interpreted in terms of the effects of stimulus-pairing, that is, in terms of the psychological process typical of classical conditioning. But there are other phenomena which cannot be so straightforwardly attributed to the classical process, and yet others which directly implicate the pay-off process of instrumental learning. In the former category is the success of 'multiple schedules' (Ferster and Skinner, 1957), in which a signal indicates which of several schedules is in operation, so that a green light may produce responding characteristics of a variable-interval schedule, but a red light typical fixed-ratio performance, in the same animal. This would appear to require at least a Thorndikean stimulus-response association, by which different patterns of response were stamped in to different discriminative stimuli.

A further very general finding with schedules of reinforcement has from time to time been put up as a useful practical touchstone by which to distinguish the operation of classical (stimulus-substitution) or instrumental (response-selection) psychological processes. This is the finding that any schedule in which there is only inconsistent and intermittent reinforcement of a given response almost invariably results in an increase in the amount of behaviour per reward during training, and also may spectacularly increase the persistence of behaviour when rewards are witheld, by comparison with the procedure of giving the identical reward consistently every time the response is performed. The effect most of interest is the persistence of unrewarded behaviour (resistance to extinction) since this is less logically necessary, but the degree to which animals will comply to the logical necessities of reward schedules is also a form of experimental evidence. When animals receive rewards only occasionally for successfully running down a straight alley or through a maze, the fact that they carry on running longer than animals rewarded continuously and consistently, when all rewards are stopped, is known as 'the partial reinforcement effect' (Amsel, 1962; Mackintosh, 1983), but this result clearly shares all the essential features of what is called intermittent reinforcement in Skinner boxes.

Pavlov (1927 pp.384ff.) found that if a dog was fed after only every other presentation of a signal or even after every third presentation, then the conditioned reflex of salivating to every signal developed quickly, but that if reinforcement was less frequent than this (food after every fourth buzzer) no conditioned response could be obtained, and the dog appeared simply to ignore the signal (not even demonstrating inhibition). The exact numbers here are probably not significant, but it has usually been claimed (e.g. Kimble, 1961) that partial reinforcement in the stimulus-pairing procedure seriously reduces the effects of this on autonomic conditioned reflexes. It would be helpful if we could say simply that intermittent reinforcement increases the effectiveness of response pay-off processes but decreases responses supported only by stimulus-substitution or other classical processes. There are two reasons why we cannot make things quite that simple. First there is the probability that classical conditioning involving motor behaviour differs in some ways from that involving autonomic responses. Intermittent pairings sometimes, it is claimed, produce more persistent behaviour in the pigeon autoshaped key-peck paradigm (Boakes, 1977; Mackintosh, 1983). A difficulty here is that the key peck is probably substantially influenced by instrumental effects (Williams, 1981; Jenkins, 1977; see pp. 180–2 above). The more serious but related complication is that there is insufficient agreement about whether intermittency in pairings should generally be regarded as weakening any classical conditioning process. In fact Pearce and Hall (1980) have proposed a theory that classical conditioning in general is more effective when there is some uncertainty attached to the reliability of the signal, and this aspect of the theory has already received considerable experimental support (e.g. Kaye and Pearce, 1984).

My own view, nevertheless, is that there are strong theoretical reasons for assuming that intermittency of associations will have rather different implications for stimulus-substitution and response-selection processes, and that a great deal of the inconsistency of experimental evidence can be circumvented by taking *degree* of intermittency into account, specifically, in accordance with Pavlov's original observation, by distinguishing uncertainty, as in the 50:50 examples, from probable absence, when intermittency is of the order of 10:1 or 100:1. There are few experimental reports I know of in which a response shown to be independent of pay-offs, and therefore an indicator of classical associations, has been found to be either learned or maintained when the signalled event follows the signal with a probability of less that 10 per cent: on the other hand I could go on quoting for the rest of the book experiments in which responses demonstrably under the control of wanted consequences are maintained, if not originally learned, when hundreds of responses are necessary before one is associated with an event of equivalent motivational significance. This may depend partly on the details of foraging strategies, but it is also likely that more general rules about stimulus-signalling and goal-seeking biological functions can be applied. There would be very little point, either for the immediate advantage of an individual dog, or for the longer-term value of the instincts to be built in to its surviving relatives, in stimulus-signalling mechanisms which ensured that dogs carried on salivating at the sound of a buzzer (and expecting food then), if the buzzer was followed by food once every 100 times. It would be a waste of the animal's mental and physical effort to pay attention to the stimulus (and in this case a waste of saliva). On the other hand, if it is the dog's own behaviour which is correlated with the receipt of food, even if only occasionally, then, if it is hungry enough, it is worth the repeated efforts of the individual animal if it persists in responding until it gets the food; and animals which have built-in characteristics of stamina and patience will enjoy certain advantages over their fellows in the circumstances of an ungenerous but eventually rewarding environment.

At fairly extreme levels of intermittency, then, the limited evidence available supports the hypothesis that the psychological processes by which an animal correlates its own motor behaviour with wanted outcomes are to some extent different and separate from the processes by which emotional, visceral and reflexive reactions are automatically shifted from one external stimulus to another. This is not to say there are no parallels at all to be seen: Dickinson (1980) was able to sustain a very orderly account of animal learning by speaking only of event-event associations ('E1–E2 associations' was the exact notation), assuming that for most purposes it is irrelevant whether the first signalling event is the receipt of an external stimulus or the performance of a motor act. What the two kinds of association have in common will be left until chapter 8; here I wish to stress my own view that whatever the kinds of association may have in common, it is arguable that the variables of volition, effort and personal involvement are related to a 'making-it-happen' system which is involved in the response-consequence association in some forms of instrumental learning.

Lea (1979, 1984a) among others, has drawn attention to the possibility that all the principles of learning examined in the abstract in the laboratory evolved under the constraint that they should produce optimal behaviour, in particular optimal foraging for food (Krebs and Davies, 1983; Kamil and Sargent, 1981; Maynard-Smith, 1984), in a given species's natural environment. This, Lea suggests, may apply both to specializations (waiting and pouncing in cats and other ambush hunters; long continued unexciting searches in grazers and browsers) and to more general principles such as the distinction between pay-off-sensitive motor behaviour and the more automatic and reflexive anticipatory response shifts referred to above. Intermediate principles, such as that of paying most attention to stimuli that are fairly closely associated with significant events, but in a way not yet totally predictable (Pearce and Hall, 1980) are also presumably only confirmable in laboratory experiments because they serve a theoretically important biological function. The problem is that the discovery of what should be a mathematically important biological or psychological function is partly a matter of the ingenuity of the theorist (Pyke *et al.*, 1977). It is rare that what is claimed to be an optimal behaviour is actually shown to be so by naturalistic experiment instead of mathematical simulation. However there is some agreement on what kinds of foraging are generally optimal, and I mention this here because of the strong possibility that the assessment of pay-offs held to be the defining feature of instrumental conditioning is in some cases theoretically necessary for individuals to adjust their foraging behaviour in natural environments.

One principle of foraging that has been found to roughly match observed behaviour applies to the simplified case of the choice between two alternative food items – whether animal or vegetable. If one is better than the other (more nutritious), then the animal ought to pick it. This sounds completely obvious, but it means that a given species must be able to detect the difference, possibly making use of post-ingestional effects, and then use sight or taste cues to make the choices. It may be that the two kinds of items are in different places, require different search strategies and so on, and in this case the choice has become more complicated and the learning-what-is-where task – forming Tolman's cognitive maps – may be needed. However, choosing the better of two alternatives can be studied from another theoretical angle, since there is the problem of when to give up on the better alternative if it becomes too scarce or difficult to get. The easiest rule to specify is that, provided there is no cost to the business of taking a food item when it is available, then the best item should always be taken when it is there, and the worse of two items should not be taken if there are plenty of the better kind, but should be taken with more and more enthusiasm as the better kind becomes scarce. The only surprising thing about this rule is that how much there is around of the less-preferred item is irrelevant – it is only the availability of the more-preferred item that really matters.

Both shorebirds (redshank) choosing to eat shrimp rather than worms (Goss-Custard, 1977) and pigeons choosing immediate rather than delayed rewards in a Skinner box (Lea, 1979) and rats with a similar task (Collier and Rovee-Collier, 1981) follow this principle roughly, but not exactly. The exactness is not at issue – the point here is that some system of choosing is used, and motor behaviours of varying degrees of complexity and novelty are required in the making of the choices (e.g. Krebs *et al.*, 1978). This provides a biological rationale for the existence of psychological processes by which behaviours are selected according to a fairly sophisticated assessment of differing reward outcomes. That laboratory animals are capable of modulating their learned behavioural choices in this general kind of way is made obvious by the research on concurrent interval schedules discussed above (pp. 133–7) among other results, whatever the precise equation used to fit the data. It seems extremely likely that both classical and instrumental processes of association would need to be appealed to in any explanation for all of these phenomena of choice between reward outcomes, and very unlikely that either one or the other alone would be sufficient. The assessment of pay-offs as an instrumental reward process would appear to one of the most obvious requirements for learned optimal foraging.

Molar and molecular correlations between behaviour and reward

There should be a good measure of agreement that learned behaviours are somehow correlated with rewarding outcomes – this after all is what Thorndike (1898) started off with. There is as yet likely to be little agreement on the exact mechanisms involved, but it is worth mentioning one area of argument. This concerns the scale of the behavioural units which are susceptible to instrumental reinforcement. The theoretical choice is between small-scale or molecular units – almost of individual muscle twitches – and larger-scale extended actions or response strategies, referred to, originally by Tolman (1932) and, Hull (1943) as 'molar' behaviours. The first question is whether the larger chunks of useful activity can be regarded as aggregates of muscle contractions, or whether, alternatively, the cognitive representations of actions are relatively independent of the small-scale co-ordination of individual muscles which are needed to put them into effect. The conclusion previously in the last chapter (e.g. pp. 140–5) has been that Tolman was right about muscle-twitches, and that, especially in spatial learning, what is actually learned consists partly of the macro-activities of 'getting to and from' rather than specific bodily movements.

In the next chapter, under the heading of 'Learned helplessness', we shall see that Seligman and others have proposed that the correlation between what an animal does and the things which happen to it as a consequence brings about not only particular goal-directed actions, but also a more general belief that doing things is useful. This comes close to an attributional theory of learning which includes various kinds of beliefs about the utility of trying to make things happen, and moods of optimism and pessimism about life in general (Miller and Norman, 1979; Seligman and Weiss, 1980). Both Alloy and Tabachnik (1984) and Dickinson (1985) have proposed that typical learning-by-pay-off tasks in the animal laboratory, as well as most of human psychology, involves initial beliefs and preconceptions as to what causes what, modified according to fairly global assessments of the validity of these beliefs in practice. The particular theoretical tack taken in these proposals is that modification of beliefs or expectancies occurs as a product of the 'assessment of covariation' between one category of events and another, such assessments having fallibility as one of their defining characteristics, in both people and animals. Dickinson (1985) has however been able to make fairly direct experimental tests of hypotheses derived by applying this speculation to the performance of rats on schedules of reinforcement, by arguing that it is experienced global correlations between variations in responding and variation in rewards received which encourages goal-sensitive behaviour.

When an animal is well-trained on any particular schedule, both its behaviour and the consequent delivery of reward occurs with great consistency, and since there is thus no longer any opportunity for the animal to assess whether changes in its behaviour lead to changes in the receipt of rewards, responding becomes a matter of habit, and can be shown to be insensitive to the de-valuing of rewards (see pp. 156–63).

Although there is strong evidence that under some circumstances animals may develop molar cognitions about what general sort of behaviour is worth making for what expected source of reward, Dickinson's own theory includes an alternative mechanism for the maintenance of consistently rewarded habits. It is therefore no threat to his theory that experimental evidence supports the view that relatively molecular and Thorndikean mechanisms of stamping in small-scale response characteristics appear to be responsible for a good deal of the

behaviour exhibited when stereotyped behaviour is established using schedules of reinforcement, at least in the case
where pigeons peck the keys in Skinner boxes for food
rewards. The difference between behaviour on variable ratio
and variable interval schedules has already been referred to
(pp. 132–3), and is relevant here because when rewards are
given for a certain number of responses, even when the
number varies randomly, it is clear that there is more correlation between rate of response and rate of getting rewards
than there is on an equivalent interval schedule, since whenever rate of response varies this will directly change reward
rate. By comparison, interval schedules specifically arrange
that there is little correlation between reward rate and
responding, since the delivery of rewards is determined
primarily by the value of the interval, and remains roughly
the same over wide variations in actual responding. Despite
this overt characteristic of interval schedules, many explanations of the 'matching law' observed for concurrent interval
schedules have emphasized that there could be some mechanism by which response efforts are adjusted according to
associated rewards received, and that assessment of correlations between response rates and reinforcements is likely to
be a part of such a mechanism (Baum, 1981; Rachlin, 1978;
Herrnstein, 1970).

The idea that variations in response-rate are assessed by
the animal according to variations in reinforcement rate that
are thus brought about is very definitely a 'molar' factor,
implying sophisticated sensitivities to average values without
necessarily specifying detailed cognitive mechanisms of calculation. An alternative, much more molecular explanation for
the effects of reinforcement schedules is that an important
element of what is learned is the time that should elapse
between successive responses (inter-response time or IRT;
Ferster and Skinner, 1957; Anger, 1956; Platt, 1979; Shimp,
1969). In this case sophisticated calculations must often be
performed by the human theorist to discover which reinforcement schedule should do what, but it is straightforward in
principle that under variable-interval schedules, the longer
the time between two responses, the more likely it is that the
second response will be reinforced (since more of the interval

will have elapsed). This does not apply to variable-ratio schedules. Thus a molecular explanation for the fact that variable-interval schedules produce slower response rates than variable ratios with equivalent frequencies of obtained reward is that longer inter-response times are selectively stamped in under the interval schedule. Theories such as this soon become elaborate and mathematical. However, a number of extremely elegant experimental comparisons, plus a computer simulation, recently conducted by Peele *et al.* (1984), suggests very strongly that the selective effect of reinforcement on particular bands of inter-response times is indeed observed after long Skinner-box training, and is the main factor responsible for the different response rates observed under variable-interval and variable-ratio schedules.

There is no reason to object to the experimental reliability of this finding. But there is every reason to resist the implication, drawn by Peele *et al.* (1984), that similar molecular explanations of instrumental conditioning will provide satisfactory accounts of all goal-directed learning, or even of all phenomena observable for the food-reinforced key-pecking of the pigeon, which is a narrow and unrepresentative paradigm, even though very widely used. The molecular explanation, that rewards stamp in the details of a preceding behaviour, is the mechanical version of the Law of Effect originated by Thorndike. Much of this chapter has been devoted to the evidence against it, for example in spatial learning and in goal-sensitive actions. The tension between the molar and molecular explanations for pay-off-controlled activities should therefore be resolved, not by choosing one or the other, but by a form of attribution which is apparently deeply uncongenial to the human intellect – by saying that we can attribute instrumental learning sometimes to one process, and at other times to another.

Levels and types of association and brain mechanisms in conditioning

Theories of learning have not always implied very much about the real neural mechanisms which many of us assume make the theories possible. One of Aristotle's most glaring bloomers was his hypothesis that the brain had no psychological functions (since he thought it was a sort of radiator for cooling the blood); he rashly did not hedge his bets on this one and declared that the brain had no more to do with mental processes than a piece of excrement. In modern times few theorists have done quite so badly on brain function, but several learning theorists have managed to ignore the brain altogether – Skinner as a matter of principle and Tolman and Hull by default. The early attempts of Pavlov and Thorndike to tie down theories of learning to putative neural mechanisms did not gain them many admirers. The most successful and influential theory of brain processes in learning is probably that of Hebb (1949), followed closely by the not dissimilar model of Konorski (1967), and these have influenced Bindra (1976) and Wagner (1976, 1978), while remaining rather remote from the theoretical comparisons of conditioning processes which have been the concern of this chapter. I shall follow the mainstream tradition of saying little or nothing about the details of the brain processes involved in learning, while expressing the hope that more will be known at some point in the distant future: however, I wish to refer briefly to brain anatomy for the purpose of buttressing my speculative conclusion to this chapter, which is predictably similar to that reached in previous chapters, since it takes the form of saying that learning involves quite different levels of representation of whatever it is that is learned. In addition, in this chapter, I have tended to stress that there are several different types of possible learned association, and that those types by which motor behaviours are connected to motivational pay-offs are what differentiate instrumental processes from classical processes, while accepting, of course, that both stimulus-pairing and response-rewarding laboratory procedures typically arouse impure mixtures of these internal processes.

Brain structures and psychological processes

The vertebrate brain consists of several identifiable parts, each containing thousands or millions of neurons. Readers unfamiliar with this fact should consult a suitable textbook of physiological psychology or, for more directly relevant discussions, Walker (1983a), Macphail (1982) or Yeo (1979). Not much more detail is needed for present purposes than was regarded as well established by Herrick or Bayliss in 1918. Primarily sensory and primarily motor tracts go up the outside and down the inside of the *spinal cord*. Stimulus-response reflexes of some degree of complexity, especially in lower vertebrates, are accomplished within the spinal cord itself, but its main function is clearly to transmit information to and from the higher centres of the brain. Just at the top of the spinal cord several cranial nerves go in and out of the medulla, first of all to various *cranial nuclei:* these control both input and output for the internal organs and some parts of the sensory and motor systems and therefore they can be involved in learned associations, as well as relaying to other parts of the brain. At the back of the brain is a large crumpled lump with grey matter on the outside and large white fibre tracts on the inside: the *cerebellum*. Although there is no agreement as to exactly what happens inside it, no one doubts that it plays a special part in balance and in fast co-ordinated muscle movements, including both learned and unlearned motor skills. Cerebellar learning is likely to be both anatomically and functionally separate from learning in other parts of the brain. Within the cerebellum, there are specialized regions dealing with different parts of the body – hindleg, foreleg, face and head, etc. (The left and right sides of the body are done on the left and right of the cerebellum, respectively.)

There are a great many known pathways in which sensory and motor information is transmitted up and down from the spinal cord and cerebellum through the *mid-brain, thalamus* and *basal ganglia*, to the top and front of the brain, where lie what are often referred to as the 'highest centres', located in mammals in the cerebral cortex. And there are other bits, connected by known neural tracts, which are identified with motivation and emotion, and happen to be called the *limbic system*. Best known of these are the hippocampus, which responds to novelty and therefore is expected to be needed for memory and for learned cognitive maps; and the hypothalamus, which controls the pituitary master-gland, and thus the autonomic nervous system, and has parts which seem specialized for hunger, sexual excitement and thirst, and thus may be regarded as necessary for drive and incentive.

There is not necessarily a one-to-one correspondence between brain anatomy and brain function, and it is true that detailed theories of brain function are not very advanced. However, what is already known and certain is sufficient to support the following crudest possible deduction: there is more than one part of the brain, and therefore there might be more than one kind of learning, depending on what or which part is most closely involved in it. A somewhat less crude theory of brain function was put forward by the father of British neurology, Hughlings Jackson (Jackson, 1888/1931; see Walker, 1986), which has yet to be contradicted, and which is one of the reasons for assuming that associated events may occur at different levels of representation. Jackson's theory was that there was a hierarchy of representation in the brain, particularly representations of movements, since localized epileptic movements were one of his medical special-izations. The hierarchy was specifically related to a vague notion of evolution, and specifically related to the question of the voluntary control of actions. An illustrative example is the case of a patient who had lost voluntary control of tongue movement and thus could not comply with the standard doctor's instruction of 'put out your tongue', but whose tongue was capable of efficient, but involuntary, licking of the lips. Thus Jackson believed that there were at least three and possibly more, separate brain representations of the tongue, the lowest being involved with reflexive movements, such as those necessary in swallowing and lip-licking, and physically based mainly on the cranial nuclei, the middle being required for more complicated movements, including those which need to be learned for speech, and the top being needed for delicate voluntary control.

Without making any unnecessarily firm commitments to Jackson's or any other detailed account of brain function, it is surely very safe to assume that bodily movements may be initiated or influenced either by the spinal cord, or by the cerebellum, or by the basal ganglia, or by various higher motor centres of the cerebral hemispheres, which are in the

frontal cerebral cortex of mammals, which have rough equivalents in the cerebral hemispheres of birds and reptiles, and
possibly though not definitely very rough equivalents indeed
in the cerebral hemispheres of the brains of frogs and fish
(Macphail, 1982; Walker, 1983a). If this assumption is
correct, it is almost equally safe to take it for granted that
there are psychological consequences of the anatomical differentiation, and that behaviours depending on one level of
representation will be demonstrably different from behaviours
characteristic of a different level. Then spinal reflexes would
be different from voluntary actions, and conditioned digestive
reflexes would be different from learned and novel methods
of goal-seeking, which gives one kind of biological basis to
the same sort of conclusion already reached about classical
and instrumental conditioning.

The types of learned association – conclusions

It is now possible to summarize the conclusions of this chapter
in terms of the biological functions and possible anatomical
implications of learned associations, categorized according to
the traditional types of S-S, S-R, and R-S, but with reser-
vations about the adequacy of the typology.

S-S associations and learning about stimuli

This is useful to begin with, since it calls into question not
only the typology but also the concept of an association that
only comes in pairs. Stimulus-stimulus associations can be
made in principle without any response, and therefore are
obvious candidates for behaviourally silent or latent learning
(p. 150). In these cases learning may be presumed to take
place simply by exposure to stimuli. This covers also perceptual learning (p. 41) and of course the learning to recognize
stimuli which is the theoretical basis of many kinds of habituation (p. 39). In both these cases it would be better to
explicitly rule out the implication that pairing two separate
stimuli engages utterly different brain processes from
exposure to one or three – that is clearly most unlikely, and S-
S is better understood as covering learned relations between,

within and about sensed events. For novelty, spatial learning, and certain kinds of memory for stimuli, it has often been suggested that the hippocampus of the mammalian brain plays a special part (see chapter 10). There are limits to the usefulness of this kind of assertion, but no one makes alternative suggestions along the lines of memory being in the spinal cord or cerebellum, and the relation of the hippocampus to the rest of the limbic system prompts a number of interesting speculations about how memory interacts with motivation (e.g. Gray, 1982). Even in the most rudimentary neural systems currently studied, associations between individual sensory nerves at synapses suggest S-S associations at a drastically simpler level of representation (Hawkins *et al.*, 1983, see p. 99), although these possibly ought to be included in the next sub-category.

Stimulus-reinforcer reflexive shifts (S-S*[1])

It is a moot question whether any stimulus is without any motivational effects at all. But there is clearly a difference of degree at least between familiar geographical and social surroundings and the commonly used motivationally significant stimuli or 'reinforcers' of food for a hungry animal and electric shocks for a fearful one. The pairing of a relatively neutral signal with another event of some moment, which elicits external or internal un-conditioned responses, is common to the various kinds of Pavlovian conditioning (chapter 3) and very similar, perhaps identical effects which occur when similar events are used as goals for instrumental responding. The theory and description of what results from these stimulus-pairings is 'stimulus-substitution' (p. 100). The essential feature of this is that it is relatively automatic and involuntary, and, as argued in this chapter, unaffected by the pay-offs, that is, the evaluated costs or benefits, of the reinforcing event. By contrast, the hedonic properties of the reinforcing event may be one of the attributes which are transmitted to the signal – the hedonic shift (Garcia *et al.*,

---

[1]The asterisk indicates that the stimulus or response which it accompanies has motivational significance

1977a, see chapter 7). In this case reactions of the limbic motivational system compose part of the set of attributes shifted to a new stimulus. These can hardly be put as a necessary part of stimulus-pairing effects if the same terms are to be used for animals such as the sea-slug which do not have a limbic system. Hawkins *et al.* (1983) suggest that there is in this animal a set of diffusely projecting 'facilitator neurons' which for this purpose is equivalent to the vertebrate limbic system. This may be so, but again it is unduly limiting to suppose that the phenomena of stimulus-substitution can only be observed with very strong defensive reflexes, or with strong motivation in any species, since it is more likely that stimulus-reinforcer pairings blend into pairings of much less powerful stimuli (e.g. second-order conditioning; see p. 86).

S-R habits

Although S-R associations have been under a cloud for several years, due to disillusion with theories in which they were the main or indeed the only component, there can be no question of leaving them out of learning theory altogether. Everyday habits, good and bad, are often describable as associations between stimulus and response, and learned skills such as swimming, driving, or riding a bicycle – and even social skills – patently require some sort of automatic pilot, which ensures that the right responses are made at the right times. The main point of doubt is whether the formation of habits is governed by strong motivational stimuli via a backwards stamping-in principle, as suggested by Thorndike, or whether some other more complex mechanism ensures the perform- ance of responses in the first place, habits being then acquired merely by repetition (e.g. Spence, 1956). It seems wisest to keep both possibilities open, since Dickinson (1980, 1985), among others, has argued strongly that there is often a shift from initial voluntary control to repeated habits, and the mechanism of repetition without massive motivational feed- back seems important for human skills: but the less-complex stamping-in device would appear to be available to the restricted neural systems, such as those possessed by decorti- cate rabbits, decerebrate duck embryos, or decapitated cockroaches, which selectively make responses with favourable outcomes (p. 158). These preparations should not be regarded as identical; indeed it is arguable that decorticate rabbits or rodents, since they retain the basal ganglia and limbic system and other subcortical structures (which certainly are involved with motivation and the control of movement, and are even said by some to contain the seat of self-awareness: Penfield and Roberts, 1959; Creutzfeldt, 1979), should possess the essential equipment for voluntary goal-directed responses, even if lacking in much sensory and motor information processing capacity. There may in fact be more than one form of stamping-in, or immediate confirmation mechanism. Anatomical evidence suggests that the cerebellum has detailed wiring for its own stamping-in of input and output connections, which may be independent of the motivational drive/satisfaction devices of the limbic system. The limbic system itself is likely to have its most direct effects on forebrain structures (e.g. the sensory thalamus and the motor basal ganglia), and the vital centres lower down in the mid-brain and brainstem have their own homeostatic imperatives which may influence reflexive associations. Eventually, for example in the mammalian spinal cord, one gets down to a level which has no obvious mechanism for stamping in by pay-offs, but which may be capable of anticipatory response shifts between closely related sensory inputs. The point is that there is a clear difference between the biological functions of the bottom and top anatomical levels of a mammal's brain, and an equally clear neurological disparity between the brain of a monkey and the ganglia of a cockroach or slug. It is merely the beginnings of any comprehensive biological account of learning to distinguish between reflexive habits, which are independent of knowledge of the goals which they may nevertheless achieve, and the possibilities of more considered, flexible and delicate adjustments of means to ends which have been offered in the course of brain evolution.

R-S* associations: responses made as means to ends

Although it is conventional to emphasize that instrumental learning is partly a matter of association between responses and their practical consequences, it is useful theoretically to reverse the order here, and say that goal-directed behaviours will ensue if, when a given end is desired, the means by which it can be obtained are activated. Thus the order of the association can be that the wanted goal comes first, and the necessary response second, and this could be regarded as the essential minimum of a voluntary behaviour – that a representation of the consequences of responding directs the performance of the response. In this sense means-to-ends associations differ from stimulus-response impulses mainly in that an internal representation of the goal is part of the stimulus. It is possible, however, that some species may be capable of acquiring if-then knowledge in a rather more elaborate form, in which what is learned is that if a certain response is made, such and such consequences follow. In principle, this could be a 'declarative representation' formed and utilized without the response ever having to be made. But for this kind of representation to be practically useful, it would need to be attached in some way to response instructions, to ensure that when the consequences of responding assumes a high priority, so also does response performance. The conclusion from experiments on latent learning (p. 150) is that this form of representation is normally available to laboratory rats, for the purposes of maze learning.

The role of motivational factors in means-ends learning is bound to be strong in the context of response performance, almost by definition, and thus the psychology of drives or the mechanisms of wanting interacts with the learning of this kind of association. It is arguable that willed actions of any kind are based on the biological mechanisms which evolved to ensure that needed goals are achieved, by a built-in set of instructions to perform activities associated with gaining those goals. There is little doubt that the limbic system of higher vertebrate brains can function as a device of this kind. Mammals rapidly learn to perform an artificial response, such as pressing a lever, if this action switches on electrical current to an electrode strategically placed in the limbic system (e.g. in the medial forebrain bundle between the septal area and the hypothalamus), but the receipt of electrical stimulation at the same location elicits goal-oriented behaviours (eating of food, copulation) and, most crucially, also arouses motivational states which are sufficient to promote the learning of new arbitrary responses to gain access to food, or to the opportunity for copulation (Olds, 1961; Caggiula, 1970; Mendelson, 1966; Roberts *et al.*, 1967). Thus this type of instrumental learning is not so much a stamping-in of habits as a form of wish fulfilment.

R-R* associations: working rewarded by doing

At this point it needs to be acknowledged that a goal can be and often is the opportunity to do something, rather than the passive receipt of external stimulation. Glickman and Schiff (1967) and Herrnstein (1977) have stressed the importance of this for instinctive behaviours in animals, and Premack's laboratory demonstrations that one activity can reward another (Premack, 1965) are often acknowledged by reference to the 'Premack principle'. A mouse will press a lever so that it can run in a wheel, but the popularity of the Premack principle is no doubt due in part to the ubiquity, and perhaps the effectiveness, of instructions to children in the form 'first do your homework, then you can ride your bicycle'.

R-S associations: feedback and latent expectancies

It would be a strong restriction to imply that means-ends relations could only be learned when the ends are being actively desired. One of the demonstrations of latent learning had rats pressing a lever for water which happened to be salty, then going back to this when they became salt-deprived (Kriekhaus and Wolf, 1968, p. 152). As a form of latent expectancy learning, or anticipation of feedback for responses where the feedback is informative without being strongly motivating, especially in motor skills, associations between responses and subsequent stimulation should be common. There are of course a number of built-in physiological mechanisms for supplying this kind of information, in proprioception, mechanisms of balance in the inner ear, and in the visual control of movement and posture (eye-hand co-ordination, also evident in the difficulty of standing on one leg with closed eyes).

R-R associations: response chains and skills

Very often, chains of responses involve a great deal of internal and external sensory feedback, and therefore can be said to include S-R and R-S associations. The function of the feedback is however to produce integrated sequences of movements – what is referred to as 'a response' may in some experiments be the twitch of a single muscle, but typically will require an unseen and unremarked feat of muscular co-ordination. Much of this is innately programmed, but most human skills demonstrate the possibility of complex learning of motor sequences. The control of some sequences without re-afference or proprioceptive feedback from response completion is evident in the playing of musical arpeggios, when this is done too fast for there to be any time for neural information to be sent back and forth. With prolonged training, the minimal form of response habits may dispense with as much feedback as possible – the early experiments by Carr and Watson (1908) on maze-running in rats were continued until the animals tried to run in the same pattern when the maze was lengthened or shortened. On the other hand, finely tuned perceptual and motor skills, such as playing arpeggios, or fast bowling, may require daily practice involving constant attention to feedback.

Conclusion: relation of classical and instrumental conditioning to other forms of learning

Under the heading of 'varieties of memory', Oakley (1983) has placed the kinds of learning covered in this chapter about half-way up on a continuum with genetically determined instincts and reflexes and learning in the course of growth below, and culturally acquired information, such as may be obtained through higher education, above. This is a wide-ranging and comprehensive account of learning, which gives classical and instrumental conditioning a context as a bridge between biology on the one hand and culture on the other.

However, even in this context, and perhaps especially in this context, it is important to recognize that what is simply described as conditioning covers a considerable variety of possible psychological processes. The general rule of thumb which applies to habituation to a single stimulus, anticipatory shifts in given responses due to stimulus pairings, and the development of new behaviours by response selection, is that these procedures correspond to biological problems for which there are vastly different psychological solutions. I have compared these solutions on a scale of levels of representation of the procedural events, which vary from responses in single neurons to cognitive representation and descriptions of perceived events and purposive actions which defy reductions to simpler levels. Cutting across these levels of representation there are however types of process which can be categorized in terms of what kinds of association are learned. Most simply, in stimulus-pairings, many of the behavioural effects of classical conditioning can be interpreted as the automatic and involuntary transfer of the properties of one stimulus to another, whereas in response-reward procedures, although there is often opportunity for this kind of stimulus-substitution effect, there is also the chance of effortful and goal-directed response-selection process, as a rudimentary form of voluntary behaviour. Not surprisingly, the system of motivated effort is more evident in motor movements than in visceral responses but the motor system also takes part in more automatic habits and skills, and the sensory systems have their own specializations of information-gathering, including the formation of associations between stimuli. Conditioning experiments may thus engage biologically useful processes of perceptual learning, motivated goal-seeking, and automatic habit formation. In later chapters I shall examine to what extent these processes overlap with mechanisms of perception and memory, and whether these more complex psychological processes can be considered as further elaborations of principles already inherent in the more basic biological solutions to the functional problems of anticipating important events, automatically ignoring irrelevant events, and discovering new ways of bringing about needed goals.

7 Reward and punishment

'What is painful is avoided and what is pleasant is pursued'.

Aristotle, *De Motu Animalium*

Appetitive and aversive motivation

Up until this point, I have discussed instrumental learning and voluntary behaviour almost entirely in terms of the pursuit of the pleasant, or more automatic versions of this concept which correspond to the seeking of positive goals. This has been in the cause of simplicity, but clearly any theory of willed action would have to include the avoidance of undesired outcomes as well as the search for wanted rewards, and any more general and less cognitive account of the effects of motivation on learning needs equally to consider at least two kinds of motivation, associated with sought-after and feared events, or with more reflexive forms of approach and avoidance behaviours.

Perhaps even more than in other chapters, the reader may here encounter confusion due to arbitrarily selected technical terms in learning theory. The most conventional distinction between putatively pleasant versus disagreeable events refers to 'appetitive' versus 'aversive' reinforcers, corresponding to appetites and aversions or appetitive and aversive motivation. These should be regarded as the most conventionally correct terms (Mackintosh, 1974, 1983), but there are many variations in usage (e.g. Gray, 1975). I shall speak fairly loosely of attractive and aversive events, or attractive and aversive emotional states, and hope that the meaning is clear from the context. However some of the terminological difficulties arise from genuine theoretical questions surrounding the degree of interchangeability of reward and punishment. It is logically possible to conceive of a single urge underlying them both; Hull (1943) for instance based his theory on the universal biological necessities of nourishing and preserving the bodily tissues, but drew an analogy between pain and hunger as the mechanisms for dealing with these needs, and was thus able to use the single concept of drive reduction for all motivation. Behaviour in Hull's theory is always impelled by goads, either internal or external, never attracted by equivalent positive goals. The best that one can hope for in this scheme is to minimize one's levels of irritation and distress. Few have been optimistic enough to make quite so thorough a job of the converse of Hull's theory – the Pollyanna conviction that the motive for response is always to make things better, life consisting of degrees of happiness, with even the most unpleasant ordeals perceived in terms of how much joyful relief the future may bring. However, Herrnstein (1969), Gray (1975), Dickinson (1980) and Mackintosh (1983) have all emphasized that escape from unpleasantness can in some cases be explained in terms of future attractions, in the context of experiments in which rats perform responses which reduce the frequency of the electric shocks they would otherwise receive.

Often there are problems in tying down the subjective aspects of positive and negative emotions to measurable behaviours, or in making even theoretical distinctions between their effects. One can imagine building a robot in which all desirable ends were represented as positive numbers, and all adverse outcomes by negative numbers: the only motivational instruction necessary for this artificial creation would be to maximize the aggregate, and any constant, positive or negative which was added to individual values would be irrelevant. A feature of this idealized system is that the rewards and punishments, or attractive and aversive reinforcers, have equal, but opposite, effects. I shall use as a theme for this chapter the question of whether, in practice, in the natural as opposed to the idealized world, reward and punishment have this sort of symmetry. To the extent that they do not, it will clearly be necessary to say in what ways the motivational systems for reward and punishment differ.

Anatomical and functional separation of attractive and aversive mechanisms

It will be as well to start with the line of evidence just appealed to in discussing types of association (chapter 6) – the biological facts of brain structures and the theories of the behavioural functions which these structures serve. It has been clear ever since Papez (1937) pointed it out that the limbic system or 'Papez circuit' of the vertebrate forebrain, which is an interconnected network of brain parts, is the place to look for motivational mechanisms. Lesioning of different parts produces different motivational effects. Amygdala lesions make the animal tame and inappropriately relaxed; septal lesions make it jumpy and aggressive; lesions of the lateral hypothalamus and pyriform cortex make it under- or over-sexed; and lesions of the ventro-medial versus lateral hypothalamic regions make it eat too much or too little. There are no agreed interpretations of precisely what this evidence means, but in the case of motivation associated with eating, then physiological theories have it in common that they are all complicated, assuming separate mechanisms for such factors as motivational states resulting from extreme hunger, the effects of food palatability, and detailed control over when an animal starts and stops a particular meal (Green, 1987). This supports the psychological expectation that eating may occur either as a reaction to strongly unpleasant inner sensations of hunger, or in the absence of physiological need, in considered and sybaritic anticipation of taste-enjoyment, or in some combination of these.

The stronger and more direct form of evidence is however that from animals' reactions to mild electrical stimulation of different points in the limbic system, which gives rise to the assumption that there are pleasure and pain centres in the brain (Olds, 1958). Olds (1961) re-affirmed his belief that these results require the addition of a pleasure-seeking mechanism to any drive-reduction or pain-avoidance formula such as that proposed by Hull. In Olds's words, pleasure has to be seen as 'a different brand of stimulation' from the mere absence of drive (1961, p. 350). On the face of it, this arises simply because there is no obvious source of a need or drive state when rats that are not deliberately deprived of anything, run to a particular place in a maze, or repeatedly press a lever, apparently because this results in their receiving electrical stimulation of the brain (via electrodes implanted through their skulls). Deutsch and Howarth (1963) proposed an *ad hoc* defence of drive theory, which relied on the assumption that the same electrical stimulation both initiated the drive and reduced it, but this cannot cope with the findings that rats will run across an electrified grid to get brain stimulation (Olds, 1961), will perform more or less normally on schedules of reinforcement for bar-pressing in Skinner boxes when long intervals intervene between successive episodes of brain stimulation (Pliskoff *et al.*, 1965; Benninger *et al.*, 1977) without any prior priming, and also appear to be comforted by appetitive positive brain stimulation received during illness in the taste-aversion paradigm (see p. 232 below; Lett and Harley, 1974).

The behavioural effects of rewarding brain stimulation thus appear to support the view that there is an attractive motivational mechanism. But few have ever doubted this; our question is to what extent the attractive mechanism is equal and opposite to the aversive one. Some asymmetries appear to be present anatomically. Olds (1961) suggests that the reward system takes up rather a large part of a rat's brain, the punishment system much less of it: out of 200 electrodes placed in the brain at random, 35 per cent had rewarding effects on behaviour, 60 per cent had no apparent motivational effects at all, and only 5 per cent had definite punishing effects. Using standard behavioural tests, the precise location of rewarding and punishing sites can be plotted; in Olds and Olds (1963) study a point was judged attractive if animals pressed a lever to turn electricity on, but aversive if, when a train of stimulation was started by the experimenter, the rat pressed a similar lever to turn this off.

The main features of the anatomical lay-out suggested by this procedure are that:

(i) points where electrical stimulation is attractive are centred generally on the hypothalmus and its main fibre tract connection with the septal area, the median forebrain bundle, with hardly any involvement of the thalamus (a sensory relay station);

(ii) conversely points with exclusively aversive behavioural effects were found frequently in the thalamus, and also in the periventrical region of the midbrain

(iii) many points which showed *both* attractive and aversive effects were found in the hypothalmus, in the medial area for instance;

(iv) 'pure' effects one way or the other were most likely in fibre bundles, while the ambivalent points, in nuclei, demonstrate that the two systems are often brought close together in physical proximity.

These physiological results do not provide strong evidence as to whether punishment is the mirror image of reward in terms of its behavioural effects, but they certainly suggest that there are two separate physiological systems, which interact, and that the aversive system is fairly directly connected to sensory input, in the thalamus and midbrain, as would be expected for pain and discomfort, whereas the attractive mechanism is intimately involved with metabolic and autonomic control, as would need to be the case if some of the attractive systems serve purposes in connection with bodily needs and homeostatic balances, and cyclical variations in behaviour. This can be related to the analysis of different types of drives (Gray, 1975) and to theoretical schemes of biological function. At a very rudimentary stage of examination of this, it would not surprise us to find that there were motivational imperatives of different degrees of urgency. A hungry animal being chased by a predator should only have one choice when internal comparisons are made between the importance of eating and the importance of escaping, but, while keeping a watchful eye open to the possibility of danger, a prey animal may need to make sophisticated adjustments about its own choices of palatable but costly versus abundant but boring items. In terms of function, it seems unlikely that the underlying mechanism for panic flight should have much in common with the incentive to fill oneself with the most energy-rich food available in times of great abundance. And in the natural world, as opposed to the laboratory, for many species the time devoted to active escape from danger or the immediate food-seeking may be short by comparison with that taken up by nest construction, complicated social interactions of several kinds, migration, and exploring and updating of unfamiliar or familiar territorial domains. All these various activities need some kind of psychological system to sustain them, and it is not likely that just one or even just two kinds of motivational apparatus would be sufficient for the whole lot.

Similarities between reward and punishment

Having established that there are grounds for expecting qualitative differences between attractive and aversive motivational systems, we ought now to inspect the contrary evidence – that the behavioural effects of the two systems are roughly equal but opposite. That is to say, attractive stimuli attract, and thus encourage the performance of responses which it has been learned will bring them about, while aversive stimuli repel, and discourage behaviours which make them more likely. The above statements may appear to be tautologous, and thus not worth experimental examination. This is almost the case, and perhaps would have been had not both Thorndike (1931) and Skinner (1953) argued the contrary. Thorndike was persuaded by some data that should have been treated more tentatively that neither young chicks nor undergraduates possessed any mechanism which would prevent them from doing again things which had previously proved disadvantageous, and from the beginning had emphasized that it was accidental successes, rather than accidental error, that was the engine of trial-and-error learning. Skinner was similarly sceptical about the ability of rats to associate unfavourable outcomes with their own behaviour, but this was linked to an idealistic and perhaps practically sound rejection of the use of punishment by parents and teachers to control the behaviour of children. Skinner's argu-

ment seems to have been that punishing a child for wrong-
doing will produce generally counter-productive emotional
upheavals, which may become transferred even more counter-
productively to associated events by classical conditioning;
but that the punishment will not act as a deterrent for any
specific response.

We may accept Thorndike's suspicions about the fallibility
of chicks and undergraduates, and Skinner's doubts about the
advisability of punitiveness in parents and teachers, without
discounting the symmetry that certainly exists to some degree
between the encouragement of responses by reward and their
deterrence by punishment, but without perhaps going quite
as far as to say that 'The most important fact about punishment is that its effects are the same as those of reward but
with the sign reversed' (Mackintosh, 1983, p. 125). The
deterrent effect of aversive stimuli on instrumental responses
can in fact be readily demonstrated in the typical Skinner box,
and indeed was so demonstrated by Estes (1944). If rats press
a lever because this delivers food pellets, they may be deterred
from pressing it by the addition of mild electric shocks,
delivered to the feet at the moment the lever is pressed.
Depending on their degree of hunger, the size of the food
pellets and the strength of the shock, they will continue to
press if rewarded with little or no punishment, and continue
to refrain from pressing if the punishment is strong enough,
and is given invariably if they occasionally try to get away
with it. Moreover, if the rewards cease, the effect of the
rewards will dissipate as the animals learn that the response
no longer brings them about, and similarly if shocks cease,
the effect of punishment will disappear as the animals learn
that these are not forthcoming: these effects are symmetrical,
since they can both be construed as learning about the consequences of responding (Mackintosh, 1974, 1983). However,
there are limits to the symmetry. First there is a logical
difference between learning about positive and negative
response consequences. Since positive consequences are
sought,and, if learning has been successful, found, then any
change in the positive consequences of responding will quickly
become apparent to the responding animal. On the other
hand, since negative consequences are withdrawn from, and,

if learning has been successful, avoided, then changes in negative consequences may not immediately present themselves to the animal which is not responding, and this is one reason why, other things being equal, we might expect the deterring effects of a temporary unpleasant consequence of responding to be somewhat more lasting than the encouraging effects of a temporary incentive with equivalent emotional force. This may be the explanation for the finding of Boe and Church (1967) that a very strong series of shocks given consistently for rats' intermittently food-rewarded lever pressing deterred further lever-pressing completely and indefinitely.

It is certainly arguable that in addition to bias against gathering new information about pain and distress, any scale of these affective qualities will be difficult to map on to a scale of the desirability of food pellets according to their size or taste, even with a change of sign. However, within limits, it is possible in behavioural experiments to construct a scale of practical equivalences, by setting off given amounts of attractiveness in a goal against degrees of unpleasantness encountered in the course of achieving it. Vast amounts of evidence were collected before the Second World War by Warner (1927, 1928a, 1928b) and Warden (1931), among others, using the 'Columbia obstruction box', in which rats were required to run across an electrified grid to obtain access to food, water or a member of the opposite sex, under systematically varied conditions. Rats were reluctant to run across the standard grid for food until they had been without food for at least two or three days, but crossed with little hesitation for water if deprived of this for 24 hours. Male rats ran across the same grid to get to a female in heat rather more often one day after previous sexual contact than four weeks after, and very much less if tested within six hours of previous copulation; females only crossed at all to males in the most receptive half of their estrus cycle, with a peak number of crossings confined to the estrus phase. The highest rates of crossing the standard electrified grid were observed in maternal rats separated from their young (Nissen, 1930; Warden, 1931).

It would be unwise to place very much emphasis on these results, but it is clear that the animals were capable (a) of learning that there was a desired goal object of a certain kind in the 'incentive compartment' on the other side of the electrified grid, and (b) of combining this knowledge, in however simple a form, with the level of their current appetite, so that, for instance, they would cross to food if very hungry, but not when moderately so. Stone (1942) was able to get essentially similar results, without using the somewhat artificial device of the shocking grid, by training rats to dig through tubes filled with sand, or to scratch their way through a succession of paper-towel barriers blocking a runway, in order to get to goal objects. More precise quantification was obtained by Brown (1942) and Miller *et al* (1943: see Miller, 1944), who trained rats to run down an alley towards food while wearing a harness with a cord attached, which allowed their movements to be carefully measured, in some cases in terms of the force with which they pulled against a calibrated spring. It was found that hungry rats, trained to run towards food, pulled against the spring with almost as much force when 2 metres away as when very much closer to the food. However other rats, who received electric shocks in the goal box instead of food, pulled vigorously to get away when subsequently placed close to the goal box, but did not pull at all when placed 2 metres away, even after extremely severe previous shocks. It would have been odd if any other result had been obtained, since hungry rats are presumably still hungry when far away from food, whereas shocked rats are not necessarily afraid once they are far away from the site of their aversive experience (see below, p. 218). The difference between the pulling towards food and away from shock is often referred to as the difference between approach and avoidance gradients, and drawn as in Figure 7.1. The argument in favour of such approach-avoidance gradients is strengthened by experiments in which the same rats are both shocked and fed in the same goal box. Subsequent behaviour at various points on the path to this goal can be predicted in terms of the strength of current hunger, and the intensity of previous shocks. With moderate values of both, animals approach about half-way towards the goal and then stop, as would be expected from Figure 7.1. Either stronger hunger or weaker shock leads to closer approach; with weak hunger

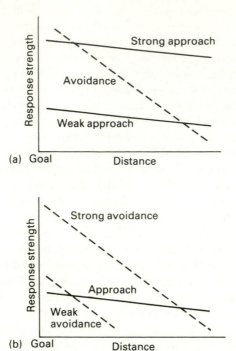

Figure 7.1   *Approach and avoidance gradients.*
Schematic plots of how the strength of approach and avoidance responses
may vary with distance from the goal object based on experiments in which
rats receive food and electric shock at the same place. In (a), it is apparent
that strong approach tendencies may result in high points of avoidance
gradients being encountered. Paradoxically, (b) demonstrates that a
reduction of avoidance tendencies in circumstances of conflict may have
the effect of raising the point at which approach and avoidance tendencies
balance out. After Miller (1944).

or more aversive shocks animals naturally keep further away.
Although this was true on average, there was considerable
variation between and within individual animals. Some rats
adopted a pattern of consistent vacillation, of increasingly
hesitant approaches followed by abrupt retreats, while others
moved forward in steps, making long pauses before each

small approach, eventually coming to a complete halt (Miller, 1944).

All this suggests that positive incentive, or the attractiveness of a goal, can be somehow weighed against the negative incentive derived from previous aversive experiences. Logan (1969) used precisely these terms in another claim that 'the effects of punishment are symmetrically opposite to the effects of reward', based on an experimental variation on the theme of conflict between reward and punishment, which included a more explicit choice between alternatives. Rats were allowed to choose between running down a black or a white alley, after having previously done 'forced trials' to ensure equal experience of what the black and white choices entailed. First, preferences were established by such differentials as seven food pellets at the end of the black alley, but only one in the white; or three pellets given at the end of both alleys, but available immediately in the white goal box, but only dropped in 12 seconds after arrival in the black goal box. Both these procedures establish strong preferences in hungry rats, since these behave as if they would rather have seven than one food pellet, and a given amount of food sooner rather than later. Logan then examined how easy it was to reverse these preferences by the obstruction box method of making the rats run over an electrified grid for 2 feet before reaching the preferred goal, and varying the intensity of the shocks thus delivered. A very orderly effect of shock intensity on percentage of choices of the originally preferred goal was observed, and a stronger shock was necessary to persuade the animals to choose one instead of seven pellets than to shift the preference for immediate versus delay rewards of the same size. This difference was even more pronounced when shock had to be endured on only 50 per cent of the approaches to the preferred goal. Choice of seven versus one pellet was very resistant to that procedure, the risk of only a very strong shock reducing preference to just under 50 per cent, whereas the choice of immediate over delay reward was still strongly determined by shock intensity, rats settling for delayed rewards fairly frequently (on about 60 per cent of choices) even with the risk of only a low-shock intensity (Logan, 1969, p. 47).

All these results, and many others (Azrin and Holtz, 1966;

Solomon, 1964; Morse and Kelleher, 1977) seem to suggest that reward and punishment are 'analogous if not equivalent processes' (Morse and Kelleher, 1977), are symmetrical but opposite in their effects, and so on. Gray (1975, pp. 135 and 229) has formalized this view first with respect to the symmetry of the possible behavioural effects of delivering or witholding attractive and aversive events; and second by presenting a theoretical model, shown in Figure 7.2, in which, as can be seen at a glance, precisely comparable mechanisms are proposed for the operation of reward and punishment, with a 'decision mechanism' which allows for the results quoted above, in which the attractive effects of reward are balanced against the aversive effects of punishment. In instrumental learning therefore, there are many reasons for assuming that punishment may sometimes operate in more or less the same way as reward, even though there are differences in anatomical factors and in ecological function. In terms of Figure 5.8, which was used to summarize the sorts of associations possible in instrumental learning with reward, all that is necessary is to substitute 'unwanted' for 'wanted'; to interpret 'appropriately associated with unwanted events' to mean that such behaviours will involve withdrawal rather than approach; and thus to suppose that the result of learning that a response has unwanted consequences (at (1) in Figure 5.8) will be an impulse to inhibit such responses rather than make them. As in Gray's model (Figure 7.2), it is necessary that rewards are automatically linked to impulses to approach, and to the repetition of rewarded responses, while aversive stimuli must be inherently linked to withdrawal, behavioural inhibition, or an internal 'stop' command. Clearly, as a consequence of this in general and in Figure 5.8, when the punishment mechanism works, punished responses are suppressed, and the relevant motivating event is notable by its absence).

The theory of avoidance learning

The symmetry of attractive and aversive events can certainly be maintained in plotting the predicted effects of increases and decreases in their frequency. Animals should behave so

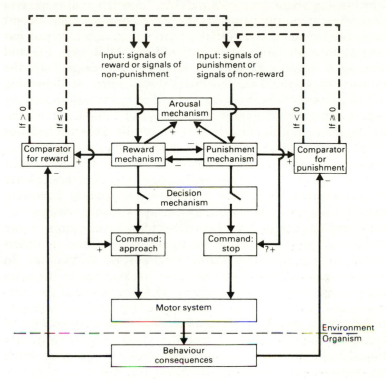

Figure 7.2   *Gray's symmetrical model of reward and punishment.*
The only difference between reward and punishment in this model is in
their differing effects on the motor system. After Gray (1975).

as to maximize their receipt of appealing experiences and
minimize their encounters with aggravation and distress: thus
they should learn to repeat responses which either bring about
or prolong rewards or prevent or cut short punishments; and
they should also learn to inhibit responses which either
prevent or truncate pleasurable or satisfying states of affairs,
and they should learn to inhibit responses which initiate or
continue pain or distress. Both this last sentence and Gray's
diagram (Gray, 1975, p. 135) may appear complex, but
they are simply behavioural elaborations of the pleasure/
pain principle. The first step in this is to say that responses

which bring about rewards should be repeated, and responses that bring about punishments should be stopped. The second step goes beyond this, to deduce that responses which prevent otherwise available rewards should be inhibited, whereas responses which prevent or truncate otherwise imposed punishments should be repeated. It has often been pointed out (Mowrer, 1939; Dickinson, 1980) that this second step is very much more demanding of the cognitive abilities of both the animal and the learning theorist, because the critical consequences of responding are unobservable – what is important is that nothing happens.

There are a number of explanations for why the absence of an event may be critical in serving as a goal or reinforcement for instrumental learning. Perhaps the most straightforward explanation for the theorist, if not for the system being explained, takes the form of assuming that the behaving system contains comparator mechanisms, which assess whether current levels of attractive or aversive stimulation are greater or less than expected. If an expected event does not take place, this fact can thus be fed into the relevant motivational device – the absence of a reward should be regarded with displeasure, but the absence of an expected punishment clocked up as something to be sought after. Such arrangements are included in Figure 7.2. The main problem with this is that it takes an enormous amount of continuous cognitive processing for granted. Whenever a normally obtained reward or punishment is missed, the system should sit up and take notice, and this implies some form of continual vigilance. But we have already seen that such comparator mechanisms, albeit of varying degrees of complexity, are a universal feature of basic learning processes. In habituation to motivationally insignificant stimuli, it is assumed that all stimulus input of this kind is compared to a 'neuronal model' of what is expected, the distinction between novel and familiar stimuli being between stimuli which do or do not match the model (Sokolov, 1963 see p. 40). For classical conditioning, it is assumed that the signalling stimulus arouses some representation of the signalled event, subsequently compared with obtained experience (Dickinson, 1980, see p. 105). For instrumental learning with rewards, we assume that the representations of wanted events are available, often before the relevant response is made (Tinkelpaugh, 1928, see p. 153). When an expected reward is not obtained for an instrumental response, most theories assume that some process of frustration or inhibition is aroused, which is responsible for the eventual decline of non-rewarded responses (Rosenzweig, 1943; Amsel, 1962; Pearce and Hall, 1980; Dickinson, 1980; Gray, 1975). On these grounds it would seem almost an aesthetic necessity that for the purpose of achieving harmony and symmetry, we should also assume that when an expected punishment is omitted this is sufficient to encourage the repetition of any response associated with the omission. Fortunately there is behavioural evidence to suggest that something of this sort does indeed take place (Herrnstein, 1969). However, there is an even greater amount of evidence to suggest that this is not the only significant process in instrumental learning motivated by aversive stimulation.

Escape learning

Little attention has been given to what is formally known as escape learning, in the case where electric shocks or other localized aversive stimuli are delivered, but most of the arguments about Thorndike's experiments on cats which escape from small boxes would apply – for instance, is the successful response an automatic habit, or is it made in knowing anticipation of its consequences? If a rat in a Skinner box is exposed to continuous painful electrical shocks from the floor, it will normally learn rapidly any response which makes this stimulus cease, whether it is moving to a part of the floor that is safe, rolling on its back to make use of the insulating properties of its fur, or pressing a standard lever which serves as the off-switch. It is arguable that responses made to relieve already present pain or discomfort are more likely to be made automatically and reflexively than topographically similar behaviours learned under the influence of rewards which follow them. First of all painful aversive stimuli may have greater motivational immediacy than others (see below, p. 230), but apart from that, there is little need to construct cognitive representations of a motivationally significant stimulus which is already present before the response is made, whereas the logical structure of learning for rewards means that there has to be an internal and cognitive representation of the motivating event, if the reason for the response is to be known while it is being initiated. In Hullian terms the drive stimulus may be rather more obvious and vivid when it is externally imposed than when it is generated by internal time-sensitive cycles (see Gray, 1975; chapter 4). Nevertheless, one of the behavioural phenomena reliably observed when rats press levers in Skinner boxes to turn off electric shocks is difficult to explain purely on a Thorndikean stamping-in basis. In all experiments of this type, it is necessary to specify how long the shock is turned off for. It can be for the rest of the day, or the rest of the experiment, but more commonly it is for something like 20 seconds, after which the shock starts again, and the lever must be pressed again (Dinsmoor and Hughes, 1956; Davis, 1977). Under these circumstances rats have a strong tendency to hold the lever firmly pressed down during the shock-free intervals. In a very large part, this is due to the species's instinctive reaction of 'freezing' or crouching very still, which is elicited by painful stimuli or signals of danger (Davis, 1977), but it is also maintained by its utility as a preparation for rapid execution of the next response (Dinsmoor *et al.*, 1958; Davis, 1977).

Apart from the emphasis on instinctive reactions, few conclusions can be drawn from the fact that animals learn rapidly to repeat naturally favoured responses which turn off shocks (Davis, 1977). A great deal more theoretical interest has been attracted to the case of avoidance learning, since by contrast with escape learning, where the motivating stimulus occurs conspicuously before each response, this event, when learning is successful, is rarely, if ever, seen.

The two-process theory of avoidance learning

The two-process theory of avoidance learning appeals to the classical conditioning of fear or anxiety as the first process, and the instrumental reduction of this unpleasant emotional state as the second. It is associated with the names of Mowrer (1940, 1960) and Miller (1948), and an apparatus known as the Miller-Mowrer shuttle box (actually used originally by Dunlap *et al.*, 1931). This is a box with two compartments, each with a floor through which electric shocks can be delivered, perhaps with a hurdle or barrier between them. Every so often, say about once every 2 minutes, a buzzer is turned on for 10 seconds. If the animal in the box stays in the compartment where it is when the buzzer starts, it receives shock at the end of the 10 seconds. However, if it jumps or otherwise shuttles to the alternative compartment before the 10 seconds are up, the buzzer is (in most experiments) turned off, and (in all experiments) no shocks are given on that trial. It is clearly greatly to the advantage of the animal concerned if it shuttles between the two compartments when it hears the buzzer, and thus the basic result is capable of explanation by the principle that behaviours which reduce the frequency of unpleasant experiences should be learned (Herrnstein, 1969).

Thus, instrumental learning, conceived as the principle of reward and punishment in an abstract logic of events, is capable by itself of explaining why avoidance learning *ought* to occur. It cannot explain why, in many instances, mainly when the required responses conflict with instinctive reactions, avoidance learning fails to occur (Bolles, 1978; Seligman and Johnston, 1973) and it misses out altogether the undeniable fact that in most cases the delivery of aversive stimuli arouses distinctive emotional states, which are highly conditionable, in the sense that predictable though not identical emotional reactions are quickly induced for other stimuli which are taken as signals for impending pain or distress (see backward conditioning, p. 87). There is thus ample reason to retain the two-process theory, to the extent that it predicts both conditioned emotional states and responses motivated by them, while also acknowledging that there is evidence for more calculated forms of avoidance learning, based on anticipation of the consequences of responding, compared to the state of affairs that might otherwise be expected to obtain (Gray, 1975; Mackintosh, 1983).

The paper 'Anxiety-reduction and learning' by O.H. Mowrer (1940) stated a simple and direct form of the two-process theory, including the assumption that anxiety reduction should qualify as a 'satisfying state of affairs' in Thorndike's Law of Effect. Behavioural responses which bring relief from anxiety should therefore be stamped in or fixated. As an experimental test of the theory, Mowrer trained several groups of rats and guinea pigs to run around a circular track composed of eight grid segments which could be independently electrified. Once a minute a tone was turned on for 5 seconds, with shock to be delivered to the segment the animal was initially standing on at the end of the tone. But as soon as the animal moved forward at least one segment the tone was turned off, and no shock was delivered. After three days of this at 24 minutes per day, the animals received only two out of the 24 potential shocks in a day, and stable performance was reached at four shocks per day which counts as about 80 per cent (20/24) correct avoidance. There were minor species differences between the rats and guinea pigs, rats learning better with random rather than fixed intervals between trials, and the guinea pigs the other way around. Mowrer (1940) argued that the running response to the tone was established because it relieved conditioned anxiety or dread, but pointed out that learning of this sort appeared to work best when the response that ended dread closely resembled the response which would be used to escape from the dreaded event itself, when it was present. This would be reasonable, even if the main process involved was the conditioning of an emotionally loaded representation of the stimulus event, but it leaves Mowrer's evidence open to the objection that no conditioned anxiety, or anxiety relief, was necessary, since more direct 'knee-jerk' conditioning of the motor response alone would account for the results.

There are many reasons why this objection could be discounted, but the clearest demonstration that avoidance learning involves more than motor response shift would require that the response made to avoid is quite different from that used in escaping from the event avoided. Such a demonstration was provided by Miller (1948), who used a procedure in which the response learned was separated from the response elicited by shock, both by topography and the lapse of time. In a two-compartment shuttle box Miller first gave 10 trials only in which rats received intermittent shock for 60 seconds in a white compartment without being able to escape, and were then confronted with continuous shock and a suddenly opened door. All the animals here learned to run through the door quickly, to the safe black compartment. Also when subsequently put in the white compartment even without shock, they ran to the black compartment. The next phases of the experiment showed that this was not just a matter of automatic running. First, the rats were left in the white compartment with the door closed, but a wheel by the door which, if turned, opened the door. All rats showed variable behaviour around the door which could be construed as attempts to get through it. Half of them (13/25) moved the wheel by accident the fraction of a turn necessary to open the door, during the first few trials, and thereafter became more and more adept at turning the wheel to open the door as soon as they were placed in the white compartment. The others tended more and more to adopt the posture of rigid crouching. These results are strong evidence that the initial phase of shocks meant that the rats thereafter were put into an aversive motivational state by being in the white compartment, and that the novel behaviour of turning a paddle-wheel device was learned by being associated with escape from the anxiety-provoking compartment. Miller (1948) then changed the procedure for the 13 rats that were turning the wheel, so that the wheel no longer worked, but the door would open if a bar, on the other side of it, was depressed. The first time this was done, the animals turned the wheel more vigorously than usual − although only a fractional turn had previously opened the door the typical (median) number of whole turns was almost 5, one rat making 530 whole turns. However, all but this one, by the fifth attempt, quickly opened the door by pressing the bar, instead of turning the wheel.

Problems for two-process theory of avoidance

The experiment by Miller (1948) and others in which animals learn to shuttle back and forth between two compartments as the signal for impending shock (Mowrer and Lamoreaux, 1946; Kamin, 1956) appear to support the two-process explanation of classical conditioning of what can loosely be called fear or anxiety to external cues, and instrumental reinforcement of responses which remove the animal from these cues, or otherwise reduce fear. The reader may however have noticed that there is a blatant contradiction between what is implied in this account and the claim made in the previous chapter (pp. 184–8) that classical conditioning is ineffective if there is only intermittent pairing of a signal with a signalled event. It is in the nature of successful avoidance learning that the signal for shock is no longer a signal for shock, because responses are made which prevent the shock happening. There are a number of ways around this contradiction. Most directly, there is 100 per cent correlation between the signal and the shock when no response is made, and the fact that a response has been made can quite properly be regarded as having altered the character of the signal – 'signal alone means shock', and 'signal plus response means no shock' are both reliable and consistent associations. There are other aspects of reactions to aversive stimulation however which indicate the need to appeal to special factors to do with strong instinctive reactions to pain and danger, and with related emotional and physiological changes involving stress.

The contradiction between the supposed sensitivity of classical conditioning to the degree of correlation between events, and the persistence of avoiding behaviours in the absence of anything to be avoided, is taken to extremes in what is called 'traumatic avoidance learning' (Solomon and Wynne, 1954; Solomon *et al*, 1953; Solomon and Wynne, 1953). This is simply a shuttle-box avoidance procedure used with dogs rather than rats, and with strong shocks. With a 3–minute interval between trials, and a 10–second signal of lights going off and the gate between compartments being raised, Solomon and Wynne (1953) reported that dogs received only seven or eight shocks before reaching the criterion of 10 consecutive avoidance responses, which involved jumping over a shoulder-high hurdle. This is not particularly exceptional – the result that is theoretically important is that once this criterion had been reached, dogs showed no sign at all of ever reducing their tendency to jump when the signal came on, even after 200 trials at 10 per day, or in one case after 490 trials. There was evidence that the animals became much less emotional as the extinction procedure (without any received or potential shocks) proceeded, but that the latency of jumping either stayed the same or decreased.

One argument is that these two reactions are connected, and that 'anxiety conservation' occurs because the continued fast jumping prevents the dog 'testing reality' by discovering that shocks will no longer occur if the signal is ignored. However, it was no simple matter to confront the dogs with reality in a way which quickly removed the conditioned response of jumping. If a glass barrier was inserted between the compartments so that successful jumping was impossible, the dogs at first appeared excited and anxious, and over 10 days quietened down, but then, if the glass barrier was removed, they immediately began jumping again. An alternative procedure of punishing the jumping response was tried, by simply arranging that shock was present in the opposite compartment to the one the dog was in, when the signal sounded. Here it was highly disadvantageous for the dogs to continue jumping, but this is precisely what most of them did. If the glass-barrier procedure and the punishment procedure were alternated, then the jumping response was finally suppressed, but its persistence in the absence of any overt benefit was clearly not predictable on the straightforward version of the two-process theory (Solomon *et al*, 1953; Solomon and Wynne, 1954; Seligman and Johnston, 1973).

It is therefore necessary to modify the two-process theory in some way to account for the persistence of avoidance responding when no further motivating events are observed. There are several possible modifications, all of which have some merit. However, it first has to be said that modification of the two-process theory is not always necessary, since avoiding behaviours are not always very persistent. For instance in Mowrer's experiment already quoted (1940), in which rats or guinea pigs ran around a circular maze at the sound of a 5–second tone, omitting all shocks from the procedure meant that many animals stopped running by the end of one session of 24 tones. Since they had previously only been receiving about four shocks per day, this implies that the first few times they waited the full 5 seconds of the tone and received no shock, this immediately led to a drop in the tendency to run. Many other experiments with rats have found conditioned avoidance responses quickly declining when shocks are no longer given (Mackintosh, 1974, 1983). In most of these the shock is not associated with the animal being in a particular location (as it was in the experiment of Miller, 1948) but with a light or sound signal. Thus the only modification in two-process theory that is necessary is the one which suggests that the signal with no response functions as the cue which is consistently associated with shock, while the signal together with a response is associated with not getting shock (Dickinson, 1980). It is already the case of course, that the instrumental part of two-process theory should be strengthened by intermittent reinforcement (see p. 183).

Habitual responding which prevents fear

As Mowrer's original formulation of two-process avoidance learning (1939) was explicitly inspired by Freud's book *The Problem of Anxiety* (1936), the next modification is no novelty. Freud of course proposed that although anxiety was a reaction to danger, the important dangers for people were internal personal conflicts, rather than external events, but whatever the source of anxiety, it is a thoroughly unpleasant and unwanted emotional state. One of Freud's main points was that 'symptoms are only formed in order to avoid anxiety' (1959, p. 144). In other word, neurotic habits keep anxiety in abeyance. The same principle appears to apply to avoidance learning. Solomon and Wynne (1954) pointed out that overt signs of emotionality (e.g. pupil dilation, excretion) in their dogs tended to decline after initial experiences, partly because the avoidance response of jumping was made so fast there was no time for the autonomic nervous system to react to the signal. But the general reactions of the animals between the signals also became much calmer. Measurement of the heart rate of dogs (Black, 1959) and of the behavioural reactions of rats (Kamin *et al.*, 1963) support the contention that with well-trained avoidance responding there is little evidence of conditioned fear (Seligman and Johnston, 1973).

Thus the two-process theory has to be extended beyond its most rudimentary formulation, which implies that fear is classically conditioning, and responses are only made when impelled by high levels of this conditioned fear. It is possible that well-learned avoidance responses may be sustained for some time purely by habit (Mackintosh, 1983, p. 168), but it is also likely that, as Freud suggested (1959, p. 162) there is a second kind of anxiety, which motivates the avoidance of full-blown fear reactions. One aspect of this 'non-fearful' motivation for avoidance responses that has been put to experimental test is that responses may be made as if they were being rewarded by safety or relief, as 'attractive events' (Dickinson, 1980, pp. 106–9). It is certainly the case that explicit environmental signals which guarantee the absence of shock facilitate performance when given as feedback for avoidance responding by rats (Kamin, 1956; Morris, 1975). However, this is only a relative kind of attractiveness: according to theoretical definitions, the absence of shock can only be attractive, indeed it can only be noticed, if there is already some form of anticipation of shock (Dickinson, 1980). Responding in anticipation of safety from pain can hardly be equivalent in its emotional connotations to responding for palatable titbits, as is suggested by the finding that even animals responding successfully on avoidance schedules may develop stomach ulcers (Weiss, 1968; Brady *et al.*, 1958). However, it seems undeniable that standard avoidance learning procedures involve the avoidance of conditioned fear, as well as escape from conditioned fear. Well-trained animals do not wait until they become afraid before they respond, they respond so as to prevent themselves becoming afraid.

Herrnstein's theory of avoidance learning

Herrnstein (1969) proposed that the notion of fear, or indeed of any emotional evaluation whatever, should be eliminated from theories of avoidance learning by adapting the hypothesis above so that it refers only to external aversive events; animals respond so as to prevent themselves from experiencing aversive events, or 'the reinforcement for avoidance behaviour is a reduction in time of aversive stimulation'

(1969, p. 67), aversive stimulation being interpreted only in terms of events observable in the environment, outside the animal. Thus one of the processes in two-process theory appears to be eliminated. However, Herrnstein recognizes that, in order for his theory to work, it must be assumed that animals first detect the changes in the likelihood of being shocked with and without a response, and secondly, learn to produce activities which have the outcome of lessened exposure to disagreeable events. His explicit alternative to ordinary two-process theory is to substitute a more bloodless cognitive assessment of shock probabilities for internal emotional states which have motivational properties. This is a technical possibility, in that once it is assumed that behaviour will be directed by the outcome of less of a certain kind of experience, it is not absolutely necessary to add in anything else by way of emotion. I shall conclude that independent evidence suggests that in practice there usually are conditioned emotional effects produced by external aversive events, but it is appropriate to give first Herrnstein's side of the argument. The usual two-process theory makes most sense when there is a clear signal which predicts an avoidable shock. Thus when the buzzer sounds in a shuttle box it appears reasonable to assume that the buzzer will at least initially arouse fear, which will motivate the learning of new responses. But it is possible to study avoidance learning by other methods, in which there is no clear signal for impending shocks. Sidman (1953) discovered a procedure known as 'free-operant' or Sidman avoidance, in which rats press a lever in a Skinner box to avoid shocks. There is no external signal. One timer ensures that a brief shock will be delivered every x seconds if there are no responses, and another timer over-rides this with the specification that shocks are only delivered after y seconds since the last response. Thus if the rats do not press the lever they will be shocked every x seconds (say 10) but if they press the lever at least once every y seconds (say 20) no shocks whatever will be delivered. It is possible to adapt two-process theory by assuming here that there is an internal timing device which serves as a signal – the sense that (y–1) seconds have elapsed since the last response could serve as a signal for impending shocks, and there is some indication that this sort of thing happens, since rats often wait for (y−1) seconds before responding. However, Herrnstein and Hineline (1966) modified this procedure to discount internal timing, by making all time intervals random. In their experiment, rats were shocked on average once every 6 seconds if they did not respond, but when they pressed a lever, they produced a shock-free period which averaged 20 seconds. They could not postpone shock indefinitely, but they could reduce the frequency of shocks significantly by lever-pressing – it is as if they could escape temporarily from trains of shocks only 6 seconds apart on average. This procedure was in fact more successful in inducing lever-pressing than Sidman avoidance (Herrnstein, 1969). Since all time intervals were probabilistic, Herrnstein argues that any internally timed process of fear would be redundant, for both the animal and the theorist, and both would do better simply to accept that lever-pressing reduces shock frequency, and is therefore a behaviour worth performing (1969, p. 59). There is something to this, as a parsimonious strategy or procedure, but there is compelling additional reason to suppose that inner emotional states may be aroused, *whether or not* they serve a useful function in a particular experimental procedure. Monkeys which perform for long periods on a Sidman avoidance response, but so successfully that they hardly ever receive shocks, nevertheless are liable to develop stomach ulceration which may prove fatal (Brady *et al.*, 1958). Seligman (1968) found that random and unpredictable shocks produced 'chronic fear' in rats, assessed both by stomach ulceration and by very substantial depression of food-reinforced responding in the 'conditioned emotional suppression' technique. These are precisely the sorts of data that suggest the involvement of a central emotional state, over and above whatever cognitive assessment of shock frequency might be sufficient grounds for instrumental behaviour. It thus seems more likely than not that even Herrnstein and Hineline's (1966) rats felt relatively relieved once they had pressed the lever, but were aversively motivated when they did not. The best tests of emotionality in these circumstances are undoubtedly physiological indices, but some aspects of the behavioural data are more suggestive of strong emotion than cognitive finesse. After experience on the schedule described above, in which lever presses were necessary to produce intervals between shocks averaging 20 seconds, the rats were left to respond with all shocks programmed at this average, irrespective of responding; in other words responding was completely without utility, and it eventually ceased. However, this extinction process was extremely prolonged, and therefore has something in common with the persistent behaviour observed in Solomon *et al.*'s (1953) dogs. One rat made 20,000 responses during 170, 100–minute sessions in which responses were useless, before slowing to a halt. This may be because of the strength of an automatic habit, but it is likely that this persistence of the behaviour is related to the emotional and motivating force of the painful aversive stimuli. With a very similar procedure, in which rats had the opportunity of distinguishing between circumstances in which randomly delivered food pellets either did or did not depend on lever-pressing, no such persistence of unnecessary behaviour was observed (Hammond, 1980). This again suggests some form of asymmetry between the motivating effects of attractive and aversive events, with, if anything, aversive stimuli having more powerful and long-lasting emotional effects than attractive ones. Herrnstein (1969) was right to point out that the behavioural evidence to define emotional effects is often lacking, and his arguments support those of Freud (1936), Mowrer (1939), Solomon and Wynne (1953) and Seligman and Johnston (1973), that behaviour which is motivated by the avoidance of aversive events can often be sustained with little overt or covert sign of high emotional arousal. But this does not mean that emotional states can simply be dropped from all discussions of the motivating effects of aversive events; behavioural evidence including posture and other instinctive forms of emotional expression and results obtained with the 'conditioned emotional response' (CER) procedure, as well as more direct physiological indications of autonomic arousal, plus all the data not included here on the effects of tranquillizing drugs on aversively motivated performance (see e.g. Gray, 1982; Green, 1987), provide ample grounds for continuing to include conditioned fear or anxiety in theories of aversive motivation.

Instincts and anticipation in avoidance responding

It is difficult to determine to what degree such responding, which avoids anxiety, is based on habit, as opposed to calculation of the undesirable consequences of not responding. It is probable that dogs and cats, if not rats, have a certain degree of anticipation of specific painful possibilities which they wish to avoid. Thus dogs or cats will strongly resist being put back into an apparatus in which they have been shocked several days before (Solomon *et al.*, 1953; Wolpe, 1958). Rats do not normally do this, in fact there is often a 'warm-up' effect, meaning that after a 24 hour break, rats do not respond in an avoidance procedure until they have received a number of shocks. Although avoidance responding of a minimal kind, usually the continuous flexing of a leg which will be shocked if it is extended, can be obtained in cockroaches and spinal mammals (Horridge, 1962; Chopin and Buerger, 1975; Norman *et al.*, 1977), it is worthy of note that decorticate rats, though they may be trained to perform many standard food-rewarded tests, have never been reported to have mastered any of the avoidance learning tasks used with normal animals (Oakley, 1979a). This proves nothing in itself, but adds to the general impression that avoidance learning, or perhaps anxiety itself, is partly a product of the imagination. Ordinary rats typically perform avoidance tasks at 80 per cent success, receiving one shock in five, while it is much more common for cats and dogs, and rhesus monkeys, to perform a response almost indefinitely after receiving just a few shocks (Solomon and Wynne, 1954; Wolpe, 1958; Brady *et al.*, 1958). Much anecdotal evidence, for instance about monkeys looking for snakes, suggests that larger mammals have specific expectancies about precisely what aversive stimulus is to be anticipated, as opposed to only unpleasant but inchoate inner feelings. An experiment by Overmeier *et al.* (1971) supplied some measure of support for this suggestion, since dogs trained to avoid shock by nosing a panel to their left at one signal, but to their right at another, did so more quickly if each signal consistently predicted shock to a particular leg (whether on the same or opposite side as the response needed to avoid it) compared with animals for which either signal was followed by shock to either leg at random. The authors of this report argue that signals predict something specific, and not only something which is quite generally a bad thing (cf. Trapold, 1970, p. 155). There is evidence that rats also, as well as dogs, may acquire reactions to a signal that are specific to particular signalled aversive events: Hendersen *et al.* (1980) found that prolonged associations between a signal and an airblast meant that the signal had little effect if was turned on while animals were responding to avoid electric shock, whereas a similar brief association, or a prolonged association long past, meant that responding to avoid electric shock was more vigorous. The suggestion is that one aspect of the association, which was the more long-lasting, was arousal or diffuse fear produced by the signal, but a second, more ephemeral part of the association linked to the signal reactions or representations specific to the airblast.

However, whatever the level of cognitive representation of specific feared events that may take part in avoidance learning, it is by definition the instinctive and built-in reaction to both the aversive events themselves and to unpleasant emotional states associated with them to withdraw and shrink from them, and to perform any response which lessens contact with them. It is completely possible also that part of the instinctive and built-in reaction to aversive events include modulation of the classical conditioning process, so that an intermittent association between an arbitrary signal and pain is taken more seriously than an intermittent association between a similar signal and food reward. This is more likely for aversive events which produce emotional reactions of very high intensity; Solomon and Wynne (1954) for instance, proposed that traumatic conditioning of anxiety might be irreversible if feedback from the periphery of the autonomic nervous system caused some kind of brain overload. This is rather vague, but some explanation is needed for the empirical evidence that only one or two associations between a signal and a powerfully aversive event may produce indefinite aversion to the signal (Wolpe, 1958; Garcia *et al.*, 1977b). The cases where only one pairing of a signal and an aversive event occurs make nonsense of the otherwise well-supported theory that only a statistically reliable correlation or contingency between the two events can lead to the formation of psychological associations (Rescorla, 1967; Dickinson, 1980). As a generality, it seems wisest to accept that the difference in the anatomical systems used to process attractive and aversive events, and, functionally, the difference between the ecological requirements for the seeking of food and drink on the one hand, and the requirements for not becoming some other animal's food on the other, will lead to asymmetries between reward and punishment beyond those logically necessitated by the outcome-testing nature of approach to significant objects and the outcome-assuming nature of withdrawal.

Part of the asymmetry may lie in the central criteria used for conditioned emotional associations, with, as it were, more stringent internal statistical criteria required for hope than for fear. But Solomon and Wynne (1954) may well be right to point to the autonomic system as well. Aversive stimuli arouse the 'fight or flight' or 'behavioural inhibition' syndromes of the sympathetic nervous system and limbic brain system respectively (Gray, 1982). Once this sort of physiological arousal has reached a certain point, it may become aversive in its own right, and thus a signal initially associated with a strong aversive stimulus may become motivationally self-sustaining (Eysenck, 1976; Walker, 1984, chapter 9). This is still somewhat speculative. There is little doubt, however, that many of the peculiarities of avoidance learning, and indeed of any form of reaction to aversive stimulation, can be attributed to the instinctive behaviours of the species involved, or 'species-specific defensive reactions' or 'SSDRs' (Bolles, 1970, 1978). It may be that fearful emotional states generally produce more rigid and reflexive behaviour than relaxed exploration or systematic foraging for nutritional necessities. In any case, it is possible to point to many specific responses, such as leaping and frightened running, or passive crouching (freezing) by laboratory rats, which, are automatically elicited by particular aversive stimuli, and therefore are likely to occur in response to associated signals for such stimuli whether they are useful or not. This has led to assertions that many kinds of learning induced by aversive stimuli are special cases, and not explicable in terms of general principles, but it is not necessary to abandon all general principles provided that included among them are principles which take into account instinctive behaviours. Taste-aversion learning is a case in point.

Taste-aversion learning

It is perhaps a measure of the persisting effects of the dust-bowl empiricism of pre-war learning theories that the phenomena of taste-aversion learning should initially have been found surprising, and that the concept of natural functional relationships between stimuli in learned associations should have taken so long to take root (Garcia, 1981). It is a fact of life that though eating is essential, eating the wrong thing can be disastrous, and to the extent that the process of learning is useful in foraging and food selection, animals, especially those with a varied diet, ought to be capable of learning from experience foodstuffs that are best avoided. Thus young jays quickly learn not to eat moths with a foul taste on the basis of visual cues, and it is well known that some species of moth which are palatable have evolved markings like those of others which are not, because of selective predation – a phenomenon known as mimicry (Maynard-Smith, 1975). The biological advantage of taste lies entirely in distinguishing what should be eaten, and when, and how eagerly, from what should not be eaten; and these categories, although they may be to some extent innate, might usefully be modified according to the post-ingestional consequences of specific eating experiences. There is a certain amount of evidence that, as Hull (1943) would have predicted, metabolic usefulness of what is eaten may lead to slight alterations in taste or smell preferences – for example protein-deprived rats increase their preference for the odour of a diet associated with receipt of balanced proteins (Booth and Simpson, 1971; Green and Garcia, 1971; Holman, 1968; see also Booth *et al.*, 1972; Booth *et al.*, 1976). There is much clearer and stronger evidence that animals very rapidly become averse to the taste of a food eaten before they became ill.

This became apparent in studies of the effects of radioactivity on animal behaviour. Exposure to radiation affects the intestinal tract and makes animals ill; after they have recovered they may refuse to eat foods previously consumed (Haley and Snyder, 1964; Rozin and Kalat, 1971). This would not have surprised Pavlov in the least, but a considerable stir was created when Garcia and Koelling (1966) published a careful experiment which suggested that the effect was selective, in that taste cues much more than visual cues appeared to acquire associations with illness. The experimental technique was to place thirsty rats in a small box containing a drinking spout for 20 minutes a day, measurements being taken of the number of times they lapped at the spout. The water might be given a sweet or a salty taste, and an attempt was made to provide audiovisual feedback of a roughly equivalent kind by arranging that a flash of light and a click would occur each time a rat lapped at the drinking spout. Rats were first pre-tested to assess rate of drinking 'bright-noisy-tasty' water under these conditions. During the training phase, on most days the animals were allowed to drink plain water undisturbed, but every three days the distinctive sight, sound and taste feedback was given, and the animals subsequently became ill, some because, while drinking sacharin-flavoured water, they were exposed to a sufficiently strong dose of X-rays, and others because lithium chloride, which tastes salty, was added to their water. For comparisons, yet other rats were allowed to drink bright-noisy-salty water while a gradually increasing shock, which eventually suppressed their drinking, was applied to the floor ('delayed shock'), and a fourth group had alternate 4 minutes of immediate shock when they drank with the three kinds of feedback, but no shock when they drank plain water without audiovisual feedback.

All the animals in this experiment (Garcia and Koelling, 1966) had very much suppressed drinking by the compound cues during the training procedure, the shock animals somewhat more than those poisoned. The crucial phase occurred when no further aversive events, either sickness or shock, were imposed, and the rats were tested separately with water that had the previously experienced taste, but no sight and sound feedback, or the sight and sound feedback with plain water. These tests showed very clearly that animals which had been shocked drank just as much of the flavoured water as they had done of plain, but drank less when plain water had the sight and sound cues. And by contrast, animals poisoned drank normally under these conditions, but drank very little of water flavoured with saccharin or with normal salt, in the absence of the light and click feedback (the sweet and salty taste having been used for the X-ray and lithium chloride groups respectively). Since all the rats received both taste and audio-visual feedback during conditioning, it would appear that there was a selective tendency to connect the internal and visceral sensations of illness with the cue of taste, and to connect the pain coming from the outer environment with some aspect of the audio-visual compound. Internal consequences were associated with the internal cue of taste, while external effects were associated with the external modalities of sight and sound. This kind of result has been very widely replicated (e.g. Domjan and Wilson, 1972; Miller and Domjan, 1981; Revusky, 1977). However, the explanation which should be given for this fairly straightforward finding has been a matter of dispute (Milgram *et al.*, 1977; Logue, 1979). It is first necessary to emphasize that the phenomenon is quantitative rather than qualitative. Pavlov (1927) reported that symptoms of illness could readily be associated with the sight of the syringe which normally preceded their induction, in dogs (see p. 73), and rats will become averse to black or white compartments (Best *et al.*, 1973) or to a compound of external cues that represents the particular box they drank in before being poisoned (Archer *et al.*, 1979). As noted in Chapter 3, extremely specialized metabolic reactions, such as those which happen to prevent the analgesic effects of morphine, are capable of being conditioned to external cues which characterize a particular room. And on the other hand, experiments such as that of Logan (1969) quoted above, indicate that peripheral electric shocks (rather than only illness) can alter food preferences. Thus there is no need to assume that certain forms of unpleasant experience can be associated *only* with biologically appropriate cues. The effects are a matter of degree: what has to be explained is a kind of selectivity, in which when there are several possible stimuli which could be taken as cues for a biologically significant event, whichever stimulus is most biologically appropriate or relevant is likely to be dominant.

There is little disagreement as to the form taken by the phenomenon, but a variety of views as to what should be concluded from it. Differing amounts of emphasis are given to the innate and built-in aspect of whatever mechanism is responsible. Garcia and Koelling (1966) refer to 'a genetically coded hypothesis' which might account for the observed predisposition, and the phenomenon of taste-aversion learning is usually taken to contradict *tabula rasa* assertions about animal behaviour (Revusky, 1977; Logue, 1979), but less specific forms of innate determination, such as a gathering together of internal and external stimuli (Revusky, 1977), perhaps as a sub-example of a principle favouring spatial continuity in the formation of associations (Mackintosh, 1983), have been defended.

Garcia himself has tended to interpret what is now frequently referred to as the 'Garcia effect' in terms of innate mechanisms, and has drawn attention to the fact that the taste system is neuroanatomically related to visceral stimuli in vertebrates, since input from the tongue and the viscera both are collected in the brainstem, and there is in fact a particular structure there, the nucleus solitarius, which receives both taste and gastro-intestinal input fairly directly (see Garcia *et al.*, 1974, 1977a, 1977b). There are thus anatomical grounds for expecting that taste should be especially likely to be affected by visceral experiences – more so even than smell, since the olfactory input is to the forebrain, where it goes to the limbic system. There is behavioural evidence (Garcia *et al.*, 1974) to support Garcia's theory that the olfactory system is used for appetitive food-seeking – it supplies information, along with vision and hearing, about objects at a distance, but is more closely connected than they are with motivational urges to find things which taste good but reject things which taste bad. The taste system of the tongue, according to Garcia *et al.* (1977a, p. 212), interacts with the limbic (and olfactory system), but is also affected by visceral receptors which 'assess the utility of the ingested material for the needs of the internal economy'. The evidence is that rats do not appear to associate a smell with illness which occurs some time afterwards (while they do so associate tastes: Hankins *et al.*, 1973), but rats do associate smell with pain, when a food substance is paired with electric shocks (Hankins *et al.*, 1976; Krane and Wagner (1975) suppressed food intake by delayed shocks but did not assess the relative contributions of taste and smell).

There is thus every indication that the ease with which taste-aversions are formed reflects innately determined mechanisms, perhaps even in the form of visible neuroanatomical circuits. How does this affect the theoretical questions of the symmetry of reward and punishment, and the validity or otherwise of the general principle of learning? Garcia *et al.* (1977b) put the case that there is a symmetry between the dislike of tastes associated with bodily distress and cravings for tastes associated with relief from distress caused by illness or nutritional deficiencies. The onset of illness tends to be sudden, and recovery gradual, which makes dislikes very much more frequent than likes, but if thiamine-deficient rats are given a thiamine (vitamin B) injection after drinking saccharin-flavoured water, they subsequently showed an increased preference for it (Garcia *et al.*, 1967). There is thus support for a 'medicine' effect, which is in the opposite direction to the taste-aversion effect. It is not necessarily equivalent in all other respects, but clearly post-ingestional (and post-injectional) relief from aversive bodily states, and associations with subsequent pleasurable internal feelings, change preferences for ingested substances, very strikingly so in the case of human addictions to alcohol or other drugs.

The charge has been made that taste-aversion learning is a specialized and circumscribed phenomenon, with little in common with other kinds of aversively motivated change in behaviours, and that principles of learning should be assumed to be specific both to particular categories of events to be associated, and specific to particular species (Rozin and Kalat, 1971; Seligman, 1970). This charge can however be effectively refuted, since it is possible to point to many similarities between taste-aversion and other forms of learning, and indeed many similarities between very different species of animal, provided that some principle of selectivity in the formation of associations is accepted, such as 'preparedness'

(Seligman, 1970) or 'relevance' (Revusky, 1977; Mackintosh, 1983) and provided that innate motivational mechanisms and innately determined instinctive behaviours are included as determinants of both learning and performance. Revusky (1977) persuasively argues that if the errors of extreme behaviourism and empiricism are renounced, and it is accepted that 'from a naturalistic point of view, all aspects of the learning process are innate' (1977, p.46), then many if not all the phenomena of learning can be subsumed under the extremely general principle that learning 'has evolved to process information about causal relationships in environments' (1977, p.46). Similarly Mackintosh (1983) suggests that 'a function view of conditioning' would readily accommodate any result showing that 'a natural causal relationship' is easily learned, but with the rider that 'To the extent that the causal laws describing the world in which we and other animals live are generally true, admitting of no exception, so there should be general laws of conditioning' (1983, pp.221–2). In a sense this is Hume's theory of the perception of cause-and-effect, turned on its head, since Hume's point was that what we believe to be causal relationships in the outer world are merely subjective impressions based on pairings of events; whereas Revusky and Mackintosh argue that the mechanisms which determine how and when an individual forms associations based on the experienced pairing of events have themselves only evolved because (more often than not) the operation of these mechanisms will ensure that learned behaviour will reflect biological truth. With this principle to hand, we need not be alarmed if animals learn to associate tastes with illness, since the mechanisms of learning evolved in a world in which illness is in fact often caused by ingested food. This still leaves us with the job of describing what the mechanisms are, and exactly how they operate, but brings in at the start not only biological function, but the assumption that some of the details of the processes of learning in any species have been tuned to the realities of that species's natural life.

Taste-aversion learning has therefore been extremely important as a theoretical *cause célèbre*, requiring much more explicit acknowledgment of innate determinants of learning than was previously thought proper. But the phenomenon itself is readily incorporated into the newly liberated versions of general learning theory, since the phenomenon is in fact readily obtainable in a wide variety of animal species, and is readily explicable as a special case of the two-process theory of avoidance learning. A general account of taste-aversion learning in several species, with a common form of explanation, has been provided by Garcia himself (Garcia, 1981; Garcia *et al.*, 1977b). An aspect of Garcia's biological approach is a respect for species differences, but these appear to be less marked than one might expect. Birds usually have few taste-buds but excellent eyes, and one might suppose on these grounds that taste-aversion learning should be subordinate to sight-aversion learning in birds. Wilcoxon *et al.* (1971) did indeed find, in a widely quoted study using bob-white quail, that if these birds became ill after drinking blue-coloured and sour-tasting water, they subsequently avoided blue water more than sour. It is clearly absurd to doubt that birds (apart from the aberrant kiwis, which are flightless and nocturnal, and use smell) use vision in food selection, but there is evidence nevertheless that there is a special connection between taste and digestive upset even in highly visual species. Extremely hungry blue jays catch even poisonous-looking butterflies in their beak, rejecting only those whose taste has been previously followed by nausea. This indicates a certain general primacy of taste (Garcia *et al.*, 1977a) and also follows the principle of matching learning to biological causality, since butterflies which look dangerous but taste normal are safe (Browner, 1969). More surprisingly, large hawks (*Buteo jamaicensis, Buteo lagopus*) which have visual receptors in their eyes measured in millions, but taste receptors on their tongue measure only in tens, also seem to use taste as the main cue for aversion to poisonous bait. A hawk used to eating white mice, and given a black mouse made bitter with quinine, and then made ill with a lithium injection, afterwards seized and tasted a black mouse, without eating it, and only after that refused to approach black mice. However, hawks given black mice which did not have a distinctive flavour, before being poisoned in the same way, required several poisoning episodes (instead of just one) to acquire an aversion, and this took the form of not eating either white or black mice. It thus appears that taste is more readily associated with illness than are some readily distinguishable visual features of food, even for the most visual of vertebrates. Although greater persistence through time of taste cues has been ruled out as an absolutely necessary aspect of taste-aversion learning in rats, which do not vomit when ill (Revusky, 1977), it is very probable that part of the salience of a strong bitter taste for avian poisoning experiences is due either to its prolonged after-effects in the mouth or to its presence during vomiting, which is a reaction seen in blue jays after eating poisonous butterflies, and in hawks after lithium injections.

Taste-aversion learning is thus not species-specific to rats. The result with hawks also contradicts the ecological hypothesis that rats show the phenomenon only because, as omnivores, they are likely to sample a wide variety of possibly dangerous substances (Revusky, 1977). There may be biological dangers in a carnivorous diet, and this would mean that the ecology was wrong rather than the relation between ecology and psychology, but results obtained with captive wolves and coyotes demonstrate that general as well as specific processes may be engaged by taste-aversions (Gustavson *et al.*, 1974). A pair of captive wolves attacked and killed a sheep immediately on the two opportunities they had before an aversion treatment of being given lithium chloride capsules mixed with sheep flesh and wrapped in woolly sheep's hide. On the next occasion that a sheep was allowed into their enclosure, they at first charged it, but never bit it. Then they became playful, but when the sheep responded with threatening charges, the wolves adopted submissive postures and gave way. Similarly, wildborn captive coyotes were deterred from attacking rabbits by being given rabbit carcasses injected with lithium chloride, although for most of them two such poisonings were necessary. By contrast, if laboratory ferrets were repeatedly made ill after they had killed and eaten mice, they did not stop killing mice, even though not only would they not eat the mice that they killed, but their aversion to mice was apparent in retching when mice were bitten, and rejection and avoidance of the dead carcass. Less than one in five laboratory rats kill a mouse put in their cage (but three out of four wild rats kept in a laboratory: Karli, 1956), but those which do will kill very consistently, except if given aversion treatments, when they are rather more flexible than ferrets, since they will stop eating mice if poisoned after eating, but will also stop killing if poisoned after killing without being allowed to eat their victim.

The theory offered to explain taste-aversion phenomena in these various species is a variant of the theory of classical conditioning, discussed in terms of a 'hedonic shift' (Garcia *et al.*, 1977a, pp. 300–6; see this volume, chapter 3, pp. 77–80). Both specific metabolic and reflexive reactions (for instance nausea and retching) and more general emotional evaluation on some like-dislike dimension become shifted to the signalling stimulus, which is usually taste in the first instance, from the later events of illness. In some species, in particular the wild canines, attack in a state of hunger is relatively well integrated with expectations of eating – in the terms of Adams and Dickinson (1981b), attack is a purposive action rather than an automatic habit. Therefore in these species an aversion to the goal has a relatively powerful inhibitory effect on behaviours which lead to the goal. In other species, or at any rate in domesticated rats and ferrets, the instinctive behaviour of killing is relatively independent of representations of the taste of the goal, and therefore aversion to the taste has less effect on responses which happen to provide the opportunity for that taste. The hedonic shift would be expected to be associated with the qualitative aspects of the unpleasant experience it resulted from, but is not always limited in that way, since the wolves with a single experience of taste-aversion modified their behaviour to the extent of adopting species-typical postures of social submission at the advance of a now-unpalatable sheep. The other example often quoted in this context is the positive social behaviour directed by hungry rats at conspecifics whose presence has become the signal for food (Timberlake and Grant, 1975). This result supports the idea that there is a motivational good-bad dimension which is partly independent of the type of attractive/aversive event experienced, whether social, oral, intestinal or tactile. Garcia *et al.* (1977b, p. 284) include as indicators of the bad end of this scale 'conditioned disgust responses' which include urinating on, rolling on or burying food associated with illness in coyotes, and a paw-shaking gesture in a cougar.

Once a motivational shift has taken place, it is conceivable that new motor responses could be learned instrumentally under its influence – an animal might learn to press a lever to allow itself to escape from close proximity to strongly disliked food. There is little evidence to show abitrary responses being learned in this way, but, as is the case for many laboratory forms of avoidance learning (Bolles, 1978), once a conditioned motivational state has been established, certain instinctive but sometimes goal-directed patterns of behaviour are likely to be elicited. A superficial similarity between aversive motivational states established by electric shock and those which result from poisoning is that both appear to elicit species-specific responses of burying unwanted objects, although only a limited amount of information is available on this. Pinel and Treit (1978, 1979) have however confirmed that rats having received only one strong electric shock from a wire-wrapped prod mounted on the wall of their test chamber thereafter appeared motivated to cover up this object, either by pushing and throwing sand or bedding material over it with the forepaws, when this was possible, or by picking up wooden blocks with their teeth and placing them in a pile in front of the prod, if only wooden blocks were available to them. Rats will also bury certain objects (a mousetrap or a flashbulb) when first exposed to them in a familiar territory, but not others (the wire-wrapped prod or a length of plastic tubing: Terlecki *et al.*, 1979). Yet another set of species-specific behaviours which may be changed when underlying motivational shifts are induced by the artificial means of electrical shocks is seen in the social behaviour of chickens. Dominance relationships or 'pecking orders' in groups of these birds are usually stable over time. However, when Smith and Hale (1959) rigged contests between successive pairs of birds in four-member groups by staging a confrontation between hungry birds over a plate of food, and delivering shocks to the initially dominant bird whenever it ate or had social interactions with its partner, they found that they could completely reverse the rankings initially observed, and that the reversals lasted for at least nine weeks without further shocks. It is thus arguable that taste-aversion learning, and related alterations in the motivational value of natural stimuli by pairings with other events, rather than weakening theories of learning, add to their generality by demonstrating that natural and instinctive behaviours are subject to learned change, as well as arbitrary or more flexible responses such as pressing a lever, or running through a maze.

Stress, learned helplessness and self-punishment

I have already had cause to comment on the fact that exposure to aversive stimuli has physiological effects, such as changes in heartbeat and in skin conductivity, which can be used as indices of emotional response, and which may thus be useful in assessing the degree to which emotional reactions to aversiveness have become conditioned to prior stimuli. There are a great many other kinds of physiological reaction, induced by exposure to aversive stimuli, including release of adrenaline and corticosteroids by the adrenal glands, and also changes in brain biochemistry, for example the release of natural opoids (Maier *et al.*, 1983; Seligman and Weiss, 1980). Many of these reactions, which are part of the body's defence against damage and disease, can usefully be subsumed under the term stress (Selye, 1950). Physiological stress is an example of an asymmetry between the motivational systems of reward and punishment. It is possible to consider emotional excitement representing hope, elation or satisfaction as being physiological arousal similar to fear, though opposite in its affective value, and conceivably corresponding positive reactions for extreme fear can be found in sufficiently intense cravings for food, drink, drugs and socially and sexually attractive goals. But there is no departure from physiological normality due to the experiencing of attractive events which serves as a counterpart to the changes under the heading of stress which can be produced by exposure to aversive stimuli.

Stomach ulceration and loss of weight in rats and other mammals is a relatively indirect way of measuring stress, but serves to indicate long-term effects. Measurements of ulceration, together with behavioural evidence, suggest that there are psychological factors in the stress produced by externally painful experience, even in rats. Seligman (1968) found that unpredictable shocks, randomly interspersed with visual or auditory stimuli, produced extensive ulceration in rats, as well as profound suppression of food-rewarded lever-pressing. Control groups receiving exactly the same physical intensity of shock, and the same audio-visual stimuli, but with the shock signalled by these cues, formed no ulcers, and kept up their usual levels of food-rewarded behaviour, except in the presence of the shock signals. Ulceration is also less in rats which receive shock only in the absence of their own avoiding response, than in animals receiving identical physical stimulation which is uncorrelated with their own behaviour, and not otherwise predictable (Weiss, J.M., 1971). Not surprisingly, in view of these findings, it has frequently been observed that rats will respond so as to be exposed to signalled and predictable, rather than to unsignalled and unpredictable shocks, when given the choice (Lockard, 1963; Miller *et al;* 1983; Badia *et al.*, 1979).

In monkeys, severe ulceration has been observed even when hardly any shocks are received, if this is only the case because the animals are responding continually for long periods (on a Sidman avoidance schedule, see p. 226) in order to prevent shocks, and may therefore be assumed to be then in a state of constant anxiety (Brady *et al*, 1958). The existence of this sort of stress response shows both that there may be distinctive physiological changes produced by aversive laboratory procedures, and that fairly complex psychological reactions also occur, particularly involving the predictability of aversive events, and therefore, of course, the predictability of their absence. Degree of predictability of events, especially their predictability on the basis of the subject's own behaviour, appears to be something which can itself be learned, with a consequent influence on more ordinary forms of learning in the future. This is a conclusion drawn primarily from research into the phenomenon known as 'learned helplessness', which has been extremely extensive, due partly to the belief held by some that this kind of learning is an important aspect of human depression, the most common form of mental illness (see Maier and Seligman, 1976; Seligman, 1975; and Seligman and Weiss, 1980, for reviews). The initial experiments were performed on dogs, using a shuttle-box avoidance test like that of Solomon *et al.* (1953; see p. 222). Normally in this apparatus, dogs learn within 2 and 3 trials to jump over the barrier as soon as shock is turned on, and eventually learn to jump to the signal before the shock. However if, before this test, dogs are placed in a harness and given at random 50 or more shocks which they cannot escape from, most of them never make even the first escape response, and few if any ever learn to avoid or even escape from the shocks consistently. Seligman's (1975) argument is that the dogs given inescapable shocks had learned to give up trying, or had learned that they were helpless to escape shocks. Something of this kind may indeed occur, but it is likely that this is not the only consequence of the large number of shocks given in the preliminary treatment. Either a general emotional exhaustion or specific and temporary biochemical changes which inhibit temporarily active learning have been proposed, with some reason, as alternative explanations (Weiss and Glazer, 1975; Seligman and Weiss, 1980). A third possibility, for which there is strong evidence where rats are concerned (Glazer and Weiss, 1976), though not with dogs (Maier, 1970), is that during the supposedly helpless phase animals are in fact learning passive motor strategies which interfere with later tasks which require highly active behaviour.

The three alternative explanations for the inability to learn which is the phenomenon which characterizes 'learned helplessness' are thus: (1) some kind of physiological debilitation; (2) an inappropriate, probably passive, response habit; and (3) a more cognitive set, which in animals must at least amount to a disinclination to appropriately associate response output with desirable consequences, and in people might form part of more elaborate atrributional processes, in which helplessness could be connected to beliefs about one's own general or specific inadequacies, or about the unyielding cruelties of an unjust and uncaring external world (Abramson *et al.*, 1978; Miller and Norman, 1979; Peterson and Seligman, 1984).

Physiological debilitation

There are certainly temporary after-effects of stressful experiences, which dissipate with time, and which can depress learning. In the first experiments with dogs, Overmier and Seligman (1967) could demonstrate 'learned helplessness' in shuttle-box training given within 24 hours of the inescapable shock treatment, but not if there was a recovery period of two days or more. Weiss and Glazer (1975) demonstrated that either shock treatment or exposure to very cold water (2°C) 30 minutes before a shuttle-learning test reduced the performance levels of rats. They attribute this to a temporary depletion of adrenalin-like chemicals in the brain, although since relatively inactive motor tasks were not affected, more peripheral forms of fatigue may also have contributed to the reduction in performance on active tasks. Temporary kinds of exhaustion may thus be important in the early stages of learned helplessness. But they are not the only factor. Dogs which have failed once in the shuttle test, given soon after inescable shocks, will fail again a month later. On the other hand dogs allowed to learn to escape first, before being given the usual stress of shocks in harness, are unaffected even immediately after the stress (Maier *et al.*, 1969).

Competing response habits

In several experiments (Maier and Testa, 1975; Seligman and Beagley, 1975; Glazer and Weiss, 1976; Jackson *et al.*, 1980) rats exposed to inescapable shocks may subsequently learn a passive response relatively well, but appear to have difficulty in performing a task differing mainly in the degree of activity involved. Therefore it is likely that deficits in readiness to perform very active responses is one of the consequences of inescapable shock treatment. But there must be more cognitive or more associative consequences as well. Maier (1970) showed that even if he explicitly trained dogs to stand still to escape shock, as a preliminary phase, there was little subsequent disruption in their ability to learn the usual active shuttling task. Jackson *et al.* (1980) observed that pre-stressed rats were just as active as others in running through a Y-maze, but nevertheless very slow to learn to turn in the same direction every time to escape from being shocked.

Associative or cognitive changes

Since alternative explanations have limited application, it seems necessary to include a more cognitive explanation of the phenomenon of learned helplessness (Maier *et al.*, 1969). A relatively non-commital way of describing this is to refer to the lack of an expectancy that attempts at active responding will lessen or terminate experiences. More positively, inescapable shocks could result in an animal acquiring the expectancy that shock termination is independent of its behaviour. This interpretation has added weight because of the finding that exposure to a zero correlation between tone cues and shocks delayed the subsequent learning of an association when the tone was now paired with shock ('learned irrelevance'). Mackintosh (1973) also found that a zero correlation between a tone stimuli and the experience of drinking water, for thirsty rats, similarly retarded the acquisition of anticipatory licking when the tone was made a signal for impending delivery of water. There are thus grounds for believing that an expectational, or associative, mechanism is affected by the experience of the lack of any correlation between events. (Maier *et al.*, 1969; Dickinson, 1980). It might be possible to distinguish the associative aspect of this from the related motivational deficit or 'reduced incentive to initiate responding' (Rosselini *et al*, 1982, p. 376). One way of doing this is to show that there are cross-motivational effects – Goodkin (1976) showed that deficits in the usual task – shuttling to escape shock – could be produced by exposure to the relatively unstressful preliminary experience of receiving deliveries of food at random, irrespective of any organized action by the animals. Inescapable shocks did not encourage rapid learning of new responses needed to obtain food in later tests (Rosselini, 1978; Rosselini and DeCola, 1981), and impaired the subsequent learning by rats of whether they should poke their nose through a left-hand or right-hand hole to produce food, even when training was long continued, the correct response being changed (reversal learning). The deficits in this case lasted for long after the animals had recovered from the temporary suppression of activity produced by receiving the shocks (Rosselini *et al.*, 1982). Experience of severe and unrelievable conditions at an early encounter with aversive stimuli may thus have long-lasting effects on future behaviour compatible with some kind of reduced confidence in the effectiveness of action, or in secure regularities of events, but it is worth noting that the effects of prior shock treatments on the subsequent behaviour of rats in the experiments quoted above were relatively minor, compared with the complete disruption of escape-learning in dogs observed by Seligman *et al.* (1968) and others.

Self-punishment, discrimination and attention

It needs to be emphasized that while an initial experience of severe and inexorable painful events leads to later passivity, exactly the same external trauma has quite different consequences if dogs have already been trained in their escape task beforehand, in the sense that there do not appear to be any consequences in this case, since the dogs' performance on the already learned task is unaffected, and they go on to escape and avoid normally (Seligman *et al.*, 1968). Therefore the order of various learning experiences is crucial, and this is particularly so when strong aversive events are involved – possibly making another special feature of punishment as opposed to reward. The long-lasting and counter-productive fixation of initial learning was apparent in the procedures of Solomon *et al.* (1953), already described (p. 222). Dogs which had learned to jump over their hurdle at a signal in order to avoid shocks in a shuttle-box were undeterred by a new arrangement in which jumping brought them towards an electrified floor instead of away from it. Some dogs made anticipatory yelps while jumping, and the experimenters concluded that the high emotionality caused by the reintroduction of shocks after the dogs had learned to avoid had strengthened rather than weakened the tendency to jump. It seems plausible that in instances of this kind, where observational evidence of autonomic arousal was described in terms of 'symptoms of terror' (Solomon *et al.*, 1953), the repetition of a previously learned response should be regarded as panic-stricken reliance on first impulses. However, it demonstrates that repeated inescapable shocks (once the animals had jumped on the electrified floor, a gate was lowered behind them) are compatible with highly active responding, as well as with the passivity of learned helplessness.

One argument is that both passivity and jumping away are alternative kinds of natural and instinctive responses to pain, one or other being selected in a very obvious way by variations in procedure, since passive animals have been prevented from moving away from shocks (in many cases by being physically restrained in a harness) and active dogs have been first trained to jump (Bolles, 1970, 1978). This is clearly a major factor, but it is worth also bringing in the difficulty for the animals of distinguishing precisely what might be the best option, especially under conditions of high emotional arousal. Solomon *et al.*'s animals (1953) had already learned that a signal might be followed by shock. They alternated from one side of the shuttle box to the other, and therefore were shocked on both sides both in early training and in the punishment procedure. Once in a state of fear, they had initially learned that jumping could reduce fear, or was otherwise advantageous in avoiding shocks. Finally, the punishing shocks were of relatively brief duration (3 seconds) and the dogs would have experience of much longer episodes early in training. Therefore it is to some extent understandable that the animals had difficulty in discriminating what was obvious to the experimenters – that jumping, which had once been required in rather similar circumstances, should now be abandoned.

The absence of discrimination between different sources of fear was implicit in the theory of self-punitive or 'vicious circle' behaviour originally put forward by Mowrer (1947), derived from the two-process theory of the effects of aversive events. If a response has been learned under the influence of conditioned fear, then punishment, especially if it involves the reinstatement of the original aversive event, may add to conditioned fear, and thus enhance the motivation for the punished response. But particular sources of confusion between necessary and unnecessary activities can sometimes be identified as adding to the likelihood of maladaptive behaviours. Brown (1969) reviewed a number of experiments in which rats ran towards a source of electric shocks, thus exposing themselves to aversive events which they could avoid by not so running. But in most cases it is clear that that activities which are elicited by the aversive stimuli, and also the responses which terminate them, are similar in topography or type to the behaviours which ensure continued exposure. For instance, in the experiment by Melvin and Smith (1967), rats first trained to run down an alley into a safe goal box, in order to avoid receiving shock from the floor of the alley, continued to run (or even started to run again after a period when no shocks were given) when the reality of the apparatus was that the middle section of the alley only was always electrified, and shocks could be avoided more completely by freezing in the start box than by running very fast over the electrified segment of the runway. The difficulty of distinguishing running towards the safe goal box, after getting shock, and running in the same direction before the shock, presumably contributed to this result.

Attention and aversive events

Since fleeing from danger is ecological necessity for many species in the wild, and even civilized life may be motivated to a substantial extent by apprehension and annoyance, it would be very odd if all forms of learning motivated by even mildly undesirable emotion led to helplessness, depression, or further unnecessary disasters. It should therefore be acknowledged that the phenomena in this section are anomalies, which may reveal an asymmetry between rewarding and punishing motivational mechanisms, in extreme or unusual circumstances, but which but do so only over and above an underlying functional similarity between the ability to seek out pleasure on the one hand and security and safety on the other. In the diagram due to Gray (1975) on p. 215 (Figure 7.2) the symmetry of rewarding and punishing mechanisms is maintained when both add to arousal of some kind. Animals ought to be alerted by receipt of either wanted or unwanted outcomes, even though subsequent learning should be directed at increasing such receipts in one instance and decreasing them in the other. The differing advantages in maintaining alertness to relatively distant negative as opposed to positive outcomes might mean that some species give higher priorities to one rather than the other case. However, the shared advantage of attention to either kind of motivating event may be responsible for the so-called paradoxical effect of mild punishment for correct choices, in increasing rather than decreasing correct choices in certain kinds of food-reinforced discrimination learning (Muenzinger, 1934; Drew, 1938; Fowler and Wischner, 1969). The belief that painful stimuli should motivate learning in general, instead of merely motivating escape, is not altogether without foundation, even though many educational practices based on this belief (for instance the 'beating of the bounds' of the City of London, when new apprentices were ceremonially whipped at a series of landmarks as an aid to memory) are very happily discontinued.

Reward and punishment: conclusions

The briefest possible summary is the assertion that rewards are wanted and punishments unwanted experiences, which implies a similarity if not an identity of motivational processes based on attractive and aversive events. However, it would not be surprising if the biological priorities differed as between flight from dangerous or painful stimuli on the one hand, and the pursuit of attractive social or consumable goals on the other. There are in fact both anatomical and behavioural grounds for assuming that strongly aversive stimuli have a greater emotional loading, and a less flexible connection with instinctive patterns of behaviour, than strongly attractive stimuli used in similar ways. But for both attractive and aversive stimuli, behavioural experiments can demonstrate automatic emotional anticipation of significant events, instinctive behaviours released as a result of this, and modification of initial behaviours according to their costs and benefits.

There are thus many similarities between rewards and punishments used as motivating events in animal learning experiments, and it is arguable that asymmetries between attractive and aversive motivation can be interpreted as matters of degree – unpleasant events merely being more likely to produce conditioned emotional states and associated instinctive reactions than pleasant stimuli of roughly the same motivational weight. This approach would certainly apply to the many experiments in which animals appear to weigh positive and negative outcomes against each other.

However, in the context of severe anxiety and stress, it seems necessary to appeal to special factors which apply to aversive but not to appetitive motivation. Some of these are undoubtedly physiological, and directly related to the reactions of the autonomic nervous system to aversive stimuli. Others may be more cognitive in nature, in the sense that they reflect either instinctive defensive reactions of particular species or more general asymmetries in the processing of attractive and aversive information.

8 Discrimination, attention and perception

'Thus, from the point of view of the conditioned reflexes, the cerebral hemispheres appear as a complex of analysers, whose purpose is to decompose the complexity of the internal and external worlds into separate elements and moments, and then to connect all these with the manifold activity of the organism.'

Pavlov (1955, p. 300)

The conditioning/extinction theory of discrimination

It is arguable that most, if not all, forms of learning involve differential reaction to certain classes of stimulus input. It is advantageous if certain response skills, such as those involved in driving a golf ball, can be called into action at will, under different external circumstances (as at different golf courses), but usually the deployment of such skills will require modification according to special kinds of informational input (as in the assessment of the desired distance and direction of the stroke). Although the learning of wild animals is often demonstrated by skilled motor accomplishments, such as the aerial acrobatics of the crow family, or the shell-cracking techniques of the oyster-catcher, laboratory analysis of animal learning can almost always be defined in terms of responses given to certain classes of environmental stimuli. Habituation can be described as the differentiation of familiar from novel events: often fine limits of discriminatory ability (for instance in human infants) can be conveniently established by habituating the first response to a certain stimulus-pattern, and discovering the smallest change in this pattern that leads to recovery of the response. Any sort of Pavlovian conditioning demonstrates at least a crude distinction between the presence or absence of the conditioned stimulus. Goal-directed or instrumental learning is less obviously tied to a given external cue, but a rat or cat inside an experimental box only goes through the motions of pressing a lever to escape when the lever is present; and it is easy to demonstrate that this or any other rewarded action can be limited to a specific external signal such as a buzzer of light, and thus made a measure of the detection by the animal of these events.

The issues in learning theory which have been covered in previous chapters cannot therefore be divorced from the sensory capacities of the species doing the learning; it is, rather, a matter of having previously taken for granted certain kinds of perceptual sensitivity which will here be examined in more detail. However, it is also true that simple conditioning experiments, such as may involve responses to buzzers or lights, rarely tax the perceptual abilities of their subjects – indeed, the buzzers and lights may be chosen precisely because they present no discriminatory problems – and that new theoretical issues may be raised by experiments which are designed to in some way stretch the limits of an animal's perceptual apparatus. Sometimes, if not always, 'discriminative experiments, by introducing the element of choice and decision, must involve some new processes' (Mackintosh, 1983, p. 259). It is thus possible to introduce the issues of discrimination learning by reference to the now thoroughly discredited theory of Spence (1936, 1937, 1940) and Hull (1952), which assumed that all of the phenomena of choice and discrimination could be explained by appeal to the strengthening and weakening of different sets of stimulus-response associations by reinforcement and non-reinforcement.

Suppose that a rat learns to press a lever for food rewards in a Skinner box while a light is on, but learns also to refrain from pressing when the light is off, in darkness, since no rewards are then delivered (Skinner, 1938). The simplest

conditioning/extinction explanation of this is that a connection between light shining in the eyes and the responses of
lever-pressing is strengthened when this conjunction of events
is followed by reward, while the absence of rewards for presses
in the dark leaves this second association weak. In practice,
Spence (1937) and Hull (1952) had to talk of 'the relative
strengthening of the excitatory tendency of a certain
component of the stimulus complex' (Spence, 1936, p. 430),
since the rat in question would not make pressing movements
if lights of appropriate brightness were to be shone in its eyes
in its home cage. It is conceivable that the explanation in
terms of direct connections between certain stimulus inputs
and response outputs, and/or the modification in terms of
response connections to elements of a stimulus complex, may
yet be needed to account for motor reflexes differentially
conditioned to tactile or olfactory stimuli in the slug *Aplysia
californica* or in other invertebrates (Carew *et al.*, 1983; Sahley
et al., 1981). But there several ways in which the
conditioning/extinction explanation of discriminative learning
is inadequate as an account of results typically obtained with
vertebrates in the laboratory. Spence (1936, 1937) originally
proposed the conditioning/extinction theory as an explicitly
defensive measure against two claims of more cognitively
inclined psychologists: first, that discrimination learning was
discontinuous, the animal being only able to start learning
once it had selected an appropriate 'hypothesis', or begun
attending to the appropriate signals (Krechevsky, 1932, 1938;
Lashley, 1942); second, that one kind of appropriate hypothesis concerned comparisons between two or more stimuli, so
that animals might select stimuli according to relative values
(by choosing the brighter, the bigger or the smaller and so
on) instead of reacting only according to the absolute physical
magnitudes of the external events (e.g. Kohler, 1925, 1929).
By 1950, Spence himself had become even more defensive,
and it is now rarely disputed that some or other analogue
of an active attentional process is typically engaged by a
discrimination task, and that in this and other ways the
animal imposes internal perceptual organization on the
physical events which may impinge on its sense organs (Sutherland and Mackintosh, 1971; Walker, 1983a, chapter 7).

Generalization along innate stimulus dimensions

Even the conditioning/extinction theories of Hull and Spence made use of the internal organizing factors implied in the notion of stimulus generalization. Pavlov (1927, p. 113) found that if a tone of a particular pitch was learned as a conditioned stimulus 'many other tones spontaneously acquire similar properties', these spontaneuously acquired properties being predictable as a systematic function of the degree of similarity of a stimulus to the already learned signal. This degree of similarity is an internal and to a large extent innately determined aspect of stimulus organization. For pitch, this is obvious in the case of species differences in upper and lower limits of sensitivity. Tactile generalization over the body surface, also observed by Pavlov (1927), requires some kind of sensory homunculus or body image. This may seem a relatively straightforward consequence of cutaneous sensation, but the brain organization required for many obvious-seeming stimulus dimensions is actually complex. Strong generalization along a dimension such as colour, much studied in pigeons, requires not only specialized receptors in the retina, but also methods of ordering and comparing the outputs from these further on in the visual system (e.g. Karten, 1979; Emmerton, 1983; Jassik-Gerschenfeld *et al.*, 1977). Position in the visual field, the location of a sound source to the left or right of the receiver, assessment of the *distance* of an auditory or visual signal from the receiver – all stimulus dimensions of this kind are only possible with the benefit of complicated internal brain circuitry (see Masterton and Glendenning, 1979). One way of acknowledging this is to talk of hypothetical 'analysers' for given stimulus dimensions, assuming these analysers to be largely innate (Sutherland and Mackintosh, 1971; Pavlov, 1927). This is a convenient, though not terribly revealing, strategy.

Generalization gradients and peak-shift

The spontaneous but systematic change in reactions over a whole stimulus dimension can be graphed as a 'generalization gradient,' which under the right conditions can be a roughly

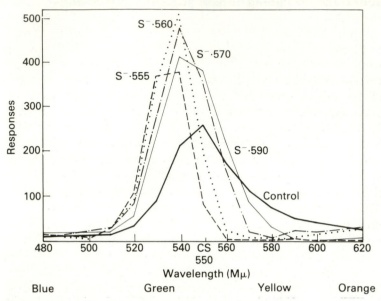

Figure 8.1   *Generalization gradients and peak shift.*
Number of responses to a range of coloured stimuli, by pigeons only ever
rewarded for pecking at a stimulus of wavelength 550. Various groups
had previous experience of a specific non-rewarded stimulus (S-) of the
wavelength value indicated. See text. After Hanson (1959).

symmetrical and bell-shaped distribution about the stimulus
value previously experienced. Smooth curves were obtained
by Hanson (1959) and easily replicated subsequently, which
show the generalization of the pigeons' key-pecking response
to other hues after being trained with a green of a particular
wavelength, and serve to demonstrate the smoothness and
cohesiveness of that species's internal scale of wavelength,
which begins peripherally with five different colours of oil-
droplets in the retina, functioning as cut-off filters, plus the
three different types of visual pigment (absorbing maximally
'red', 'green' or 'blue' light) in the retinal cone cells, which
are more reminiscent of the primate system (see Figure 8.1).

The heavy line in Figure 8.1 shows data from birds which
were trained on a variable interval schedule to peck a key
illuminated with light at a wavelength of 550 nm, which

appears to the human observer as a rather yellowy leaf-green. After this they were shown the complete range of 13 hues, in random order, no further rewards being given, and responded to these at rates indicated on the figure. In this case the roughly bell-shaped curve was asymmetrical, with more responses being given to the green side than the yellow side of the yellowy-green maximum, but the usual result is a neatly symmetrical curve around this hue (Guttman and Kalish, 1956). Other birds were given up to 25 days' extra discrimination training, after the initial experience with 550 nm, in which half the time they continued to be shown this particular yellow-green, getting rewards on the same schedule, but for the other half an even more yellow colour was presented (560, 570 or 590 nm for separate groups) with no rewards at all obtainable in its presence. This procedure produces behavioural evidence of discrimination, since the birds learn to respond when rewards are available, but not when they aren't. However, the dotted lines on Figure 8.1 show data obtained following the discrimination training (with two stimuli), when all 13 hues were shown randomly, and rewards never given at all. In this test, pigeons with previous experience that a greeny-yellow was bad news, even though yellowy-green had remained a signal for reward, showed relatively little responding to the exact stimulus they had been rewarded for (550nm) but had a high peak level of responding for 540 nm, a much greener green. A reduced effect of this kind was observed after training with a more orangy yellow (590 nm) as the previously negative stimulus. The fact that the peak level of responding in a generalization test is not given to the originally rewarded stimulus is referred to in the name given to this phenomenon, which is 'peak shift'. Curves are not always so clear and consistent as those obtained for pigeons after colour discriminations, but a roughly similar change in generalization gradients following reward/no reward or 'GO/NO GO' successive discriminations has been found for line tilt with pigeons (Bloomfield, 1966) and children (Nicholson and Gray, 1972), for visual intensities with pigeons (Ernst *et al.*, 1971) for auditory intensities with rats (Pierrell and Sherman, 1960), and for gravitational forces (produced in a centrifuge) with squirrel monkeys (McCoy and Lange, 1969).

The explanation of the peak shift effect may vary, but it is always powerful and incontrovertible evidence that the physical dimensions being experimentally varied are indeed sensed by the species concerned and are moreover internally organized on some kind of interval scale, so that for one reason or another suppression of responding to one side of a standard stimulus can be converted to an increase on the opposite side. Terrace (1966) showed that the result obtained by Hanson (1959) was temporary – if the two-value discrimination is continued for long enough (up to 60 sessions in the experiment by Terrace, 1966) then the subsequent generalization gradient is symmetrical exactly about the rewarded value. This piece of evidence implicates a temporary emotional and inhibitory effect of non-reward, and thus suggests that a version of the inhibition/excitation formula originally proposed by Spence (1937) is responsible for the peak shift effect. The general idea is that there are two separate generalization gradients, an excitatory, pro-response gradient produced about the exact stimulus value present for rewards; and an inhibitory, anti-response gradient centred on the negative stimulus which signals reward absence. When the inhibitory gradient overlaps with the rewarded stimulus, but only just, then it is possible to perform a subtraction of inhibitory influence from excitatory influence which results in a shift of peak response values (see Figure 8.2). Thus Spence's theory of simple gradients about absolute stimulus values has merits in the context of the successive, GO/NO GO discrimination procedure.

Generalization and transposition

But there is general agreement that Spence was wrong to assume that all perception can be explained in terms of learning restricted to exact stimulus values, and that his inhibition/excitation theory does not work for the task he designed it for, that of explaining transposition, and the discrimination of relative stimulus values (Riley, 1968; Mackintosh, 1983). Early work on stimulus discrimination (e.g. Coburn, 1914; Johnson, 1914) had suggested that animals often discriminate relative values, especially if given a simul-

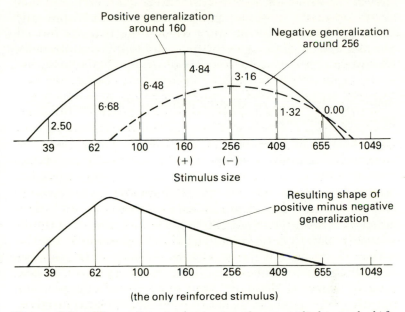

Figure 8.2 *The conditioning/extinction theory applied to peak shift.*
Uniform generalization of both positive and negative response tendencies
could produce asymmetrical generalization gradients. See text. After
Spence (1937).

taneous choice between two displays. Thus a rat or chicken
rewarded for choosing the darker of two shades of grey card
is likely to transpose this relationship immediately to vastly
different pairs – if it has learned to choose the darker of two
fairly light greys it is more than likely to choose also the
darker of two much darker ones, even though in an absolute
sense this is further away from the brightness originally
rewarded. Kohler (1929) emphasized this as an aspect of the
Gestalt theory of perception. In a sense this should be quite
uncontroversial, since brightness contrast, and other forms of
context effect, are accepted as basic perceptual phenomena,
as indeed are other Gestalt principles of grouping by proximity and similarity (Dember and Warm, 1979). Although
animal discrimination learning often reveals good abilities for
exact sensory discriminations, many species have demon-

strated capacities for also discriminating relational cues such as 'darker than', 'greener than' or 'larger than'. In primates certainly, and possibly in other species, this extends to such abstract aspects of perceived displays as oddity and similarity (Bernstein, 1961; Wright *et al*, 1968; see pp. 278–9 below).

Selective attention to simple stimulus dimensions and problem reversals

The theories of Spence and Hull could be regarded as attempts to minimize the role of the animal in discrimination learning. Physical events impinge on the animals' sense organs, and may or may not find their way through a network of stimulus-response connections to emerge as behaviour potentials – as little as possible is said about active processes of search, inference and judgment as organizing factors in animal learning: 'what has been termed intelligent or insightful learning differs only in degree from blind or slow learning' (Spence, 1940, pp. 287–8). There was a long-drawn-out argument between supporters of this sort of stimulus-response theory and their opponents, initially Lashley (1929, 1942), Krechevsky (1932, 1938) and Tolman (1932, 1948), which at the time was referred to as the 'continuity-noncontinuity controversy' (see Osgood, 1953, pp. 446ff. and Sutherland and Mackintosh, 1971, chapter 4). Lashley (1929) had noticed that rats in discrimination experiments often appeared to change suddenly from random behaviour to their maximally efficient performance. Thus he proposed that learning was *not* a continuous process of strengthening correct responses; rather, in the case of discrimination learning, it was a case of selecting or attending to the appropriate sensory features. In Krechesvky's experimental studies (1932, 1938) rats were given a visual discrimination task such as choosing a black rather than a white card (placed to the right or left at random) for successive choices. It appeared that there were rapid shifts between 'hypotheses' which first were wrong – for instance position habits such as always going left, or always going right. Lashley (1942) took the extreme view that hypotheses were switched on and off as an 'all-or-nothing' process, only one being possible at a time. Spence (1940) was from the start willing to admit that for choices between visual stimuli animals must point their eyes and head in the appropriate direction, as a preliminary to learning the task, but wished to include such 'receptor exposure adjustments' as merely another kind of gradually learned stimulus-response process. As Hull (1952, p. 93) put it in his chapter on discrimination learning, 'exposing the receptors to the relevant stimuli in such a problem situation, will be referred to as *receptor adjustment acts*. The detailed theory of the evolution of this type of habit will be presented later in connection with an account of compound trial-and-error learning, of which it is a small-scale example.'

The continuity-noncontinuity controversy is partly a matter of terminology, and it is now conventional to talk of selective attention in discrimination learning, or of the switching in and out of perceptual analysers (Sutherland and Mackintosh, 1971), or of changes in the associability of certain classes of stimuli (Mackintosh, 1983). In terms of experimental predictions, the continuity-noncontinuity question boils down to the question of exactly how quickly and how abruptly such attentional processes change, and the answer, perhaps surprisingly, is that the changes tend to be moderately continuous (Sutherland and Mackintosh, 1971).

If the change in attention from an irrelevant to a relevant cue is an all-or-nothing discrete process, then it should not matter to animals if a problem is changed before they have hit on the correct solution. Thus if rats are being trained to choose a black but not a white door, because food is found behind the black one, but are responding at random, if this is because they are paying no attention at all to the nature of the visual cues it will not delay learning if the discrimination is reversed, food being always put behind the white door instead. This is termed 'presolution reversal'. As it turns out, changing the problem in this way almost always delays learning, and this implies both that learning to pay attention to the correct cue is gradual, and that animals may show some sensitivity to the correct cue before they have begun to use it efficiently (Sutherland and Mackintosh, 1971). It should be pointed out that although rapid changes in discrimination performance are observed occasionally, as a rule the degree of correctness in discrimination learning improves gradually, even for monkeys and chimpanzees, on the initial experiences with the tasks (Harlow, 1950).

A second straightforward experimental test might be called 'post-solution reversal', if a U-turn in choice is required after correct performance has become established. Two phenomena are observed in this case, one rather ephemeral but the other highly reliable, both of which support the proposition that attentional processes may change very gradually if not continuously. The 'overtraining reversal effect' appears to be obtained only in rats, and only when this species learns a moderately difficult discrimination for an appreciably large reward (Mackintosh, 1974, pp.602–4). Little theoretical weight should therefore be attached to it, but its occurrence is consistent with assumptions amply confirmed by different kinds of tests. If, once rats have learned to choose a black door instead of a white door, irrespective of spatial position, the task is switched so that the white door is correct, rats may take an inordinate amount of time to alter their original preference for black (100 or more trials). In some circumstances, however, prolonged experience with the original problem (overtraining) results in a more speedy alteration of performance when the problem is eventually switched (70 instead of 138 trials to reversal in the original report by Reid, 1953). It is possible to argue that this is because the period of overtraining enhances attention to the relevant stimulus dimension, although what this involves precisely is unclear (Mackintosh, 1974, 1983).

Although the effects of extra experience on the first reversals of a two-choice discrimination are only occasionally obvious, gradual improvements in performance on repeated reversals of the same discrimination is virtually certain in mammals and birds (see Figure 8.3). It is not clear whether gradual improvements in performance on serial reversal learning are due to increased attention to a particular stimulus dimension, as opposed to more elaborate learned changes such as the development of win-stay/lose-shift response strategies (Mackintosh, 1974; Mackintosh *et al.*, 1985). However, the improvements must in some way be attentional even in the later case, since this strategy requires that attention is concentrated on

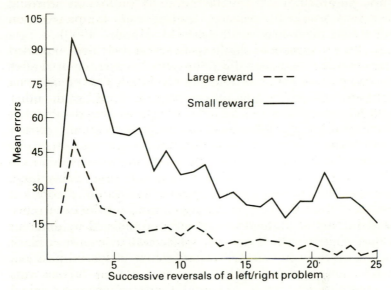

Figure 8.3 *Gradual improvements in serial reversal learning.*
The performance of homing pigeons which received either a large reward
(4 seeds) or a small reward (1 seed) for displacing the correct choice of
2 blocks which covered left and right foodwells. The birds received 20
trials per day of training to respond to their non-preferred side, until
they reached a criterion of less than 3 errors per day. Then the correct
side was switched until the same criterion was reached, and this was
continued for 24 reversals. After Gossette and Hood (1968).

the choice made and its outcome on the immediately
preceding trial. It is thus difficult to disentangle the perceptual from the memorial aspects of this phenomenon, but it is
none the less of considerable theoretical interest, as there are
reasonably consistent differences in serial reversal performance between fish, which show very limited improvements,
birds and mammals, which generally improve more dramatically, and monkeys and apes, who are likely to demonstrate
exceptionally accurate performance under these conditions
(Mackintosh *et al.*, 1985; Gossette *et al.*, 1966, 1968; see
'Learning sets', p. 270 below).

It is always difficult to be sure that minor variations in

procedural detail are not the source of species differences in accuracy or speed of learning, leading some to conclude that all species differences are illusory (Macphail, 1982), but there are strong suggestions that fish show relatively little improvement when two-choice discriminations are serially repeated, by comparison with rats, and that commonly studied primates (rhesus monkeys, chimpanzees and children) show much greater improvement, again by comparison with rats (see Mackintosh *et al.*, 1985; Harlow, 1949, 1959; Woodard *et al.*, 1971; Gossette *et al.*, 1968). One of the advantages of the serial reversal procedure for species comparisons is that such factors as the level of motivation and the discriminability of the stimulus choices used are to some extent controlled for in the data from the very first discrimination. If this is learned without undue difficulty, but leaving room for significant improvements which are not forthcoming, it seems fair to conclude that the species in question is lacking not in any basic capacity for discrimination but in some higher-order change in attentional strategy or use of memory, which enables the serial reversal improvement seen in other species to take place (see 'Learning sets', pp. 270–4 below).

Selective attention to stimulus dimensions and transfer effects

The reversal of two-stimulus discrimination tasks may not in fact be the most suitable way to demonstrate selective attention to a particular perceptual dimension. A rat or pigeon which has just learned to respond to a black but not a white card for its food rewards has considerable difficulty when the rule is first changed, and could be forgiven for ignoring the appearance of the cards altogether. In practice there is evidence that greater attention is paid to card appearance over a series of reversals, but at the same time the animals need to develop a form of cynicism about reliability of the dimension they are attending to. There are several other lines of evidence which bear on theories of selective attention in discrimination learning, and one of these concerns transfer effects when two or more problems are learned in succession, the different problems not being simple reversals of the same two stimuli.

It was typical of experiments in Pavlov's laboratory that the same dog should experience many different signals. One of the main reasons for this was most dogs only stayed awake during experiments if a wide variety of stimuli was used each day (Pavlov, 1927, pp. 285–6 – this precaution is not usually necessary with hungry rats and pigeons, even if they are restrained), which points to the connection between processes of selective attention and overall arousal or alertness (Sokolov, 1963). Pavlov took it for granted that a major aspect of brain function was that 'it selects out of the whole complexity of the environment those units which are significant' (1927, p. 110), and did not need to be convinced of the importance of attention in dogs, but noted two results which apply also to other species, and which indicate something about the details of attentional processes. First is the fact that a contrast between positive and negative stimuli produces an overwhelmingly more rapid and precise discriminative behavioural reaction than merely the repetition of a single positive stimulus (Pavlov, 1927, p. 117). This is explicable in terms of a mechanism by which discrepancies between expected and experienced outcomes are resolved, or which reduces more general uncertainties about motivationally significant outcomes. Any such mechanism would be involved in changes in arousal and alertness, and in selective attention to those stimulus dimensions containing information which reduce uncertainty (Sutherland and Mackintosh, 1971; see pp. 105–13 chapter 4).

Transfer from easy to difficult cases

A second phenomenon noted by Pavlov specifically implies that attention to a particular dimension can somehow be usefully switched in (1927, pp. 121–3; 396). Dogs shown a circle of white paper as a signal for food continued to salivate to an off-white circle of the same size even when this had invariably signalled the absence of food on dozens of occasions. If, however, a dark grey circle was first used as the negative signal, and then a couple of lighter shades of grey, the original off-white circle could be readily and completely accurately distinguished from the white circle – in that it elicited no salivation. This might be regarded as the use of the traditional 'method of limits' in establishing just noticeable differences in animal sensation – Hodos and Bonbright (1972) used a graded series of intensity filters for precisely this purpose, and established that pigeons could detect whether or not a plain glass slide was inserted between them and a light source. But a more important inference for present purposes is that, although the dogs may in the first instance have been looking at the white and off-white circles (since they salivated only when they were presented) and thus have had appropriate peripheral 'receptor adjustments' (Spence, 1940), training with a brief progression of easier cases seems to have encouraged the switching in of a more central analyser. Transfer from easy to difficult cases is a reliable result (Lawrence, 1952; Mackintosh, 1974; Terrace, 1966) with many species. It applies not only to brightness, of course, but to colour (Marsh, 1969) and to shape (Pavlov, 1927, p. 122 used easy and then more difficult circle/ellipse discriminations). Vision in particular (but other senses also) involves many different stimulus dimensions, which reflect different methods of internal analysis of the same input, and not necessarily selection between different sources of input (noticing the colour as opposed to the shape of a circle does not require greatly different methods of inspecting the stimulus, especially in species with limited eye-movements). Separate brain mechanisms may of course be involved in different sorts of perceptual analysis (Walker, 1983a) and therefore the switching in of analysers may be almost literal, although on the grounds of behavioural evidence alone the analyser is a hypothetical though convenient construct (Sutherland and Mackintosh, 1971).

Transfer to alternative problems using the same dimension

The effects of transfer from an easy to a hard discrimination may be particularly noticeable, since performance on the hard discrimination without prior training is often extremely poor. But statistical comparison can reveal transfer effects in other instances. For instance, when rhesus macaque monkeys are allowed to find food under one of two objects presented together, they make significantly fewer errors on the later pairs if they are trained first to choose a red object instead of a green one, then a black form instead of blue one, then an orange rather than a brown, that is, if they are given four colour problems in succession. However, if they are given two colour problems and two shape problems (e.g. circle versus square, cross versus 'T'), shape and colour alternating, no improvements are observed (Shepp and Schrier, 1969). This kind of experiment is described as a comparison between 'intradimensional and extradimensional shifts', and it is very frequently found that the intradimensional shifts are learned more easily than extradimensional shifts, implying that consistent attention to the same dimension is an advantage (Mackintosh, 1974, p. 597).

Two carefully designed and influential experiments were reported by Lawrence (1949, 1950). In these, transfer was studied between problems in which very similar pairs of stimuli had to be responded to rather differently. In the first case rats were initially trained to enter one of two side-by-side compartments in a simultaneous discrimination. For different groups choice was on the basis of the walls being black or white, or on the floor being made of fine or coarse wire mesh, or in response to the compartments being of different widths. After this, the animals were trained on successive discriminations in an enclosed T-maze in which only one stimulus value was present at a time, and the rule was of the form, 'turn left if the walls are white, turn right if the walls are black.' In the initial simultaneous discrimination the most obvious equivalent rule would be 'choose the black compartment whether it is on the left or the right', and therefore the animals could not transfer exactly what they had learned on the first problem to the second. However, all rats trained on a black-white discrimination initially showed positive transfer (made fewer errors) in learning the second kind of black-white discrimination. The experiment was balanced so that each of the three stimulus dimensions used in the first problem was tested with either of the other two present but irrelevant in the second problem: the expected positive transfer was observed in all six cases, by comparison with control groups. A second experiment confirmed that positive transfer of a similar kind also occurred when the first problem was a successive discrimination (one stimulus at a time) and the second was a two-choice simultaneous discrimination, in the same apparatus (Lawrence, 1950).

It may perhaps seem odd that such results should require systematic confirmation – being trained on a black-white discrimination in one context certainly ought to be of use in learning further black-white problems. But the experiments were performed at Yale, with the advice of Clark Hull, and were therefore a very careful and quantitative analysis of what Lawrence called 'the acquired distinctiveness of cues'. This is a useful descriptive term, but clearly the physical cues themselves do not change, or acquire new characteristics, except in the sense that prior experience leads animals to treat them differently. Lawrence made the theoretical distinction between selection via 'orientation behaviour' such as moving the head or focusing the eyes, and 'mediating processes' which are internal and unobservable. He pointed out that although changes in orienting behaviour could not be eliminated as an explanation for his results, his choice of diffuse stimuli – wall colour, floor texture, and apparatus width – made it highly unlikely that overt peripheral bodily adjustments were important. His mediating processes might of course just as well be referred to as selective attention.

Transfer to alternative problems using different dimensions – learning sets

For theories of selective attention, the most convenient results are those demonstrating that prior experience with one particular dimension, such as visual intensity or colour, facilitates performance on subsequent tasks involving that particular dimension, but *not* on similar tasks requiring discriminations on alternative dimensions. Lawrence's results (1949, 1950) and many other results comparing performance across stimulus dimensions (for instance, intra– versus extra-dimensional shifts, Mackintosh, 1974) provide unequivocal evidence for some processes of transfer which are indeed selective. However this does not exclude the possibility of more general transfer effects. Learning not to attend to a single wrong dimension, such as the left-right position of displays which are always left-right randomized, may obviously improve performance on every other relevant dimension – for instance any individual visual feature which happens to be made relevant on the left-right displays. It is also conceivable that the learning of one discrimination problem produces non-specific changes in alertness or attentiveness, which are of benefit in any subsequent task. Thomas *et al.* (1970, 1971) have suggested a factor of non-specific attentiveness on the grounds that a second GO/NO GO successive discrimination is likely to be more quickly learned than the first, but in these cases just the learning that rewarded and non-rewarded periods alternate over time may be responsible for part of the improvement. Rogers and Thomas (1982) found that non-specific transfer effects only occurred when discrimination tasks were unaltered (i.e. when one successive task was followed by another), and suggested that what may appear to be transfer of general attentiveness is better described as transfer of 'task-appropriate response tendencies'.

Harlow (1959) would have been able to include all effects like these in what he called 'error factor theory'. He pointed out that there are a number of general features of correct performance in discrimination learning tasks which the experimenter may take for granted, but which the animal may have to learn gradually by trial and error, and which may be responsible for errors until they are learned. Even learning to expect a reward for a correct response is necessary in the first instance; usually the next phase is learning that there is a class of stimuli to which responses should not be made. Depending on the exact experimental procedure, there may be other general features of task solution such as the location of stimuli, the frequency of stimulus changes and the necessary strategy of responding which, when learned during prior tasks, may facilitate performance on future tasks. None of this is problematical – the question is simply exactly which features are responsible for particular transfer of training effects, and if and when selective attention to a salient stimulus dimension should be put down as one of these general features of task solution. The phenomenon that Harlow (1959) was concerned with was his previous discovery (1949) of 'learning sets'. This is a transfer of training effect which on the face of it cannot involve selective attention, since it involves progressive improvement over a succession of problems which explicitly require that there is no single salient dimension.

Learning sets

These may be observed in a succession of standard two-choice simultaneous discriminations. Typically they are obtained when primates are presented with a tray on which there are two objects, a raisin or peanut being under one of these. The monkey (or ape) then reaches out an arm and pushes away an item, to retrieve its food incentive if it is correct. The apparatus is known as the WGTA (Wisconsin General Test Apparatus) (see Figure 8.4). A wide range of stimulus items is needed for the study of learning sets, which may vary on known dimensions – stars, circles, squares, pyramids and so on, varying in colour, height and size – or which may be more easily discriminable 'junk objects' – cups, bottles, toys, kitchen implements and other human artifacts. Whichever pair of objects is chosen for a monkey's first discrimination problem, the animal will take a considerable number of trials – certainly more than four or five – before it settles to the habit of always pushing away first the one which the experimenter has chosen to associate with the food incentive on this problem. The learning set effect is observed only in animals who have received practice on literally dozens of different pairs of stimulus items. As experience is gained on different pairs, the rate of learning each new pair gradually speeds up, to the extent that, after 200 or 300 pairs, learning is instantaneous. The first time a new pair is presented the animal has only a 50 per cent chance of making a correct choice. But theoretically, the second time a new pair is presented, the animal has 100 per cent chance of being correct, provided it remembers the results of the first trial and makes its choice accordingly. Harlow's finding (1949) was that rhesus monkeys did indeed become 100 per cent

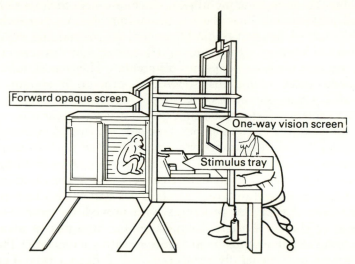

Figure 8.4   *The Wisconsin General Test Apparatus (WGTA).*
A widely used method of testing visual or spatial discriminations in
primates is to conceal food under only one of two or more objects
presented to the animal on a given trial. The development of this method
at the University of Wisconsin has led to the use of the acronym WGTA.
Similiar object-displacement methods can be used with some non-primate
species (see Figure 8.3). After Harlow (1959).

correct (or virtually so, at over 97 per cent) on the second trial
of all new problems, but only after they had had experience of
learning with 250 previous pairs of objects.

There are two important theoretical aspects to this finding,
which Harlow initially described as 'learning to learn'. First,
although avoiding simple sources of error such as fixed
position habits may be useful in the early improvement of
performance, the explanation for the eventual high level of
performance is probably that the animals have adopted a
strategy of making full use of their memory of the immediately
preceding trial – since this high level of performance can be
seriously disrupted merely by lengthening the interval
between successive trials (Deets *et al.*, 1970; Bessemer and
Stollnitz, 1971). In a sense the only question here is the effect

of time on immediate memories, since how else could second-trial performance be correct if the animal did not remember the result of the first trial? However, the second theoretical aspect of learning set is more controversial, and this concerns its use as a measure of species differences. Hayes *et al.* (1953) trained three chimpanzees with a procudure similar to Harlow's and obtained over 95 per cent performance after 150 problems. Fisher (1962), using the same apparatus, but pictures cut from magazines instead of three-dimensional objects, found less impressive performance in two young gorillas (80 and 84 per cent correct on trial 2 after 232 problems), but there is good evidence that Old World monkeys and apes can generally reach over 90 per cent correct performance after 200 or 300 problems with procedural details like those in Harlow's original experiments. Attempts to obtain learning sets in analogous procedures with species other than primates have generally produced trial 2 figures very much less than 90 per cent correct even after 500 or more problems, and both Harlow (1959) and Warren (1965) deduced that Old World primates must possess some quantitatively superior capacity which allowed for this difference in performance. Warren (1973) and others (e.g. Macphail, 1982) have since maintained that this was unjustified, and that the better performance of the Old World primates, in so far as it stands up to detailed comparisons, is due only to better visual perception or to some similar relatively peripheral or contextual advantage.

It is certainly difficult to use learning set performance on its own to argue for some fundamental intellectual superiority in our closest relatives. However, critics of the comparative use of learning sets may have overstated their case. For example, one study which was procedurally appropriate in other respects, and appeared to show that mink and ferrets could reach primate levels of performance, failed to control for olfaction, since these carnivores demonstrated their abilities only by pushing with their nose at that door of the two avilable behind which a piece of meat had been placed (Doty *et al.*, 1967). The tuning in of a very acute sense of smell may be as biologically advantageous to carnivores of the weasel family as immediate visual memory is to primates, but it is not the same thing. Slotnik and Katz (1974) showed that rats could rapidly be trained to make almost immediate discriminations between members of 16 pairs of smells delivered to them alternately in 5–second puffs in a special apparatus, using a GO/NO GO discrimination procedure. It is fair to regard this as evidence that rats are likely to learn olfactory discriminations much faster than visual ones, but it is naive to suppose that this rapid learning results from the same kind of cognitive capacity as that employed by primates during learning set tasks. One-trial learning can be observed in many laboratory paradigms, including avoidance of objects or locations associated with electric shock, and in the taste-aversion procedure (see pp. 232ff.). But it is not the one-trial aspect of learning at the end of a learning set experiment which accounts for Harlow's initial interest in the phenomena, but the very gradual improvements which indicate 'learning to learn'. The present theoretical position is that primate learning set performance should be explained by switches in attentional processes, which lead eventually to the use of immediate memory of the choice made and the resulting outcome on the previous trial.

Claims that the intellectual capacities necessary for this cognitive strategy are widely distributed in the animal kingdom should be treated with caution. For instance, Morrow and Smithson (1969) reported that they had discovered 'learning sets in an invertebrate' on the grounds that they had succeeded in training eight small wood louse-like crustaceans to creep round a 'T'-maze, and observed a statistical decline in the errors made over several reversals of the direction of the correct turn. There are a number of possible accounts of how the nervous systems of these creatures might accomplish improvements in locomotor adjustments of this kind, but it is surely unlikely that any of them would have a great deal in common with the explanation of primate learning sets. In this case the behavioural test reported as 'learning set' hardly justified the term. (The major features of the training set phenomenon are: (a) eventual performance on a given problem is well above chance on the *second trial*; and (b) this performance develops gradually as a result of experience with several hundred pairs of objects.)

However, others have taken care to use a primate-style procedure when testing non-primate species. Hunter and Kamil (1971) used 700 pairs of junk objects in two-choice discrimination problems presented to blue jays, which obtained an invertebrate reward (half a mealworm) only if they displaced the object designated as correct on any given problem. This is closely analogous to the two-choice discriminations rewarded with raisins or peanuts for monkeys, and there appears to be a genuine improvement of a learning set kind in blue jays, since trial 2 performance improved from chance on the first few problems to 73 per cent correct after 700 problems. It is thus reasonable to claim that blue jays and also mynah birds (Kamil and Hunter, 1970; Kamil *et al*, 1977) are capable of learning to employ win-stay, lose-shift strategies which make use of memories of immediately preceding trials. But this is hardly a challenge to the assumption of primate superiority, since the level of performance achieved – roughly 70 per cent after up to 1,000 problems – is no match for the almost perfect performance in rhesus monkeys after 250 problems that was reported by Harlow (1949). It ought always to be remembered that chance performance on these tasks is 50 per cent, and that therefore that 90 per cent can be regarded as double the improvement on chance represented by 70 per cent.

Direct switching of selective attention

Transfer experiments like those of Lawrence (1949, 1950), in which training on one problem with a certain kind of stimulus improves performance on a second problem with the same kind of stimulus, strongly suggest that an active, 'top-down' change in the receiving system during the first problem modifies the way in which external stimuli are detected during the second problem. They thus support two-stage theories, such as that of Sutherland and Mackintosh (1971), in which the receipt of external stimuli is a variable process subject to learning (and the output of certain responses governed by stimuli as received is a second process of learning). But transfer experiments are certainly not the only, and perhaps not even the best, form of support for the hypothesis of selective attention in discrimination learning. Several quite different types of experimental manipulation can be used to examine variations in responsiveness to chosen categories of stimuli. Bond (1983) performed very straightforward experiments on visual search in pigeons, which he suggests support a hypothesis of attentional thresholds; he supposes that attention to a particular stimulus category can be switched in when this category is frequently encountered. His technique was to present birds with 20 grains consisting of various proportions of two types, black gram beans and red wheat, placed on a background of mixed gravel of a similar size, allowing them enough time to peck up about half the 20 grains available. The data show a clear bias in the proportion of each type of grain taken; when a 50:50 mixture was presented the birds retrieved equal amounts of the two types, and responded relatively slowly; but when, say, 80 per cent of the grain presented was of one type, then the birds had an exaggerated preference for this type, picking it on more than 95 per cent of their successful pecks, and also responded much faster. The theory is that the animals are able to switch in selective attention to a particular stimulus category when the frequency of discovery of the category exceeds some threshold. (Conversely, the speed at which a single instance of a certain stimulus type can be found in a visual display may be progressively and adversely affected as the number of alternative 'distractor elements' is increased: Blough, 1977, 1984).

Conditional discriminations

A similar sort of explanation, in terms of the switching-in of a stimulus analyser, or the temporary turning-on of sensitivity to a particular configurational cue, has been applied to many other kinds of discrimination learning. Pavlov's method of contrasts itself, requiring a distinction between rewarded and non-rewarded stimuli, is the simplest possible demonstration of the conditional nature of reactivity to stimulus variation. Another well-known example was reported by Jenkins and Harrison (1960). Pigeons rewarded for pecking at a key when a 1,000 Hz tone is on are subsequently indifferent to large changes in the frequency of this tone. But if the tone is made a signal for reward, because its absence indicates no rewards are obtainable, then this appears to enhance attention to the tone considerably, since the birds show sharp drops in responding whenever the frequency of the tone is changed, in either direction, producing very steep generalization gradients. Although it is usually concluded that pigeons are poor at utilizing auditory cues, the correlation of an auditory stimulus with food rewards appears to greatly increase auditory analysis. We may confidently expect pigeons to be normally indifferent to the music of both Bach and Stravinsky, but if the distinction between Bach and Stravinsky is a necessary preliminary to food, pigeons learn to make it, or rather, they analyse heard sounds sufficiently to generalize from Bach to Buxtehude (Porter and Neuringer, 1984; see below).

The rapid switching in and out of attention to alternative aspects of the outer environment is sometimes appealed to as an explanation for various kinds of effect under the heading of conditional discrimination. Lashley (1938) trained rats to jump towards an upright triangle on a black background, and to an inverted triangle on a striped background, but not towards an upright triangle on a striped background, or an inverted triangle on a black background. A probable explanation of this effect in rats is that each compound cue is learned separately (Sutherland and Mackintosh, 1971). However, there are other cases of conditional discrimination which look as though one kind of stimulus has become a signal for attention to be paid or not paid to another kind. For instance Yarczower (1971) studied how often pigeons pecked at stimuli made up of a white line which could be tilted at five different angles and projected on either a red or a green background. The training procedure specified that food could be obtained by pecking the green background, irrespective of the angle of the line projected thereon, but that when the background was red, reward could be obtained by pecking at it only when the background contained a vertical white line – a similar line at a 40° slant meant that pecks would go unrewarded. As one might expect, when the key was red, any deviation of the white line from the vertical suppressed the level of responding; but a consistent rate of response was given to the green key, whatever the tilt of a white line superimposed on it. This led Yarczower to suggest that something had been learned which was roughly equivalent to 'if red, pay closer attention to line tilt than if not red'.

Blough (1972) reported a much more elaborate set of data, in which wavelength of a visual stimulus was combined with the frequency of a tone, or a timing variable. He concluded that the interactions between any pair of dimensions were multiplicative, in that if one component of a compound stimulus was very different from the value which signalled reward, then changes in the other component had little effect – this can be taken as implying attentional changes in the context of the statistics of signal-detection theory. On the face of it, a much more direct use of attentional processes is implied by the simpler experiment performed by Reynolds (1961), who trained pigeons with four stimuli presented on the same key for 3 minutes each, in cycles which allowed for each stimulus to get 12 3–minute presentations in a daily session. The four compound stimuli consisted of white triangles and circles on blue or red backgrounds. One of these compound stimuli, the red triangle, always signalled reward; another, the blue circle, never did. The consequences of the other two compound stimuli varied, since there was an additional rule: there were two sidelights, and when one was on redness signalled reward, and when the other was on the presence of the triangle signalled reward. The main result of this training was that birds responded to the red circle and the blue triangle only when these stimuli signalled reward, as well as always responding to the red triangle and never responding to the blue circle. The simplest mechanism of accomplishing this differentiation, as it would appear to the human observer, involves selective attention to either the figure or the ground of the compound stimulus, according to the additional cues, one of which indicates that any triangle would be rewarded, and the other that any red background signals reward. It is not clear however that this is what occurred. A replication of a very similar compound discrimination by Reynolds and Limpo (1969) found inconsistent patterns of response when the coloured backgrounds or white forms were presented alone, with the birds responding more to coloured backgrounds alone than to the white forms alone.

The simpler method of demonstrating conditional discrimination with compound stimuli is that of Lashley (1938). This was used by Born *et al.* (1969). A circle and a triangle in white outline were projected with either a red or a green background. Only two of these four possibilities signalled reward for any one of the pigeon subjects: for instance the red circle and the green triangle might signal reward, but the red triangle and the green circle not. After this rule had been learned in Born *et al.*'s experiment, uniform red- and green-coloured stimuli and circle and triangle outlines on a dark background were presented alone as a test. None of the subjects responded to the colours alone, but all three responded vigorously to one of the shapes, but not to the other. This is exactly what would be expected if the colours were being used as the first stage of a two-stage strategy, to indicate which of the two shapes should be responded to, there being a bias towards one or other of the shapes in the absence of the usual colour cue.

There is an alarming variety of visual discrimination experiments on pigeons, and also on laboratory monkeys: the most reliable conclusion is probably that no single explanation will account for all results. Both the learning of elaborate compounds (see below) and isolated learning of individual elements of compound stimuli are well substantiated, in both species. However there is some support for the notion that pigeons respond most to the literal appearance of individual visual displays while by comparison laboratory monkeys are capable of more abstract representations. This is clearest in the case of the rules of responding according to similarity of oddity in 'matching to sample' tests, using three displays. Suppose the middle of three displays is illuminated red. This display is touched or pecked, and goes off, but the two side displays are now lit red and green. A rule of similarity or matching to the sample would require that the red display be chosen, whatever side it was on, such choices being the only ones rewarded. A rule of oddity would require that the green alternative be chosen after a red sample, but a red alternative chosen after a green sample. Primates are generally capable of abstracting such rules, in that after being trained with several colours they can immediately apply the rules to new colours, or two new sorts of visual stimuli (Bernstein, 1961: Premack, 1983). Although there is not a complete consensus on how data obtained from pigeons should be interpreted, obtaining evidence for any degree of abstract learning in this context is very difficult. A review of previous experimentation by Carter and Werner (1978) concludes that pigeons in these circumstances amost invariably learn a set of 'sample-specific rules'. That is, for matching to sample, they learn that if a red sample, choose a red alternative, and if a green sample, choose a green alternative, without being able to apply a general rule of similarity when other visual stimuli are tested (Mackintosh *et al.*, 1985; Wilson *et al.*, 1985). This sounds very much like a form of temporary priming for recognition of particular stimulus displays, but since it works just as well, if not better, for the oddity rule, it might be regarded as a very quick and temporary switching-in of receptivity to particular stimulus patterns.

Theories of attention in conditioning

Although the more complicated procedures of discrimination learning experiments may bring into play mechanisms not normally activated in the simplest of conditioning experiments (Mackintosh, 1983), there are a number of points of contact between theories of discrimination learning and theories of basic associative processes such as those of Rescorla and Wagner, (1972), Mackintosh (1975), Wagner (1978) and Pearce and Hall (1980) which were discussed in chapter 4 (pp. 105 ff.). A very general feature of all these theories is that they are attempts to account for the waxing and waning of the 'effectiveness' or 'associability' of the conditioned and unconditioned stimuli (CS and US) in classical conditioning procedures. In terms of behavioural predictions to be made, there is rarely anything to choose between theories which refer to variations in the effectiveness or associability of stimuli and those which make similar points in terms of selective attention given to stimuli, or analysers for these same stimuli being switched in (thus making the stimuli more effective and more capable of being associated

with other things). Mackintosh (1975) notes that there is
a formal equivalence between assuming that change in the
associations made to specific stimuli vary according to a
'learning rate parameter' which depends on previous experience, and assuming that the probability of learning anything
about a stimulus varies according to the amount of attention
given to it, which also depends on previous experience. The
main advantages in continuing to use the phraseology of
attention are that, first, it allows easier comparisons with the
present concerns of discrimination learning, and second, that
it points to additional sources of evidence, such as variations
in the observed degree of alertness of animals, or in their
orienting behaviour to specific sights and sounds. Thus, the
theory of Pearce and Hall (1980) was proposed primarily in
terms of 'variations in effectiveness' of conditioned stimuli,
but informally they suggest that the variations in effectiveness
arise because associations depend on a limited capacity
processor, and that potential conditioned stimuli will compete
for access to this central processor, which is very much
compatible with a selective attention approach (Broadbent,
1958, 1984). And in practice, some of the support for the Hall
and Pearce model is provided by overt measures of attention,
such as bodily orientation towards and physical contact with
a light source (Kaye and Pearce, 1984).

Therefore there is a case that both the phenomena of
discrimination learning, more usually discussed in terms of
attention, and the findings of simpler conditioning experiments should be applied as tests to the same theories. The
theories examined in chapter 4 in the context of classically
conditioned associations may be reviewed as follows.

Rescorla and Wagner (1972)
The equation given on p. 106 above is usually interpreted
in terms of the powers of the unconditioned stimulus (US)
(Dickinson, 1980). The acquisition of a conditioned response
reaches a limit in this account because only surprising or
unpredicted motivationally significant events influence
previous stimuli. In the early stages of learning, food received
by a Pavlovian dog is relatively unexpected – therefore extra
associations are formed to a preceding buzzer signal: in the

final stages of learning however the dog now expects food because of the buzzer – the buzzer will have reached its limit and any other signals added in conjunction with the buzzer will *not* acquire further predictive properties. Nothing much is said here about selective attention to the signalling stimuli, because the explanation is in terms of the predictability of the reinforcement.

Mackintosh (1975)
Mackintosh proposed (as did Sutherland and Mackintosh, 1971) that subjects increase attention to relevant stimuli and decrease attention to irrelevant ones, relevance being defined in terms of the degree to which a stimulus dimension can be used to predict the occurrence or non-occurrence of reinforcement. The factor of predictability of motivationally significant stimuli, as used by Rescorla and Wagner (1972), is included by assuming that attention to a stimulus dimension is increased only if it allows for the prediction of otherwise unexpected reinforcement (or predicts the omission of otherwise expected ones).

Pearce and Hall (1980)
These authors emphasized what is implicit in some earlier theories – that attention to a particular signal will be reduced when it has very high predictive accuracy, and maximum attention will be given to a stimulus when its outcome is uncertain.

Wagner (1976, 1981)
Wagner's elaborate theorizing makes use of several concepts derived from studies of human information-processing, including: the shift from controlled to automatic processing (Shiffrin and Schneider, 1984) which may be related to the decline in active attention given to a well-learned condition stimulus, emphasized by Pearce and Hall (1980); the active representation of to-be-associated events ('rehearsal', after Atkinson and Shiffrin, 1968) in a short-term memory store; and the decrease of such activity produced as a consequence of the presentation of a particular stimulus if its representation has already been 'primed', which is similar to the notion

involved in the other theories above that an already expected event will not arouse much additional attentional effort.

Discrepancy and expectancy theories and discrimination learning

Of the theories very briefly encapsulated above, none except that of Mackintosh (1975) was designed to handle the basic phenomena of discrimination learning, and therefore few specific predictions from the theories about discrimination learning are made. It is however possible to list some sources of overall consensus and a few points of disagreement.

Paradoxes of knowledge and arousal

All the theories above include some kind of acknowledgment that when learning is complete the flow of information into the learner is somehow restricted. In the extreme case, in Pearce and Hall's (1980) theory, a signal which predicts an event of great motivational significance with perfect accuracy is at some level no longer processed. This is in conflict with the initial assumption of Sutherland and Mackintosh (1971) that an analyser capable of predicting rewards perfectly should at the limit of learning be switched in to the maximum extent possible. A number of arguments arise from this conflict. The discriminability of the signal, and the question of exactly what is switched in or out, require further specification (see below). But it will always have to be acknowledged that the early stages of learning, when curiosity and uncertainty are highest, may involve more rapid change in knowledge, or more rapid formation of associations, than the later stages of learning, when the prior acquisition of knowledge may only be rewarded by routine and automatic (but correct) responses. There may thus be more learning actually going on in the early stages. But this does not mean that information has been lost in the later stages: performance which appears to be routine, with little sign of alertness or strong orientation to relevant stimuli, can change very rapidly when accustomed outcomes are changed, for instance when a discrimination is reversed. For this reason, it may be necessary for theories of attention to distinguish between arousal and orientation and the switching in of an analyser – it may be necessary to allow for an analyser to be fully switched in when there are few signs of active attention. This is of course implicit in theories of habituation which are able to account for the 'missing stimulus effect' – no response at all may be given to a predictable train of stimuli, but the minimal but functionally vital degree of attention usually given is revealed by arousal and orientation when the stimulus is missed out (see p. 51).

This can be related to two phenomena of discrimination learning, the 'errorless learning technique' (Terrace, 1963) and the effect of unrewarded exposure to shape stimuli on subsequent shape discrimination learning (Channell and Hall, 1981). Terrace's errorless learning result suggests that high arousal and orientation to stimuli in the early stages of learning is not strictly necessary. Very gradual changes to the stimuli in a easy discrimination task allow for the animal to learn painlessly and without apparent arousal a more difficult discrimination that might otherwise be difficult or impossible (cf. Pavlov, 1927, p. 122). The orientation and arousal part of attention is involved in searches for the correct predicting cue – once the correct predicting cue is known, it is no longer so necessary. Gibson and Walk (1956) reared young rats in cages containing cut-out triangles and circles and showed that these animals were better able than others to learn a subsequent circle/triangle discrimination. However in other cases prior exposure to the stimuli to be used in a discrimination retards learning (Hall, 1980; Bateson and Chantrey, 1972). Channell and Hall (1981) demonstrated that rats exposed to stimulus objects in their home cages learned a subsequent simultaneous discrimination (in a Lashley jumping stand, between horizontal and vertical stripes) better than control subjects; but if animals were given experience of the stimuli in the discrimination apparatus itself, but without differential reward or punishment, the learning of the discrimination was retarded. This might be interpreted in terms of the learning in the home cage of processes of perceptual analysis ('formation of a neuronal model' in the version of Sokolov, 1975) which turn out to be useful if applied in the discrimination apparatus. But when animals encounter the stimuli in the experimental apparatus itself, any perceptual learning may be vitiated by the additional factor of learned irrelevance (see below) – having become accustomed to the stimuli in the absence of differential reward, there will be less reason for these animals to attend to these now relevant sources of information when differential rewards are introduced, by comparison with those introduced to the whole task at the same time (see Dickinson, 1985 for a hypothesis about the correlation between signalling experiences and outcome experiences as a necessary factor in learning).

Learned irrelevance

Mackintosh (1975) pointed out that learning to ignore irrelevant stimuli may be as much part of selective attention as learning to pay more attention to those stimuli which are useful. The term 'latent inhibition' is usually used for cases where, for instance, unrewarded presentation of a buzzer retards subsequent learning that the buzzer is a signal for food. If this is interpreted as due mainly to habituation of attention to the initially irrelevant signal, then clearly the effect should apply just as well to discrimination learning. Halgren (1974) reported that prior exposure to either the positive or the negative stimulus retarded learning of a subsequent discrimination. 'Learned irrelevance' may refer to a stronger effect, in which a stimulus and a reinforcer are both experienced prior to conditioning, but with no correlation between them (Baker and Mackintosh, 1977). Thus if a dog receives food occasionally and hears a buzzer occasionally, without any statistical relationship between one and the other, it may be even slower to respond to a signalling relationship when one is introduced than a dog that has merely become habituated to a tone without food. Mellgren and Öst (1969) showed that the same effect occurs in the context of discrimination learning, in that rats which experienced alternations of a tone and a light, with water reinforcements given at random during both, afterwards took longer to learn to press a bar for water during one stimulus but not during the other, by comparison with others that had the same prior experience of the stimuli but without random reinforcements. Generally speaking, either as a function of habituation (in a particular context) or as a function of habituation due to lack of correlation with reward, the decline in attention to a stimulus dimension has similar consequences in straightforward conditioning (with one positive stimulus) or in discrimination learning (with one positive and one negative stimulus), and the same theory, whatever its details, could apply in both cases (Mackintosh, 1983, p. 251).

Learned relevance and attentional sharpening

With learning to pay *more* rather than less attention to a particular set of stimuli, something remarkably different occurs when one negative (non-rewarded) stimulus is added to one positive (rewarded) signal, as Pavlov (1927, p. 117; see p. 265 above) first pointed out. This brings up the question of 'what is the stimulus?', the complete answer to which, it was said long ago (Stevens, 1951, p. 31), would solve all the problems that there are in psychology. The answer is therefore unlikely to be an easy one. But it is worth emphasizing that 'the stimulus' which in theory becomes more effective, more associable, or has more attention paid to it, is difficult to define, both for the subject of an experiment and for the theorist. If a light signals the arrival of a food pellet to a rat, is it the position of the light bulb, the overall change in light intensity, or the shadow cast, that is important? There is more than one answer, since different animals, and different experimenters, may quite justifiably come to different conclusions. Now, if a light on the left signals food, but a similar light on the right does not, the number of possible answers to Stevens's famous question is reduced. Even more so if, for one of Pavlov's dogs, a metronome which has only clicked at 100 beats a minute before food deliveries now beats half as fast and there is no food. Before this contrast was introduced, a dog, and therefore an experimenter, had no way of knowing whether the speed of click was important, whether a click was needed at all or if any noise from that direction would do. Once a single alternative stimulus has been introduced, it can then become clear to the receiving animal that the rate of clicking is a relevant part of the correct signal. Given a big enough range of perceptual capacities in the receiving subject, then in a sense a stimulus dimension *has* to be defined by two separate stimulus instances, just as a line must be defined by two points. And in attentional theory, it is first a dimension, or rather dimensions, of the outer environment that must be specified.

The method of contrast between two stimuli can in practice sharpen attention to a particular stimulus dimension or quality, so that the exact rate of clicking of a metronome will have a pronounced effect on the exact number of drops of saliva secreted by the Pavlovian dog (see 'intradimensional shifts, p. 267 above). It is possible also that differential reward and punishment may set up particular values on stimulus dimensions as being especially wanted (or unwanted). The animal may not so much be paying attention to clicks in general as waiting hopefully for clicks of 100 but not 50 beats per minute. The dog listening to his master's voice is not so much sampling various phonetic dimensions as identifying a particular pattern of sound, which is very probably associated with characteristic patterns of smells and sights as well.

Information-processing strategies

A dog given food after tape recordings of its master's voice could be said to be undergoing a simple conditioning procedure, but might very well encode the information received in an unnecessarily complex fashion, because of its prior experience (and innate dog-like predispositions): the use of a simple conditioning procedure does not guarantee only simple responses to it (Davey, 1983, 1986). However, other things being equal, the procedures of discrimination learning are such as to allow and to encourage the development of more complex processes of perception and learning than those which might on occasion suffice for the acquisition and extinction of a simpler conditioned response (Mackintosh, 1983, chapter 9). The procedure of repeating simultaneous, two-choice discriminations, with an endless succession of pairs of objects, may, it has been argued here, result in the development of a strategy of taking detailed note of the results of the immediately preceding choice, in a way that does not occur *ab initio* and which may never occur at all in sufficiently lowly species (see 'Learning set, pp. 270–4). When a two-stimulus discrimination procedure is modified into a four-stimulus task (peck at the red triangle or the blue circle; but not at the blue circle or the red triangle) then new (and not yet answered) questions arise about the possibility of learning configurations, as the conjunction of specified levels of more than one dimension, and the alternative possibility of using individual levels of one stimulus dimensions to set global or particular scans in motion (if blue respond only to small circles; if red responding according to angularity). Thus various procedures under the heading of conditional discriminations can be expected to arouse internal reactions to environmental circumstances that may be conveniently described (although by no means satisfactorily explained) by reference to strategies of information-processing. This also applies to the evidence described below, in which the behavioural procedures may be as straightforward as is possible for discrimination learning, but the classes of stimuli chosen require that theories be couched in terms of pattern recognition, and perceptual complexity.

Perceptual complexity in animal learning

The natural environment of most species tested in the animal laboratory requires perceptual capacities vastly different from those engaged merely by tones of different pitch, or lights of different colours. For instance, recognition of individual conspecifics, for species such as the pigeon or monkey which do not take much interest in smells, is roughly as demanding a task for them as it is for us, although they may not necessarily accomplish it in precisely the same way. It should not therefore occasion much surprise or alarm if these species, when presented with discrimination tasks of the same order of difficulty as those which they are confronted with in the wild, display considerable expertise. On the contrary, this provides an opportunity for framing and testing hypotheses about discriminatory capacities which are more closely related to a species' evolutionary and ecological opportunities than those of traditional learning theory. Visual pattern recognition, of one sort or another, takes up most of this section, since it is both theoretically challenging and practically convenient. Many animals specialize in touch (especially via whiskers) or olfaction, as opposed to vision, and these modalities are not as extensively researched. However, it is possible to quote evidence from hearing to begin with, to demonstrate that perceptual complexity is not exclusive to the modality of vision.

Music discriminations by pigeons and speech perception by monkeys

A rather charming report by Porter and Neuringer (1984) suggests that pigeons' responses to auditory events may be more complex than is usually assumed, on the grounds that several individual birds were demonstrated to respond differentially to any of Bach's 'Toccatas and Fugues in D minor and F' on the one hand, and Stravinsky's 'Rite of Spring' on the other. This is not a very powerful reason for assuming similarity between pigeon and human hearing, but the experiments performed suggest that auditory pattern recognition in the pigeon may go beyond coos and clicks. With many other birds apart from *Columba livia*, we should expect sophisticated hearing because of their own vocal productions; although pigeons' own vocalizations are limited, they are distantly related to parrots, and have no noticeable degeneration of the auditory apparatus.

After some preliminary relevant experience, the birds used by Porter and Neuringer (1984) were tested in the following manner. In a conventional Skinner box, tape-recorded music was played continuously, either from the 20-minute selection of Bach organ music, or from Stravinsky's 'Rite of Spring' for orchestra. These two alternatives alternated at random intervals, but on average once per minute. During Bach, pecks on the left key were occasionally rewarded by access to grain (VI-30 seconds), but right-key pecks were not; conversely, while the Stravinsky was playing, right keys occasionally paid off, but left-key pecks were wasted effort. Occasionally, novel pieces of music were inserted: pre-1750 works by Buxtehude, Scarlatti and Vivaldi for organ, harpsichord and violin and orchestra respectively; and twentieth-century pieces for organ and chamber group, plus Stravinsky's 'Firebird Suite' for orchestra. The results were that performance on the standard Bach v. Stravinsky was reasonable but not perfect, about 70-75 per cent of responses being made on the correct key. It is impossible to say exactly what auditory cue or pattern of cue was responsible for the results. Overall loudness was controlled, but it is likely that harmonic differences between organ and orchestra were detected, since during Vivaldi excerpts all the birds made 80 per cent of their pecks on the right (Stravinsky) key. However, this cannot have been the only source of discrimination, since the pigeons did the same thing when they heard the modern piece for organ, Walter Piston's 'Chromatic Study on the Name of Bach'. It is certainly not necessary to conclude that pigeons have any notion of musical style; but it is equally unnecessary to assume that their auditory system can detect only pitch and intensity, and nothing about sound patterns. Others have shown that the chinchilla (a not especially vocal rodent) can discriminate human speech sounds; or to be more specific, that the stop consonants 't' and 'd' can be successfully used as positive and negative stimuli in a discrimination task (Kuhl and Miller, 1975). However, the training required the animals to distinguish 't' and 'd' sounds associated with three different vowels, and as produced by four different talkers, and the discrimination generalized to new talkers and other vowels. Further evidence indicated that the rodents, like humans, detected the difference between these voiced and unvoiced consonants on the basis of the timing of the onset of voicing, and did this also, at slightly different boundaries, for the other stop-consonant pairs of 'b' versus 'p' and 'g' versus 'k'. Rhesus monkeys have also been trained to discriminate 'b' from 'p' and 'g' from 'k', using synthesized speech stimuli that are convincing for people (Waters and Wilson, 1976) and, without training, strongly react to changes between 'd', 'b' and 'g' during an habituation series (Morse and Snowdon, 1975). The primary interest of these studies is in suggesting that experience of producing speech sounds oneself, though undoubtedly helpful, is by no means necessary for the accomplishment of basic phonetic auditory discriminations, and that the evolution of any specialized human subsystem for speech perception must have been made very much easier by the fact that mammalian auditory pathways were already capable of prerequisite forms of categorization. None the less, these results are equally useful in emphasizing that few perceptual systems evolved under pressures to detect differences between pure tones, or between black and white cards. On the contrary, perceptual systems evolved while they performed complex but necessary discriminations in natural environments, such as immediately detecting the location of the sound of a cracking twig, which requires binaural comparisons (either for time of arrival, or frequency spectrum differences; Harrison, 1978). Thus it may be necessary to use naturalistic stimuli in order to discover some of the essential characteristics of discrimination learning. Conversely, discrimination learning techniques may be useful in analysing the bases of natural perceptual abilities. It comes as no surprise, for instance, that monkeys can learn an auditory discrimination task which requires them to respond differentially according to the functional category of the tape-recorded cries of their own species, but specialized laboratory techniques are needed in order to assess whether they might have a right ear advantage in this task, as people do for human speech (Peterson *et al.*, 1978), and more directly, whether left-hemisphere rather than right-hemisphere lesions cause greater reductions in the accuracy of performance (Heffner and Heffner, 1984).

Visual pattern recognition

The method of operation of biological visual systems presents several puzzles, since they still outperform artificial apparatus by a wide margin (Marr, 1982; Frisby, 1979; Ballard *et al*, 1984; Feldman, 1985). Visual discrimination learning by animals provides necessary evidence about the limits and the plasticity of recognition performance, and its relation to specific physiological mechanisms, and has added theoretical interest because it separates visual perception from language, and from any other uniquely human cognitive specializations.

Letter stimuli

Recognition of letters is an example of this – although there
can be no human specialization for letter perception, as there
might be for speech perception, human letter recognition must
be more than a visual detection task, as it is bound up with
the skills of reading and language, and the phonetic organization of speech. Both Morgan *et al.* (1976) and Blough (1984)
have examined letter perception in pigeons, where neither of
these complications need be considered.

Morgan *et al.*'s procedure was unusual in that free-living
pigeons responded to stimuli projected to a screen in a
window of a laboratory, but apart from this the training
followed a conventional GO/NO GO discrimination schedule.
Positive stimuli alternated with negative stimuli, each
projected for varying intervals averaging 30 seconds. At the
end of positive stimuli only, rewards were obtained by pecking
the stimulus screen. During training, positive stimuli could
be any of 18 different 'A's, and negative stimuli any of 18
different '2's, differing because they were made up from
different typefaces. When birds were clearly responding very
much more to positive than to negative stimuli, new 'A's and
'2's from 22 further typefaces were introduced, each presented
only once. All birds continued to respond vigorously to 'A's
but not to '2's with little difficulty despite considerable variation in the appearance of the new 'A's (see Figure 8.5).

This suggests that something about the pattern of an 'A'
was being distinguished from something about the pattern of
a '2', but does not provide much information about how
this discrimination might have been accomplished. Further
evidence was sought by presenting partial and rotated forms
of 'A's and '2's. An inverted 'A', an upright 'A' with no cross
bar and an upright triangle all elicited a high response rate,
but on the other hand 'A's lying on their sides and an inverted
triangle were hardly responded to at all. After this two birds
were tested with all the letters of the alphabet in the same
unelaborate typeface (Helvetica Medium). The order of preference was   R,H,X,K,W,N,M,B,U,Y,T,F,D,V,O,P,Q,E,S,
C,G,I,J,L,Z, with the first nine letters (R – U) eliciting
appreciable responding and the last nine (Q – Z) virtually

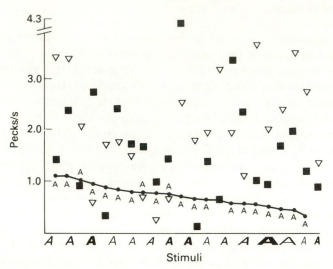

Figure 8.5   *Discrimination of 'A's in 22 typefaces.*
Rates of response for 3 pigeons to slides of the letter 'A' in 22 novel typefaces. All had previously been trained to respond to 'A's, but not to '2's, in 18 other typefaces. The scores for the 3 birds are plotted as circles, squares and triangles, with the stimuli ordered according to the responses plotted as circles. After Morgan *et al.* (1976).

none at all. As the authors of this report point out, there does not appear to have been a single feature of the stimuli which determined response. However, the features of 'legs' and 'apex' in positive stimuli, and 'curvature' and 'flat bottom' in negative displays, would go a long way towards accounting for the results of transfer tests, apart from the relatively high level of reponse to 'B' and 'U'. Therefore, they argue that the basis of the pattern recognition performance is not a single critical feature, but rather a 'polymorphous concept' utilizing several features, which may occur in several combinations.

Blough (1982, 1985) used a choice procedure to train pigeons to in turn discriminate each letter of the alphabet from all other letters. The target letter, suppose 'E', could appear on any one of three keys, and another distractor letter, say 'O' would be in the other two positions, the distractor letter varying from trial to trial. A limited amount of time was given with each of the 26 letters as a target, so that error data was used from a stage when easy pairs (e.g. E and O) were usually distinguished correctly, but difficult pairs (e.g. U and V) often confused. Computer programs were then used to analyse the error data. These confirmed Morgan *et al.*'s (1976) suggestion that a number of different features are used by the pigeon for letter discriminations. Thus straight letters, such as I, T and L, were often confused with each other, and there were also clusters of confusions around M,N and W; A,R,P and B; C,G and S; and D,O and Q, which seem likely to be related to the features of oblique angularity, small enclosed regions, curved openness to the right, and large loops (Blough, 1984, 1985).

Human reaction time data also give this sort of picture of letter similarity (Podgorny and Garner, 1979). It is arguable that only extremely peculiar algorithms for letter recognition would not, but Anderson and Mozer (1981) have in fact proposed such a system for letter recognition, based on the counting of squares touched by standard letters on a standard-sized grid, and even this produces confusions between F and P, G and S, and N and W; but it also produced clumps such as G,O and S with V, and Q with Y, which can less obviously be derived from a feature analysis system (Neisser, 1967) for letter recognition.

Anderson and Mozer (1981) argue against the existence of specific feature analysers in the nervous system, and for a rather more diffuse and global method of categorization by inter-connected matrices of neurons. The data certainly supports the view that, if there are features analysed, then categorization such as that needed for letter recognition makes use of multiple features, in many combinations. An even more direct experimental demonstration of this has been provided by Gaffan (1977a) who trained rhesus monkeys on a form of GO/NO GO discrimination with the visual 'wordlike' displays of RIM, LID, RAD and LAM, as alternative positive stimuli, and RID, LIM, RAM and LAD, as alternative negative stimuli. The monkeys learned to respond to all four positive stimuli (being then rewarded by sugar pellets) and not to respond to any of the negative displays, with a high degree of accuracy (over 90 per cent correct trials). The point is that it would be impossible for them to do this by adding up positive and negative weights for any individual letter, or pair of letters, since all letters and pairs of letters were equally often positive and negative, as may be checked by inspecting the lists above. The only way to solve the problem is by learning to recognize each individual combination of letters – in Gaffan's terms, by using 'visual configurational cues arising from the interaction of the stimulus elements' (p.594) unless, as seems most unlikely, there is some mysterious visual property which is common to all of RIM, LID, RAD and LAM, and none of RID, LIM, RAM and LAD. It is thus fair to assume that the monkeys learned a number of different complex patterns, rather than one or two key features.

Picture stimuli

An appeal to the learning of complex patterns is hardly very satisfactory as an explanation for anything, and becomes even less useful when the patterns become large in number and variable in structure. A large amount of data from problems which answer this description has been reviewed by Herrnstein (1984, 1985) and Cerella (1982). Herrnstein and Loveland (1964) trained pigeons to distinguish coloured slides containing people from an otherwise similar set not containing people. With a conventional GO/NO GO successive discrimination procedure, 80 slides were presented to the birds each day, one at a time, for roughly a minute each, with a random order of those containing people and those not. Food rewards could be obtained by pecking a key only when slides containing people were being shown, and then only on a variable interval schedule (VI-1 minute). After several weeks of this training (by no means exceptionally long for a visual discrimination), the birds had a high response rate for most of the positive slides and a much lower response rate, in some cases zero, for the negative slides. It should be noted that this is not perfect or 100 per cent correct performance, but it is certainly sufficiently accurate to justify a claim for a categorization process depending on the presence of people; the phrase often used, but rarely clearly defined, is that 'pigeons have a concept of' people. This result appears to be replicable, and not artifactual (e.g. Mallott and Sidall, 1972) but has as yet no agreed theoretical interpretation (Herrnstein, 1985). It is quite clear, however, that the pigeon's capacity for classific-ation of large numbers of slides is not confined to detection of the human form. Herrnstein *et al.* (1976) used several hundred slides in each case to demonstrate classification on the basis of tree versus non-tree scenes, and similarly bodies of water versus none. They also showed learning of slides containing one particular person as against similar scenes containing other persons. There is a temptation to assume that the pigeon's recognition of water and trees is innate, but clearly no pattern recognitions schema or template for individual persons could be innate in the pigeon. There is also the question of how far previous experience before the experiment had established the discriminatory capacities then demonstrated. Herrnstein and de Villiers (1980) conclusively eliminated both the possibility of innate conceptual categories and the influence of previous individual experience by using a set of slides taken by a scuba diver, only half of which showed the presence of a fish. Thus although the perceptual *processes* involved in categorization and visual recognition may be innate (and probably are; Weiskrantz, 1985), the *content* of individual categories cannot possibly be, and therefore must be learned or constructed on the spot.

Cerella (1979, 1982) has performed similar experiments with pigeons, using line drawings of cubes, drawings of Charlie Brown and other characters from the 'Peanuts' comic strip, and silhouette outlines of oak and other trees' leaves. The birds are good at oak leaves, reasonable at whole or partial or scrambled sections of Charlie Brown, but no good at recognizing line drawings of cubes depicting the cube at a substantially different orientation from the one they had already learned. Cerella (1982) concludes that fairly local features of two-dimensional patterns are responsible for the categorical discriminations. This may be too limited a theory, but one of the results which led to it should be noted. With slightly more stringent conditions than in the other cases (requiring the birds to peck directly at the positive stimulus), it was possible for pigeons to make general classifications of any oak leaf outline as opposed to the outline of leaves from other trees, after having had only the experience of being rewarded for pecks at a single oak leaf, with no negative instances, that is without the benefit of the method of contrasts (see p. 265 above). On the other hand, under similar conditions birds failed to discriminate between one particular oak leaf and outlines of other leaves from the same species. This implies that the categorization process is not necessarily inductive, that is, it does not have to be cumulatively developed on the basis of numerous instances, providing that there is a strongly salient perceptual feature – in this case the lobulation of the oak-leaf outline.

As Herrnstein (1984) stresses, the results obtained in his laboratory are sufficient to contradict frequently expressed views of the type, 'the human visual system is the only effective pattern classification system known' (Howard and Campion, 1978, p. 32). But does this imply that we need to attribute to pigeons a large dose of high-level intellectual abstraction? Not necessarily. Herrnstein (1984) appeals to a rather powerful-sounding process of categorization. But Greene (1983) and Vaughan and Greene (1984) have provided evidence for a model which is weak on abstraction and very strong on visual memory, in order to account for the classificatory abilities of pigeons. The experimental result on which this model rests is that, after very extensive training, birds can perform adequately with up to 160 pairs of slides in the same procedure as the categorization experiments, but where there is no known category of pattern which links the set of positive or the set of negative slides (Vaughan and Greene, 1984). It is thus necessary to assume that pigeons can make use of a large visual recognition memory for individual slides, or individual features. Now, this would not in itself explain the transfer of classificatory performance when one set of already learned displays is replaced by a large new set (Cerella, 1982; Herrnstein, 1985). But there is a limit to the degree of physical difference between the already learned set in these cases and the transfer set. It is therefore not implausible to propose that what might be attributed to 'abstraction of a concept' is accomplished by a brute force

mechanism of exact memorization 'coupled with generalization along certain physical dimensions' (Vaughan and
Greene, 1984).

While this is a very useful theoretical model, it is less
explanatory than it appears to be, since a large role is given
to 'generalization' which in a sense is what must itself be
explained. It is likely, however, that visual memory is an
extremely important component of visual classificatory
performance, even if, as Lea and Ryan (1983) emphasize,
there is also good evidence for abstraction in the sense of
feature analysis, when known visual features of letters (in
quite different typefaces) can be isolated from experimental
data.

For comparison with human visual pattern recognition
performance it is undoubtedly more sensible to select data
from primates rather than pigeons (even though birds have
a superior ratio of visual ability to maintenance cost). There
is strong evidence that when great apes (chimps and orangutans) look at pictures, they recognize familiar objects in a
way which allows transfer to touch and manipulation, and
that this is more humanlike than rote memory of individual
pictures (Hayes and Hayes, 1953; Davenport *et al.*, 1973,
1975). However, there is relatively little data showing classificatory ability for large numbers of pictures in primates, by
comparison with pigeons. Schrier *et al.* (1984) have now
reported on the performance of stump-tailed macaque
monkeys in procedures closely analogous to those used by
Herrnstein and others with pigeons. Categories classified were
humans present or absent in slides, monkeys present or
absent, and the letter A versus the figure 2 in many typefaces.
It is, as always, difficult to make exact comparisons of the
performance of the different species in this case. Schrier *et al.*
summarize their data by saying that the level of transfer of
classificatory skill to new sets of slides of 'humans' and
'monkeys' was lower in their monkeys than had been reported
in pigeons, but seemed to have used a higher criteria for their
animals in that no response at all was allowed on negative
trials. The transfer tests make it quite clear, though, that the
monkeys had come to depend to a large extent on the learning
of individual slides during initial training, which would

support the application of Greene's (1983) rote-memory theory to monkeys. The monkeys appeared to have much greater transfer to the classification of 'A's versus '2's to new typefaces than they did with the more naturalistic categories, and for 'A's versus '2's Schrier *et al.* (1984) suppose that the performance of their monkeys was at least as good as that reported for pigeons. On the basis of Schrier *et al.*'s data, all that can be properly concluded about cross-species comparisons between pigeons and macaque monkeys is that there is as yet little evidence for substantial differences in performance in two-way classifications of large numbers of visual displays. For both species, however, theories of classificatory performance increasingly involve loose reference to visual memory. Further discussion of cognitive organization in animal memory will be found in the next chapter. However, it is appropriate here to mention the general theoretical contrast between accounts of pattern recognition based on template-matching and those which rely instead on feature analysis (e.g. Neisser, 1967), since the issues involved are very similar to those arising in the case of class-concept learning by some sort of abstraction of common features on the one hand or by rote-learning of all class members on the other. Yet another instance of a similar contrast is that between 'viewer-centred' and 'object-centred' internal descriptions in the computational theory of visual perception (e.g. Marr, 1982). In all cases it is arguable that templates, rote-learning and viewer-centred descriptions are inadequate by themselves, since we (or an animal) would need far too many of them to do any good, and in any case they could never help with novel examples of a known concept, mental rotations and other kinds of creative imagination, or simply with unusual or occluded views of a familiar object. Without denying the sense of these arguments, it is worth pointing out that the empirical evidence from discrimination learning experiments suggest that the rote-learning of large numbers of individual examples seems to be a common perceptual strategy, both in pigeons (Vaughan and Greene, 1984) and in primates (e.g. Gaffan, 1977b, p. 509; Schrier *et al.*, 1984). Recent physiological evidence obtained from primates points to the usefulness of relatively non-abstract, concrete representations of the visual scene. In the studies of Perrett *et al.* (1985) macaque monkeys were first extensively trained on a visual discrimination task. Real objects or photographs were presented behind a large aperture shutter. If either a monkey or a human face or head, at any angle or position, was seen, the experimental monkeys could lick a tube to obtain sweetened water. If any other class of object was seen (food, parts of the body, junk objects including a football, a fur coat and so on) then the monkeys were trained not to lick. Hence this is a form of the usual GO/NO GO discrimination task. When the monkeys were well-trained, recordings were made via brain electrodes from individual cells in the temporal lobe (in the anterior superior temporal sulcus). This is a long way from the main visual reception area, but has been known for some time to be an important site for visual categorization (Weiskrantz, 1974; Rolls *et al.*, 1977). Many cells were found which fired when faces or heads were shown, but did not fire or fired much less for other objects. There are many important aspects of the results obtained, since visual transformations that make it difficult for people to recognize faces (e.g. use of photographic negatives) reduced the response of face-sensitive cells, and it is thus likely that these cells correspond to a late stage in human face perception. However, for present purposes it is especially interesting that authors of these reports (Perrett *et al.*, 1985) stress the large proportion of cells sensitive to particular views of the head (e.g. either full-face or profile, viewed from above or below) and argue that viewer-centred descriptions may be valuable even at high levels of visual analysis. Faces may be something of a special case, since it is not clear that any object-centred description derived from a small number of canonical views would be able to generate adequate information about other views – it would be very difficult to predict someone's profile from knowledge of their full face, and much simpler to recognize profile and full face separately in the first instance. At any rate, this is what seems to happen in the brain of the monkey, on the evidence to hand.

It is a useful general point, that may apply to many other kinds of object recognition, that category identity may be established by pooling a number of very different descriptions.

This is what is implied by the term 'polymorphous concept'
– it has often been observed that a lower-case and an upper-
case 'A' have little in common, and that many easy-to-use
words, such as 'chair', 'dog', or 'game', apply to an extremely
wide variety of instances (Lea, 1984b). Thus what end up as
seemingly natural and homogeneous concepts may be held
together by initially quite arbitrary associations – flame and
heat going together only in so far as we have experienced
their conjunction. Associationists such as Hume and Hull
may have overstressed this possibility, but it remains true that
very general learning abilities, which allow for the stringing
together of initially unlike elements, may be exceedingly
useful in nature, and are certainly demonstrated by pigeons
and monkeys learning to identify certain letters with food
in laboratory experiments. Generalization across typefaces is
something different, and amounts to association by similarity
as opposed to association by contiguity. But in discrimination
learning at least, there may be no clear-cut point where arbitrary associations based on contiguity end and extensions and
generalization based on similarity begin, and therefore the
notions of template versus feature abstraction, or rote memory
versus concept learning, may turn out to be complementary
in practice, even though contradictory in theory.

Discrimination, attention and perception – conclusions

The main theoretical conclusion to be derived from the study
of animal discrimination learning is that processes which can
be referred to in terms of selective attention, while not necessarily absent from any other kind of learning, are made much
more obvious by specialized training techniques. Several
experimental results all point to differential sensitivity to
physically constant environmental cues caused by prior
experience, which has to be interpreted as a switching in or
out of internal perceptual processes, or at the very least as a
stage of learning which is separate from response selection,
and which results in changes to the effectiveness or associability of external stimuli. Most of these results are obtained
by transfer experiments of one kind or another – training with
one stimulus value shows up in generalization gradients along

many other values; there is transfer from easy to difficult cases or from one position to another on the same stimulus dimension; and attention to a stimulus dimension seems to transfer from one response requirement to another. But much more subtle and rapid variation in attentional processes can be inferred from performance on more complex discrimination tasks: both using conditional combinations of relatively straightforward stimulus dimensions such as colour or line orientation, and when the patterning of stimuli to be distinguished is sufficiently elaborate to require theories proposing that in one form or another a special set of stimulus dimensions is processed simultaneously.

9 Memory and cognition in animal learning

'If someone had bought a coat, but wasn't wearing it, we'd say that he didn't have it, but did possess it. – Well now, ask yourself whether knowledge, too, is something that it is possible to possess but not to have.'

Plato, *Theaetetus*, 197d

The meaning of memory

It is possible to use the word memory to refer to any conceivable kind of retention of information – wax tablets retain an impression of any words inscribed upon them, a lock stores an ability to recognize its key, and metallic oxides on videotapes or floppy discs can be made to function as memories for just about anything. The genetic material of all life forms can reasonably be regarded as consisting of memories of instructions for growth and structure, and the nervous systems of all animals as memories of instructions for behaviour. In some sense or other the brains of vertebrates record memories of events in the life of the individual animal. That is to say, events in the life of an individual animal will determine its future behaviour, and therefore a physical change must store information over the intervening period of time. But clearly, psychologists should want to know most about the kinds of changes responsible for human memory, and these are known to a large extent verbally and subjectively, and are therefore difficult if not impossible to be sure about in other species – which makes it dangerous to transfer the term memory to and fro between experiments on human and animal subjects.

For many years the dangers were acknowledged by reserving the term memory for the human case, allowing 'learning' to cover all cases of animal behaviour changed by prior experience. There is now however a very liberal use of terminology derived from work on human memory in the context of what was formerly called learning (e.g. Medin *et al.*, 1976; Roitblat, 1982; Roitblat *et al.*, 1984; Walker, 1983a). Is there any justification for throwing caution to the winds in this way?

Several of the experiments described later on in this chapter have attempted to replicate closely both the procedures and the results of investigations of human memory – thus we have probe recognition techniques revealing serial position curves in pigeons and monkeys (Sands *et al.*, 1984). There is no ground for assuming that similar-looking curves in error data necessarily imply similar casual mechanisms (Gaffan, 1983), but it is certainly more excusable to be making hypotheses about memory mechanisms when specialized techniques provide ostensibly supportive data.

Other theorists (Wagner, 1981; Honig, 1981, 1984) have found it convenient to adopt the phrases and assumptions of human cognitive psychology, even when discussing data of a reflexive type: Wagner (1978, 1981) attributing modifications of shock-induced eyeblinking in rabbits to rehearsal in short-term memory, and Honig applying a theory of working memory to temporal discriminations made by rats. While in some instances borrowings of this kind may seem premature, there can be no denying that an enormous amount of new experimental work and theoretical discussion has been stimulated by these theoretical developments, and therefore caution in accepting strong claims for animal memory mechanisms should be combined with tolerance for those who make them.

The wisest course, however, would seem to be to try to make distinctions between phenomena which most justify an appeal to memory mechanisms of a more or less human type, and those which can safely be attributed to humbler psychological processes, and perhaps left in the charge of some of the old favourites among principles of animal learning. For instance, the conditioning/extinction theory of animal discrimination learning, while failing to account satisfactorily for many of the more sophisticated achievements of higher vertebrates, may still be needed in cases involving their more basic responses (perhaps in metabolic and emotional conditioning) and might well provide the best explanation for all of the discriminatory performances of slugs (Sahley *et al.*, 1981; Carew *et al.*, 1983; see p. 353 below). As Thorndike (and Herbert Spencer and William James before him) was fond of pointing out, much human behaviour based on learning is habitual, in the sense that memories of the relevant prior experiences are either never available in the first place, or become progressively lost or unused. Since we do not need to explain all human learning in terms of memories it is unlikely that any concept of animal memory ought to be applied universally. Thus although there are advantages in the tactic employed by Roitblat (1982) and Hawkins *et al.*, (1983) of referring to all effects of experience on later behaviour as representations, and all representations as memories, I shall try to differentiate between habit-based skills and automatic performances, and behavioural phenomena which seem to call more strongly for an explanation in terms of representations which are conditional and flexible tokens of prior experiences, not tied to any particular response output (Walker, 1983a). Weiskrantz (1985) has drawn a similar distinction between 'reflexive' and 'reflective' psychological processes, reflexive processes being associations, however complex, between a stimulus and a response to it, and reflective processes being associations in which learned information can be ordered and re-ordered without any behavioural response occurring. Weiskrantz (1985) and Johnson-Laird (1983) have both stressed that conscious human memories can be seen as a system that monitors stored categorical knowledge and associations, and that an enormous amount of extremely sophisticated cognitive processing can and does go on in the human brain, remaining forever unmonitored. A cognitive representation might thus qualify as a reflective process by Weiskrantz's definition therefore without being subjectively and verbally remembered in the usual human sense, and to attribute any animal learning performance to retention of a cognitive representation does not necessarily imply that an identity with human psychological processes is being claimed (Terrace, 1985).

Nevertheless, a strong area of interest in studies of animal memory concerns questions about portions of brain anatomy that, when damaged, appear to result in disorders of memory in human clinical patients. The hippocampus, otherwise implicated in the storage of information about experienced events in theories of habituation (Sokolov, 1963, 1975; see pp. 50-2 in chapter 2) attracts most of this interest (O'Keefe and Nadel, 1978; Olton *et al.*, 1979; Gaffan, 1977b; Gaffan *et al.*, 1984c) although of course other brain structures, particularly the anterior thalamus, may lead to certain syndromes of memory loss when damaged and it is important to avoid the temptation of assuming that any single brain structure can perform a psychological function on its own. The anatomical and the behavioural evidence concerning hippocampal function can however take up the whole of very large books on its own (e.g. Gray, 1982) and therefore I will say very little about it here; but I shall mention the hippocampus occasionally in passing, and it is worth bearing in mind that one of the reasons for distinguishing between habit and memory is that different kinds of brain processes are apparently required for each – certainly there is considerable evidence that human patients with severe disorders of memory can continue to exercise old skills, can learn new ones, and can acquire, for instance, the ability to play a new tune on the piano, without having the usual human ability to recall recent events. (Starr and Phillips, 1970; Cohen and Squire, 1980). Learning how is not the same as learning that.

Memories versus maps of mazes

One of the most familiar differentiations between response-based habits or gradually acquired skills on the one hand, and more cognitive representations of experience on the other, is that made by Tolman (1948) between stimulus-response association and 'cognitive maps' as explanations for the learning of mazes. In chapter 5 I concluded that there was overwhelming evidence, from the phenomenon of 'latent learning' by casual exploration and from 'place-learning' tests, that spatial representations of geographical information are commonly the basis for correct performance by rats given maze tests. It is not sufficient however to suppose that all maze-learning involves memories rather than habits and leave it at that. In some cases, of course, stimulus-response habits influence maze performance, especially after long training. But there is also a very productive distinction to be drawn between firmly fixed geographical knowledge and comparatively transient memories of spatial experiences. We would normally say that we know *how* to travel from home to work and back again, by a variety of routes, but say we may vaguely remember *that* the hotel was on the second street on the left coming up from the beach when revisiting the scene of a brief and long-distant holiday.

A not entirely dissimilar distinction is possible between the relatively well-learned and permanent knowledge that rats have of familiar mazes, and their memory of moment-to-moment changes in the location of food rewards in those mazes, and of their own recent activities in them. This distinction has come most to the fore in the context of the effect of brain lesions on maze performance, and in the context of performance on a particular kind of apparatus known as a *radial maze* (Olton and Samuelson, 1976), discussed in chapter 5.

Performance on a radial maze.

The radial maze was used in the first instance as a test of recent memory. Olton and Samuelson (1976) in a paper titled 'Remembrance of places passed' described the behaviour of rats place on an elevated maze of the design shown in Figure 5.1. The point of this apparatus is that it allows for a direct and straightforward assessment of a rat's memory for where it has recently been. A rat is simply placed in the middle of the maze, with a single food pellet (out of sight) at the end of each arm. The most efficient thing for it to do is to go down each arm just once, retrieving all the food pellets with the minimum distance travelled. Olton and Samuelson found that with experience (after 40 tests) rats were almost perfectly efficient, choosing an average of about 7.5 arms in their first eight choices. Careful control tests established that they were not doing this by smelling the food, or smelling their own scent on previously used arms, but were using geographical landmarks of some kind in the room where the maze was placed (called 'extra-maze cues') to supply place-memories of their previous choices. The controls included rebaiting already tried arms, and confining the rat in the centre of the maze after each arm was explored, during a short period in which individual arms of the maze might be swopped over, so than an already tried arm could be put in a not-yet-tried place (Olton and Collison, 1979). Rats sometimes adopt a stereotyped response strategy on the radial maze of always going into the next arm around in a particular direction, but this is not at all necessary for efficient performance, as may be gathered from several of the other experiments with the radial maze mentioned below.

Reference versus working maze memory

In discussions of human memory, a distinction is often drawn between short-term and long-term memory. A similar distinction is drawn between forms of cognition which may contribute to maze performance by animals, although different authors have used different terminology here. Honig (1978), Olton *et al.* (1979) and Olton (1979) draw a distinction between 'reference memory', which contains information used on most or many trials on the maze, and 'working memory', which contains only information pertaining to a particular trial – that is, on the usual radial maze, working memory contains a record of the places the rat has been to and eaten a food pellet, during that trial or run. Thomas and Spafford (1984) refer to 'dispositional memory' for long-term information, which conveniently links with the possibility of long-term control and may be partly accomplished via routine habits, and 'representational memory' for more vivid short-term cognitions. Walker and Olton (1984) have however stressed that long-term information may be in the form of relatively permanent cognitive maps rather than individual response habits, and this is important since it means we have to allow both for cognitive maps of the environment and for a working memory of recent movements within that cognitive map.

These terms are to some extent interchangeable – I would find 'working memory' versus 'dispositional memory' the most versatile contrast – but of greater moment than the terms themselves is the fact that experimental evidence supports a distinction between two types of process, whatever names they may be given. Olton and Papas (1979) provided such evidence with an experiment on a 17-arm radial maze, which differs from the 8-arm version only in having more arms. This makes it more difficult for the animals to perform perfectly; the usually quoted maximum level of performance is 15 different choices in the first 17 choices (Olton *et al.*, 1977). Random selection of arms would allow for only 11 different arms in the first 17 choices, and it has been estimated that being able to make 15 out of 17 correct choices would actually require a memory of about 12 of the items (Olton, 1979). However accurate that may be, it is clear that performance on a 17-arm maze should be fairly demanding of memory capacity, and Olton and Papas complicated matters by using a procedure in which nine of the arms were always empty. Thus on a particular trial, a rat has to remember both not to go into any of the arms which have always been empty in the past, and not to go into any of the arms which always start off with food present but which have recently been visited. For some animals all the unbaited arms were bunched on one side of the maze; for the others they were randomly mixed with baited arms. The experimental data followed for two kinds of distinction between 'reference' and 'working' memory. Entries into the never-baited arms could be counted as errors of reference, and entries into already tried baited arms could be counted as errors of working memory; both kinds occurred and working memory errors became more likely as successive choices were made in a trial, whereas reference errors did not show this trend. (Reference errors were much more frequent in the 'mixed' group.)

Olton and Papas (1979) were interested in a second kind of distinction between reference and working memory errors. After training, they performed brain operations on all the rats, damaging parts of the hippocampal memory circuit (lesions to the fimbria of the hippocampus and of the fornix, the hippocampal output tract). Large memory-system lesions of this kind had much more effect on working-memory errors (increasing them substantially) than on reference-memory errors (which were unaffected). This supports an anatomical distinction between memory processes, with dysfunction of the hippocampal memory circuits strongly associated with errors attributable to lack of information about the recent past, with rats (Olton *et al.*, 1979). There is plenty of evidence that ordinary radial maze performance shows a severe and enduring deficit after memory system lesions, even though response skills and habits remain unaffected (Becker and Olton, 1982; Walker and Olton, 1979; Walker and Olton, 1984).

Memory-system lesions cause deficits in temporary memory

Lesions to the septo-hippocampal structures and pathways in the rat limbic system produce deficits in performance on a variety of tasks, many of which involve memory for spatial information. O'Keefe and Nadel (1978) thus proposed that in animals the hippocampal system is responsible for the formation of cognitive maps – that is, it is devoted to spatial information, but not to other kinds of memories. There is considerable evidence, however, that this is largely an acci-dental consequence of the ubiquity of spatial tasks in tests of memory given to rats (Olton *et al.*, 1979).

The general form of a test sensitive to memory-system damage in rats is to allow the animals to find food (Thomas and Spafford, 1984) or water (Sinnamon *et al.*, 1978) in a particular location, on a particular day, and then to give them a choice between going to that or to an alternative location very soon thereafter. Rats can learn to accurately repeat their previous choice up to two hours after learning trials (Sinnamon *et al.*, 1978), or can learn to repeat or not to repeat their immediately preceding choice in a T-maze, a few minutes later (Stanton *et al.*, 1984); but these abilities are severely impaired by memory-system lesions, even though the usual dispositions involved in attempting to solve the task

– running from the starting place to a goal site – remain unaffected.

In all these cases involving temporary memory for reward location, it is difficult to exclude the possibility that it is map-forming or map-reading abilities that have suffered, rather than a more general memory system. But there are other kinds of test in which spatial mapping abilities are less crucial, or in which they can be shown to be unaffected by memory-system lesions. Meck *et al.*, (1984) used tests of stimulus duration discrimination based on choice of pressing one of two levers, with a single location of rewards, and concluded that memory-system lesions interfere with the retention of either spatial or temporal information over a short (5-second) delay even though there is no effect on discrimination of the duration of a sustained signal. Ross *et al.* (1984) used the Pavlovian conditioning procedure developed by Holland and Rescorla, (1975; see chapter 3, p. 86) in which lights and/or sounds are used as signals that food is to be delivered at an unvarying location, rats being observed to jerk their heads from side to side when a sound signals food, and to rear up on their hind legs at the illumination of a localized light source, when this is the signal. Rats with memory-system lesions appeared to be perfectly well able to learn simple associations and discrimination of this type; but the lesions seemed to permanently prevent the formation of conditional discriminations requiring the sensitivity to the joint presence of two signals separated by a time interval (5 seconds again). Rats can usually learn that if a tone is sounded 5 seconds after a light signal has just been turned off, food is to be expected, but that the same tone sounded without a prior light signal is to be ignored; hippocampal damage prevented the initial learning or the subsequent continuation of this discrimination based on a serial but separated compound positive signal (Ross *et al.*, 1984).

There are thus selective effects of memory-system damage on tasks not specifically spatial, but specifically requiring temporary retention of information over time intervals. Walker and Olton (1984) provide evidence that memory-system lesions do not prevent success on spatial tasks, if these make use of relatively long-term spatial knowledge. They used

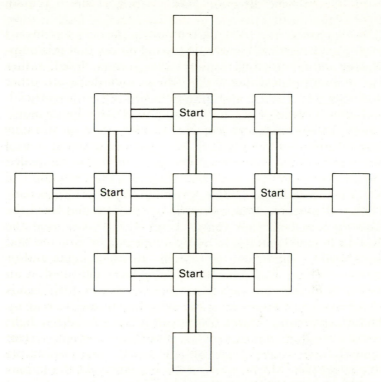

Figure 9.1 *A compound maze for working and reference memory.*
Spatial habits can be distinguished from spatial memory. If rats are
trained to run from all four start boxes, they can either be rewarded for
always going north (relatively difficult) or for always going to the central
goal box (relatively easy). Both these habits survive damage to the
hippocampal memory system of the brain much better than the ability to
choose whichever of 2 available paths from one of the start boxes had
been taken a few seconds previously. After Walker and Olton (1984).

a difficult form of maze with 12 separate locations divided
into four starting points and eight goals (see Figure 9.1) In
one spatial task, rats had to learn to always go to the centre
goal box, being trained with two choices from each of three
of the four possible starting places, and given transfer tests
from the fourth. In a second spatial task, rats learned always

to run in the same direction (say north in Figure 9.1) from
three of the starting places (in this case finding food in three
different goal boxes), being tested for transfer by being placed
in the fourth starting box with the usual two choices available.
Walker and Olton (1984) report that the same-direction task
was more difficult to learn than the same-location task, but
that rats could learn and transfer correct performance on
both these tasks after memory-system lesions (fimbria/fornix).
Similar lesions prevented correct performance on a spatially
much simpler task, using just two goal boxes and two start
boxes of the same apparatus, which required rats to choose
(or not to choose) the goal box they had been rewarded in
on an immediately preceding forced-choice information trial.
Thus a distinction between working memory and reference
memory is sustained for spatial tasks. It has to be admitted
that the lesioned animals in one of Walker and Olton's (1984)
experiments took as long to relearn spatial tasks after brain
damage as they had done to initially learn the same tasks
before the operation and there may be some spatial tasks
which are too difficult to learn after hippocampal damage.
The Morris muddy-water test requires rats to learn to swim
to an invisible underwater platform in a circular tank.
Animals with severe hippocampal damage seem not to be
able to do this (Morris *et al.*, 1982). It may be that the only
way for a rat to find the invisible platform here is to remember
exactly where it was on immediately preceding tests, with
respect to distant cues, dispositional habits being of less use
for free-swimming than for running down narrow paths in
mazes. In any event it is not necessary to assume that the
hippocampal system is never useful in spatial tasks in order
to reject the hypothesis that this brain structure is used exclusively for spatial knowledge.

Alternative views of connections between limbic systems and memory

I have endorsed the claim of Olton *et al.* (1979) that maze-
learning and other tasks performed by rats provide evidence
for qualitatively different processes of memory, with brain
systems centred on the hippocampus providing an anatomical

key to the difference, as damage to these appears to selectively disturb the proper functioning of working memory, or the temporary information store. It is fair to say that there are conflicting claims. Gray (1982) has proposed an elaborate theory in which the septo-hippocampal system is functionally related to anxiety, although since the central assumption in this theory is that the septo-hippocampal system acts as a comparator for actual and expected events Gray is able to incorporate results which support the working memory hypothesis into his grander scheme. It is unlikely in the extreme that the limbic system as a whole is involved only with memory processes, since many kinds of motivation and emotion are related to limbic function as well (Green, 1987), but for present purposes, the main point is that some kinds of limbic damage produce selective behavioural effects, showing a distinction between long-term behavioural disposition and moment-to-moment temporary memory. Mishkin (1978, 1982) has on anatomical grounds suggested wider brain circuits, involving notably the amygdala, ought to be involved in all memory functions.

Outstanding alternatives to the working memory hypothesis remain O'Keefe and Nadel's (1978) proposal that hippocampal damage always and only affects spatial memory, Gaffan's (1974) suggestion that the crucial distinction is between associative learning and recognition memory, and Gaffan's more recent alternative theory (Gaffan *et al.*, 1984a, 9; Gaffan, 1985) that the line is between the learning of stimulus configurations and the learning of conditional motor responses, with damage to the hippocampus producing only 'an increase in confusability', as normally it 'keeps track of specific responses in specific contexts'. It is therefore premature to suppose that Olton *et al*'s (1979) working memory hypothesis is the final word on the matter, but some or other version of the temporary/long-term division of memory processes is likely to remain alive and kicking for a great deal longer (see Rawlins, 1985). We may note that the results reported by Gaffan (1977b, 1977c) still give some support to the notion of a temporary store for fairly recent experiences; while the new evidence provided by Gaffan (1985) does not unequivocally contradict it.

Gaffan (1977b) trained monkeys to observe the same 25 coloured slides every day, each presented twice in a random sequence, the animals only being rewarded if they pressed a response button several times during the *second* presentation of any slide. After considerable training they were able to distinguish between the first and second presentations of all individual slides with 90 per cent accuracy (during the middle part of the session) even when an average of nine other slides might have intervened between the two sights of the same picture. Disabling the hippocampus (by lesions of the fornix) produced a devasting loss in this ability, even though the monkeys were able to recognize the pictures and respond correctly when the same slide was shown twice in succession. A similar pattern of medium-term memory loss with intact very short-term recognition was apparent when monkeys were shown lists of one, two or three colours before a 'probe' item which they had to respond to differentially according to whether it had been on the list or not. (Gaffan, 1977c). Fornix-lesioned monkeys had difficulties in identifying the earlier colours in lists of two or three, even though they were able to perform normally with lists of one. Difficulties in this sort of task are primarily due to interference between lists, which is especially prominent when lists of different lengths are used (Wright *et al.* 1984b; see below) and therefore it is difficult to sort out the relative contributions of absolute time values as opposed to number of confusable items as limiting factors in the hypothetical temporary store, as has been apparent for many years in studies of human short-term memory (Gregg, 1986).

Gaffan *et al.* (1984a, 1984b, 1984c) report the results of several experiments, which have led them to emphasize a distinction between the learning of actions and automatic dispositions to respond to standard stimulus configurations. In the first place several experiments show that fornix-lesioned monkeys perform as normals on tasks in which varied stimulus rules have to be rote-learned. For instance, in a Wisconsin General Test apparatus (see p. 271) they learned to choose one member of five pairs of junk objects if they were given a free reward to start with, but the alternative member of these five pairs if they were not. This demonstrates an impressive storing of information, but it is of a long-term, dispositional or 'reference memory' kind and therefore is consistent with the view that only temporaily relevant information should become unavailable after this kind of memory system lesion (Walker and Olton, 1984; Rawlins, 1985). It was also the case however that fornix-lesioned monkeys performed unexpectedly badly on two tasks in which the nature of the response might plausibly be thought to be one of the items that needed to be remembered. In one task 60 objects were presented singly in random order each day, half with a reward under them and half not. Following this phase (which was split into six lists of 10), the same objects were presented as pairs. The monkey's task was to choose only those members of these pairs which had *not* just recently been rewarded. In this case lesioned animals performed badly, though not disastrously, while in an otherwise identical experiment in which the choice rule was to choose objects which *had* just been rewarded, they were not impaired. The problem for the working memory hypothesis is only to explain why no impairments were seen in the second case, but it would not seem particularly surprising if a rapid Thorndikean stamping-in process provided a mechanism for repeating rewarded (but not unrewarded) choices in the absence of working memories of the previous choices themselves. A second task which proved difficult for fornix-lesion monkeys was to choose (in a WGTA) always the left-hand choice of one pair of objects, but always the right-hand member of a second pair. Thus correct choices were the left-hand member of A:B and B:A, but the right-hand member of C:D and D:C. It would have been difficult to predict that impairments of working memory should reveal themselves on this task but not the conditional choice among members of five pairs of junk objects referred to above (p. 314). However, it is clearly a task which involves conflicting rather than consistent cumulative response dispositions (sometimes A is chosen, sometimes B, sometimes the correct response is left and sometimes right) and therefore it is at least possible, if not conclusive, to suggest that unlesioned animals made fewer errors than lesioned monkeys in this case because they were able to consult working memories of the precise outcomes of individual previous trials.

Gaffan *et al.* (1984b, 1984c) propose that the special property of memory that is affected by fornix lesions is memory of response actions as opposed to any kind of memory of the presence or absence of objects. It certainly seems to be the case that monkeys thoroughly trained before this lesion, even on quite difficult tasks, are able to sustain or even improve on a high level of correct performance. Monkeys shown two objects, say A and B, without any reward, but then rewarded if they choose these two from immediately following pairs with alternatives (i.e. from A with C and B with D), could perform this task at a level of 80 or 90 per cent correct after fornix lesions. Gaffan *et al.* (1984c) interpret this to mean that the lesions did not impair the working memory of the stimulus objects seen at the beginning of a trial, a conclusion it is difficult to avoid. However, it is not inconceivable that correct performance would be obtained on this task by an automatic learning strategy which did not require working memory. Whatever this might be, it did not appear to be possible when two monkeys were given a test which could be solved on the basis of memory of their own responses. At the beginning of each trial one object (A) was presented over a baited foodwell and the monkeys pushed it away in order to retrieve a peanut. Then a second object was presented 8 cm behind the baited foodwell – the animals reached out for the peanut but did not have to touch this second object (B). Then they were given a choice between A and B, the correct choice being to choose A, which they had just touched. The two animals were each about 10 per cent worse on this task after than before fornix lesions, and one of them was about 10 per cent worse on a more difficult version of this task (which the other animal could not perform even before the lesion). This is a rather limited amount of data on which to reject the more general 'working memory' interpretation of hippocampal function, but it may very well be that memory of the animal's own activities often, but not always (e.g. Ross *et al.*, 1984), forms a prominent part of the memory content which is disturbed by surgical damage to the hippocampal system.

Comparison of present with recent stimuli, and the serial position effect

The working memory hypothesis implies that the retention of temporarily relevant information over short periods (which may be in seconds, minutes, or even hours) is subject to different constraints from those which apply to the longer-lasting retention of information in the case of motor skills, or of habits or dispositions of responding to standard stimulus configurations, even those which may take quite complex forms, as in a reference memory of spatial knowledge. Within this hypothesis, it is quite possible that several shorter-term processes contribute to working memory – for instance, there may be modality effects with special characteristics of short-term retention of visual auditory or olfactory information, and also stimulus dimension specificity, with selective attention to, for instance, the analysis of colour and shape (see pp. 275-9 above). In human short-term memory, there are undoubtedly many effects which depend upon verbal factors, and to some extent the whole system can be regarded as a device for the receipt and output of speech, involving a unique degree of similarity between stimulus items and response items. Tests of human memory may appropriately rely on measuring verbal recall. Mishkin (1982), among others, has proposed that all mental associations might be considered as forms of recall, and that therefore there is a neural hierarchy of separate systems for recognition of individual stimuli and associations with other events in animal brains, but for purposes of experimental measurement there are no worthwhile analogies to verbal recall available for studies of animal memory, except in 'language-trained' chimpanzees (see below).

Therefore, studies of temporary memory in animal learning have had to rely very heavily on recognition techniques, though it is of course possible to devise tests of an animal's memory for its own recent actions (Morgan and Nicholas, 1979; Shimp, 1976, 1984).

Delayed matching-to-sample procedures (DMTS)

A standard procedure by which temporary retention of information may be investigated requires merely the insertion of a delay between the sample stimulus and the two comparison choices in the matching-to-sample procedure described in the previous chapter (p. 278). If a centre key is lit red, but then goes out for a minute before two side keys are lit red and green, and a pigeon pecks the red side key reliably (but would equally peck green if the sample had been green), then we have good grounds for assuming that temporary information is retained in some way during the delay interval, although there is nothing in this basic result to indicate in what form the information is retained. The simplest suggestion is a trace theory, which supposes that an internal analogue of the sample decays gradually, and remains available at the time of choice to direct a matching (or non-matching) decision (Roberts and Grant, 1976). There has been general agreement, however, that theories of this type do not suffice even to explain the delayed matching performance of the pigeon, since for the pigeon 'what's past is prologue', and sample stimuli initiate active remembering in specific codes of 'what to do next', as much as of 'what just happened' (Carter and Werner, 1978; Honig, 1981; Grant, 1981; Maki, 1981; Roitblat, 1982; Urcioli and Zentall, 1986).

The sort of performance which might initially suggest a simple trace theory is shown in Figure 9.2. Well-trained pigeons were shown single samples that might be red, green, blue or yellow, at various intervals before being required to choose between red/green or blue/yellow pairs of side keys (in random left/right positions) with the length of sample-presentation time varied from day to day. As Figure 9.2 demonstrates, even without any delay (the choice being made available as soon as the sample was turned off), performance was only 100 per cent correct with the longest sample presentation of 14 seconds, declining to 80 per cent with 1-second samples; and this difference was retained when long delays were required, all samples being followed by less accurate choices as the retention delay was increased to 60 seconds. Such regular data, and the sharp drop in accuracy with delays of only a few seconds, suggest a process of temporal decay. No one doubts that time makes a difference, but there is considerable evidence against any simple form of trace decay. First there is a proactive interference effect, since if a wrong

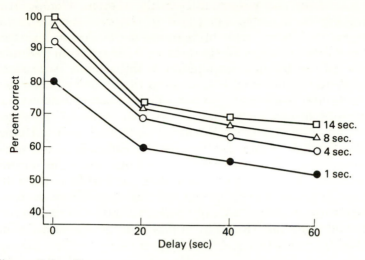

Figure 9.2   *Short-term memory in pigeons as a function of recency and stimulus duration.*
Per cent correct responses when pigeons were required to choose whichever of 2 colours had been presented at the beginning of a delay period. The length of the delay period is given on the horizontal axis and the duration of the stimulus presentation before the delay is indicated on the figure. See text. After Grant (1976).

choice has recently or often been right it is much more likely to be chosen (Roberts and Grant, 1976). Second there are retroactive inference effects of the type that brief changes in lighting intensity during the delay interval have a detrimental effect on performance, whether the changes are increases (Grant and Roberts, 1976) or decreases (Cook, 1980). Third, surprising (relatively rare) samples are better remembered over longer delays than when the same samples are usual instead of unusual (Roberts, 1980; Grant *et al.*, 1983), and fourth, there is a phenomenon called 'directed forgetting' (Maki, 1981), where on a proportion of trials a brief signal given after the sample normally indicates that there will be no choice to follow, and when choice stimuli are presented as probes after this 'forget' stimulus, accuracy is reduced.

These findings all suggest that what is remembered is not

an automatic and passive trace of the sample. That what is remembered is not in fact coded in terms of the sample at all, but usually in terms of prospective choices, is indicated in the first instance by the lack of necessity that eventual choices bear any obvious relation to the sample. After a red sample the animal could be required to choose a vertical, not a horizontal black line, and after a green sample the vertical (this sort of procedure may be referred to as a conditional discrimination, or as 'symbolic matching to sample'; Honig, 1984; Roitblat, 1982). Elaborations of this task to include a third easily confusible sample (e.g., orange) and a third easily confusible choice item (e.g., a nearly vertical line) allow for the observation that errors are more likely to reflect prospective coding of choices than retrospective coding of the sample, for both pigeons (Roitblat, 1982) and monkeys (Gaffan, 1977c).

The limits of temporary visual memory

The experimental procedures used to study retention over a delay by the conditional discrimination or matching-to-sample principles typically lead to the frequent presentation of the same small set of stimulus items, and typically suggest a retention span for accurate performance of the order of seconds for both monkeys and pigeons (D'Amato, 1973; D'Amato and Worsham, 1974; D'Amato and Cox, 1976; Roberts and Grant, 1976; Grant, 1981). Overman and Doty (1980) provided evidence to support the intermittently expressed suspicion that the second of these typicalities depends upon the first. To produce the standard result they used one pair of coloured slides. One member of this pair was presented on a centre display panel, and the subjects (macaque monkeys) were required to touch this 9 times; it then went off, and after a delay the pair slide was projected on two side screens (left/right randomized) and a reward of orange juice could be obtained by pressing the member of the pair which had most recently been given as the centre sample. Under these conditions accuracy was only 70 per cent with a 5-second delay, quickly declining to chance levels of performance at 30-second delay intervals (Figure 9.3). At the

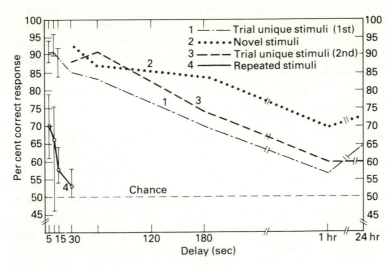

Figure 9.3 *Short-term visual memory in monkeys as a function of delay and interference.*

If only one pair of coloured slides is presented to monkeys, and they are repeatedly required to choose whichever one of these two had just been shown to them a few seconds earlier, their choice accuracy drops precipitously after 10 seconds' delay. However, if slides were used only once per day ('trial unique'), or if the correct choice was always a novel slide, then 'short-term' memory could be measured in hours instead of seconds. See text. After Overman and Doty (1980).

other extreme, the same monkeys had previously been tested under the constraint that every trial began with a novel slide, never seen by the animal before, and after the delay interval there was a choice between this once-seen slide and an alternative never-seen picture (most slides were of human artifacts: a shoe, a mug, spectacles and so on). Here, by contrast, performance was relatively resistant to temporal delays, even when the animals were removed from the apparatus after seeing the sample, and returned to it an hour or a day later (Figure 9.3). Only slightly less resistant was the monkeys' initial performance with a set of 100 slides used repeatedly for several days, but with each pair of slides being used only once a day. This would appear to be conclusive evidence that the time constraint on the memory processes assessed by sample and choice comparison procedures interacts very strongly with interference or confusibility between alternative possibilities, at least as far as visual cognition in primates is concerned.

Memorable attributes

Allowing that there may be active retention of prospective codes during a delay interval, and that confusions between several physically similar possibilities may lower the accuracy of choices, does not amount to a very strong hypothesis about the properties of the memory process involved. However, it is likely that at least one more specific proposition about the nature of the remembered representations can be rejected, namely the idea that these are restricted to physical imagery of the sample or the choice stimuli. Parkinson and Medin (1983) suggest this on the basis of experiments on the role of the novelty or familiarity of the stimuli used in delayed-matching-to-sample experiments with monkeys in the WGTA apparatus (see p. 271). Selections made from several hundred common manufactured objects repainted in uniform colours were used as stimulus categories: 10 objects seen repeatedly several times each day were designated 'familiar'; stimuli seen once within a day and not re-used for several days were 'novel'; and stimuli which were seen several times in a given day but only ever used on one day were termed 'moderately familiar'. Overman and Doty's (1980) result that accuracy is higher with novel than with familiar stimuli was replicated, but Parkinson and Medin (1983) also argued that the degree of familiarity itself became a discriminative cue, since the animals were highly accurate at always rejecting a novel choice, whether the sample had been itself novel, familiar, or moderately familiar. Also, with practice the monkeys became better at choices between a moderately familiar and a novel stimulus than they were at choices between two moderately familiar items. The experiment by Gaffan using repetitions of extremely familiar slides (1977a; p. 314) also suggests that fine distinctions in degree of familiarity can be available as cues for choice.

A much more direct suggestion that the immediate sensory properties of events are not the only contributors to memory processes can be obtained from the experiment of Weissman *et al.* (1980), who begin their report with a reference to William James's dictum that 'a succession of feelings, in and of itself, is not a feeling of succession'. On the basis of a carefully designed experimental procedure they are then able to conclude that pigeons can, at least briefly, remember a feeling of succession. The birds were required to distinguish between the sequence of orange followed by green and that of green followed by orange, indicating this by pecking at a vertical line after the former, but at a horizontal line after the latter. The fact that they refrained from pecking at various alternatives offered to them (without reward), such as two green flashes followed by a vertical line, or two orange flashes followed by a horizontal line, was sufficient to establish that detection of the temporal order of the two-event sequences, rather than alternative sources of information, was responsible for their correct discriminations. It seems probable that various selected attributes of stimulus events and various relationships between them, such as those discussed in the previous chapter (bigger than, brighter than, etc.: p. 260) might be retained as part of working memory processes and that memorial coding should be selective in very much the same way that attention to and discrimination of the remembered events is selective in the first place.

The serial position effect in choice and recognition

In human verbal memory, an extremely reliable difference between the accuracy of recalling words from the beginning, middle and end of a memorized list has been obtained in countless experiments, and this serial position effect has occasionally been used to provide purely behavioural support for a distinction between long-term and short-term memory stores which might rest otherwise on neurological data (e.g. Kintsch, 1970). It is usually assumed that words at the end of a list are remembered well just afterwards because they are still available in some kind of short-term store, whereas words at the beginning of a list have been stored elsewhere, but have the advantage of being put there first, thus acquiring a certain distinctiveness, and also suffering least from proactive interference. On this model, hippocampally damaged human patients suffer most from interferences, or have difficulties inserting new items into long-term memories, and can thus remember only the very end, but not the beginning, of a long list, and that only just after hearing or seeing it (Milner *et al.*, 1968: Weiskrantz, 1977).

Kesner and Novak (1982) described a procedure that would be theoretically capable of revealing serial position effects in rats, and report results, replicated by Cook *et al.* (1985), suggesting that it does so in practice. A radial maze (p. 144 above) is used, equipped with doors enabling the experimenter to allow access to only one of the eight arms at a time. A rat may thus be given the chance to enter the arms in a particular random order, and then given a choice between two of them, being rewarded only if it chooses the one it has least recently entered. After training animals to choose the first rather than the seventh arm in any random previous list of arms entered (an easy discrimination first, see p. 265 chapter 8) Kesner and Novak (1982) compared rats' performance in choosing the first over the second, the fourth over the fifth, and the seventh over the eighth, of any preceding list, finding that choices between the middle pair were at chance levels, but that the earliest of the first and last pairs could be chosen successfully, by normal rats. On the other hand, animals with hippocampal lesions never performed above chance on the first pair, and could only manage the last pair if tested just after they had experienced it. Slightly different methods of immediate testing have confirmed that more information is retained by rats about places in a maze they have most recently visited than about places visited earlier (Roberts and Smythe, 1979).

A more elaborate technique for obtaining serial position effects from visual recognition performed by monkeys was reported by Sands and Wright (1980a, 1980b). The animals were first trained on a simultaneous same/different discrimination, using 211 coloured slides of objects such as flowers, fruit and human artifacts. Slides were presented in pairs, one above the other. When an identical pair was shown, the

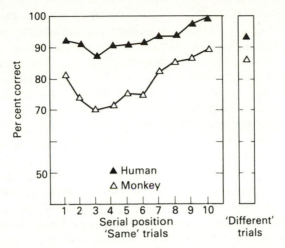

Figure 9.4   *The serial position effect in a monkey's memory for lists.*
See text. After Sands and Wright (1980b).

correct response was to move a lever to the right, and if, alternatively, the slides were obviously different, the same lever was to be pushed to the left. Various food rewards were given intermittently for correct responses. With sufficient training on this same/different principle, it was possible to move on to what is referred to as 'serial probe recognition', in which a 'list' of 10 slides were shown serially on the top screen, followed by a single slide on the bottom screen, and occasional rewards were obtained by pressing the lever to the right if the bottom slide had appeared on the previous top list, and to the left if it had not. The data resulting from this training are shown in Figure 9.4, along with data obtained from a single human subject performing without any reward or previous experience on the task. A more pronounced bowing of the serial position curve is apparent for the rhesus monkey than for the human subject, due no doubt to the ceiling affect produced by the greater accuracy of the latter. When the list was lengthened to 20 slides, the human and monkey curves became more similar.

What should be concluded from this result? First, we must note that both primacy and recency effects in similar procedures have been reproduced in other monkeys by Roberts and Kraemer (1981) and by Wright *et al.* (1984a) and in a chimpanzee by Buchanan *et al.* (1981), and that therefore the effect shown in Figure 9.4 is replicable. But does this mean that, as Wright *et al.* (1984a, p.527) conclude, such primacy and recency effects make it more likely that 'animals process information and think in ways basically similar to humans'? Only up to a point. Gaffan (1983) argues that quite different factors might be responsible for the production of the primacy effect in the monkey procedure and in human verbal learning, on the grounds that the monkeys were allowed to initiate all lists by depressing their lever on hearing a 'ready' signal. It is certainly true that this is likely to enhance attention to the first items on the list – one of the reasons for requiring animals to make a response before or after a stimulus is presented is to make sure that they notice it. However, as Wright *et al.* (1983) do not fail to mention in their rejoinder to Gaffan (1983), the primacy effect in human learning may be due to a variety of factors, among them greater attention paid to the beginning of a list, and the combination of both recency and primacy effects is unlikely to have a single cause in any species. There must surely be extra factors to consider in human performance: a superficially trivial matter mentioned by Santiago and Wright (1984) is that animals have difficulties in 'trial separation' whereas humans bring to all experiments a whole set of expectations, sets and attributions which may influence even the most basic of conditioning processes (Lowe, 1983; Davey, 1986). The now unfortunately common practice of referring to a hypothetical process of animal memory as 'rehearsal' should not disguise the fact that some at least of human verbal learning depends on a unique articulatory loop, to say nothing of deeper and more mysterious linguistic matters. Nevertheless, providing one retains a sense of proportion, it is not merely reasonable but obligatory to consider whether some of the phenomena of human cognitive performance might share both properties and causes with similar happenings observable in humbler species, and Sands and Wright (1980a) have every justification for urging that models of memory for complex images have much to offer to the comparative psychologist.

One of the strongest empirical points made by Sands and Wright (1980a) was that monkeys are more strongly influenced than people by the problems of confusion ('proactive interference') that arise from using the same stimulus items repeatedly. This seems to apply also to pigeons, since Santiago and Wright (1984) discovered that pigeons given the opportunity to look through a window of a Skinner box at the same slides as those used in parallel experiments on monkeys, projected on similar screens, were able to develop roughly similar serial position curves in the serial probe recognition procedure (see Figure 9.5). It should at once be said that Wright *et al.* (1984a, 1984b) were more than adequately seized by the differences between pigeon and monkey capabilities. (i) The birds showed little sign of generalizing their same/different responses (on right and left-hand keys) to new stimuli, whereas monkeys eventually showed near perfect transfer to completely new pairs of slides. (ii) The pigeons have so far only performed above chance on lists of four, whereas monkeys have got up to lists of 20. (iii) Monkeys appear to tolerate longer delays between the end of a list and its probe. (iv) Unlike the monkeys, pigeons demonstrated only random responding when lists of variable length were used. (v) As a plus for the pigeons, they showed no sign of developing the short cuts, circumventing the purpose of the experiment, which had to be guarded against in monkeys, such as memorizing correct responses to individual probes whenever this is possible, or making fast and correct 'different' responses to probes based on novelty. (vi) Summarizing these differences, Wright *et al.* (1984b) suggest that monkeys are better able than pigeons to quickly and flexibly adopt new and efficient cognitive strategies.

Therefore, the similarity of the data for monkeys and pigeons in Figure 9.5 should not be taken as reflecting a similar similarity in overall cognitive capacity. But it serves to indicate strongly that there may be reasonably general principles behind primacy and recency effects in probe recognition performance, of the archetypal form that the recency effect is based on a short-term or more transitory store, since

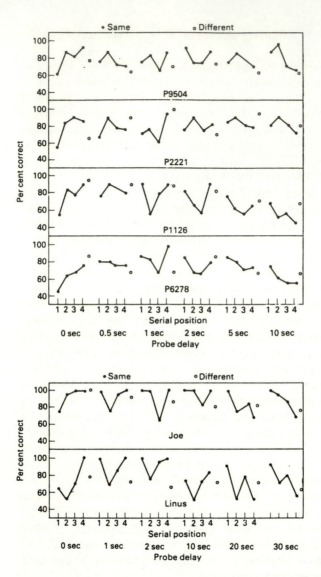

Figure 9.5 *Serial position effect in pigeons and monkeys as a function of probe delay.*

Serial position curves for 4 pigeons (above) and 2 monkeys (below) obtained using the same stimulus materials (coloured slides of objects) in lists of 4, and with various delays intervening between the list and the probe test, at which the animals were required to indicate whether a probe stimulus had been present in the previous list. See text. After Santiago and Wright (1984) and Wright *et al.* (1984a).

it is a decreasing function of delay, whereas the primacy effect is related to interference, attention, or possibly some form of consolidation, since it actually increases with time past since the list was seen, during the intervals under consideration.

The ecology of memory

It is not immediately obvious that the variations in memorial accuracy that produce the serial position effect have in themselves a useful function. It is more likely that they reflect general principles of the operation of memory mechanisms, which arise from natural necessities, but which are not specialized to particular species or particular tasks. It is a very general feature of perceptual systems that a change in stimulation is strongly marked, especially if it represents an increase, and thus the special attention given to the beginning of a list, in either storage or retrieval, is to be expected. Similarly, it would be difficult to design any perceptual system without some form of transitory sensory buffer, and recency effects should not therefore come as any surprise in studies of animal memory.

However, although specialized laboratory testing of memory may seem both very general and very artificial, few doubt that both the acquisition of a long-term store of knowledge (reference memory) and memory in the form of running commentaries on recent events (working memory) may serve useful purposes in real life. In the natural life of animal species the most obvious function of both kinds of memory is producing optimum patterns of foraging for food (Olton *et al.*, 1981; Krebs and Davies 1983; Olton, 1979). We may imagine a hypothetical animal which learns that food may be temporarily available at 10 different locations with a much larger territory (reference memory) and also takes note of which of these have been recently exploited (working memory). A special case of memory for food locations arises when animals themselves place food in particular hiding places, returning to retrieve it at a later date. The hoarding of nuts by squirrels is an example, though not one usually taken to indicate very efficient use of memory. In other species, however, rigorous experimental testing has indicated that memory for the location of hoarded food is very accurate. Shettleworth and Krebs (1982) studied the behaviour of captive marsh tits (*Parus palustris* – actually a woodland bird) in an artificial aviary, in which old tree branches had a total of 97 holes drilled in them and were covered with cloth flaps. An experienced bird placed in the aviary with a bowl of hemp seeds would hide 12 seeds in some of these hiding places (as well as eating other seeds) within seven or eight minutes. It was then removed from the aviary for two or three hours, before being allowed a 12-minute recovery test to see how many of the seeds it had stored it could find (the bowl of free seeds having been taken out). The average performance of four birds on this task was 8 out of 12 seeds recovered, with a total of 30 of the hiding places inspected, over a total of 12 tests each. This is very much less than perfect, but substantially better than chance. The birds did better at the beginning of a test – five of the first 10 holes inspected had seeds previously hidden in them, but there was no relation between the order in which seeds were stored and the order of their recovery. Occasionally the birds missed a seed even though they inspected the hole it was in.

In the course of a second experiment (Shettleworth and Krebs, 1982) birds were given two hiding places, a couple of hours apart – in each case a bowl of seeds was available and they were allowed to hide eight seeds before being removed. Then they were given a 12-minute retrieval test three hours after the second hiding phase. The first additional result here was that the birds almost never attempted to put two seeds in the same hole, even in the second hiding phase – this strongly suggests that they were avoiding already used sites, although the chances of revisiting one of the previous eight sites is fairly low, even at random. A second additional result was that some birds showed a tendency to find first those seeds which they had hidden last (that is, in the second storage phase). The data were not unequivocal for these additional results (the experiment was curtailed by the advance of spring – the birds only bother to hide food in the winter) but there seems little doubt that 'marsh tits can use memory for individual storage sites in recovering hoarded food' (Shettleworth and Krebs, 1982). For this species and other extremely small tits the rigours of winter must combine with the dangers of heat loss (due to their high surface area/volume ratio) to make it worthwhile for them to exploit occasional superabundant food sources by systematic caching. It is not clear, however, whether this requires a specialized development of memory capacities, as opposed to the specialized behaviour of hiding as well as eating food.

Crows, jays and other corvids often perform well on tests of learning and memory (e.g. learning sets, see p. 274). It appears that a certain North American corvid, Clark's nutcracker, may have developed a spectacular memory for the location of stored food, since in order to cope with the harsh winters of alpine environments it may store upwards of 30,000 pine nuts in 2,500 locations during the autumn, returning to these throughout the winter, during its early breeding season, and in some cases much later in the following year (Van der Wall, 1982; Balda and Turek, 1984; Kamil and Balda, 1985). Studies of individual captive birds suggest that non-local landmarks of some kind must be used in coding the location of food stores, since birds performed accurately if experimenters removed food or pushed away local signs when pine nuts had been buried under sand, but made systematic errors if obvious features of the test environment, such as logs and stones, were all moved (Balda and Turek, 1984). Since in the wild food caches are often retrieved when buried under snow, it seems necessary to assume that this species forms a particularly detailed cognitive map of its surroundings, possibly with food caches referred to particular large landmarks or 'focal points' (Balda and Turek, 1984).

That species other than those which habitually hide food may possess memory for food location in considerable detail is illustrated by the semi-naturalistic experiments reported by Menzel (1973, 1978) on chimpanzees who were thoroughly familiar with the test environment of a 1-acre field, having already lived in it for a year before the tests began. One straightforward test was to carry a single chimpanzee around the field to watch while 18 pieces of fruit were hidden by another experimenter in holes in the ground, tree stumps and so on, all the other animals having been removed and caged outside, allowing the observation that when all the animals (six) were put back in the field a couple of minutes later, the observer chimpanzee could demonstrate its remembered knowledge of the location of food by finding it (on average 12 out of 18 pieces), the uninformed animals providing a control comparison (and typically finding only one piece between them). The chimpanzees, like nutcrackers (Balda and Turek, 1984), are capable of re-organizing spatial knowledge, since they recovered hidden food according to a least-distance principle rather than in the order in which it was hidden (except when the food was half food and half vegetables, in which case they travelled greater distances in order to be able to recover fruit rather than vegetables first). Another example demonstrating some use of geometry was obtained when the experimenters adopted the device of hiding only two pieces of food, at symmetrically opposite locations about the midline of the field, drawn from the point where all animals were released into it, but with the exact position of the hiding places varying considerably from trial to trial. The same procedure of showing only one chimpanzee the hiding places on a given trial was used, but in this case the control animals were able to improve their performance by watching the test animal and, on seeing it find one of the two food locations, running directly towards the symmetrically opposite one (Menzel, 1978, p. 409).

Inference and intentional communication in *Anthropoidea*

Menzel (1978) reported a number of results which confirm the essential features of the observations of Kohler (1925): chimpanzees, given suitable opportunities for play and practice, demonstrate manipulations of objects which appear to indicate considerable knowledge of spatial relationships, and insights into how these may be altered. Thus some of Kohler's apes used sticks to drag in otherwise out-of-reach bananas on the ground outside their cage, and piled up old crates to reach an out-of-reach banana suspended from the roof.

The *Anthropoidea* is the suborder of primates made up of New World monkeys (*Ceboidea*, e.g. marmosets, capuchins and squirrel monkeys), Old World monkeys (*Cercopithecoidea*, e.g. rhesus, Japanese, pig-tailed or other macaques, baboons, guenons and langurs), and the *Hominoidea* superfamily which includes lesser apes (gibbons and siamangs), great apes (gorillas, chimpanzees and the orang-utan) and all the *Hominidae*, of which the only surviving species is *Homo sapiens*. The other primates, prosimians, including the lemurs of Madagascar, bushbabies and tarsiers, are mostly nocturnal, lacking colour vision, and smaller-brained than the *Anthropoidea*, and are phylogenetically earlier and more remote from human ancestry. On the grounds of both behaviour and anatomy, it is clear that the great apes collectively are more closely related to the present human species than any other group of animals, although opinions vary as to which one of four great apes (chimpanzee, pigmy chimpanzee, gorilla and orang-utan) should receive the dubious accolade of being most human.

The chimpanzee is usually given the edge by anatomists and physiologists, and is in any case selected most often for study by comparative psychologists partly because of its availability. Because of its close biological relationship to people, some comparative psychologists have been tempted to assume that a reverse-Tarzan effect should be possible, that is that by rearing a young chimp in the company of a human family, it should be possible to inculcate in it all significant human qualities, up to and including articulate speech. However, the husband and wife teams of Kellogg and Kellogg (1933/1967) and Hayes and Hayes (1951), though observing for several years the development of lively, sociable and otherwise imitative infant chimpanzees, were unable to report any significant progress by these animals towards the acquisition of a human language. (More recent accounts have been given by Kellogg, 1968 and Hayes and Nissen, 1971.) The Hayeses were initially encouraged by the fact that their animal, Viki, appeared to go through a 'babbling' stage of experimental noise-making when a few months old, but their efforts to explicitly train up normal speech had minimal success. It is now believed that the shape of the chimpanzee throat precludes the production of more than a single general-purpose vowel, but that a range of consonants should be anatomically possible (Lieberman, 1977). However Viki appeared to have great difficulty in establishing any voluntary control of the vocal apparatus. In order to assist with consonant production, the experimenters manually held Viki's lips together. Viki subsequently demonstrated a surely adequate degree of motivation by holding her lips in the required position with her own hands. However, by the time of her death (at age 6½), she had, by even the most charitable criteria, learned only seven words. 'Mama', 'Papa', 'up' and 'cup' were approximations to vocal English, used in approximately correct contexts. Three sounds which she produced spontaneously in the first instance, two clicks and a 'tsk', were trained as requests for a ride in the car, a cigarette, and to go outside. No other investigator, before (Furness, 1916; Cunningham, 1921) or since (Premack, 1976; Gardner and Gardner, 1971; Patterson, 1978) has claimed that intensively trained young simians can better Viki's limited performance, and it seems safe to conclude that the motor skills necessary for learned vocalization are beyond the capacities of the great apes.

Inappropriate anatomy, and the lack of specializations for the voluntary control of tongue, palate, lips and lungs, might conceivably prevent the acquisition of speech without rendering impossible meaningful communication via other modalities, as certainly may be the case for human beings with similar motor handicaps. Similarly inhibition of speech in human children by profound deafness may necessitate-recourse to visual sign languages. Herculean efforts have therefore been expended in attempts to train chimpanzees up to human levels of competence in the use of gesture sign language (Gardner and Gardner, 1969, 1971, 1985), communication by the manipulation of plastic tokens (Premack, 1971, 1976); and communication via special symbols on computerized keyboards (Rumbaugh and von Glaserfeld, 1973; Savage-Rumbaugh *et al.*, 1980; Savage-Rumbaugh *et al.*, 1985).

There is now a very extensive literature on these attempts, which has frequently been reviewed (e.g. Terrace *et al.*, 1979; Passingham, 1982; Walker, 1986). No detailed account of this research will therefore be given here. A very general conclusion is that, although there is much of interest in the data gathered, there is little to suggest that the natural abilities of apes verge on human competence, requiring only a helping hand from a persistent experimenter to reveal much more than is immediately obvious; and much which supports the hypothesis of Lenneberg (1967) and Chomsky (1976) that linguistic ability depends not only on biological specializations of hearing and voice, but also on genetically determined intellectual capacities of some kind which are not shared by any non-hominid primates. The communicative performance of trained apes differs from human speech in, among other possibilities, modality (it is not vocal); syntactic complexity (it is not sequentially ordered); disengagement from context (reference is usually to present or imminent stimuli); and separation from tangible goals (communication in apes is typically impelled by ulterior motives, and is rarely an end in itself).

However, attempts to train apes in language-like communication, and spin-offs from these attempts, have raised a number of questions about the limits of animal learning, and the transition between basic and universal associative processes and primate cognitive superiorities (Rumbaugh and Pate, 1984). Although apes cannot talk, or communicate in an equivalent manner with gestures, this does not necessarily mean that all their learning abilities can be adequately accounted for in terms of mechanisms available to invertebrates, or even in terms of mechanisms available to the pigeon or rat. Terrace *et al.*, (1979) were inclined to the view that, since their gesture-trained chimpanzee, Nim Chimpsky, failed to produce evidence of sentence construction, the associations they observed between certain gestures and appropriate objects referred to did not differ from associations between discriminative stimuli and instrumental responses and rewards obtained in Thorndikean experiments (see p. 118). Savage-Rumbaugh *et al.*, (1983) have however given both a theoretical and an experimental demonstration that there is a wide variety of possible kinds of association between a gesture and an object, or a visual symbol and an object. Simple labelling demands an association between symbol and object, but 'reference' as an act of naming involves considerably more than knowledge as an association. The conclusion supported by Savage-Rumbaugh *et al.* is that 'symbolization is not a unitary skill but rather a combination of diverse productive and receptive skills': it is possible however to suppose roughly that naming usually involves an agreement among several participants that a particular symbol 'stands for' a corresponding object or event, with all parties knowing that the symbol is only a symbol, but a real event is not.

The most rudimentary form of reference is perhaps to draw someone else's attention to a particular object by pointing at it, or holding it up for inspection. Children often do this before they know conventional names for individual objects. Without special training, young chimpanzees do not point things out with the arm or finger, but they do exhibit objects by holding them out to a human companion. After a certain age children hold things out to give as well as to show, but this seems not to happen with chimps, since it is reliably reported that psychologists are frequently bitten when assuming that they are intended to take possession of objects held out in this manner (Savage-Rumbaugh *et al.*, 1983, p. 462).

Thus although chimpanzees can be trained by rote-learning to associate a set of visual symbols or gestures with a set of objects, they do not normally demonstrate what these authors take to be the preliminary features of the 'protodeclarative' in the human child: indicative pointing, giving objects to others, and the use of nonsense vocalization in association with these activities. Further, chimpanzees may after learning a set of symbols in one context, be unable to transfer this training to another. Often they are trained to give the symbol for a food object under conditions when they always receive that food object after they have named it. Not surprisingly, they then become confused if they are shown chocolate, and produce the chocolate symbol, but receive beancake. If chimpanzees are trained in a productive skill, that is to produce consistent symbols for real objects which they are shown (either by gesturing, or by pressing the correct key on a keyboard), they do not necessarily perform correctly when tested on a corresponding receptive task, namely selecting a single item from a collection when given the symbol. A similar dissociation may however be observed in very young infants; Rice (1980) trained normal 2- and 3-year-olds who did not already know this to say the right words when shown red, green and yellow objects. Some infants took hundreds of trials before they did this correctly, and after that still performed at random when asked to choose named objects – choosing at random when asked 'Give me the red one' yet responding correctly when asked 'What colour is this?' Even as adults, these skills are in one sense highly separated, since brain damage (for instance, after strokes) may frequently affect productive but not receptive skills or vice versa, as in the traditional classification of Broca's and Wernicke's aphasia (Goodglass and Geschwind, 1976; Walker, 1986; Harris and Coltheart, 1986).

Whatever the final verdict on these matters, it is obvious that the human act of naming involves more than a simple association between two events, and most probably requires a whole complex of social skills and cognitive assumptions. Nevertheless, two chimpanzees, Austin and Sherman, who had previously demonstrated a functional form of communication between themselves (Savage-Rumbaugh *et al.*, 1978b) by requesting and donating various tools required to procure concealed foods, satisfied what Savage-Rumbaugh *et al.* (1983) regarded as fairly stringent criteria for an act of naming which includes intentional reference to objects. In the first experiment the animal subject had to look at a table on which an experimenter had placed a selection of five to seven foods, changed from trial to trial. Then it had to walk round a screen to a keyboard out of sight of the foods, key in a particular item (by pressing a single key), return to the table, and pick up the item it had previously indicated. When this was done correctly the subject was allowed to share the indicated food with the other chimpanzee. This provides additional evidence to that previously reported for ability to label previously seen food objects (Savage-Rumbaugh *et al.*, 1978a) since the stimulus for the choice of label was not simply a single object but the animal's own decision about its intended future choice from among a given selection.

A second and similar experiment used an object set of photographs of 20 foods and 10 objects; two experimenters (one of whom placed a random selection of five objects on the table each trial, and the other, who did not know which five objects were present, to receive the animal's eventual choice); and a longer distance between the table of objects and the remote keyboard. Pains were taken that all these trials were 'blind', that is, that human experimenters could not inadvertently signal to the animals which objects they should choose or which key they should press. The task also differed from the first in that the food rewards given to the animal did not correspond to the objects previously indicated. Possibly because photographs of food were used, whereas sometimes real objects rather than photographs of objects were present, the choices were more often of non-food objects than of foods. Thus on a typical trial the animal would inspect a table on which was present a straw and a wrench, and photographs of cake, melon and banana, walk round a screen to a distant keyboard (sometimes after the animal had reached the keyboard it would have to return to the table to refresh its memory), press the arbitrary visual pattern for 'wrench', return to the table, select the wrench, take the wrench around another screen to an experimenter who knew only that 'wrench' had been indicated, and receive praise and yoghurt.

This sort of one-word indication of intended action is one of the earliest vocal skills achieved by human children and the surprise is perhaps only that its demonstration in chimpanzees should have been so long delayed – these animals were 9 and 10 years old and had been in training together for eight years. It does not of course follow that the eight years of training were all necessary, but the trouble taken over this result does not suggest that more creative and lengthy conversations with chimpanzees will readily be achieved. Is it possible therefore to conclude that the obvious superiority of humans at human language tasks should be attributed to a core of grammatical or syntactical competence, rather than to a larger plexus of social, emotional and vocal predispositions? There is no reason to suppose that human predispositions for language do not include all the above and more besides, and it is unlikely that the difficulties encountered by those trying to train non-human primates in language arise from a single cause. The detection of grammatical regularities by human infants may require the utilization of a powerful and special-purpose problem-solving device (Wexler, 1982), but the normal routines of early life and more particular forms of support in social relationships no doubt aid its activities (Bruner, 1983; Harris and Coltheart, 1986). It is certainly unlikely that merely the detection of word order (or morpheme order) supplies a great deal of force in itself to language-learning in human infants. No theory should come to harm, therefore, from the discovery that apes, having become sensitive to a limited number of visual or gestural symbols, can detect limited changes to the order within two– or three-symbol messages.

Muncer and Ettlinger (1981) trained a single 5–year-old female chimpanzee for one year in the production and comprehension of a small number of the hand and arm gestures which make up the American Sign Language used with the human deaf. Correct use of the prepositions 'in' and 'behind' was trained by rewarding the animals for using the correct function word, with the correct order of nouns, in describing displays such as 'apple in bag', or 'apple behind bag' (the bag was transparent). Comprehension of similar phrases was taught by compliance with instructions always beginning with push – thus 'push apple in bag', 'push bag behind apple'. Double-blind trials were given regularly both in training and in the subsequent tests. These were made up of a small number of probe trials, on which words were presented in novel orders. There were 14 of these new sequences, of the form 'bag in box', 'bag behind box', and 'push apple behind box', 'push bag behind peanut'. Performance on these novel trials was significantly better than chance, though far from perfect. The chimpanzee appeared to have little difficulty in always putting the preposition second, in groups of three signs, and in fact more errors were due to choice of the wrong preposition than to errors of sequence, possibly because both 'bag in box' and 'bag behind box' entail the occlusion of the bag by the box. In any event, in this limited context the chimpanzee's syntactical abilities were not negligible.

In a second experiment, the same chimpanzee was trained in similar fashion to produce and comprehend gestures for 'and', 'or' and 'not'. Presented with displays of four items, the animal might be instructed to 'take peanut and carrot', while leaving the other two (perhaps a banana and an apple), or alternatively 'take peanut or carrot'. For production of 'and' the animal had simply to put this between 2 appropriate object gestures when 2 objects were presented. For production of signs for 'or' and 'not', the chimpanzee was encouraged to gesture 'Graham not take Banana', or 'Graham take banana or apple', if one or two items were present respectively, by being allowed to take herself what Graham left. Selfishly, the chimpanzee, Jane, failed to produce the sign for 'or' correctly even after six months of training, but comprehension for all three gestures appeared to be good. Comprehension test trials were therefore given in which, for the first time, 'not' was combined with 'or' or 'and', using objects not previously experienced with conjunctions; these took the form of instructions such as 'not paper and bag' or 'not paper or bag'. The reader may care to consider for a moment which responses should be regarded as correct in these circumstances. The chimpanzee's response was to refrain from taking raisins from objects signed immediately after the gesture for 'not', but to pick up the raisins placed on all other objects. This would seem to me to be one plausible interpretation of the 'not' sign, given that there was nothing which corresponded to a set of brackets. However, Muncer and Ettlinger intended that 'not paper or bag' should mean neither object should be responded to, and therefore conclude that a response to the second object indicates a 'failure to negate conjunctions'. It certainly seems likely that a very simple strategy, of not taking rewards from the first object after 'not' was responsible for the chimpanzee's choices, and this also appeared to apply when instructions of the type 'not A and not B' were successful in preventing responses to both objects. However, it should be noted that even the application of this simple rule (to novel combinations of 'not' with objects) placed a load on visual memory, since the serial gestures were transitory. The results of the first experiment, in which 'in' and 'behind' were applied correctly, suggest that the chimpanzee was capable of interpreting order of gestures in visual memory in terms of object relations in space (and vice versa), and this represents a considerable cognitive, if only a trivial syntactical, achievement.

Theoretical interpretations of ape-training experiments

There are a number of theoretical questions which arise from the limited success of experiments in training apes to communicate, most of them not within sight of being clearly answerable. (i) The most secure conclusion at present is that the innate difference between the other *Anthropoidea* and *Homo sapiens* with regard to propositional communication and thought can be only a little blurred by the best efforts of the latter to educate the former; (ii) despite this, special coaching of young apes promotes intellectual accomplishments not normally exhibited spontaneously; (iii) there being little basis for comparison, it is not clear whether this is possible because apes have innate abilities which are significantly in excess of those of other large mammals; (iv) it is uncertain whether the special coaching of apes allows already present cognitive processes to be revealed to human observers, or whether the artificial educational procedures build in new mental strategies which could never arise in their absence.

Communication in non-primate mammals

The succeful employment of sheepdogs and working elephants to perform economically productive tasks, and also the use of performing animals such as dolphins or seals for the purposes of human entertainment, all require some degree of comprehension by the animals concerned of human commands (e.g. Williams, 1950). There is considerable difficulty, however, in determining whether such reliable following of instructions is due to instrumental learning of the Thorndikean type – that is, stamped-in routine responses to discriminative signals – as opposed to psychologically more complex transmission of information about goals to be achieved. Productive skills of course suffer from the same ambiguity, but the combination of both receptive and productive use of meaningful signals, as appears to be demonstrated in certain of the chimpanzee experiments (e.g. Savage-Rumbaugh *et al.*, 1978b) is more impressive than the following of instructions alone, especially as the instructions given to domestic and working animals are usually of the very simple 'go', 'stop', 'turn left', 'turn right' type, which are easily interpretable in terms of conditioned responses to stimuli.

Various experimental studies have however suggested that non-primate mammals may be trained in comprehension exercises not wholly dissimilar to some of those given greater publicity when performed by chimpanzees, although in neither case is any strong theoretical conclusion made possible. Schusterman and Krieger (1984) used a specially developed system of gesture-signs, composed of both arm and hand positions, of a trainer sitting on the side of a pool (very like a whole-word, sitting semaphore), to convey three-sign instructions to California sea lions. The first sign was always a 'modifier' such as black, white, grey, large, small; the second was a noun indicating which of several items floating in the pool was to be operated on – including pipe, ball, disc, waterwings and chlorox bottle; and the third was the required action – such as flipper-touch, tail-touch, mouth-touch, fetch, or toss. After two years on gradual training with these signals, one animal was judged to follow correctly 190 three-sign combinations, involving five modifiers, 10 objects and five actions, and another 64 three-sign combinations, involving two modifiers, eight objects and six actions. Very small pieces of fish (15 g) were given for correct responses. It is certainly possible to view this kind of training as merely a very elaborate form of stimulus-response, instrumental conditioning, but whether or not this is appropriate, successful performance undoubtedly requires (a) significant short-term visual memory, to allow a series of signs to be responded to jointly, and (b) a highly conditional relationship between the immediate stimulus objects (balls, bottles, and so on, since several different objects were always present) and the organized response categories, as both the gesture-signs and the stimulus objects jointly determined motor actions. The internal organization of a large number of putative stimulus-response associations becomes a separate problem from merely that solved by the existence of a mechanism for forming associations, and thus to some extent behavioural complexity alone is a criteria for cognitive achievement.

Herman (1980) reported rather similar learned instruction-following in a bottle-nosed dolphin, again demonstrating at least an extremely flexible and large capacity for forming associations. The same dolphin was also successfully trained in a limited type of sign-production in object labelling (Richards *et al.*, 1984). The animal was first trained to mimic vocally computer-generated sounds within the range of its whistle mode of sound production, but unlike any noises it had previously been heard to make. Then, by presenting a certain object together with one of the computer-generated sounds, as a condition for reward, and then requiring the correct sound to be present for reward, but decreasing the probability that it would be made artificially, the animal was persuaded to produce five sounds selectively according to which of five object categories it observed (ball, pipe, hoop, frisbee and person). There were however no checks that these vocal labels served any referential functions (of the kinds discussed by Savage-Rumbaugh *et al.*, 1983; see p. 335ff) and the five associations are therefore of less theoretical interest here than the cognitive skills of sound mimicry and object recognition. It is however worth noting that the *range* of learned behaviours of this kind is much greater in dolphins and seals than it is in rats and pigeons (or in invertebrates), and that quantitative factors in learning may be important as an underlay for the achievement of performances which appear qualitatively more impressive.

The brain size, both absolutely and in relation to body weight, of marine mammals (typically over 1,000 grams for dolphins and several hundred grams for sea lions) would provide an anatomical substrate for the storage of large quantities of information. It is far from being the case, though, that learning abilities are always perfectly correlated with brain size. Imitation of human vocalization, which is beyond the ability of chimpanzee, partly because of limitations of their vocal organs, is well within the specialized capabilities of parrots and mynah birds. Such imitative species usually have average to high brain/body weight proportions by mammalian standards, even with the necessary mathematical adjustments for scale (Jerison, 1973), but in absolute size, the brain of even a large parrot is small by mammalian standards. A budgerigar, with a brain of 1 gram, can produce far better imitations of human speech sounds than any chimpanzee, with a brain of hundreds of grams. The vocal imitation should clearly be regarded as a specialized, though not a negligible, skill. Its use gives an appealing apparent plausibility to tests of cognitive discrimination conducted on parrots, since they can give clearly formed verbal answers to verbal questions. Thus Pepperberg (1981) trained an African grey parrot to give appropriate vocalizations when presented with 40 kinds of object – a performance quantitatively in excess of that so far observed in the bottle-nosed dolphin (Richards *et al.*, 1984). Later, the same parrot was trained to give different answers when presented with the same object (e.g. a yellow triangle) depending on whether it was asked 'what colour?' (answer 'yellow') or 'what shape?' (answer 'three-corner') – an arbitrary imitation of human answers given in training). The experimental controls in this investigation leave something to be desired, and Pepperberg (1983) claims only limited accuracy and understanding by the bird with the two perceptually easy dimensions of colour and shape. However, the study serves at least as a reminder that the rote-learning of large amounts of information is not confined to large-brained mammals (see also Vaughan and Greene, 1984).

Visual inference and reasoning

Communicative skills are one thing, internal manipulation of mental symbols another. At least, one should expect that to be the case with species in which language is not obviously the main vehicle of thought. Several tests have been designed to discover not whether a chimpanzee exhibits explicit linguistic skills, but whether it is capable of solving intellectual problems which can be of other kinds.

Transitive inference

One kind of inferential and logical extrapolation is of the type that if A is greater than B, and B is greater than C, this contains the implication that A is greater than C, even if no perceptual comparison between A and C is possible. There is some disagreement as to whether people detect such implications on the basis of linguistic formulae or because of some more concrete internal imagery (Clark and Clark, 1977). Gillan (1981) reports examples of choices by a chimpanzee without special training in communication, which he believes demonstrated a form of transitive inference. If this is the case, the choice must certainly represent transitive inference on the basis of figural, rather than linguistic, mental models (Johnson-Laird, 1983). The aim of Gillan's training (1981) was to set up an arbitrary selection of colours in an internal ordered series, the test of this series being choices between colours not paired together before. Thus, in a random series of trials, a chimpanzee was trained to choose orange from orange/white, white from white/red, red from red/black and black from black/blue (by putting food in only one of pairs of containers presented with coloured lids). Strictly speaking, there is no logical reason for concluding anything from such a series of trials, apart from noting the relative frequency of food location in each individual pair. However, since orange is always rewarded, and blue is never rewarded, it would be possible to code appropriate choices on a single scale of preference with the order orange, white, red, black, blue — this would be a more economical way of representing previous experience than memories of the outcome with each pair. A consequence of this sort of mental scale of preference should be that white is preferred to black, if these two colours are presented together, even though no experience has been gained with exactly this pair. Only one chimpanzee out of the three studied by Gillan (1981) in fact chose white over black consistently in this sort of test. But for this animal strong and statistically reliable choices suggestive of internal serial ordering of colours was obtained even when a longer sequence was used. (One other animal made similar choices after longer training.) The most revealing control test was that, if the linearity of the inferred sequence was distorted by contradictory trials with the two end-points — that is, in the example above, if blue was rewarded in blue/orange pairings, then the inferred preference (of white over black) disappeared. This supports the hypothesis that the chimpanzee is capable of constructing an internal mental model from a limited sample of experience, the mental model determining subsequent choices (see Johnson-Laird, 1983 for the theory of mental models in human inference and cognition).

Analogical reasoning

A form of reasoning quite different from transitive inference, frequently elicited by paper-and-pencil tests of human intelligence, requires, at least ostensibly, a comparison between two instances of an abstract two-point relationship. Thus, 'hand is to arm as blank is to leg' demands a comparison between arms and legs, with respect to the relationship of extremities to limbs, but might conceivably be solvable in a less formal way, by more concrete mental analogies. However, according to Premack (1983), chimpanzees can only solve this sort of problem *if* they have had formal training in the use of symbols to denote the logical relationships of similarity and dissimilarity. It may be, therefore, that what appears to us subjectively to be concretely obvious may in fact depend upon covert use of abstract, linguistically coded concepts of likeness.

Analogical reasoning was reported by Gillan *et al.* (1981) for the chimpanzee Sarah, who had experienced thorough training with the use of plastic tokens to indicate other objects and relations between them 10 years previously, with intermittent use of the plastic tokens for the concepts of 'same/ and 'different' in the intervening period (Premack, 1971; Premack and Woodruff, 1978; Woodruff *et al.*, 1978; Premack *et al.*, 1978). This animal was thus already extensively trained to place the token 'same' between two identical objects, or between an object and another token normally associated with it (as its 'name'), with similar but contrasting use of the token for 'different'. For the analogies training these tokens for likeness and difference had to be applied either with geometric figures (differing in size, shape, colour and marking) or with household objects already familiar to the animal (most of whose 16 years had been spent in academic captivity). The chimpanzee was able to answer questions of analogy in two related ways, which I shall describe in the case of examples of household objects.

The chimpanzee's task (Gillan *et al.*, 1981) was always to produce a consistent array of four objects with 'same' or 'different' tokens placed between them. Thus if given on one side apple peel together with a peeled apple, and on the other orange peel with a peeled orange, and the two tokens to choose from, the correct response (successfully made) was to insert the 'same' token in the middle. In the alternative form of the test, the 'same' token was already present, with a banana and banana peel on one side of it, and an orange alone on the other, a choice having to be made between orange peel and a peeled orange for the completion of the array (the animals's choice, judged correct, being the peel: thus orange peel is to orange as banana peel is to banana).

A range of problems of this type were tested, Sarah being correct in her choices more often than not, but making the occasional apparent error. Given a paintbrush and a piece of painted wood on one side and a piece of marked and torn paper, she choose tape rather than the correct crayon – the target relationship being 'marking'. This might cast some doubt on the validity of the correct choice of tape to go with marked torn paper when the comparison was with a torn cloth together with a needle and thread – the target relationship being 'repair'. On the other hand, who is to say that a paintbrush should not be construed as 'repair'? Clearly the interpretation of the roughly 80 per cent correct choices made by the animal is exceedingly difficult – a variety of cognitive strategies, all falling short of human understanding, may have been employed by Sarah, based on her extensive previous experience. It is however very hard to imagine an explanation for the relatively accurate performance in terms of simple conditioning processes along the lines of the theory of discrimination learning put forward by Spence (1936) and Hull (1952), and to a large extent the intercourse with common objects and tools as well as arbitrary indicators for the concepts of 'same' and 'different' ought to qualify as an analogy for human reasoning, at least by comparison with an analogy to conditioned spinal reflexes.

In 1983, Premack reported that Sarah was the only chimpanzee to have performed successfully on the above tests of analogical reasoning (and that by comparison with the performance on similar tasks by human infants, she was at the 6–year-old rather than the 4–year-old level). However, there was one other test which three 'language-trained' (with plastic tokens) chimpanzees passed, while four similar but not thus trained animals failed. They were presented with two objects from a meaningful series of three, for example, an apple and a knife, and given the opportunity to complete the series, for example by choosing a cut apple to add instead of alternatives of a cut orange, or an apple with a nail in it. Premack (1983) supposed that the 'language-training' facilitated performance on this task by enhancing an already present abstract mental code. Alternative, or complementary, possibilities are that: (i) since the training with tokens took the form of placing objects in meaningful arrays, the attentional and conceptual learning involved in this transferred fairly directly to the choosing of correct items to make up meaningful groups of three; and (ii) in the case of extensive training with tokens for 'same' and 'different', the mental representations of these tokens supply a completely new abstract code, which serves as a new tool for thought, and enables animals thus trained to make conceptual choices not otherwise available to them.

Biological bases of animal cognition

One sort of basis for conditioning, learning, and cognition, is the anatomical apparatus of the central nervous system, without which there would be little by way of suitable phenomena available for study. Oakley (1979a, 1983, 1985) has provided several surveys of relationships between the central nervous system and learning and memory, and I shall not pursue this topic in detail here (see Walker, 1983a, chapters, 4,5,7 and 8). The main organizing principle adopted by Oakley (1979a, 1983) has, however, been alluded to in previous chapters (3, 4 and 5) and is worth emphasizing again now: different sorts of internal computation, of different orders of complexity, can be expected to be performed at successive levels of the vertebrate brain. Rather different mechanisms for accomplishing superficially similar behavioural ends may therefore be employed by disparate vertebrate species, and we are entitled to expect, on these grounds alone, that the capacities of a chimpanzee for

receiving, ordering and interpreting the results of life experience will not be identical to that of a lamprey or tadpole,
because very different weights apply to the functions of the
cerebral hemispheres in the two cases. It might not be worth
belabouring this point were it not for the fact that Macphail
(1982, 1985) is not entirely alone in seeking to minimize, or
to ignore, the factor of species differences in animal learning
and cognition (e.g. Mackintosh, 1974, 1983; but see Mackintosh *et al.*, 1985). The evidence from cross-species comparisons of cognitive abilities, like the evidence from comparative
studies of brain size (Jerison, 1973), remains equivocal and
ambiguous in many respects, but we can rest assured that
even the most ardent advocates of species equality in learning
are as unlikely to produce data demonstrating analogical
reasoning about household objects from laboratory rats and
pigeons as they are to produce evidence for the serial position
effect using lists of four coloured slides from the sea-slug
Aplysia, or from lampreys or tadpoles.

An alternative theoretical basis for biological differences in
psychological processes which ought to be more fundamental
than brain mechanisms, but which in practice is far more
elusive, concerns the evolutionary rationale for species differences, either in terms of the functioning of psychological
processes in behavioural ecology or in terms of phylogenetic
development. This perhaps is best left as a goal for the future,
since there is so little agreement on either the possibility or the
desirability of this kind of theoretical basis for psychological
matters, but one or two attempts to construct theoretical
frameworks for cross-species comparisons may be mentioned.
Although obscure, Piaget's *Biology and Knowledge* (1971) has
the virtue of emphasizing natural continuities in information-
processing mechanisms, while clearly not losing sight of
human cognitive excellences (Boden, 1979). The continuities
are empirically confirmed by findings such as those reported
by Redshaw (1978), who gave tests of intellectual development designed for human babies to infant gorillas in the first
year of life. Human babies progress in a predictable order
through tasks such as: following moving objects with their
eyes; finding a toy after it has been hidden behind a screen;
pulling in a toy resting on a flannel; and knowing to desist

from pulling the flannel in the same task when the toy is held just above the flannel. Gorilla babies progress through exactly the same tasks in very much the same order, but at a slightly faster rate, failing on only one or two of the tests used for human infants up to the point, at about 18 months of age, when human infants begin to acquire speech, but gorilla infants don't. Like chimpanzees, the gorillas do not spontaneously point to familiar persons, or hand over toys to human observers (as babies do), activities which have been mentioned above as aiding the development of spoken communication (Savage-Rumbaugh *et al.*, 1983). Neither did the infant gorillas observed by Redshaw (1978) use sticks to retrieve otherwise out-of-reach toys, or pile up building blocks into towers, although adult chimpanzees will gradually learn to do these things to obtain food (Kohler, 1925).

As growth (and formal education) proceeds, the differences between ape and human young of course expand enormously: without minimizing these it was possible for Piaget (1971) to conclude that the development of cognition in the two cases has some common biological roots, with more primitive forms of learning of a sensory-motor kind, in particular associations formed in classical or instrumental conditioning being retained when higher forms of cognition, depending on the internal classification, comparison, and ordering of perceived objects, are successively added in. The details of these theories are perhaps less important than the fact that experimental classification and comparison of animal learning abilities is possible when tests of the development of object perception are conducted. Gradual development of the concept of object permanence can be observed in kittens as well as chimpanzees, at least up to the point of the recovery of play-objects hidden under cloths (Gruber *et al.*, 1971). With infant monkeys it is still possible to use tests of object perception roughly similar to those employed with human babies, and to observe a form of object permanence of some cognitive significance (Wise *et al.*, 1974). The experimental limit of this, which would appear to require both good visual memory and some form of visual inference, is the 'empty container' test. A peanut is put into an opaque container, such as a large cup, within an infant monkey's sight; the container is then slowly passed behind a screen, afterwards being turned towards the monkey so that it can see whether the peanut is still there or not. If, on seeing that the container is empty, the animal immediately looks behind the screen for the peanut, it has passed the test. Premack (1983) termed this sort of performance in young chimpanzees' 'natural reasoning', and found that both language-trained (with plastic tokens) and non-language-trained chimpanzees performed at roughly the same level as 4- to 5-year-old children on several different tests of this kind. In one of these, the chimpanzee watches while an apple is put in one bucket, and a banana in another. It is then briefly taken away, returning to find a human individual standing between the buckets and eating either an apple or a banana. Older chimpanzees, and children, immediately go to the bucket in which the other type of fruit had been put; younger ones learn to do this very quickly. Obviously one of the reasons for getting this task wrong could be a failure of memory. However Premack (1983) found that younger subjects were more likely to give wrong responses because they did not seem to make a 'similarity assumption' – the hypothesis (not necessarily correct) that the banana being eaten is the same one that had recently been put in a bucket. This assumption of object similarity – or of consistency and stability in the environment, and relatedness between events – is even more apparent in a more complicated test used by Premack (1983). In this, the animal is shown one or two pieces of the same kind of fruit in the trainer's hands. Then the trainer goes to a different room, or out to a field, and puts whatever fruit there is in a container, in the absence of the animal, going back, manifestly empty-handed, to the animal, which is then taken out to the container to see a single piece of fruit removed from it, and confiscated. Now, if the chimpanzee had seen only one piece of fruit in the first place, it merely grooms itself or stares into the distance. If, on the other hand, two pieces of food had been in the possession of the trainer to begin with, the chimpanzee goes directly to the container to retrieve the piece of fruit which remains in it.

It would of course be possible to perform correctly on this task, given enough training, by differential habits controlled by the two initial stimuli of one and two pieces of fruit. It is however likely that both children and apes react to the problem by incorporating such isolated stimulus events into a more coherent narrative, or network of related events, though not necessarily to the same degree. A particular narrative constraint on a series of simple events, or, alternatively, a development of the concept of object permanence which occurs at a relatively advanced age in human children, demands that a given object does not spontaneously change certain of its quantitative characteristics over time. Thus 7- or 8-year-old children, but not 3- or 4-year-olds, know that orange juice poured from a wide to a narrow glass must in some important sense remain 'the same' (provided none is spilt or added), and passing a range of such tests, for conservation of volume and number over a variety of physical transformations, is heralded as an important stage in cognitive development (Piaget and Inhelder, 1969). It is thus of interest that two individual female chimpanzees, Sarah trained with plastic tokens as symbols, and Jane trained with a limited number of sign-language gestures, have satisfied reasonably rigorous tests for conservation of volume (Woodruff *et al.*, 1978; Muncer, 1982), without much special training. By explicit and protracted training on rewarded and unrewarded choices between changed and unchanged displays, Pasnak (1979) demonstrated that rhesus monkeys were capable of arduously acquiring the habit of paying attention to whether an experimenters did or did not add or subtract something to the volume of one of two displays (whether of modelling clay, straws, sponge cubes, or of many other substances) before further changes to the shape of the displays were made.

All of these experimental details could be regarded as supporting the uncontentious claim that the biological function of the vertebrate brain is to regulate the animal's interaction with the external world, if not Piaget's (1971) particular discussions of this function. A necessary addition to this bald truism is however some or other scheme for classifying the variety of ways and means by which the useful regulation of animal behaviour is brought about. The experiments and theories reviewed in previous chapters have presented many possibilities, with emphasis on a cognitive dimension or hierarchy, ranging from simple reflexes to complex ideas. Concern with species comparisons and evolutionary progression has always suggested at least one more dimension of classification: that ranging from the utterly innate to the entirely learned. There is sometimes a temptation to conflate these two dimensions – supposing that all reflexes are innate, and all complex ideas learned. The evidence is quite to the contrary, much experimental work on conditioning and habituation (chapters 2,3 and 4) demonstrating that the most reflexive of behaviours (including knee-jerk spinal reflexes and internal metabolic processes) are subject to learning, since they become attached to widely varying sets of controlling stimuli, depending on life experiences; while most work on memory and cognition in animal learning suggests that the more complex the mental operation, the more likely it will be constrained by species membership, and thus by inherited predisposition if not by inherited mental content.

Many learning theorists have been guilty of ignoring both variations in information-processing capacity, as between single reflex circuits (Hull, 1943; Carew *et al.*, 1983) and the possibilities presented by whole brains, as well as of ignoring information-processing specializations (such as colour vision in birds and primates, echolocation in bats and dolphins, speech in *Homo*?) whose style and range of operation must be unlearned, even if all the information thus gathered is not (Fodor, 1983). However, most of the guilty parties have been apprehended (Seligman, 1970) and current trends are towards far more realistic incorporation of biological facts of life into idealized and relatively abstract accounts of the learning process (Lea, 1984a; Krebs and Davies, 1983; Staddon, 1983; Staddon and Simmelhag, 1971).

The evolution of learning

Increasingly, attention is being given to the more fundamental question of how and why the learning process itself should have evolved (as an alternative to the more reliable but less flexible instinctive methods of producing useful behavioural strategies: Maynard-Smith, 1984). Plotkin and Odling-Smee (1981) provide a necessary overview of the problems of applying evolutionary theories to behavioural and psychological questions. They propose that these problems should be made explicit by distinguishing several different levels in a 'multi-level, multi-process model of evolution'. The first level of this is that at which natural selection operates on the genes – often the only level considered even in analyses of behaviour (Maynard-Smith, 1984; Hamilton, 1964). The second level they call 'variable epigenesis': genes are only important in so far as they direct growth and bodily change, and normal growth (epigenesis) is determined by many other factors (including nutrition, temperature, chance) as well. At a third level they put all forms of learning, by which the individual organism is to some extent affected in its own experience of life, rather than by the genetic consequences of the experiences of its ancestors; and at a fourth level, the 'cultural pool', by means of which the mechanism of individual learning becomes a means of transmitting information both across and within generations, while bypassing the relatively slow and painful route of genetic selection.

It is undeniable that processes denoted as learning stretch from changes barely distinguishable from physical growth and maturation (especially early in life) to the nowadays virtually instantaneous transmission of information that may be made possible by human rumour, fashion, scholarship or science. Within the biological context of learning theories, the lesson has gradually sunk in that the animal world contains a hierarchy of strategies for behavioural change, many individual strategies all serving roughly the same purpose and many individual strategies accomplishing a broadly similar function, all being possible in the same species. Thus it is biologically possible to arrange for the decline of responsiveness to a repeated stimulus by a mechanisms of sensory adaptation, by a process more like response fatigue, or by a more complicated procedure of setting up a central representation of the detailed characteristics of sensory input which will allow a repeated stimulus to be recognized as familiar. All these operations might be performed for a single item of behaviour, inexorably linked to only one form of stimulus input, even though a sufficiently rich internal representation of familiar stimuli should qualify as an advanced form of memory. Similarly, to allow individual responses of muscles or glands to become triggered by many alternative inputs, according to various and unforeseen circumstances of life, a number of associative mechanisms might be employed: arrangements might be made for links to be formed between stimulus inputs adjacent in time, between the response as made and whatever input happens then to be present, or between central representations of the environment as perceived and global emotional or cognitive states. And for actions and reactions to change, as surely they should, as a consequence of the costs and benefits which they immediately bring, in so far as these can be assessed by the evaluative procedures of a given brain, then alterations might be made, on the basis of their results, to one or all of reflexes, impulses, habits and intentions.

The detailed evidence in previous chapters suggests that any laboratory study of learning is likely to call into play a large number of these possible processes of behavioural change, crossing boundaries between functional categories such as habituation or anticipatory conditioning, as well as between putative levels of complexity such as reflexive and cognitive learning. However this does not mean it is impossible to separate out such processes, according to experimental variables of species, physiology and behavioural procedure. A simple example discussed in this chapter (p. 310) is that the process of conditioning signal A for a standard motivating event may no longer apply when what is required is the conditional relationship that stimulus A should serve as a signal if and only if stimulus B is present as well. This is the biological range of learning in microcosm – in the animal kingdom as a whole there is clearly a somewhat more vivid contrast between learning processes which change reactions to the world by means of minor adjustments to the strengths of certain reflexes, and those by which an animal internalizes knowledge about the world in ways which lead to theories of its mental models or cognitive representations. Although the evidence is as yet fragmentary rather than systematic, it is possible to argue that progressive changes in the course of evolution are reflected in the degree to which species can acquire internal knowledge of the experienced environment, as well as the degree to which they demonstrate physical mastery of it. (Gottlieb, 1984; Mackintosh *et al.*, 1985; Rensch, 1959; Walker, 1986). Whether this argument is correct in the sense that progressive changes are actually visible in the capacities of monkeys and apes, but not of fish or frogs, to perform the experimental tasks involving memory and inference, is still in doubt (Passingham, 1982; Macphail, 1982, 1985). However, it is certainly safe to claim that any more advanced or more cognitive learning abilities that may be used by primates or other mammals must co-exist with older and simpler associative mechanisms, since these undoubtedly remain (Oakley, 1979a, 1985).

Irrespective of any hierarchies within processes of animal learning, there is a distinction between human verbal and cultural learning and all other possibilities that should arouse little dissent. However the question of whether there are nevertheless points of contact between human skills and principles of conditioning has never been easy to resolve. The learning-theory tradition of Pavlov and Thorndike is of course to see most if not all of human psychology as more elaborate and extreme manifestations of universal underlying necessities. Some subtler account is now clearly called for in order to accommodate both the objections from above, that history and civilization make human learning less biological, and the objections from below, that genetically inherited species differences of some kind mean that human cognition is biologically not dependent on learning (Chomsky, 1976; Fodor, 1983), or that all cross-species comparisons are invalid (Seligman, 1970; Hodos and Campbell, 1969; Johnston, 1981). If a hierarchy of processes of learning is involved in the biological context, it is perhaps easier to propose that learning processes collectively provide the interface between the natural physiology of human growth and form and the cultural possibilities that limit the relevance of any strictly biological approach to human learning. Since, from the time of William James and Sigmund Freud, it has been unexceptional to assume that human psychology itself is composed of more varied and less refined preliminaries than the end-product of rational thought, it is in some ways surprising that there should be any resistance to the assumption that the components of human habits and motives are not necessarily all immune to natural influences.

Therefore the surrender of general process learning theorists to the claims of species-specializations and human cultural uniqueness does not need to be permanently abject. Principles of learning are not fundamental to everything else in the way that Pavlov (1927), Hull (1943) and Skinner (1953) supposed that they must be, but neither are they biological curiosities that apply only in arbitrary laboratory procedures. If there is a multitude of specialized forms of learning appropriate to a variety of ecological niches, if there is a range of learning strategies between invertebrate reflexes and the social awareness of primates, and if human intellectual abilities will always have to be a special case – then this means that Pavlov and Skinner were wrong in some of their claims, but not that all subsequent theories of learning are doomed to be equally mistaken. Modern emphases on the ecological details and biological functions of natural behaviours, and on differences obtainable in laboratory experiments between reflexive associations and more cognitive forms of learning and memory, both lead to divergences of theory and practice, with a wider spread of types of investigation than I have been able to cover in this book. The divergence is in some ways less satisfying than the simple underlying certainties which all theorists seek for, but the compensation for the variousness of explanation, that now seems inevitable, may be that the variousness is closer to the truth.

Bibliography

Abramson, L. Y., Seligman, M. E. P., and Teasdale, J. D. (1978). Learned helplessness in humans: critique and reformulation. *Journal of Abnormal Psychology*, *87*, 49–74.

Adams, C. D. (1982). Variations in the sensitivity of instrumental responding to reinforcer devaluation. *Quarterly Journal of Experimental Psychology*, *34B*, 77–98.

Adams, C. D. and Dickinson, A. (1981a). Instrumental responding following reinforcer devaluation. *Quarterly Journal of Experimental Psychology*, *33B*, 109–21.

Adams, C. D. and Dickinson, A. (1981b). Actions and habits. In Spear, N. E. and Miller, R. R. (eds). *Information Processing in Animals*. Lawrence Erlbaum Associates: Hillsdale, New Jersey, 143–65.

Adams, R. M. and Walker, S. F. (1972). Stimulus control of counting-like behaviour in rats. *Psychonomic Science*, *29*, 167–9.

Ader, R. (1976). Conditioned adrenocortical steroid elevations in the rat. *Journal of Comparative and Physiological Psychology*, *90*, 1156–63.

Alloy, L. B. amd Tabachnik, N. (1984). Assessment of covariation by humans and animals: the joint influence of prior expectations and current situational information. *Psychological Review*, *91*, 112–49.

Alvarez-Buylla, R. and Alvarez-Buylla, E. R. (1975). Hypoglycemic conditioned reflex in rats. *Journal of Comparative and Physiological Psychology*, *88*, 155–60.

Amsel, A. (1962) Frustrative nonreward in partial reinforcement and discrimination learning. *Psychological Review*, *69*, 306–28.

Anderson, J. A. and Mozer, M. C. (1981). Categorization and selective neurons. In Hinton, G. E. and Anderson, J. A. (eds). *Parallel Models of Associative Memory*. Lawrence Erlbaum Associates: Hillsdale, New Jersey, 213–36.

Andrews, A. E. and Braveman, N. S. (1975) The combined effects of dosage level and interstimulus interval on the formation of one-trial poison-based aversions in rats. *Animal Learning and Behaviour*, 3, 287–9.

Anger, D. (1956). The dependence of interresponse times upon the relative reinforcement of different interresponse times. *Journal of Experimental Psychology*, 52, 145–61.

Archer, T., Nilsson, L. G. and Carter, N. (1979) Role of exteroceptive background context in taste-aversion conditioning and extinction. *Animal Learning and Behaviour*, 7, 17–22.

Aristotle (c. 350 BC/1927–52). *The Works of Aristotle*. Clarendon Press: Oxford.

Asch, S. E. (1956). Studies of independence and submission to group pressure: I. A minority of one against a unanimous majority. *Psychological Monographs*, 70, no. 416.

Asratyan, E. A. (1953). *I. P. Pavlov: His Life and Work*. Foreign Languages Publishing House: Moscow.

Asratyan, E. A. (1965). *Conditioned Reflex and Compensatory Mechanisms*. Pergamon: Oxford.

Atkinson, R. C. and Shiffrin, R. M. (1968). Human memory: a proposed system and its control processes. In Spence, K. W. and Spence, J. T. (eds). *The Psychology of Learning and Motivation*. Vol. 2. Academic Press: New York, 89–195.

Azrin, N. A. and Holz, W. C. (1966). Punishment. In Honig, W. K. (ed.), *Operant Behaviour*. Appleton-Century-Crofts: New York, 380–447.

Babkin, B. P. (1949). *Pavlov, A Biography*. University of Chicago Press.

Badia, P., Harsh, J. and Abbott, B. (1979). Choosing between predictable and undpredictable shock conditions: data and theory. *Psychological Bulletin*, 86, 1107–31.

Baernstein, H. D. and Hull, C. L. (1931). A mechanical model of the conditioned reflex. *Journal of General Psychology*, 5, 99–106.

Baker, A. G. and Mackintosh, N. J. (1977). Excitatory and inhibitory conditioning following uncorrelated presentations of CS and UCS. *Animal Learning and Behaviour*, 5, 315–19.

Baker, M. C. and Cunningham, M. A. (1985). The biology of bird-song dialects. *Behavioural and Brain Sciences*, 8, 85–134.

Balda, R. P. and Turek, R. J. (1984). The cache-recovery system as an example of memory capabilities in Clark's nutcracker. In Roitblat, H. L., Bever, T. G. and Terrace, H. S. (eds). *Animal Cognition*. Lawrence Erlbaum Associates: London, 513–32.

Ballard, D. H., Hinton, G. E. and Sejnowski, T. J. (1984). Parallel visual computation. *Nature*, 306, 21–6.

Barber, P. J. and Legge, D. (1986). *Information and Human Performance*. Methuen: London.

Barlow, H. B. (1972). Single units and sensation: a neuron doctrine for perceptual psychology?. *Perception, 1,* 371–94.

Bateson, P. P. G. (1966). The characteristics and content of imprinting. *Biological Review, 41,* 177–220.

Bateson. P. P. G. (1973). Preferences for familiarity and novelty: a model for the simultaneous development of both. *Journal of Theoretical Biology, 41,* 249–59.

Bateson, P. P. G. (1979). How do sensitive periods arise and what are they for? *Animal Behaviour, 27,* 470–86.

Bateson, P. P. G. and Chantry, D. F. (1972). Retardation of discrimination learning in monkeys and chicks previously exposed to both stimuli. *Nature, 237,* 173–4.

Baum, W. M. (1974). On two types of deviation from the matching law: bias and undermatching. *Journal of the Experimental Analysis of Behaviour, 22,* 231–42.

Baum, W. M. (1981). Optimization and the matching law as accounts of instrumental behaviour. *Journal of the Experimental Analysis of Behaviour, 20,* 387–403.

Becker, J. T. and Olton, D. S. (1982). Cognitive mapping and hippocampal function. *Neuropsychologia, 19,* 733–41.

Beggs, A. L., Steinmetz, J. E., Romano, A. G. and Patterson, M. M. (1983). Extinction and retention of a classically conditioned flexor nerve response in acute spinal cat. *Behavioural Neuroscience, 97,* 530–40.

Bendig, A. W. (1952). Latent learning in a water maze. *Journal of Experimental Psychology, 43,* 143–7.

Benninger, R. J., Bellisle, F. amd Milner, P. M. (1977). Schedule control of behaviour reinforced by electrical stimulation of the brain. *Science, 196,* 547–9.

Berlyne, D. E. (1960). *Conflict, Arousal, and Curiosity.* McGraw-Hill: New York.

Bernstein, J. S. (1961). The utilization of visual cues in dimension-abstracted oddity by primates. *Journal of Comparative and Physiological Psychology, 54,* 243–7.

Bessemer, D. W. and Stollnitz, F. (1971). Retention of discriminations and an analysis of learning set. In Schrier, A. M. and Stollnitz, F. (eds). *Behaviour of Nonhuman Primates: Vol. IV.* Academic Press: New York, 1–58.

Best, P. J., Best, M. R. and Mickley, G. A. (1973). Conditioned aversion to distinct environmental stimuli resulting from gastro intestinal distress. *Journal of Comparative and Physiological Psychology, 85,* 250–7.

Bindra, D. (1968). Neuropsychological interpretation of the effects of drive and incentive-motivation on general activity and instrumental behaviour. *Psychological Review, 75,* 1–22.

Bindra, D. (1976). *A Theory of Intelligent Behaviour.* Wiley: London.

Black, A. H. (1959). Heart rate changes during avoidance learning i·i dogs. *Canadian Journal of Psychology, 13,* 229–42.

Blodgett, H. C. (1929). The effect of the introduction of reward upon the maze performances of rats. *University of California Publications in Psychology, 4,* 113–34.

Blodgett, H. C. and McCutchan, K. (1948). Relative strength of place and response learning in the T-maze. *Journal of Comparative and Physiological Psychology, 41,* 17–24.

Bloomfield, T. M. (1966). Two types of behavioural contrast in discrimination learning. *Journal of the Experimental Analysis of Behaviour, 9,* 155–61.

Blough, D. S. (1972). Recognition by the pigeon of stimuli varying in two dimensions. *Journal of the Experimental Analysis of Behaviour, 18,* 345–67.

Blough, D. S. (1977). Visual search in the pigeon: hunt and peck method. *Science, 196,* 1013–4.

Blough, D. S. (1979). Effect of the number and form of stimuli on visual search in the pigeon. *Journal of Experimental Psychology: Animal Behaviour Processes, 5,* 211–23.

Blough, D. S. (1982). Pigeon perception of letters of the alphabet. *Science, 218,* 397–8.

Blough, D. S. (1984). Form recognition in pigeons. In Roitblat, H. L., Bever, T. G. and Terrace, H. S. (eds). *Animal Cognition.* Lawrence Erlbaum Associates: London, 277–89.

Blough, D. S. (1985). Discrimination of letters and random dot patterns by pigeons and humans. *Journal of Experimental Psychology: Animal Behaviour Processes, 11,* 261–80.

Boakes, R. A. (1977) Performance on learning to associate a stimulus with positive reinforcement. In Davis, H. and Hurwitz, H. M. B. (eds). *Operant-Pavlovian Interactions.* Lawrence Erlbaum Associates: Hillsdale, New Jersey, 67–97.

Boakes, R. A. (1984). *From Darwin to Behaviourism.* Cambridge University Press.

Boakes, R. A., Poli, M., Lockwood, M. J. and Goodall, G. (1978). A study of misbehaviour: token reinforcement in the rat. *Journal of the Experimental Analysis of Behaviour, 29,* 115–34.

Boden, M. A. (1979). *Piaget.* Fontana: London.

Boe, E. E. and Church, R. M. (1967). Permanent effects of punishment during extinction. *Journal of Comparative and Physiological Psychology, 63,* 486–92.

Boice, R. (1984). Packrats (*Neotoma albigula* and *N. micropus*) compared in an operant anologue of foraging behaviours. *Journal of Comparative Psychology, 98,* 115–18.

Bolles, R. C. (1970). Species-specific defense reactions and avoidance learning. *Psychological Review, 77,* 32–48.

Bolles, R. C. (1978). The role of stimulus learning in defensive behaviour. In Hulse, S. H., Fowler, H. and Honig, W. K. (eds). *Cognitive Processes in Animal Behaviour*. Lawrence Erlbaum Associates: Hillsdale, New Jersey, 89–108.

Bond, A. B. (1983). Visual search and selection of natural stimuli in the pigeon: the attention threshold hypothesis. *Journal of Experimental Psychology: Animal Behaviour Processes, 9*, 292–305.

Booth, D. A. and Simpson, P. C. (1971). Food preferences acquired by association with variations in amino acid nutrition. *Quarterly Journal of Experimental Psychology, 23*, 135–45.

Booth, D. A., Lovett, D. and McSherry, G. M. (1972). Post-ingestive modulation of the sweetness preference gradient in the rat. *Journal of Comparative and Physiological Psychology, 78*, 485–512.

Booth, D. A., Lee, M. and McAleavey, C. (1976). Acquired sensory control of satiation in man. *British Journal of Psychology, 67*, 137–47.

Boring, E. G. (1950). *A History of Experimental Psychology*. Appleton-Century-Crofts: New York.

Born, D. G., Snow, M. E. and Herbert, E. W. (1969). Conditional discrimination learning in the pigeon. *Journal of the Experimental Analysis of Behaviour, 12*, 119–25.

Brady, J. V., Porter, R. W., Condrad, D. G. amd Mason, J. W. (1958). Avoidance behaviour and the development of gastroduodenal ulcers. *Journal of the Experimental Analysis of Behaviour, 1*, 69–72.

Breland, K. and Breland, M. (1961). The misbehaviour of organizms. *American Psychologist, 16*, 681–4.

British Psychological Society, Scientific Affairs Board (1979). Report of the Working Party on Animal Experimentation. *Bulletin of the British Psychological Society, 32*, 44–52.

Broadbent, D. E. (1958). *Perception and Communication*. Pergamon: Oxford.

Broadbent, D. E. (1984). The Maltese cross: a new simplistic model for memory. *Behavioural and Brain Sciences, 7*, 55–94.

Brogden, W. J. (1939). Sensory pre-conditioning. *Journal of Experimental Psychology, 25*, 323–32.

Brown J. S. (1942). Factors determining conflict reactions in difficult discriminations. *Journal of Experimental Psychology, 31*, 272–92.

Brown, J. S. (1969). Factors affecting self-punitive locomotor behaviour. In Campbell, B. A. and Church, R. M. (eds). *Punishment and Aversive Behaviour*. Appleton-Century-Crofts: New York, 467–514.

Brown, P. L. and Jenkins, H. M. (1968). Autoshaping of the pigeon's key peck. *Journal of the Experimental Analysis of Behaviour, 11*, 1–8.

Browne, M. P. (1976). The role of primary reinforcement and overt movements in auto-shaping in the pigeon. *Animal Learning and Behaviour, 4*, 287–92.

Browner, L. P. (1969). Ecological chemistry. *Scientific American, 220,* 22–9.

Bruce, V. and Green, P. (1985). *Visual Perception: Pysiology, Psychology and Ecology.* Lawrence Erlbaum Associates: London.

Bruner, J. (1983). *Child's Talk: Learning to Use Language.* Oxford University Press.

Buchanan, J. P., Gill, T. V., and Braggio, J. T. (1981). Serial position and clustering effects in chimpanzees' 'free recall'. *Memory and Cognition, 9,* 651–60.

Bullock, T. H. (1974). Comparisons between vertebrates and invertebrates in nervous organization. In Schmitt, F. O. and Worden, F. G. (eds). *The Neurosciences. Third Study Program.* MIT Press: London, 343–6.

Burghardt, G. M. (1984). On the origins of play. In Smith, P. K. (ed.). *Play in Animals and Humans.* Basil Blackwell: Oxford, 5–41.

Butler, R.A. (1953). Discrimination learning by rhesus monkeys to visual-exploration motivation. *Journal of Comparative and Physiological Psychology, 46,* 95–8.

Caggiula, A. R. (1970). Analysis of the copulation-reward properties of posterior hypothalamic stimulation in male rats. *Journal of Comparative and Physiological Psychology, 70,* 399–412.

Capaldi, E. J., Nawrocki, M. and Verry, D. R. (1984). Stimulus control in instrumental discrimination learning and reinforcement schedule situations. *Journal of Experimental Psychology: Animal Behaviour Processes, 10,* 46–55.

Carew, T. J. and Kandel, E. (1973). A cellular analysis of acquisition and retention of long-term habituation in *Aplysia. Science, 182,* 1158–60.

Carew, T. J., Pinsker H. M., and Kandel, E. R. (1972). Long-term habituation of a defensive withdrawal reflex in *Aplysia. Science, 175,* 451–4.

Carew, T. J., Walters, E. T. and Kandel, E. R. (1981). Classical conditioning in a simple withdrawal reflex in *Aplysia californica. Journal of Neuroscience, 1,* 1426–37.

Carew, T. J., Hawkins, R. D. and Kandel, E. R. (1983). Differential classical conditioning of a defensive withdrawal reflex in *Aplysia californica. Science, 219,* 397–400.

Carlson J. G. and Wielkiewicz, R. M. (1976). Mediators of the effects of magnitude of reinforcement. *Learning and Motivation, 7,* 184–96.

Carr, H. A. and Watson, J. B. (1908). Orientation in the white rat. *Journal of Comparative Neurology and Psychology, 18,* 27–44.

Carter, D. E. and Werner, T. J. (1978). Complex learning and information processing by pigeons: a critical analysis. *Journal of the Experimental Analysis of Behaviour, 29,* 565–601.

Castellucci, V. and Kandel, E. (1976). An invertebrate system for the cellular study of habituation. In Tighe, T. J. and Leaton, R. N. (eds). *Habituation.* Lawrence Erlbaum Associates: Hillsdale, New Jersy, 1–47.

Catania, A. C. (1963). Concurrent performances: reinforcement interaction and response independence. *Journal of the Experimental Analysis of Behaviour,* 6, 253–63.

Catania, A. C. and Reynolds, G. S. (1970). A quantitative analysis of the responding maintained by interval schedules of reinforcement. *Journal of the Experimental Analysis of Behaviour,* 11, 327–83.

Cerella, J. (1979). Visual classes and natural categories in the pigeon. *Journal of Experimental Psychology: Human Perception and Performance,* 5, 68–77.

Cerella, J. (1982). Mechanisms of concept formation in the pigeon in Ingle, D. J., Goodale, M. A. and Mansfield, R. J. W. (eds). *Analysis of Visual Behaviour.* MIT Press: London, 241–60.

Channell, S. and Hall, G. (1981). Facilitation and retardation of discrimination learning after exposure to the stimuli. *Journal of Experimental Psychology: Animal Behaviour Processes,* 7, 437–46.

Charnov, E. L. (1976). Optimal foraging: the marginal value theorem. *Theoretical Population Biology,* 9, 129–36.

Chen, J. S. and Amsel, A. (1980). Recall (versus recognition) immunization against aversive taste anticipations based on illness. *Science,* 209, 851–3.

Chomsky, N. (1957). *Syntactic Structures.* Mouton: The Hague.

Chomsky, N. (1976). *Reflections on Language.* Fontana: London.

Chomsky, N. (1980). *Rules and Representations.* Columbia University Press: New York.

Chopin, S. F. and Beurger, A. H. (1975). Graded acquisition of an instrumental avoidance response by the spinal rat. *Physiology and Behaviour,* 15, 155–8.

Clark, H. H. and Clark, E. V. (1977). *Psychology and Language.* Harcourt Brace: New York.

Coburn, C. A. (1914). The behaviour of the crow *Corvus Americanus Aud. Journal of Animal Behaviour,* 4, 185–201.

Cohen, N. J. and Squire, L. R. (1980). Preserved learning and retention of pattern analyzing in amnesia: dissociation of knowing how and knowing that. *Science,* 210, 207–10.

Collier, G. H. and Rovee-Collier, C. K. (1981). A comparative analysis of optimal foraging behaviour: laboratory simulations. In Kamil, A. C. and Sargent, T. D. (eds). *Foraging Behaviour.* Garland Books: New York.

Collier, G., Hirsch, E. and Hamlin, P. H. (1972). The ecological determinants of reinforcement in the rat. *Physiology and Behaviour,* 9, 705–16.

Cook, R. G. (1980). Retroactive interference in pigeon short-term memory by a reduction in ambient illumination. *Journal of Experimental Psychology: Animal Behaviour Processes,* 6, 326–38.

Cook, R. G., Brown, M. F. and Riley, D. A. (1985). Flexible memory processing by rats: use of prospective and retrospective information in the radial maze. *Journal of Experimental Psychology: Animal Behaviour Processes, 11,* 453–68.

Coover, B. D., Sutton, B. R. and Heybach, J. P. (1977). Conditioning decreases in plasma cortico-sterone levels in rats by pairing stimuli with daily feedings. *Journal of Comparative and Physiological Psychology, 91,* 716–26.

Cormier, S. M. (1986). *Basic Processes of Learning, Cognition and Motivation: A Match-Mismatch Theory.* Lawrence Erlbaum Associates: London.

Cornell, E. H. (1974). Infants' discrimination of photographs of faces following redundant presentations. *Journal of Experimental Child Psychology, 18,* 98–106.

Couvillon, P. A. and Bitterman, M. E. (1982). Compound conditioning in honey bees. *Journal of Comparative and Physiological Psychology, 96,* 192–9.

Couvillon, P. A. and Bitterman, M. E. (1984). The over learning-extinction effect and successive negative contrast in honey bees. *Journal of Comparative Psychology, 98,* 100–9.

Cowan, P. E. (1976). The new object reaction of *Rattus rattus L.:* the relative importance of various cues. *Behavioural Biology, 16,* 31–44.

Crespi, L. P. (1942). Quantitative variation in incentive and performance in the white rat. *American Journal of Psychology, 55,* 467–517.

Creutzfeldt, O. D. (1979). Neurophysiological mechanisms and consciousness. In *Brain and Mind,* Ciba Foundation Symposium 69. Excertpa Medica: Amsterdam, 217–33.

Croze, H. J. (1970). Searching images in carrion crows. *Zeitschrift für Tierpsychologie, 5,* 1–85.

Cunningham, A. (1921). A gorilla's life in civilization. *Zoological Society Bulletin, New York, 24,* 118–24.

D'Amato, M. R. (1973). Delayed matching and short-term memory in monkeys. In Bower, G. H. (ed.) *The Psychology of Learning and Motivation. Vol. 7.* Academic Press: New York, 227–69.

D'Amato, M. R. and Cox, J. K. (1976). Delay of consequences and short-term memory in monkeys. In Medin, D. L., Roberts, D. A. and Davis, R. T. (eds). *Processes in Animal Memory.* Lawrence Erlbaum Associates: Hillsdale, New Jersey, 49–78.

D'Amato. M. R. and Worsham, R. W. (1974). Retrieval cues and short-term memory in capuchin monkeys. *Journal of Comparative and Physiological Psychology, 86,* 274–82.

Darwin, C. (1872/1965). *The Expression of the Emotions in Man and Animals.* Chicago University Press.

Dashiell, J. F. (1930). Direction orientation in maze running by the white rat. *Comparative Psychology Monographs, 7,* 1–72.

Davenport, R. K., Rogers, C. M. and Russell, I. S. (1973). Cross modal perception in apes. *Neuropsychologia, 11,* 21–8.

Davenport, R. K., Rogers, C. M. and Russell, I. S. (1975). Cross modal perception in apes: altered visual cues and delay. *Neuropsychologia, 13* 229–35.

Davey, G. (1983). An associative view of human classical conditioning. In Davey, G. C. L. (ed.). *Animal Models of Human Behaviour*. Wiley: Chichester, 95–114.

Davey, G. (ed.). (1986). *Conditioning in Humans*. Wiley: Chichester.

Davis, H. (1977). Response characteristics and control during lever press escape. In Davis, H. and Hurwitz, H.M.B. (eds). *Operant-Pavlovian Interactions*. Lawrence Erlbaum Associates: Hillsdale, New Jersey, 233–66.

Davis, M. (1972). Differential retention of sensitization and habituation of the startle response in the rat. *Journal of Comparative and Physiological Psychology, 78*, 210–67.

Davis, M. and Wagner, A. R. (1969). Habituation of startle response under incremental sequence of stimulus intensities. *Journal of Comparative and Physiological Psychology, 67*, 486–92.

Davis, P. (1976). Conditioning after-images: a procedure minimizes the extinction effect of normal test trials. *British Journal of Psychology 67*, 181–9.

Dawkins, R. (1976). *The Selfish Gene*. Oxford University Press: London.

Dawkins, R. (1982). *The Extended Phenotype*. Freeman: Oxford.

Day, R. H. (1972). Visual spatial illusions: a general explanation. *Science, 175*, 1335–40.

Deese, J. (1951). Extinction of a discrimination without performance of the choice response. *Journal of Comparative and Physiological Psychology, 44*, 362–6.

Deets, A. C., Harlow, H. F. and Blomquist, A. J. (1970). Effects of intertrial interval and Trial 1 reward during acquisition of an object-discrimination learning set in monkeys. *Journal of Comparative and Physiological Psychology, 73*, 501–5.

DeLong, R. E. and Wasserman, E. A. (1981). Effects of different reinforcement expectancies on successive matching-to-sample performance in pigeons. *Journal of Experimental Psychology: Animal Behaviour Processes, 7*, 394–412.

Dember, W. N. and Warm, J. S. (1979). *Psychology of Perception*, 2nd edn. Holt, Rinehart & Winston: London.

Dethier, V. G. (1963). *The Physiology of Insect Senses*. Methuen: London.

Deutsch, J. A. (1960). *The Structural Basis of Behaviour*. Cambridge University Press.

Deutsch, J. A. and Deutsch, D. (1963). Attention: some theoretical *considerations*. *Psychological Review, 70*, 80–90.

Deutsch, J. and Howarth C. I. (1963). Some tests of a theory of intracranial self-stimulation, *Psychological Review, 70*, 444–60.

De Villiers, P. A. and Herrnstein, R. J. (1976). Toward a law of response strength. *Psychological Bulletin, 83*, 1131–53.

Dews, P. B. (1962). The effect of multiple S^Δ periods on responding on a fixed-interval schedule. *Journal of the Experimental Analysis of Behaviour, 5,* 369–74.

Dews, P. B. (1970). The theory of fixed-interval responding. In Schoenfeld, W. N. (ed.). *The Theory of Reinforcement Schedules.* Appleton-Century-Crofts: New York, 43–61.

Dickinson, A. (1980). *Contemporary Animal Learning Theory.* Cambridge University Press.

Dickinson, A. (1985). Actions and habits: the development of behavioural autonomy. *Proceedings of the Royal Society, B. 308.* 67–78.

Dickinson, A. (1986). Re-examination of the role of the instrumental contingency in the sodium-appetite irrelevant incentive effect. *Quarterly Journal of Experimental Psychology,* 38B, 161–72.

Dickinson, A., Nicholas, D. J. and Adams, C. D. (1983). The effect of the instrumental training contingency on susceptibility to reinforcer devaluation. *Quarterly Journal of Experimental Psychology, 35B,* 35–51.

Dinsmoor, J. A. and Hughes, H. L. (1956). Training rats to press a bar to turn off shock. *Journal of Comparative and Physiological Psychology, 49,* 235–8.

Dinsmoor, J. A., Matsuoka, Y. and Winograd, E. (1958). Barholding as a preparatory response in escape-from-shock training. *Journal of Comparative and Physiology, 51,* 637–9.

Distenhoff, J. F., Haggerty, R. and Corning, V. C. (1971). An analysis of leg position learning in the cockroach yoked control. *Physiology and Behaviour, 7,* 359–62.

Domjan, M. and Galef, B. G. Jr. (1983). Biological constraints on instrumental and classical conditioning: retrospect and prospect. *Animal Learning and Behaviour, 11,* 151–61.

Domjan, M. and Wilson, N. E. (1972). Specificity of cue to consequence in aversion learning in the rat. *Psychonomic Science, 26,* 143–5.

Doty, B. A., Jones, C. N., and Doty, L. A. (1967). Learning-set formation by mink, ferrets, skunks and cats. *Science, 155,* 1579–80.

Drent, R. H. (1982). Risk-benefit assessment in animals. In Griffin, D. R. (ed.). *Animal Mind – Human Mind.* Springer-Verlag: Berlin.

Drew, G. C. (1938). The function of punishment in learning. *Journal of Genetic Psychology, 52,* 257–67.

Dunham, P. J. (1968). Contrasted conditions of reinforcement: a selective critique. *Psychological Bulletin, 69,* 295–315.

Dunlap, K., Gentry, E. and Zeigler, J. W. (1931). The behaviour of white rats under food and electric shock stimulation. *Journal of Comparative Psychology, 12,* 371–8.

Dworkin, B. R. and Miller, N. E. (1986). Failure to replicate visceral learning in the acute curarized rat preparation. *Behavioural Neuroscience,* *100*, 299–314.

Eikelboom, R. and Stewart, J. (1982). The conditioning of drug-induced physiological response. *Psychological Review, 89*, 507–28.

Elliot, M. H. (1928). The effect of change of reward on the maze perform-ance of rats. *University of California Publications in Psychology, 4*, 19–30.

Ellison, G. D. (1964). Differential salivary conditioning to traces. *Journal of Comparative and Physiological Psychology, 57*, 373–80.

Emmerton, J. (1983). Vision. In Abs, M. (ed.). *Physiology and Behaviour of the Pigeon.* Academic Press: London, 245–66.

Epstein, R. Kirschnit, C. E., Lanza, R. P. and Rubin, L. C. (1984). Insight in the pigeon: antecedents and determinants of an intelligent performance. *Nature, 308*, 61–2.

Erlich, A. (1970). Response to novel objects in 3 lower primates: greater galago, slow-loris, and owl monkey. *Behaviour, 37*, 55–63.

Ernst, A. J., Engerg, L. and Thomas, D. R. (1971). On the forms of stimulus generalization curves for visual intensity. *Journal of the Exper-imental Analysis of Behaviour, 16*, 177–80.

Estes, W. K. (1944). An experimental study of punishment. *Psychological Monographs, 57*, no. 3.

Evans, S. (1936). The role of kinaesthesis in the establishment and control of the maze habit. *Journal of Genetic Psychologys, 48*, 177–98.

Ewert, J.-P. (1976). The visual system of the toad: behavioural and physio-logical studies of a pattern recognition system. In Fite, K. V. (ed.). *The Amphibian Visual System.* Academic Press: New York, 141–202.

Ewert, J.-P. (1982). Neuronal basis of configurational prey selection by the common toad. In Ingle, D. J., Goodale, M. A. and Mansfield, R. J. W. (eds.). *Analysis of Visual Behaviour.* MIT Press: Cambridge, Mass., 1–45.

Eysenck, H. J. (1975). A note on backward conditioning. *Behaviour Research and Therapy, 13*, 201.

Eysenck, H. J. (1976). The learning theory model of neurosis – a new approach. *Behaviour Research and Therapy, 14*, 251–67.

Eysenck, M. W. (1977). *Human Memory: Theory, Research and Individual Differ-ences.* Pergamon: Oxford.

Fantino, E. (1967). Preference for mixed versus fixed-ratio schedules. *Journal of the Experimental Analysis of Behaviour, 10*, 35–43.

Fantino, E. and Logan, C. (1979). *The Experimental Analysis of Behaviour: A Biological Perspective.* W. H. Freeman: San Francisco.

Feldman, J. A. (1985). Four frames suffice: a provisional model of vision and space. *Behavioural and Brain Sciences, 8*, 265–89.

Ferrier, D. (1878). *The Localization of Cerebral Disease.* Smith Elder: London.

Ferster, C. B. and Skinner, B. F. (1957). *Schedules of Reinforcement.* Appleton-Century-Crofts: New York.

Finch, G. (1938). Salivary conditioning in atropinized dogs. *American Journal of Physiology*, *124*, 136–41.

Fisher, G. J. (1962). The formation of learning sets in young gorillas. *Journal of Comparative and Physiological Psychology*, *55*, 924–5.

Fodor, J. A. (1980). Fixation of belief and concept acquisition. In Piatelli-Palmarini, M. (ed.). *Language and Learning: The Debate between Jean Piaget and Noam Chomsky*. Harvard University Press: Cambridge, Mass.

Fodor, J. A. (1983). *The Modularity of Mind.*. MIT Press: London.

Fowler, H. and Wischner, G. J. (1969). The varied functions of punishment in discrimination learning. In Campbell, B. A. and Church, R. M. (eds.). *Punishment and Aversive Behaviour*. Appleton-Century-Crofts: New York, 375–420.

Fraenkel, G. S. and Gunn, D. L. (1940). *The Orientation of Animals: Kineses, Taxes and Compass Reactions*. Clarendon Press, Oxford.

Fragaszy, D. M. and Mason, W. A. (1983). Comparisons of feeding behaviour in captive squirrel and Titi monkeys (*Saimiri sciureus* and *Callicebus moloch*). *Journal of Comparative Psychology*, *97*, 310–26.

Freud, S. (1936). *The Problem of Anxiety*. Norton: New York.

Freud, S. (1959). Inhibitions, symptoms and anxiety. In Strachey, J. (ed.). *The Standard Edition of the Complete Psychological Works of Sigmund Freud*. *Vol. XX*. Hogarth Press: London, 87–174.

Frisby, J. P. (1979). *Seeing*. Oxford University Press.

Furness, W. H. (1916). Observations on the mentality of chimpanzees and orangutans. *Proceedings of the American Philosophical Society*, *65*, 281–90.

Gaffan, D. (1974). Recognition impaired and association inact in the memory of monkeys after transection of the fornix. *Journal of Comparative and Physiological Psychology*, *86*, 1100–9.

Gaffan, D. (1977a). Discrimination of word-like compound visual stimuli by monkeys. *Quarterly Journal of Experimental Psychology*, *29*, 589–96.

Gaffan, D. (1977b). Monkeys' recognition memory for complex pictures and the effect of fornix transection. *Quarterly Journal of Experimental Psychology*, *29*, 505–14.

Gaffan, D. (1977c). Recognition memory after short retention intervals in fornix-transected monkeys. *Quarterly Journal of Experimental Psychology*, *29*, 577–8.

Gaffan, D. (1983). A comment on primacy effects in monkeys' memory lists. *Animal Learning and Behaviour*, *11*, 144–5.

Gaffan, D. (1985). Hippocampus: memory, habit and voluntary movement. *Philosophical Transactions of the Royal Society*, *B*, *308*, 87–99.

Gaffan, D., Saunders, R. C., Gaffan, E. A., Harrison, S., Shields, C. and Owen, M. J. (1984a). Effects of fornix transection upon associative memory in monkeys: role of hippocampus in learned action. *Quarterly Journal of Experimental Psychology*, *36B*, 173–221.

Gaffan, D., Gaffan, E. A. and Harrison, S. (1984b). Effects of fornix transection on spontaneous and trained non-matching by monkeys. *Quarterly Journal of Experimental Psychology, 36B*, 285–303.

Gaffan, D. Shields, C., and Harrison, S. (1984c). Delayed matching by fornix-transected monkeys: the sample, the push and the bait. *Quarterly Journal of Experimental Psychology, 36B*, 305–17.

Garcia, J. (1981). Tilting at the paper mills of academe. *American Psychologist, 36*, 149–58.

Garcia, J. and Koelling, R. A. (1966). Relation of cue to consequence in avoidance learning. *Psychonomic Science, 4*, 123–4.

Garcia, J., Ervin, F., Yorke, C. and Koelling, R. (1967). Conditioning with delayed vitamin injections. *Science, 155*, 716–18.

Garcia, J., Hankins, W. and Rusiniak, K. (1974). Behavioural regulation of the *milieu interne* in man and rat. *Science, 185*, 824–31.

Garcia, J., Rusinak, K. W., and Brett, L. P. (1977b). Conditioning food-aversions in wild animals: caveant canonici. In Davis, H. and Hurwitz, H. M. B. (eds), *Operant-Pavlovian Interactions*. Lawrence Erlbaum Associates: London, 273–316.

Garcia, J., Hankins, W. G. and Coil, J. D. (1977a). Koalas, men and other conditioned gastronomes. In Milgram, N. W., Krames, L. and Alloway, T. M. (eds). *Food Aversion Learning*. Plenum Press: London, 195–218.

Gardner, R. A. and Gardner, B. T. (1969). Teaching sign language to a chimpanzee. *Science, 165*, 664–72.

Gardner, B. T. and Gardner, R. A. (1971). Two-way communication with an infant chimpanzee. In Schrier, A. M. and Stollnitz, F. (eds). *Behaviour of Nonhuman Primates. Vol. 4.* Academic Press: New York, 117–83.

Gardner, B. T. and Gardner, R. A. (1985). Signs of intelligence in cross-fostered chimpanzees. *Philosophical Transactions of the Royal Society, B, 308*, 159–176.

Gibbon, J. (1977). Scalar expectancy theory and Weber's law in animal timing. *Psychological Review, 84*, 279–325.

Gibson, E. J. and Walk, R. D. (1956). The effect of prolonged exposure to visually presented patterns of learning to discriminate them. *Journal of Comparative and Physiological Psychology, 49*, 239–42.

Gillan, D. J. (1981). Reasoning in the chimpanzee: II. Transitive inference. *Journal of Experimental Psychology: Animal Behaviour Processes, 7*, 150–64.

Gillan, D. J., Premack, D. and Woodruff, G. (1981). Reasoning in the chimpanzee: I. Analogical reasoning. *Journal of Experimental Psychology: Animal Behaviour Processes, 7*, 1–17.

Glazer, H. I. and Weiss, J. M. (1976). Long-term interference effect: an alternative to 'Learned Helplessness'. *Journal of Experimental Psychology: Animal Behaviour Processes, 2*, 202–13.

Glickman, S. E. and Schiff, B. B. (1967). A biological theory of reinforcement. *Psychological Review*, *74*, 81–109.

Goodlass, A. and Geschwind, N. (1976). Language disorders (aphasia). In Carterette, E. C. and Friedman, M. P. (eds). *Handbook of Perception, Vol. VII*. Academic Press: London, 389–428.

Goodkin, F. (1976). Rats learn the relationship between responding and environmental events: an expansion of the learned helplessness hypothesis. *Learning and Motivation*, *7*, 382–93.

Gormezano. I. (1965). Yoked comparisons of classical and instrumental conditioning of the eyelid response; and an addendum on 'voluntary responders'. In Prokasy, W. F. (ed). *Classical Conditioning: A Symposium* Appleton-Century-Crofts: New York, 48–70.

Goss-Custard, J. D. (1977). The energetics of prey selection by redshank, *Tringa totanus* (L.), in relation to prey density. *Journal of Animal Ecology*, *46*, 1–19.

Gossette, R. L. and Hood, P. (1968). Successive discrimination reversal measures as a function of variation of motivational and incentive levels. *Perceptual and Motor Skills*, *26*, 47–52.

Gossette, R. L., Gossette, M. F. and Riddell, W. (1966). Comparisons of successive discrimination reversal performances among loosely and remotely related avian species. *Animal Behaviour*, *14*, 560–4.

Gossette, R. L., Kraus, G. and Speiss, J. (1968). Comparison of successive discrimination reversal (SDR) performances of seven mammalian species on a spatial task. *Psychonomic Science*, *12*, 193–4.

Gottlieb, G. (1984). Evolutionary trends and evolutionary origins: relevance to theory in comparative psychology. *Psychological Review*, *91*, 448–56.

Grant, D. G., Brewster, R. G. and Stierhoff, K. A. (1983). 'Surprisingness' and short-term retention in the pigeon. *Journal of Experimental Psychology: Animal Behaviour Processes*, *9*, 63–79.

Grant, D. S. (1976). Effect of sample presentation time on long-delay matching in the pigeon. *Learning and Motivation*,:17, 580–90.

Grant, D. S. (1981). Short-term memory in the pigeon. In Spear, N. E. and Miller, R. R. (eds). *Information Processing in Animals*, Lawrence Erlbaum Associates: Hillsdale, New Jersey, 226–56.

Grant, D. S. and Roberts, W. A. (1976). Sources of retroactive inhibition in pigeon short-term memory. *Journal of Experimental Psychology: Animal Behaviour Processes*, *2*, 1–16.

Gray, J. A. (1975). *Elements of a Process Theory of Learning*. Academic Press: London.

Gray, J. A. (1979). *Pavlov*. Fontana: London.

Gray, J. A. (1982). *The Neuropsychology of Anxiety: An Enquiry into the Functions of the Septo-Hippocampal System*. Oxford University Press.

Gray, J. A. (1984). The hippocampus as an interface between cognition and emotion. In Roitblat, H. L., Bever, T. G. and Terrace, H. S. (eds). *Animal Cognition*. Lawrence Erlbaum Associates: London.

Green, K. F. and Garcia, J. (1971). Recuperation from illness: flavour enhancement for rats. *Science, 173*, 249–51.

Green, S. (1987). *An Introduction to Physiological Psychology*. Routledge & Kegan Paul: London.

Green, S. and Marler, P. (1979). The analysis of animal communication. In Marler, P. and Vandenbergh, J. G. (eds). *Handbook of Behavioural Neurobiology, Vol. 3*. Plenum Press: London, 73–158.

Greene, S. (1983). Feature memorization in pigeon concept formation. In Commons, M. L., Herrnstein, R. J. and Wagner, A. R. (eds). *Quantititive Analyses of Behaviour: Discrimination Processes*. Balinger: Cambridge, Mass., 209–29.

Gregg, V. (1986). *An Introduction to Human Memory*. Routledge & Kegan, Paul: London.

Griffin, D. R. (1984). *Animal Thinking*. Harvard University Press: London.

Grossberg, S. (1982). Processing of expected and unexpected events during conditioning and attention: a psychophysiological theory. *Psychological Review, 89*, 529–72.

Groves, P. M. and Thompson, R. F. (1970). Habituation: a dual-process theory. *Psychological Reivew, 77*, 419–50.

Gruber, H. E., Girgus, J. S. and Banuazizi, A. (1971). The development of object permanence in the cat. *Developmental Psychology, 4*, 9–15.

Grzimek, B. (1974). *Animal Life Encyclopedia, Vol. 5*. Van Nostrand: London.

Gustavson, C. R., Garcia, J., Hankins, W. G. and Rusiniak, K. W. (1974). Coyote predation control by aversive conditioning. *Science, 184*, 581–3.

Guttman, N. and Kalish, H. I. (1956). Discriminability and stimulus generalization. *Journal of Experimental Psychology, 51*, 79–88.

Hailman, J. P. (1962). Pecking of laughing gull chicks at models of the parental head. *Auk, 79*, 89–98.

Haley, T. J. and Snyder, R. S. (eds). (1964). *The Response of the Nervous System to Ionizing Radiation*. Little Brown: Boston.

Halgren, C. R. (1974). Latent inhibition in rats: associative or non-associative. *Journal of Comparative and Physiological Psychology, 86*, 74–8.

Hall, G. (1980). Exposure learning in animals. *Psychological Bulletin, 88*, 535–50.

Hall, G. (1983). *Behaviour*. Academic Press: London.

Hall, G. and Pearce, J. M. (1979). Latent inhibition of a CS during CS-US pairings. *Journal of Experimental Psychology: Animal Behaviour Processes, 5*, 31–42.

Hamilton, W. D. (1964). The genetical theory of social behaviour. I and II. *Journal of Theoretical Biology, 7*, 1–32.

Hammond, L. J. (1980). The effect of contingency upon the appetitive conditioning of free-operant behaviour. *Journal of the Experimental Analysis of Behaviour, 34*, 297–304.

Hankins, W. G., Garcia, J. and Rusiniak, K. (1973). Dissociation of odour and taste in baitshyness. *Behavioural Biology, 8*, 407–19.

Hankins, W. G., Rusiniak, K. W. and Garcia, J. (1976). Dissociation of odor and taste in shock avoidance learning. *Behavioural Biology, 18*, 345–58.

Hanson, H. M. (1959). Effects of discrimination training on stimulus generalization. *Journal of Experimental Psychology, 58*, 321–34.

Harlow, H. F. (1949). The formation of learning sets. *Psychological Review, 56*, 51–65.

Harlow, H. F. (1950). Analysis of discrimination learning by monkeys. *Journal of Experimental Psychology, 40*, 26–39.

Harlow, H. F. (1958). The nature of love. *American Psychologist, 13*, 673–85.

Harlow, H. F. (1959). Learning set and error factor theory. In Koch, S. (ed.). *Psychology: A Study of a Science. Vol., 2.* McGraw-Hill: New York, 492–537.

Harlow, H. F. (1962). The heterosexual affectional system in monkeys. *American Psychologist, 17*, 1–9.

Harlow, H. F. and Harlow, M. K. (1965). The affectional systems. In Schrier, A., Harlow, H. F. and Stollnitz, F. (eds). *Behaviour of Nonhuman Primates, Vol. 2.* Academic Press: London, 287–334.

Harlow, H. F. and Suomi, S. J. (1970). The nature of love simplified. *American Psychologist, 25*, 161–8.

Harlow, H. F., Harlow, M. K. and Meyer, D. R. (1950). Learning motivated by a manipulation drive. *Journal of Experimental Psychology, 40*, 228–34.

Harris, J. D. (1943). Studies on non-associative factors inherent in conditioning. *Comparative Psychology Monographs, 18(1)*, 1–74.

Harris, M. and Coltheart, M. (1986). *Language Processing in Children and Adults.* Routledge & Kegan Paul: London.

Harrison, J. M. (1978). Functional properties of the auditory system of the brain stem. In Masterton, R. B. (ed.). *Handbook of Behavioural Neurobiology, Vol. I.* Plenum Press: London, 409–458.

Hawkins, R. D. and Kandel, E. R. (1984). Is there a cell-biological alphabet for simple forms of learning?. *Psychological Review, 91*, 375–91.

Hawkins, R. D., Abrams, T. W., Carew, T. J. and Kandel, E. R. (1983). A cellular mechanism for classical conditioning in *Aplysia:* Activity-dependent amplification of pre-synaptic facilitation. *Science, 219*, 400–5.

Hayes, K. J. and Hayes, C. (1951). The intellectual development of a home raised chimpanzee. *Proceedings of the American Philosophical Society, 95*, 105–9.

Hayes, K. J. and Hayes, C. (1953). Picture perception in a home raised chimpanzee. *Journal of Comparative and Physiological Psychology, 46*, 470–4.

Hayes, K. J. and Nissen, C. H. (1971). Higher mental functions of a home raised chimpanzee. In Schrier, A. M. and Stollnitz, F. (eds). *Behaviour of Nonhuman Primates, Vol. 4.* Academic Press: New York, 59–115.

Hayes, K. J., Thompson, R. and Hayes, C. (1953). Discrimination learning sets in chimpanzees. *Journal of Comparative and Physiological Psychology, 46,* 99–104.

Heaton, M. B., Galleher, E. L., Baker, R. T., Otero, J. M. and Alvarez, I. M. (1981). Operant escape learning in decerebrate duck embryos. *Journal of Comparative and Physiological Psychology, 95,* 199–204.

Hebb, D. O. (1949). *The Organization of Behaviour.* Chapman & Hall: London.

Heffner, H. E. and Heffner, R. S. (1984). Temporal lobe lesions and perception of species-specific vocalizations by macaques. *Science, 226,* 75–6.

Helson, H. (1927). Insight in the white rat. *Journal of Experimental Psychology, 10,* 378–97.

Hendersen, R. W., Patterson, J. M. and Jackson, R. L. (1980). Acquisition and retention of control of instrumental behaviour by a cue signalling airblast: how specific are conditioned anticipations?. *Learning and Motivation, 11,* 40.

Herb, F. H. (1940). Latent learning – non-reward followed by food in blinds. *Journal of Comparative Psychology, 29,* 247–56.

Herman, L. M. (1980). Cognitive charactersitics of dolphins. In Herman, L. M. (ed.). *Cetacean Behaviour: Mechanisms and Functions.* Wiley-Interscience: New York, 363–429.

Herrick, R. M. (1964). The successive differentiation of a lever displacement response. *Journal of the Experimental Analysis of Behaviour, 7,* 211–15.

Herrnstein, R. J. (1961). Relative and absolute strength of response as a function of frequency of reinforcement. *Journal of the Experimental Analysis of Behaviour, 4,* 267–72.

Herrnstein, R. J. (1969). Method and theory in the study of avoidance. *Psychological Review,, 76,* 46–69.

Herrnstein, R. J. (1970). On the law of effect. *Journal of the Experimental Analysis of Behaviour, 13,* 243–66.

Herrnstein, R. J. (1977). The evolution of behaviourism. *American Psychologist, 32,* 593–613.

Herrnstein, R. J. (1984). Objects, categories, and discriminative stimuli. In Roitblat, H. L., Bever, T. G. and Terrace, H. S. (eds). *Animal Cognition.* Lawrence Erlbaum Associates: Hillsdale, New Jersy, 233–61.

Herrnstein, R. J. (1985). Riddles of natural categorization. *Philosophical Transactions of the Royal Society, B, 308,* 129–44.

Herrnstein, R. J. and de Villiers, P. A. (1980). Fish as a natural category for people and pigeons. In Bower, G. H. (ed.). *The Psychology of Learning and Motivation. Vol. 14.* Academic Press: New York, 60–97.

Herrnstein, R. J. and Hineline, P. N. (1966). Negative reinforcement as shock frequency reduction. *Journal of the Experimental Analysis of Behaviour,* 9, 421–30.

Herrnstein, R. J. and Loveland, D. H. (1964). Complex visual concept in the pigeon. *Science, 146,* 549–51.

Herrnstein, R. J., Loveland, D. H. and Cable, C. (1976). Natural concepts in pigeons. *Journal of Experimental Psychology. Animal Behaviour Processes, 2,* 285–302.

Hess, E. H. (1959). Imprinting. *Science, 130,* 133–41.

Heth, C. D. (1976). Simultaneous and backward fear conditioning as a function of number of CS-US pairings. *Journal of Experimental Psychology: Animal Behaviour Processes, 2,* 117–29.

Heth, C. D. and Rescorla, R. A. (1973). Simultaneous and backward fear conditioning in the rat. *Journal of Comparative and Physiological Psychology,* 82, 434–43.

Hinde, R. A. (1960). Energy models of motivation. *Symposia of the Society for Experimental Biology, 14,* 199–213.

Hinde, R. A. (1970). *Animal Behaviour: A Synthesis of Ethology and Comparative Psychology.* McGraw-Hill: London.

Hinde, R. A. and Stevenson-Hinde, J. (eds). (1973). *Constraints on Learning.* Academic Press: London.

Hodos, W. (1961). Progressive ratio as a measure of reward strength. *Science, 134,* 943–4.

Hodos, W. and Bonbright, J. C. (1972). The detection of visual intensity differences by pigeons. *Journal of the Experimental Analysis of Behaviour, 18,* 471–9.

Hodos, W. and Campbell, C. B. G. (1969). *Scale Naturae:* why there is no theory of comparative psychology. *Psychological Review, 76,* 337–50.

Hodos, W. and Kalman, G. (1963). Effects of increment size and reinforcer volume on progressive ratio performance. *Journal of the Experimental Analysis of Behaviour, 6,* 387–92.

Holding, D. H. and Jones, D. D. (1976). Delayed one-trial extinction of the McCullough effect. *Quarterly Journal of Experimental Psychology, 21,* 683–7.

Holland, P. C. (1977). Conditioned stimulus as a determinant of the form of the Pavlovian conditioned response. *Journal of Experimental Psychology: Animal Behaviour Processes, 3,* 77–104.

Holland, P. C., and Rescorla, R. A. (1975). Second-order conditioning with food unconditioned stimulus. *Journal of Comparative and Physiological Psychology, 88,* 459–67.

Holman, E. W. (1975). Some conditions for the dissociation of consummatory and instrumental behaviour in rats. *Learning and Motivation, 6,* 358–66.

Holman, G. L. (1968). Intra gastric reinforcement effect. *Journal of Comparative and Physiological Psychology, 69,* 432–41.

Honig, W. K. (1978). Studies of working memory in the pigeon. In Hulse, S. H., Fowler, H. and Honig, W. K. (eds). *Cognitive Processes in Animal Behaviour.* Lawrence Erlbaum Associates: Hillsdale, New Jersey, 211–48.

Honig, W. K. (1981). Working memory and the temporal map. In Spear, N. E. and Miller, R. R. (eds). *Information Processing in Animals.* Lawrence Erlbaum Associates: Hillsdale, New Jersey, 167–97.

Honig, W. K. (1984). Contributions of animal memory to the interpretation of animal learning. In Roitblat, H. L., Bever, T. G. and Terrace, H. S. (eds). *Animal Cognition.* Lawrence Erlbaum Associates: London, 29–44.

Honzik, C. H. (1933). Maze learning in rats in the absence of specific intra– and extra-maze stimuli. *University of California Publications in Psychology, 6,* 99–144.

Honzik, C. H. (1936). The sensory basis of maze learning in rats. *Comparative Psychology Monographs, 13,* 1–113.

Horn, G. (1967). Neuronal mechanisms of habituation. *Nature, 215,* 707–11.

Horowitz. L. M., Lippman, L. G., Norman, S. A. and McConkie, G. W. (1964). Compound stimuli in paired-associate learning. *Journal of Experimental Psychology, 67,* 132–141.

Horridge, G. A. (1962). Learning of leg position by the ventral nerve cord in headless insects. *Proceedings of the Royal Society, B, 157,* 33–52.

Howard, J. M. and Campion, R. C. (1978). A metric for pattern discrimination performance. *IEEE Transactions on Systems, Man, and Cybernetics, 8,* 32–7.

Hudson, B. B. (1939). One-trial learning in rats. *Psychological Bulletin, 36,* 642.

Hudson, B. B. (1950). One-trial learning in the domestic rat. *Genetic Psychology Monographs, 41,* 99–145.

Hull, C. L. (1934). The concept of habit-family hierarchy and maze learning. *Psychological Review, 41,* 33–54.

Hull, C. L. (1937). Mind, mechanism and adaptive behaviour. *Psychological Review, 44,* 1–32.

Hull, C. L. (1943). *Principles of Behaviour.* Appleton-Century-Crofts: New York.

Hull, C. L. (1952). *A Behaviour System.* Yale University Press: New Haven.

Hulse, S. H., Fowler, H. and Honig, W. K. (eds). (1978). *Cognitive Process in Animal Behaviour.* Lawrence Erlbaum Associates: Hillsdale, New Jersey.

Hume, D. (1777/1970). *Enquiries Concerning the Human Understanding and Concerning the Principles of Morals.* Oxford University Press: London.

Humphrey, G. (1930). Le Chatelier's rule and the problem of habituation and dehabituation in *Helix albolaris*. *Psychologiche Forschung, 13*, 113–27.

Humphrey, G. (1933). *The Nature of Learning in Relation to Living Systems*. Kegan Paul, Trench & Trubner: London.

Hunter, M. W. and Kamil, A. L. (1971). Object-discrimination learning set and hypothesis behaviour in the Northern Bluejay (*Cyanocitta cristata*). *Psychonomic Science, 22*, 271–3.

Hunter, W. S. (1930). A consideration of Lashley's theory of the equipotentiality of cerebral action. *Journal of General Psychology, 3*, 455–68.

Hurvich, L. M. and Jameson, D. (1974). Opponent process as a model of neural organization. *American Psycholgist, 29*, 88–102.

Hurwitz, H. M. B. (1955). Response elimination without performance. *Quarterly Journal of Experimental Psychology, 7*, 1–7.

Ince, L. P. Brucker, B. S. and Alba, A. (1978). Reflex conditioning of a spinal man. *Journal of Comparative and Physiological Psychology, 92*, 796–802.

Ingebritsen, O. C. (1932). Maze learning after lesion in the cervical cord. *Journal of Comparative Psychology, 14*, 279–94.

Ingle, D. J. (1982). Organization of visuomotor behaviours in vertebrates. In Ingle, D. J., Goodale, M. A. and Mansfield, R. J. W. (eds). *Analysis of Visual Behaviour*. MIT Press; London, 67–109.

Jackson, J. H. (1888/1931). *Selected Writings. Vol. 1*. J. Taylor, ed. Hodder & Stoughton: London.

Jackson, R. L., Alexander, J. H. and Maier, S. F. (1980). Learned helplessness, inactivity, and associative deficits: effects of inescapable shock on response choice escape learning. *Journal of Experimental Psychology: Animal Behaviour Processes, 6*, 1–20.

James, W. (1890/1983). *The Principles of Psychology*. Harvard University Press: London.

Jassik-Gerschenfeld, D., Lange, R. V. and Robert, N. (1977). Response of movement detecting cells in the optic tectum of pigeons to change of wavelength. *Vision Research, 17*, 1139–46.

Jeffrey, W. E. (1968). The orienting reflex in cognitive development. *Psychological Review, 75*, 323–34.

Jeffrey, W. E. and Cohen, L. B. (1971). Habituation in the human infant. In Reese, H. (ed). *Advances in Child Development and Behaviour*. Academic Press: New York, 63–97.

Jenkins, H. M. (1977). Sensitivity of different response systems to stimulus-reinforcer and response-reinforcer relations. In Locurto, C. M., Terrace, H. S. and Gibbon, J. (eds). *Autoshaping and Conditioning Theory*. Academic Press: London, 47–66.

Jenkins, H. M. and Harrison, R. H. (1960). Effect of discrimination training on auditory generalization. *Journal of Experimental Psychology, 59*, 246–53.

Jenkins, H. M. and Moore, B. R. (1973). The form of the autoshaped response with food or water reinforcers. *Journal of the Experimental Analysis of Behaviour, 20,* 163–81.

Jenkins, H. M., Barrera, F. J., Ireland, C., and Woodside, B. (1978). Signal-centred patterns of dogs in appetitive classical conditioning. *Learning and Motivation, 9,* 272–96.

Jerison, H. J. (1973). *Evolution on the Brain and Intelligence.* Academic Press: London.

Johnson, H. M. (1914). Visual pattern discrimination in the vertebrates. *Journal of Animal Behaviour, 6,* 169–88.

Johnson-Laird, P. N. (1983). *Mental Models.* Cambridge University Press.

Johnston, T. D. (1981). Contrasting approaches to a theory of learning. *Behavioural and Brain Sciences, 4,* 125–73.

Jones, P. D. and Holding, D. H. (1975). Extremely long-term persistence of the McCullough effect. *Journal of Experimental Psychology: Human Perception and Performance, 1,* 323–7.

Kamil, A. C. and Balda, R. P. (1985). Cache recovery and spatial memory in Clark's nutcrackers (*Nucifraga columbiana*). *Journal of Experimental Psychology: Animal Behaviour Processes, 11,* 95–111.

Kamil, A. C. and Hunter, M. W. (1970). Performance on object-discrimination learning set by the Greater Hill Myna (*Gracula religiosa*). *Journal of Comparative and Physiological Psychology, 73,* 68–73.

Kamil, A. C. and Roitblat, H. L. (1985). The ecology of foraging behaviour: implications for animal learning and memory. *Annual Review of Psychology, 36,* 141–69.

Kamil, A. C. and Sargent, T. D. (eds). (1981). *Foraging Behaviour: Ecological, Ethological, and Psychological Approaches.* Garland Press: London.

Kamil, A. C., Jones, T. B., Pietrewicz, A. and Maudlin, J. E. (1977). Positive transfer from successive reversal training to learning set in blue jays (*Cyanocitta cristata*). *Journal of Comparative and Physiological Psychology, 91,* 79–86.

Kamin, L. J. (1956). The effects of termination of the CS and avoidance of the US on avoidance learning. *Journal of Comparative and Physiological Psychology, 49,* 420–4.

Kamin, L. J. (1969). Predictability, surprise, attention and conditioning. In Campbell, B. A. and Church, R. M. (eds). *Punishment and Aversive Behaviour.* Appleton-Century-Crofts: New York, 279–96.

Kamin, L. J., Brimer, C. J. and Black, A. H. (1963). Conditioned suppression as a monitor of fear of the CS in the course of avoidance training. *Journal of Comparative and Physiological Psychology, 56,* 497–501.

Kandel, E. R. (1976). An invertebrate system for the cellular analysis of simple behaviours and their modifications. In Schmitt, F. O. and Worden, F. G. (eds). *The Neurosciences: Third Study Program.* MIT Press: London., 347–70.

Kant, I. (1781/1979). *Critique of Pure Reason.* Everyman's Library, Dent: London.

Karli, P. (1956). The Norway rat's killing response to the white mouse; an experimental anaylsis. *Behaviour, 10,* 81–103.

Karten, H. J. (1979). Visual leminiscal pathways in birds. In Granda, A. M. and Maxwell, J. H. (eds). *Neural Mechanisms of Behaviour in the Pigeon.* Plenum: New York, 409–30.

Kaye, H. and Pearce, J. M. (1984). The strength of the orienting response during Pavlovian conditioning. *Journal of Experimental Psychology: Animal Behaviour Processes, 10,* 90–109.

Keith-Lucas, J. and Guttman, N. (1975). Robust single-trial delayed backward conditioning. *Journal of Comparative and Physiological Psychology, 88,* 468–76.

Kelleher, R. T. and Gollub, L. R. (1962). A review of positive conditional reinforcement. *Journal of the Experimental Analysis of Behaviour, 5,* 543–97.

Kellogg, W. N. (1947). Is 'spinal conditioning' conditioning? Reply to 'A comment'. *Journal of Experimental Psychology, 37,* 264–5.

Kellogg, W. N. (1968). Communication and language in the home-raised chimpanzee. *Science, 162,* 423–7.

Kellogg, W. N. and Kellogg, L. A. (1933/1967). *The Ape and the Child: A Study of Envrionmental Influence on Early Behaviour.* Haffner: New York.

Kesner, R. P. and Cook, D. G. (1983). Role of habituation and classical conditioning in the development of morphine tolerance. *Behavioural Neuroscience, 97,* 4–12.

Kesner, R. P. and Novak, J. M. (1982). Serial position curve in rats: role of the dorsal hippocampus. *Science, 218,* 173–5.

Kimble, G. A. (1961). *Hilgard and Marquis' Conditioning and Learning.* Appleton-Century-Crofts: New York.

Kintsch, W. (1970). *Learning, Memory and Conceptual Processes.* Wiley: London.

Klinghammer, E. (1967). Factors influencing choice of mate in altricial birds. In Stevenson, H. W., Hess, E. H. and Rheingold, H. L. (eds), *Early Behaviour.* Wiley: New York.

Kohler, W. (1925). *The Mentality of Apes.* Kegan Paul, Trench & Trubner: London.

Kohler, W. (1929). *Gestalt Psychology.* Loveright: New York.

Konorski, J. (1948). *Conditioned Reflexes and Neuron Organization.* Cambridge University Press.

Konorski, J. (1967). *Interactive Activity of the Brain.* University of Chicago Press.

Konorski, J. and Miller, S. (1937). On two types of conditioned reflex. *Journal of General Psychology, 16,* 264–72.

Krane, R. V. and Wagner, A. R. (1975). Taste aversion learning with a delayed shock US: implications for the 'Generality of the laws of learning'. *Journal of Comparative and Physiological Psychology, 88*, 882–9.

Krebs, J. R. (1979). Foraging strategies and their social significance. In Marler, P. and Vandenbergh, J. G. (eds). *Handbook of Behavioural Neurobiology: Vol. 3. Social Behaviour and Communication.* Plenum Press: New York, 225–70.

Krebs, J. R. and Davies, N. B. (eds). (1983). *Behavioural Ecology. An Evolutionary Approach.* 2nd ed. Blackwell Scientific Publications: Oxford.

Krebs, J. R., MacRoberts, M. H. and Cullen J. M. (1972). Flocking and feeding in the great tit: an experimental study. *Ibis. 114*, 505–30.

Krebs, J. R., Kacelnik, A. and Taylor, P. (1978). Tests of optimal sampling by foraging great tits. *Nature, 275*, 27–31.

Krechevsky, I. (1932). 'Hypotheses' in rats. *Psychological Review, 39*, 516–32.

Krechevsky, I. (1938). A study of the continuity of the problem-solving process. *Psychological Review, 45*, 107–33.

Kriekhaus, E. E. and Wolf, G. (1968). Acquisition of sodium by rats: interaction of innate mechanisms and latent learning. *Journal of Comparative and Physiological Psychology, 65*, 197–201.

Krueger, R. C. and Hull, C. L. (1931). An electro-chemical parallel to the conditioned reflex. *Journal of General Psychology, 5*, 262–9.

Kruse, J. M., Overmeier, J. B., Konz, W. A. and Rokke, E. (1983). Pavlovian conditioned stimulus effects upon instrumental choice behaviour are reinforcer specific. *Learning and Motivation, 14,,* 165–81.

Kuhl, P. K. and Miller, J. D. (1975). Speech perception by the Chinchilla: voiced-voiceless distinction in alveolar plosive consonants. *Science, 190*, 69–72.

Kuo, Z. Y. (1924). A psychology without heredity. *Psychological Review, 31*, 427–51.

Kuo, Z. Y. (1932). Ontogeny of embryonic behaviour. IV: The influence of embryonic movements on behaviour after hatching. *Journal of Comparative Psychology, 14*, 109–22.

Lashley, K. S. (1929). *Brain Mechanisms and Intelligence.* University of Chicago Press.

Lashley, K. S. (1938). The mechanism of vision: XV. Preliminary studies of the rat's capacity for detail vision. *Journal of General Psychology, 18*, 123–93.

Lashley, K. S. (1942). An examination of the 'continuity theory' as applied to discrimination learning. *Journal of General Psychology, 26*, 241–65.

Lashley, K. S. and Ball, J. (1929). Spinal conduction and kinaesthetic sensitivity in the maze habit. *Journal of Comparative Psychology, 9*, 71–106.

Lawrence, D. H. (1949). Acquired distinctiveness of cues: I. Transfer between discriminations on the basis of familiarity with the stimulus. *Journal of Experimental Psychology, 39*, 770–84.

Lawrence, D. H. (1950). Acquired distinctiveness of cues: II. Selective association in a constant stimulus situation. *Journal of Experimental Psychology, 40*, 175–88.

Lawrence, D. H. (1952). The transfer of a discrimination along a continuum. *Journal of Comparative and Physiological Psychology, 45*, 511–6.

Lea, S. E. G. (1978). The psychology and economics of demand. *Psychological Bulletin, 85*, 441–66.

Lea, S. E. G. (1979). Foraging and reinforcement schedules in the pigeon: optimal and non-optimal aspects of choice. *Animal Behaviour, 27*, 875–86.

Lea, S. E. G. (1981). Correlation and contiguity in foraging behaviour. In Harzem, P. and Zeiler, M. D. (eds). *Predictability, Correlation and Contiguity*. Wiley: Chichester, 355–406.

Lea, S. E. G. (1984a). *Instinct, Environment and Behaviour*. Methuen: London.

Lea, S. E. G. (1984b). In what sense do pigeons learn concepts?. In Roitblat, H. L., Bever, T. G. and Terrace, H. S. (eds). *Animal Cognition*. Lawrence Erlbaum Associates: Hillsdale, New Jersey, 263–76.

Lea, S. E. G. and Ryan, C. (1983). Feature analysis of pigeons' acquisition of concept discrimination. In Commons, M. L., Herrnstein, R. J. and Wagner, A. R. (eds). *Quantititive Analyses of Behaviour: Discrimination Processes*. Ballinger: Cambridge, Mass., 239–53.

Leger, D. W., Owings, D. H. and Coss, R. G. (1983). Behavioural ecology of time allocation in California ground squirrels (*Spermophilus beecheyi*): microhabitat effects. *Journal of Comparative Psychology, 97*, 283–91.

Lenneberg, E. H. (1967). *Biological Foundations of Language*. Wiley: New York.

Lett. B. T. and Harley, C. W. (1974). Stimulation of lateral hypothalamus during sickness attenuates learning flavour aversions. *Physiology and Behaviour, 12*, 79–83.

Levey, A. B. and Martin, I. (1975). Classical conditioning of human evaluative response. *Behavioural Research and Therapy, 13*, 221–6.

Levey, A. B. and Martin, I. (1983). Cognitions, evaluation and conditioning: rules of sequence and rules of consequence. *Advances in Behaviour Research and Therapy, 4*, 181–95.

Lieberman, P. (1975). *On the Origins of Language*. Macmillan: New York.

Lieberman, P. (1977). The phylogeny of language. In Sebeok, T. A. (ed.). *How Animals Communicate*. Indiana University Press: Bloomington, 3–25.

Lockard, J. A. (1963). Choice of a warning signal or no warning signal in an unavoidable shock situation. *Journal of Comparative and Physiological Psychology, 56*, 526–30.

Locke, J. (1689/1982). *An Essay Concerning Human Understanding*. Clarendon Press: Oxford.

Locurto, C. M., Terrace, H. S. and Gibbon, J. (1976). Autoshaping, random control, and omission training in the rat. *Journal of the Experimental Analysis of Behaviour*, *26*, 451–62.

Logan, F. A. (1969). The negative incentive value of punishment. In Campbell, B. A. and Church, R. M. (eds). *Punishment and Aversive Behaviour*. Appleton-Century-Crofts: New York, 43–56.

Logue, A. W. (1979). Taste aversion and the generality of the laws of learning. *Psychological Bulletin*, *86*, 276–96.

Lore, R. and Flannelly, K. (1978). Habitat selection and burrow construction by wild *Rattus norvegicus* in a landfill. *Journal of Comparative and Physiological Psychology*, *92*, 888–96.

Lorenz, K. (1967). *On Agression*. Methuen: London.

Lorge, I. and Sells, S. B. (1936). Representative factors in the rat under 'changed-incentive' techinique. *Journal of Genetic Psychology*, *49*, 479–80.

Lovibond, P. F., Preston, G. C. and Mackintosh, N. J. (1984). Context specificity of conditioning, extinction, and latent inhibition. *Journal of Experimental Psychology: Animal Behaviour Processes*, *10*, 360–75.

Lowe, C. F. (1983). Radical behaviourism and human psychology. In Davey, G. C. L. (ed.). *Animal Models of Human Behaviour*. Wiley: Chichester, 71–93.

Lumsden, C. J. and Wilson, E. O. (1981). *Genes, Mind and Culture: The Coevolutionary Process*. Harvard University Press: Cambridge Mass.

McCoy, D. F. and Lange, K. O. (1969). Stimulus generalization of gravity. *Journal of the Experimental Analysis of Behaviour*, *12*, 111–18.

McCullough, C. (1965). Colour adaptation of edge detectors in the human visual system. *Science*, *149*, 115–16.

Mackintosh, N. J. (1969). Further analysis of the overtraining reversal effect. *Journal of Comparative and Physiological Psychology. Monographs*, *67*, no. 2, part 2.

Mackintosh, N. J. (1973). Stimulus selection: learning to ignore stimuli that predict no change in reinforcement. In Hinde, R. A. and Stevenson Hinde, J. (eds). *Constraints on Learning*. Academic Press: London, 75–96.

Mackintosh, N. J. (1974). *The Psychology of Animal Learning*. Academic Press: London.

Mackintosh, N. J. (1975). A theory of attention: variations in associability of stimuli with reinforcement. *Psychological Review*, *82*, 276–98.

Mackintosh, N. J. (1983). *Conditioning and Associative Learning*. Clarendon Press: Oxford.

Mackintosh, N. J., Wilson, B. and Boakes, R. A. (1985). Differences in mechanisms of intelligence among vertebrates. *Philosophical Transactions of the Royal Society*, *B*, *308*, 53–65.

Macphail, E. M. (1982). Brain and Intellegince in Vertebrates. Clarendon Press: Oxford.

Macphail, E. M. (1985). Vertebrate intelligence: the null hypothesis. *Philosophical Transactions of the Royal Society, B, 308*, 37–51.

MacFarlane, D. A. (1930). The role of kinaesthesis in maze learning. *University of California Publications in Psychology, 4*, 277–305.

Maier, S. F. (1970). Failure to escape traumatic electric shock: incompatable skeletal-motor responses or learned helplessness. *Learning and Motivation, 1*, 157–69.

Maier, S. F. and Seligman, M. E. P. (1976). Learned helplessness: theory and evidence. *Journal of Experimental Psychology, General, 105*, 3–46.

Maier, S. F. and Testa, T. J. (1975). Failure to learn to escape by rats previously exposed to shock is partly produced by associative interference. *Journal of Comparative and Physiological Psychology, 88*, 554–64.

Maier, S. F., Seligman, M. E. P. and Solomon, R. L. (1969). Pavlovian fear conditioning and learned helplessness. In Campbell, B. A. and Church, R. M. (eds). *Punishment and Aversive Behaviour*. Appleton-Century-Crofts: New York, 299–342.

Maier, S. F. Shermanm J. E., Lewis, J. W., Terman, G. W. and Liebeskind, J. C. (1983). The opoidnonopoid nature of stress-induced analgesia and learned helplessness. *Journal of Experimental Psychology: Animal Behaviour Processes, 9*, 80–90.

Maki, W. S. (1981). Directed forgetting in animals. In Spear, N. E. and Miller, R. R. (eds). *Information Processing in Animals*. Lawrence Erlbaum Associates: Hillsdale, New Jersy, 199–225.

Mallott, R. and Sidall, J. (1972). Acquisition of the people concept in pigeons. *Psychological Reports, 31*, 3–13.

Marler, P. (1970). A comparative approach to vocal learning: song development in white-crowned sparrows. *Journal of Comparative and Physiological Psychology Monograph, 71*, pt. 2, 1–25.

Marler, P. and Waser, M. S. (1977). Role of auditory feedback in canary song development. *Journal of Comparative and Physiological Psychology, 91*, 8–16.

Marr, D. (1982). *Vision*. W. H. Freeman: San Francisco.

Marsh, G. (1969). An evaluation of three explanations for the transfer of discrimination effect. *Journal of Comparative and Physiological Psychology, 68*, 268–75.

Marwine, A. and Collier, G. (1979). The rat at the water hole. *Journal of Comparative and Physiological Psychology, 93*, 391–402.

Maslach, C. (1979). Negative emotional biasing of unexplained arousal. *Journal of Personality and Social Psychology, 37*, 953–69.

Mason, W. A. (1967). Motivational aspects of social responsiveness in young chimpanzees. In Stevenson, H. W., Hess, E. H. and Rheingold, H. L. (eds). *Early Behaviour*. WileyL: London, 103–26.

Mason, W. A. (1979). Ontogeny of social behaviour. In Marler, P. and

Vandenburgh, J. G. (eds). *Handbook of Behavioural Neurobiology. Vol. 3. Social Behaviour and Communication.* Plenum Press: London, 1–28.

Masterton, R. B. and Glendenning, K. K. (1979). Phylogeny of the vertebrate sensory systems. In Masterton, R. B. (ed.). *Handbook of Behavioural Neurology. Vol. I.* Plenum: New York, 1–38.

Matsuzawa, T. (1985). Use of numbers by a chimpanzee. *Nature, 315,* 57–9.

May, J. G. and Matteson, H. H. (1976). Spatial frequency contingent colour after effects. *Science, 192,* 145–6.

Maynard-Smith, J. (1975). *The Theory of Evolution.* Penguin: Harmondsworth.

Maynard-Smith, J. (1984). Game theory and the evolution of behaviour. *Behavioural and Brain Sciences, 7,* 95–126.

Mechner, F. (1958). Probability relations within response sequences under ratio reinforcement. *Journal of the Experimental Analysis of Behaviour, 1,* 109–21.

Meck, W. H. and Church, R. M. (1984). Simultaneous temporal processing. *Journal of Experimental Psychology: Animal Behaviour Processes, 10,* 1–29.

Meck, W. H., Church, R. M. and Olton, D. S. (1984). Hippocampus, time, and memory. *Behavioural Neuroscience, 98,* 3–22.

Medin, D. L., Roberts, W. A. and Davis, R. T. (eds). (1976). *Processes of Animal Memory* Lawrence Erlbaum Associates: Hillsdale, New Jersey.

Melgren, R. L. and Ost, J. W. P. (1969). Transfer of Pavlovian differential conditioning to an operant discrimination. *Journal of Comparative and Physiological Psychology, 67,* 390–4.

Melvin, K. B. and Smith, F. H. (1967). Self-punitive avoidance behaviour in the rat. *Journal of Comparative and Physiological Psychology, 63,* 533–5.

Mendelson, J. (1966). Role of hunger in T-maze learning for food by rats. *Journal of Comparative and Physiological Psychology, 62,* 341–9.

Menzel, E. W. (1973). Chimpanzee spatial memory organization. *Science, 182,* 943–5.

Menzel, E. W. (1978). Cognitive mapping in chimpanzees. In Hulse, S. H., Fowler, H. and Honig, W. K. (eds), *Cognitive Processes in Animal Behaviour.* Lawrence Erlbaum Associates: Hillsdale, New Jersey, 375–422.

Menzel, E. W. and Juno, C. (1985). Social foraging in marmoset monkeys and the question of intelligence. *Philosophical Transactions of the Royal Society, B, 308,* 145–58.

Milgram, N. W., Krames, L. and Alloway, T. M. (1977). *Food Aversion Learning.* Plenum Press: New York.

Miller, I. W. and Norman, W. H. (1979). Learned helplessness in humans: a review and attribution theory model. *Psychological Bulletin, 86,* 93–118.

Miller, N. E. (1944). Experimental studies of conflict. In Hunt, J. McV.

(ed.). *Personality and the Behaviour Disorders. Vol. I.* Ronald Press: New York, 431–65.

Miller, N. E. (1948). Studies of fear as an acquirable drive. *Journal of Experimental Psychology, 38*, 89–101.

Miller, N. E. (1969). Learning of visceral and glandular responses. *Science, 163*, 434–44.

Miller, N. E. (1978). Biofeedback and visceral learning. *Annual Review of Psychology, 29*, 373–404.

Miller, N. E. and Dicara, L. (1967). Instrumental learning of heart-rate changes in curarized rats: shaping, and specificity to discrimininative stimulus. *Journal of Comparative and Physiological Psychology, 63*, 12–19.

Miller, N. E. and Weiss, J. M. (1969). Effects of the somatic or visceral responses to punishment. In Campbell, B. A. and Church, R. M. (eds). *Punishment and Aversive Behaviour.* Appleton-Century-Crofts: New York, 343–72.

Miller, R. R. and Balaz, M. A. (1981). Differences in adaptiveness between classically conditioned and instrumentally acquired responses. In Spear, N. E. and Miller, R. R. (eds). *Information Processing in Animals.* Lawrence Erlbaum Associates: Hillsdale, New Jersey, 49–80.

Miller, R. R., Greco, C., Vigorito, M. and Marlin, N. A. (1983). Signalled tailshock is perceived as similar to a stronger unsignalled tailshock: implications for a functional analysis of classical conditioning. *Journal of Experimental Psychology: Animal Behaviour Processes, 9*, 105–31.

Miller, V. and Domjan, M. (1981). Specificity of cue to consequence in aversion learning in the rat: control for US-induced differential orientations. *Animal Learning and Behaviour, 9*, 339–45.

Milner, B., Corkin, S. and Teuber, H.-L. (1968). Further analysis of the hippocampal amnesic syndrome: 14 year follow-up study of H. M. *Neuropsychologia, 6*, 215–34.

Miranda, S. B. and Fanz, R. L. (1974). Recognition memory in Down's syndrome and normal children. *Child Development, 45*, 651–60.

Mishkin, M. (1978). Memory in monkeys severely impaired by combined but not separate removal of amygdala and hippocampus. *Nature, 273*, 297–8.

Mishkin, M. (1982). A memory system in the monkey. *Philosophical Transactions of the Royal Society, B. 298.* 85–95.

Moore, B. R. (1973). The role of directed Pavlovian reactions in simple instrumental learning in the pigeon. In Hinde, R. A. and Stevenson-Hinde, J. (eds). *Constraints on Learning.* Academic Press: London, 159–86.

Morgan, C. L. (1894). *An Introduction to Comparative Psychology.* Walter Stott: London.

Morgan, M. J. (1974). Do rats like to work for their food?. *Learning and Motivation, 5*, 352–6.

Morgan, M. J. (1979). Motivational processes. In Dickinson, A. and Boakes, R. A. (eds). *Mechanisms of Learning and Motivation*. Lawrence Erlbaum Associates: Hillsdale, New Jersey, 171–201.

Morgan, M. J. and Nicholas, D. J. (1979). Discrimination between reinforced action patterns in the rat. *Learning and Motivation, 10*, 1–27.

Morgan, M. J., Fitch, M. D., Holman, J. G. and Lea, S. E. G. (1976). Pigeons learn the concept of an 'A'. *Perception, 5*, 57–66.

Morris, R. G. M. (1975). Preconditioning of reinforcing properties to an exteroceptive feedback stimulus. *Learning and Motivation, 6*, 289–98.

Morris, R. G. M. (1981). Spatial localization does not require the presence of local cues. *Learning and Motivation, 12*, 239–60.

Morris, R. G. M., Garrud, P., Rawlins, J. N. P. and O'Keefe, J. (1982). Place navigation impaired in rats with hippocampal lesions. *Nature, 297*, 681–3.

Morrow, J. G. and Smithson, B. L. (1969). Learning sets in an invertebrate. *Science, 164*, 850–1.

Morse, W. A. and Kelleher, R. T. (1977). Determinants of reinforcement and punishment. In Honig, W. K. and Staddon, J. E. R. (eds), *Handbook of Operant Behaviour*. Prentice-Hall, Englewood Cliffs, NJ, 174–200.

Morse, P. A. and Snowdon, C. J. (1975). An investigation of categorical speech discrimination by rhesus monkeys. *Perception and Psychopysics, 17*, 9–16.

Mowrer, O. H. (1939). A stimulus-response analysis of anxiety and its role as a reinforcing agent. *Psychological Review, 46*, 553–65.

Mowrer, O. H. (1940). Anxiety reduction and learning. *Journal of Experimental Psychology, 27*, 497–516.

Mowrer, O. H. (1947). On the dual nature of learning – a reinterpretation of 'conditioning' and 'problem solving'. *Harvard Educational Review, 17*, 102–48.

Mowrer, O. H. (1960). *Learning Theory and Behaviour*. Wiley: New York.

Mowrer, O. H. and Lamoreaux, R. R. (1946). Fear as an intervening variable in avoidance conditioning. *Journal of Comparative Psychology, 39*, 29–50.

Muenzinger, K. F. (1934). Motivation in learning: I. Electric shock for correct response in the visual discrimination habit. *Journal of Comparative Psychology, 17*, 267–77. Muncer, S. J. (1982). 'Conservations' with a chimpanzee, *Developmental Psychobiology, 16*, 1–11.

Muncer, S. J. (1982). 'Conversations' with a chimpanzee. *Developmental Psychobiology, 16*, 1–11.

Muncer, S. J. and Ettlinger, G. (1981). Communication by a chimpanzee: first trial mastery of word order that is critical for meaning, but failure to negate conjunctions. *Neuropsyhcologia, 19*, 73–8.

Munn, N. L. (1950). *Handbook of Psychological Research on the Rat*. Houghton Mifflin: Boston.

Neisser, U. (1967). *Cognitive Psychology*. Appleton-Century-Crofts: New York.

Neuringer, A. J. (1969). Animals respond for food in the presesnce of free food. *Science*, *166*, 399–401.

Nicholson, J. N. and Gray, J. A. (1972). Peak shift, behavioural contrast and stimulus generalization as related to personality and development in children. *British Journal of Psychology*, *63*, 47–62.

Nicolai J. (1959). Familientradition in der Gesangesentwicklung des Gimpels (*Pyrrhula pyrhula L.*. *Journal fur Ornithologie*, *100*, 39–46.

Nissen, H. W. (1930). A study of maternal behaviour in the white rat by means of the obstruction method. *Journal of Genetic Psychology*, *37*, 377–93.

Norman, R. J., Buchwald, J. S. and Villablanca, J. R. (1977). Classical conditioning with auditory discrimination of the eyeblink in decerebrate cats. *Science*, *96*, 551–3.

Norton-Griffiths, M. (1967). Some ecological aspects of the feeding behaviour of the oystercatcher on the edible mussel. *Ibis*, *109*, 412–24.

Norton-Griffiths, M. (1969). The organization, control and development of parental feeding in the oyster catcher. *Behaviour*, *34*, 55–114.

Oakley, D. A. (1979a). Instrumental reversal learning and subsequent fixed ratio performance on simple and go/no-go schedules in neodecorticate rabbits. *Physiological Psychology*, *7*, 29–42.

Oakley, D. A. (1979b). Cerebral cortex and adaptive behaviour. In Oakley, D. A. and Plotkin, H. (eds). *Brain, Behaviour and Evolution*. Methuen: London, 154–88.

Oakley, D. A. (1983). The varieties of memory: a phylogenetic approach. In Mayes, A. (ed.). *Memory in Animals and Humans*. Van Nostrand: Wokingham, 20–82.

Oakley, D. A. (1985). Cognition and imagery in animals. In Oakley, D. A. (ed.). *Brain and Mind*. Methuen: London, 99–131.

Oakley, D. A. and Russell, I. S. (1976). Subcortical nature of Pavlovian differentiation in the rabbit. *Physiology and Behaviour*, *17*, 947–54.

Ohman, A., Ericksson, B. and Loftberg, I. (1975a). Phobias and preparedness: phobic versus neutral pictures as conditioned stimuli for human autonomic responses. *Journal of Abnormal Psychology*, *84*, 41–5.

Ohman, A., Ericksson, G. and Olofsson, C. (1975b). One trial learning and superior resistance to extinction of autonomic responses conditioned to potentially phobic stimuli. *Journal of Comparative and Physiological Psychology*, *88*, 619–27.

O'Keefe, J. (1979). A review of hippocampal place cells. *Progress in Neurobiology*, *13*, 419–39.

O'Keefe, J. and Nadel, L. (1978). *The Hippocampus as a Cognitive Map.* Clarendon Press: Oxford.

Olds, J. (1958). Self-stimulation of the brain. *Science, 127,* 315–24.

Olds, J. (1961). Differential effects of drives and drugs on self-stimulation at different brain sites. In Sherr, D. E. (ed.). *Electrical Stimulation of the Brain.* University of Texas Press: Austin, 350–66.

Olds, J. and Milner, P. (1954). Positive reinforcement produced by electrical stimulation of septal areas and other regions of rat brains. *Journal of Comparative and Physiological Psychology, 47,* 419–27.

Olds, M. E. and Olds, J. (1963). Approach avoidance analysis of the rat diencephalon. *Journal of Comparative Neurology, 120,* 259–95.

Olson, G. M. (1976). An information-processing analysis of visual memory and habituation in infants. In Tighe, T. J. and Leaton, R. N. (eds). *Habituation.* Lawrence Erlbaum Associates: Hillsdale, New Jersey, 239–77.

Olton, D. S. (1979). Mazes, maps, and memory. *American Psychologist, 34,* 583–96.

Olton, D. S. and Collison, C. (1979). Intramaze cues and 'odor trails' fail to direct choice behaviour on an elevated maze. *Animal Learning and Behaviour, 7,* 221–3.

Olton, D. S. and Papas, B. C. (1979). Spatial memory and hippocampal function. *Neuropsychologia, 17,* 669–82.

Olton, D. S. and Samuelson, R. J. (1976). Remembrance of places passed: spatial memory in rats. *Journal of Experimental Psychology: Animal Behaviour Processes, 2,* 97–116.

Olton, D. S., Collison, C. and Werz, M. A. (1977). Spatial memory and radial arm maze performance in rats. *Learning and Motivation, 8,* 289–314.

Olton, D. S., Becker, J. T. and Handelmann, G. E. (1979). Hippocampus, space, and memory. *Behavioural and Brain Sciences, 2,* 313–65.

Olton, D. S., Handelman, G. E. and Walker, J. A. (1981). Spatial memory and food searching strategies. In Kamil, A. C. and Sargent, T. O. (eds). *Foraging Behaviour.* Garland Press: New York, 333–54.

Osgood, C. E. (1953). *Method and Theory in Experimental Psychology.* Oxford University Press: New York.

Overman, W. H. and Doty, R. W. (1980). Prolonged visual memory in macaques and man. *Neuroscience, 5,* 1825–31.

Overmier, J. B. and Seligman, M. E. P. (1967). Effects of inescapable shock upon subsequent escape and avoidance learning. *Journal of Comparative and Physiological Psychology, 63,* 28–33.

Overmier, J. B., Bull, J. A. and Trapold, M. A. (1971). Discriminative cue properties of different fears and their role in response selection in dogs. *Journal of Comparative and Physiological Psychology, 76,* 478–82.

Papez, J. W. (1937). A proposed mechanism of emotion. *Archives of Neurology and Psychiatry*, *38*, 725–43.

Park, T. J. and Dooling, R. J. (1985). Perception of species-specific contact calls by budgerigars (*Melopsittacus undulatus*). *Journal of Comparative Psychology*, *99*, 391–402.

Parkinson, J. K. and Medin, D. L. (1983). Emerging attributes in monkey short-term memory. *Journal of Experimental Psychology: Animal Behaviour Processes*, *9*, 31–40.

Pasnak, R. (1979). Acquisition of prerequisites to conservation by macaques. *Journal of Experimental Psychology: Animal Behaviour Processes*, *5*, 194–210.

Passingham, R. (1982). *The Human Primate*. W. H. Freeman: Oxford.

Patterson, F. G. (1978). The gestures of a gorilla: language acquisition in another pongid. *Brain and Language*, *5*, 72–99.

Patterson, M. M. (1976). Mechanisms of classical conditioning and fixation in spinal mammals. In Riesen, A. H. and Thompson, R. F. (eds). *Advances in Psychobiology*, *Vol, 3*. Wiley: New York.

Pavlov, I. P. (1927). *Conditioned Reflexes: An Investigation of the Physiological Activity of the Cerebral Cortex*. Dover: New York.

Pavlov, I. P. (1955). *Selected Works*. Foreign Languages Publishing House; Moscow.

Pearce, J. M. and Hall, G. (1980). A model for Pavlovian learning: variations in the effectiveness of conditioned but not of unconditioned stimuli. *Psychological Review*, *87*, 532–52.

Peeke, H. V. S. (1983). Habituation, sensitization, and redirection of aggression and feeding behaviour in the three-spined stickleback (*Gasterosteurs aculeatus L.*). *Journal of Comparative Psychology*, *97*, 43–51.

Peeke, H. V. S. and Petrinovich, L. (1984). *Habituation, Sensitization, and Behaviour*. Academic Press: London.

Peele, D. B., Casey, J., and Silberger, A. (1984). Primacy of IRT reinforcement in accounting for rate differences under variable-ratio and variable-interval schedules. *Journal of Experimental Psychology: Animal Behaviour Processes*, *10*, 149–67.

Penfield, W. and Roberts, L. (1959). *Speech and Brain Mechanisms*. Princeton University Press.

Pepperberg, I. M. (1981). Functional vocalizations by an African grey parrot (*Psittacus erithacus*). *Zeitschrift für Tierpsycholgoie*, *55*, 139–60.

Pepperberg, I. M. (1983). Cognition in the African grey parrot: preliminary evidence for auditory/vocal comprehension of the class concept. *Animal Learning and Behaviour*, *11*, 179–85.

Perkins, C. C. (1968). An analysis of the concept of reinforcement. *Psychological Review*, *75*, 155–72.

Perrett, D. I., Smith, R. A. J., Potter, D. D., Mistlin, A. J., Head, A. S.,

Milner, A. D. and Jeeves, M. A. (1985). Visual cells in the temporal cortex sensitive to face view and gaze direction. *Proceedings of the Royal Society, B, 223,* 293–317.

Petersen, M. R., Beecher, M. D., Zoloth, S. R., Moody, D. and Stebbins, W. L. (1978). Neural lateralization of species-specific vocalizations by Japanese Macques (*Macaca fusata*). *Science, 202,* 324–7. Piaget, J. (1971). *Biology and Knowledge.* Edinburgh University Press.

Peterson, C. and Seligman, M. E. P. (1984). Causal explanations as a risk factor for depression: theory and evidence. *Psychological Review, 91,* 347–74.

Peterson, G. B. (1984). How expectancies guide behaviour. In Roitblat, H. L., Bever, T. G. and Terrace, H. S. (eds). *Animal Cognition.* Lawrence Erlbaum Associates: Hillsdale, New Jersey, 135–48.

Peterson, G. B., Wheeler, R. L. and Armstrong, G. D. (1978). Expectancies as mediators. *Animal Learning and Behaviour, 6,* 279–85.

Piaget, J. (1971). *Biology and Knowledge.* Edinburgh University Press.

Piaget, J. and Inhelder, B. (1969). *The Psychology of the Child.* Routledge & Kegan Paul: London.

Pierrel, R. and Sherman, J. G. (1960). Generalization and discrimination as a function of the S^D – $S\Delta$ difference. *Journal of the Experimental Analysis of Behaviour, 5,* 67–71.

Pinel, J. P. J. and Treit, D. (1978). Burying as a defensive response in rats. *Journal of Comparative and Physiological Psychology, 92,* 708–12.

Pinel, J. P. J. and Treit, D. (1979). Conditioned defensive burying in rats: availability of burying materials. *Animal Learning and Behaviour, 7,* 392–6.

Pinsker, H., Kupfermann, I., Castellucci, V. and Kandel, E. (1970). Habituation and dishabituation of the gill withdrawal reflex in *Aplysia. Science, 167,* 1740–2.

Plato (c. 400 BC/1917–37). *Plato with an English Translation.* Heinemann: London.

Platt, J. R. (1979). Interresponse time shaping by variable-interval like reinforcement contingencies. *Journal of the Experimental Analysis of Behaviour, 31,* 3–14.

Pliskoff, S. S., Wright, J. E. and Hawkins, B. T. (1965). Brain stimulation as a reinforcer: intermittent schedules. *Journal of the Experimental Analysis of Behaviour, 8,* 75–88.

Plotkin, H. C. and Odling-Smee, F. J. (1981). A multiple-level model of evolution and its implications for sociobiology. *Behavioural and Brain Sciences, 4,* 225–268.

Podgorny, P. and Garner, W. R. (1979). Reaction time as a measure of inter– and intraobject visual similarity. *Perception and Psychophysics, 26,* 37–52.

Polit, A. and Bizzi, E. (1978). Processes controlling arm movements in monkeys. *Science, 201,* 1235–7.

Porter, D. and Neuringer, A. (1984). Music discrimination by pigeons. *Journal of Experimental Psychology: Animal Behaviour Processes*, *10*, 138–48.

Powell, R. W. (1979). The effect of reinforcement magnitude upon responding under fixed-ratio schedules. *Journal of the Experimental Analysis of Behaviour*, *12*, 605–8.

Prelec, D. (1982). Matching, maximizing, and the hyperbolic reinforcement feedback function. *Psychological Review*, *89*, 189–230.

Prelec, D. (1984). The assumptions underlying the generalized matching law. *Journal of the Experimental Analysis of Behaviour*, *41*, 101–7.

Premack, D. (1965). Reinforcement theory. In Levine, D. (ed.). *Nebraska Symposium on Motivation*. University of Nebraska Press, 123–80.

Premack, D. (1971). Language in chimpanzee. *Science*, *172*, 808–22.

Premack, D. (1976). *Intelligence in Ape and Man*. Lawrence Erlbaum Associates: Hillsdale, New Jersey.

Premack, D. (1983). The codes of man and beasts. *Behavioural and Brain Sciences*, *6*, 125–37.

Premack, D. and Woodruff, G. (1978). Chimpanzee problem solving: a test for comprehension. *Science*, *202*, 532–5.

Premack, D., Woodruff, G. and Kennel, K. (1978). Paper-marking test for chimpanzee: simple control for social cues. *Science*, *202*, 903–5.

Pryor, K. W., Haag, R. and O'Reilly, J. (1969). The creative porpoise: training for novel behaviour. *Journal of the Experimental Analysis of Behaviour*, *12*, 653–61.

Pyke, G. H., Pulliam, H. R. and Charnov, E. L. (1977). Optimal foraging: Biology, *52*, a selective review of theory and tests. *Quarterly Review of Biology*, *52*, 137–54.

Rachlin, H. (1978). A molar theory of reinforcement schedules. *Journal of the Experimental Analysis of Behaviour*, *30*, 345–60.

Rachlin, H. and Baum, W. M. (1969). Response rate as a function of amount of reinforcement for a signalled concurrent response. *Journal of the Experimental Analysis of Behaviour*, *12*, 11–16.

Rachlin, H., Battalio, R., Kagel, J. and Green, L. (1981). Maximization theory in behavioural psychology. *Behavioural and Brain Sciences*, *4*, 371–417.

Rachman, S. (1977). The conditioning theory of fear-acquisition a critical examination. *Behaviour Research and Therapy*, *15*, 375–87.

Rawlins, J. P. N. (1985). Associations across time: the hippocampus as a temporary memory store. *Behavioural and Brain Sciences*, *8*, 479–96.

Reason, J. and Mycielska, K. (1982). *Absent-Minded?: The Psychology of Mental Lapses and Everyday Error*. Prentice-Hall: Englewood Cliffs, NJ.

Redshaw, M. (1978). Cognitive development in human and gorilla infants. *Journal of Human Evolution*, *7*, 133–41.

Reid, L. S. (1953). The development of noncontinuity behaviour through continuity learning. *Journal of Experimental Psychology, 46,* 107–12.

Rensch, B. (1959). *Evolution Above the Species Level.* Methuen: London.

Rescorla, R. A. (1967). Pavlovian conditioning and its proper control procedures. *Psychological Review, 74,* 71–80.

Rescorla, R. A. (1978). Some implications of a cognitive perspective on Pavlovian conditioning. In Hulse, S. H., Fowler, H. and Honig, W. K. (eds). *Cognitive Processes in Animal Behaviour.* Lawrence Erlbaum Associates: London, 15–50.

Rescorla, R. A. (1979). Aspects of the reinforcer learned in second-order Pavlovian conditioning. *Journal of Experimental Psychology: Animal Behaviour Processes, 5,* 79–95.

Rescorla, R. A. (1980). *Pavlovian Second-Order Conditioning.* Lawrence Erlbaum Associates: Hillsdale, New Jersey.

Rescorla, R. A. and Durlach, P. (1981). Within-event learning in classical conditioning. In Spear, N. E. and Miller, R. R. (eds). *Information Processing in Animals.* Lawrence Erlbaum Associates: Hillsdale, New Jersey, 81–111.

Rescorla, R. A. and Solomon, R. L. (1967). Two-process learning theory: Relationship between Pavlovian conditioning and instrumental learning. *Psychological Review, 74,* 151–82.

Rescorla, R. A. and Wagner, A. R. (1972). A theory of Pavlovian conditioning: variations in the effectiveness of reinforcement and nonreinforcement. In Black, A. H. and Prokasy, W. F. (eds). *Classical Conditioning II: Current Research and Theory.* Appleton-Century-Crofts: New York, 64–9.

Revusky, S. (1977). Learning as a general process with an emphasis on data from feeding experiments. In Milgram, N. W., Krames, L. and Alloway, T. M. (eds). *Food Aversion Learning.* Plemun Press: London.

Reynolds, G. S. (1961). Attention in the pigeon. *Journal of the Experimental Analysis of Behaviour, 4,* 203–8.

Reynolds, G. S. and Limpo, A. J. (1969). Attention and generalization during a conditional discrimination. *Journal of the Experimental Analysis of Behaviour, 12,* 911–16.

Rice, M. (1980). *Cognition to Language: Categories, Word Meanings, and Training.* University Park Press: Baltimore.

Richards, D. G., Wolz, J. P. and Herman, L. M. (1984). Vocal mimicry of computer-generated sounds and vocal labelling of objects by a bottle-nosed dolphin *Tursiops Truncatus. Journal of Comparative Psychology, 98,* 10–28.

Riley, D. A. (1968). *Discrimination Learning.* Allyn & Bacon: Boston.

Rilling, M. and McDiarmid, C. (1965). Signal detection in fixed-ratio schedules. *Science, 148,* 526–7.

Rizley, R. C. and Rescorla, R. A. (1972). Associations in second-order conditioning and sensory preconditioning. *Journal of Comparative and Physiological Psychology*, *81*, 1–11.

Roberts, R. and Church, R. M. (1978). Control of internal clock. *Journal of Experimental Psychology: Animal Behaviour Processes*, 4, 318–37.

Roberts, S. (1981). Isolation of an internal clock. *Journal of Experimental Psychology: Animal Behaviour Processes*, 7, 242–69.

Roberts, S. and Church, R. M. (1978) Control of an internal clock. *Journal of Experimental Psychology: Animal Behaviour Processes*, 4, 318–37.

Roberts, W. A. (1980). Distribution of trials and intertrial repetition in delayed matching to sample with pigeons. *Journal of Experimental Psychology: Animal Behaviour Processes*, 6, 217–37.

Roberts, W. A. and Grant, D. S. (1976). Studies of short-term memory in the pigeon using the delayed matching to sample procedure. In Medin, D. L., Roberts, D. A. and Davis, R. T. (eds). *Processes of Animal Memory*. Lawrence Erlbaum Associates: Hillsdale, New Jersey, 79–112.

Roberts, W. A. and Kraemer, P. J. (1981). Recognition memory for lists of visual stimuli in monkeys and humans. *Animal Learning and Behaviour*, 9, 587–94.

Roberts, W. A. and Smythe, W. E. (1979). Memory for lists of spatial events in the rat. *Learning and Motivation*, *10*, 313–36.

Roberts, W. W., Steinberg, M. L. and Means, L. W. (1967). Hypothalamic mechanisms for sexual, aggressive and other behaviours in the opposum. *Journal of Comparative and Physiological Psychology*, *64*, 1–15.

Rogers, J. P. and Thomas, D. R. (1982). Task specificity in nonspecific transfer and in extradimensional stimulus generalization in pigeons. *Journal of Experimental Psychology: Animal Behaviour Processes*, 8, 301–12.

Roitblat, H. L. (1982). The meaning of representation in animal memory. *Behavioural and Brain Sciences*, 5, 353–406.

Roitblat, H. L., Bever, T. G. and Terrace, H. S. (eds) (1984). *Animal Cognition*. Lawrence Erlbaum Associates: London.

Rolls, E. T., Judge, S. J. and Sanghera, M. I. C. (1977). Activity of neurones in the inferotemporal cortex of the alert monkey. *Brain Research*, *130*, 229–38.

Romanes, G. J. (1883). *Mental Evolution in Animals*. Kegan Paul, Trench: London.

Romanes, G. J. (1886). *Animal Intelligence*. 4th ed. Kegan Paul, Trench: London.

Roper, T. J., Edwards, L. and Crossland, G. (1983). Factors affecting schedule-induced wood-chewing in rats: percentage and rate of reinforcement, and operant requirement. *Animal Learning and Behaviour*, *11*, 35–43.

Rosenfeld, H. M. and Baer, D. M. (1969). Unnoticed verbal conditioning of an aware experimenter by a more aware subject: the double-agent effect. *Psychological Review*, *76*, 425–32.

Rosenzweig, S. (1943). An experimental study of 'repression' with special reference to need-persistive and ego-defensive reactions to frustration. *Journal of Experimental Psychology, 32,* 64–74.

Ross, R. T., Orr, W. B., Holland, P. C. and Berger, T. W. (1984). Hippocampectomy disrupts acquisition and retention of learning conditional responding. *Behavioural Neuroscience, 98,* 211–25.

Rosselini, R. A. (1978). Inescapable shock interferes with the acquisition of a free appetitive operant. *Animal Learning and Behaviour, 6,* 155–9.

Rosselini, R. A. and DeCola, J. P. (1981). Inescapable shock interferes with the acquisition of a low-activity response in an appetitive context. *Animal Learning and Behaviour, 9,* 487–90.

Rosselini, R. A., DeCola, J. P., and Shapiro, N. R. (1982). Cross-motivational effects of inescapable shock are associative in nature. *Journal of Experimental Psychology: Animal Behaviour Processes, 8,* 376–88.

Rozin, P. and Kalat, J. W. (1971). Specific hungers and poison avoidance as adaptive specializations of learning. *Psychological Review, 78,* 459–86.

Rumbaugh, D. M. and Pate, J. L. (1984). The evolution of cognition in primates: a comparative perspective. In Roitblat, H. L., Bever, T. G. and Terrace, H. S. (eds). *Animal Cognition.* Lawrence Erlbaum Associates: London, 568–87.

Rumbaugh, D. M. and von Glaserfeld, E. (1973). Reading and sentence completion by a chimpanzee. *Science, 182,* 731–3.

Russell, B. (1940). *An Inquiry into Meaning and Truth.* Allen & Unwin: London.

Russell, B. (1946). *The History of Western Philosophy.* Allen & Unwin: London.

Russell, M., Dark, K. A., Cummins, R. W., Ellman, G., Calloway, E. and Peeke, H. V. S. (1984). Learned histamine release. *Science, 225,* 733–4.

Sahley, C., Rudy, J. W. and Gelperin, A. (1981). An analysis of associative learning in a terrestial mollusc: I. Higher order conditioning, blocking, and a transient US pre-exposure effect. *Journal of Comparative Physiology, A, 144,* 1–8.

Sands, S. F. and Wright, A. A. (1980a). Primate memory: retention of serial list items by a rhesus monkey. *Science, 209,* 938–40.

Sands, S. F. and Wright, A. A. (1980b). Serial probe recognition performance by a rhesus monkey and a human with 10– and 20–item lists. *Journal of Experimental Psychology: Animal Behaviour Processes, 6,* 386–96.

Sands, S. F., Urcuioli, P. J., Wright, A. A. and Santiago, H. C. (1984). Serial position effects and rehearsal in primate visual memory. In Roitblat, H. L., Bever, T. G. and Terrace, H. S. (eds). *Animal Cognition.* Lawrence Erlbaum Associates: London, 375–88.

Santiago, H. C. and Wright, A. A. (1984). Pigeon memory: *same/different* concept learning, serial probe recognition acquisition, and probe delay effects on the serial position function. *Journal of Experimental Psychology: Animal Behaviour Processes*, *10*, 498–512.

Savage, G. E. (1980). The fish telencephalon and its relation to learning. In Ebbesson, S. O. E. (ed.). *Comparative Neurology of the Telencephalon.* Plenum Press: New York, 129–74.

Savage-Rumbaugh, E. S., Rumbaugh, D. M. and Boysen, S. (1978a). Symbolic communication between two chimpanzees. *Science*, *201*, 641–4.

Savage-Rumbaugh, E. S., Rumbaugh, D. M. and Boysen, S. (1978b). Linguistically mediated tool use and exchange by chimpanzees (*Pan troglodytes*). *Behavioural and Brain Sciences*, *1*, 539–54.

Savage-Rumbaugh, E. S. Rumbaugh, D. M., Smith, S. T. and Lawson, J. (1980). Reference: the linguistic essential. *Science*, *210*, 922–5.

Savage-Rumbaugh, E. S., Pate, J. L., Lawson, J., Smith, S. T. and Rosenbaum, S. (1983). Can a chimpanzee make a statement?. *Journal of Experimental Psychology: General*, *112*, 457–92.

Savage-Rumbaugh, E. S., Sevik, R. A., Rumbaugh, D. M. and Rubert, E. (1985). The capacity of animals to acquire language: do species differences have anything to say to us?. *Proceedings of the Royal Society*, *B, 308*, 177–85.

Schachter, S. and Singer, J. E. (1962). Cognitive, social and physiological determinants of emotional state. *Psychological Review*, *69*, 379–99.

Schneider, J. W., (1973). Reinforcer effectiveness as a function of rate and magnitude: a comparison of concurrent performances. *Journal of the Experimental Analysis of Behaviour*, *20*, 461–71.

Schneider, W. and Shiffrin, R. M. (1977). Controlled and automatic human information processing: I. Detection, search, and attention. *Psychological Review*, *84*, 1–66.

Schrier, A., Angarella, R. and Povar, M. (1984). Studies of concept formation by stumptailed monkeys: concepts humans, monkeys, and letter A. *Journal of Experimental Psychology: Animal Behaviour Processes*, *10*, 564–84.

Schusterman, R. J. and Krieger, K. (1984). California sea lions are capable of semantic comprehension. *Psychological Record*, *34*, 3–23.

Seligman, M. E. P. (1968). Chronic fear produced by unpredictable electric shock. *Journal of Comparative and Physiological Psychology*, *66*, 402–11.

Seligman, M. E. P. (1970). On the generality of the laws of learning. *Psychological Review*, *77*, 406–18.

Seligman, M. E. P. (1975). *On Depression, Development and Death*. W. H. Freeman: San Francisco.

Seligman, M. E. P. and Beagley, G. (1975). Learned helplessness in the rat. *Journal of Comparative and Physiological Psychology*, *88*, 534–41.

Seligman, M. E. P. and Hager, J. C. (1972). *Biological Boundaries of Learning*. Appleton-Century-Crofts: New York.

Seligman, M. E. P. and Johnston, J. C. (1973). A cognitive theory of avoidance learning. In McGuigan, F. J. and Lumsden, D. B. (eds). *Contemporary Approaches to Conditioning and Learning*. Winston-Wiley: Washington, DC.

Seligman, M. E. P. and Weiss, J. M. (1980). Learned helplessness, physiological change, and learned inactivity. *Behaviour Research and Therapy, 18*, 459–73.

Seligman, M. E. P., Maier, S. F. and Geer, H. H. (1968). Alleviation of learned helplessness in the dog. *Journal of Abnormal Psychology, 73*, 256–62.

Selye, H. (1950). *The Physiology and Pathology of Exposure to Stress*. Acta: Montreal.

Seward, J. P. (1949). An experimental analysis of latent learning. *Journal of Experimental Psychology, 39*, 177–86.

Shapiro, M. and Miller, T. M. (1965). On the relationship between conditioned and discriminative stimuli and between instrumental and consummatory responses. In Prokasy, W. F. (ed.). *Classical Conditioning*. Appleton-Century-Crofts: New York, 269–301.

Sheffield, F. D. (1965). Relation between classical conditioning and instrumental learning. In Prokasy, W. F. (ed.). *Classical Conditioning*. Appleton-Century-Crofts: New York, 302–22.

Sheffield, F. D. and Roby, T. B. (1950). Reward value of a non-nutritive sweet taste. *Journal of Comparative and Physiological Psychology, 43*, 471–81.

Sheffield, F. D., Wulff, J. J. and Backer, R. (1951). Reward value of copulation without sex drive reduction. *Journal of Comparative and Physiological Psychology, 44*, 3–8.

Shepp, B. E. and Schrier, A. M. (1969). Consecutive intradimensional and extradimensional shifts in monkeys. *Journal of Comparative and Physiological Psychology, 67*, 199–203.

Sherman, J. A. and Thomas, J. R. (1968). Some factors controlling preference between fixed-ratio and variable-ratio schedules of reinforcement. *Journal of the Experimental Analysis of Behaviour, 11*, 689–702.

Sherrington, C. S. (1906). *The Integrative Action of the Nervous System*. Yale University Press: New Haven.

Shettleworth, S. J. (1983). Memory in food-hoarding birds. *Scientific American, 3*, (March), 86–94.

Shettleworth, S. J. and Krebs, J. R. (1982). How marsh tits find their hoards: the roles of site preference and spatial memory. *Journal of Experimental Psychology: Animal Behaviour Processes, 8*, 354–75.

Shiffrin, R. M. and Schneider, W. (1984). Automatic and controlled processing revisited. *Psychological Review, 91*, 269–76.

Shimp, C. P. (1969). Optimal behaviour in free-operant experiments. *Psychological Review, 76*, 97–112.

Shimp, C. P. (1976). Short-term memory in the pigeon: the previously reinforced response. *Journal of the Experimental Analysis of Behaviour, 26,* 487–93.

Shimp, C. P. (1984). Self report by rats of the temporal patterning of their behaviour: a dissociation between tacit knowledge and knowledge. In Roitblat, H. L., Bever, T. G. and Terrace, H. S. (eds). *Animal Cognition.* Lawrence Erlbaum Associates: London, 215–29.

Shurrager, P. S. and Culler, E. A. (1940). Conditioning in the spinal dog. *Journal of Experimental Psychology, 26,* 133–59.

Sidman, M. (1953). Avoidance conditioning with brief shock and no exteroceptive signal. *Science, 118,* 157–8.

Siegel, S. (1975). Evidence from rats that morphine tolerance is a learned response. *Journal of Comparative and Physiological Psychology, 89,* 498–506.

Siegel, S. (1976). Morphine analgesic tolerance: its situation specificity supports a Pavlovian conditioning model. *Science, 193,* 323–5.

Siegel, S. (1977). Morphine tolerance acquisition as an associative process. *Journal of Experimental Psychology: Animal Behaviour Processes, 3,* 1–13.

Siegel, S., Hinson, R. E., and Krank, M. D. (1978). The role of pre-drug signals in morphine analgesis tolerance: support for a Pavlovian conditioning model of tolerance. *Journal of Experimental Psychology: Animal Behaviour Processes, 4,* 188–96.

Silberberg, A. and Fantino, E. (1970). Choice, rate of reinforcement, and the change-over delay. *Journal of the Experimental Analysis of Behaviour, 13,* 187–97.

Sinnamon, H. M., Freniere, S., and Kootz, J. (1978). Rat hippocampus and memory for places of changing significance. *Journal of Comparative and Physiological Psychology, 92,* 142–55.

Skinner, B. F. (1938). *The Behaviour of Organisms.* Appleton-Century-Crofts: New York.

Skinner, B. F. (1953). *Science and Human Behaviour.* Macmillan: New York.

Skinner, B. F. (1972). *Beyond Freedom and Dignity.* Jonathan Cape: London.

Skinner, B. F. (1977). Herrnstein and the evolution of behaviourism. *American Psychologists, 32,* 1006–12.

Slotnik, B. M. and Katz, H. M. (1974). Olfactory learning-set formation in rats. *Science, 185,* 796–8.

Small, W. S. (1901). Experimental study of the mental processes of the rat. II. *American Journal of Psychology, 12,* 206–39.

Smith, P. K. (1986). *Play in Animals and Humans.* Oxford: Basil Blackwell.

Smith, W. amd Hale, E. B. (1959). Modification of social rank in the domestic fowl. *Journal of Comparative and Physiological Psychology, 52,* 373–5.

Sokolov, E. N. (1963). *Perception and the Conditioned Reflex.* Pergamon Press: Oxford.

Sokolov, E. N. (1975). The neuronal mechanisms of the orienting reflex.

In Sokolov, E. N. and Vinogradova, O. S. (eds). *Neuronal Mechanisms of the Orienting Reflex*. Lawrence Erlbaum: Hillsdale, New Jersey, 217–35.

Sokolov, E. N. and Vinogradova, O. S. (eds). (1975). *Neuronal Mechanisms of the Orienting Reflex*. Lawrence Erlbaum: Hillsdale, New Jersey, 217–35.

Solomon, R. L. (1964). Punishment. *American Psychologist, 19*, 239–53.

Solomon, R. L. (1980). The opponent-process theory of acquired motivation. *American Psychologist, 35*, 691–712.

Solomon, R. L. and Corbit, J. D. (1974). An opponent process theory of motivation: I. Temporal dynamics of affect. *Psychological Review, 81*, 119–45.

Solomon, R. L. and Wynne, L. C. (1953). Traumatic avoidance learning: acquisition in normal dogs. *Psychological Monographs, 67*, no. 4.

Solomon, R. L. and Wynne, L. C. (1954). Traumatic avoidance learning: the principle of anxiety conservation and partial irreversibility. *Psychological Review, 61*, 653–85.

Solomon, R. L., Kamin, L. J. and Wynne, L. C. (1953). Traumatic avoidance learning: the outcomes of several extinction procedures with dogs. *Journal of Abnormal and Social Psychology, 48*, 291–302.

Sorabji, R. (1972). *Aristotle on Memory*. Duckworth: London.

Spear, N. E. and Miller, R. R. (1981). *Information Processing in Animals: Memory Mechanisms*. Lawrence Erlbaum Associates: Hillsdale, New Jersey.

Spence, K. W. (1936). The nature of discrimination learning in animals. *Psychological Review, 43*, 427–49.

Spence, K. W. (1937). The differential response in animals to stimuli varying within a single dimension. *Psychological Review, 44*, 430–44.

Spence, K. W. (1940). Continuous versus non-continuous interpretations of discrimination learning. *Psychological Review, 47*, 271–88.

Spence, K. W. (1951). Theoretical interpretation of learning. In Stevens, S. S. (ed.), *Handbook of Experimental Psychology*. Wiley: New York, 690–729.

Spence, K. W. (1956). *Behaviour Theory and Conditioning*. Yale University Press: New Haven.

Spence, K. W. and Lippit, R. (1946). An experimental test of the sign-Gestalt theory of trial-and-error learning. *Journal of Experimental Psychology, 36*, 491–502.

Staddon, J. E. R. (1983). *Adaptive Behaviour and Learning*. Cambridge University Press.

Staddon, J. E. R. and Simmelhag, V. L. (1971). The 'superstition' experiment: a reexamination of its implications for the principles of adaptive behaviour. *Psychological Review, 78*, 3–43.

Stanton, M. E., Thomas, G. J. and Brito, G. N. O. (1984). Posterodorsal septal lesions impair performance on both shift and stay working memory tasks. *Behavioural Neuroscience, 98*, 405–15.

Starr, A. and Phillips, L. (1970). Visual and motor memory in the Mnestic Syndrome. *Neuropsychologyia, 8*, 75–88.

Stevens, S. S. (1951). Mathematics, measurement, and psychophysics. In Stevens, S. S. (ed.). *Handbook of Experimental Psychology.* Wiley: New York, 1–49.

Stevenson, J., Hutchison, R. E., Hutchison, J., Bertram, B. L. R. and Thorpe, W. H. (1970). Individual recognition by auditory cues in the Common Tern (*Sterna hirundo*). *Nature,* London, 226, 562–3.db.

Stewart, J., de Wit, H. and Eikelboom, R. (1984). Role of unconditioned and conditioned drug effects in the self-administration of opiates and stimulants. *Psychological Review, 91*, 251–68.

Stone, C. P. (1942). Motivation. In Moss, F. A. (ed.). *Comparative Psychology.* Prentice-Hall: New York, 62–97.

Sulloway, F. J. (1979). *Freud, Biologist of the Mind.* Basic Books: New York.

Sutherland, N. S. (1960). Outlines of a theory of pattern recognition in animals and man. *Proceedings of the Royal Society, B, 171*, 297–317.

Sutherland, N. S. and Mackintosh, N. J. (1971). *Mechanisms of Animal Discrimination Learning.* Academic Press: London.

Taub, E. and Berman, A. J. (1968). Movement and learning in the absence of sensory feedback. In Freedman, S. J. (ed.). *The Neuropsychology of Spatially Oriented Behaviour.* Dorsey Press: Homewood, Ill., 173–92.

Taub, E., Bacon, R. C. and Berman, A. J. (1965). Acquisition of trace-conditioned avoidance response after deafferentation of the responding limb. *Journal of Comparative and Physiological Psychology, 59*, 275–9.

Terlecki, L. J., Pinel, J. P. L. and Triet, D. (1979). Conditioned and unconditioned defensive burying in the rat. *Learning and Motivation, 10*, 337–50.

Terrace, H. S. (1963). Discrimination training with and without 'errors'. *Journal of the Experimental Analysis of Behaviour, 6*, 1–27. 283.

Terrace, H. S. (1966). Behavioural contrast and the peak shift: effects of extended discrimination training. *Journal of the Experimental Analysis of Behaviour, 9*, 613–7.

Terrace, H. S. (1981). Introduction: autoshaping and two-factor learning theory. In Locurto, C. M., Terrace, H. S. and Gibbon, J. (eds), *Autoshaping and Conditioning Theory*, Academic Press: London, 1–18.

Terrace, H. S. (1985). Animal cognition: thinking without language. *Philosophical Transactions of the Royal Society, B, 308*, 113–28.

Terrace, H. S., Pettito, L. A., Sanders, R. J. and Bever, T. G. (1979). Can an ape create a sentence. *Science, 206*, 891–902.

Thistlethwaite, D. (1951). A critical review of latent learning and related experiments. *Psychological Bulletin, 48*, 97–129.

Thomas, D. R. and Switalski, R. W. (1966). Comparison of stimulus generalization following variable-ratio and variable-interval training. *Journal of Experimental Psychology, 76,* 365–76.

Thomas, D. R., Freeman, F., Svinicki, J. G., Burr, D. E. S. and Lyons, J. (1970). Effects of extradimensional training on stimulus generalization. *Journal of Experimental Psychology, Monograph, 83,* no. 1, part 2.

Thomas, D. R., Miller, J. T. and Svinicki, J. G. (1971). Nonspecific transfer effects of discrimination training in the rat. *Journal Of Comparative and Physiological Psychology, 74,* 96–101.

Thomas, G. J. and Spafford, P. S. (1984). Deficits for representational memory induced by septal and cortical lesions (singly and combined) in rats. *Behavioural Neuroscience, 98,* 394–404.

Thompson, R. F. and Glanzman, D. L. (1976). Neural and behavioural mechanisms of habituation and sensitization. In Tighe, T. J. and Leaton, R. N. (eds). *Habituation.* Lawrence Erlbaum Associates: Hillsdale, New Jersey, 49–93.

Thompson, R. F. and Spencer, W. A. (1966). Habituation: a model phenomenon for the study of the neuronal substrates of behaviour. *Psychological Review, 73,* 16–43.

Thon, B. and Pauzie, A. (1984). Differential sensitization, retention, and generalization of habituation in two response systems in the blowfly (*Calliphora vomitoria*). *Journal of Comparative Psychology, 98,* 119–30.

Thorndike, E. L. (1898). Animal intelligence: an experimental study of the associative processes in animals. *Psychological Review, Monograph Supplements, 2(8),* 1–109.

Thorndike, E. L. (1901). The mental life of the monkeys. *Psychological Review, Monograph Supplements, 3(5),* 1–57.

Thorndike, E. L. (1931). *Human Learning.* Century: London.

Thorpe, W. H. (1963). *Learning and Instinct in Animals.* 2nd ed. Methuen: London.

Tighe, T. J. and Leaton, R. N. (1976). *Habituation: Perspectives from Child Development, Animal Behaviour, and Neurophysiology.* Lawrence Erlbaum Associates: Hillsdale, New Jersey.

Timberlake, W. and Grant, D. I. (1975). Autoshaping rats to the presentation of another rat predicting food. *Science, 190,* 690–2.

Tinbergen, J. M. (1981). Foraging decisions in Starlings *Sturnus vulgaris L. Ardea, 69,* 1–67.

Tinbergen, N. (1951). *The Study of Instinct.* Oxford University Press: London.

Tinbergen, N. (1953). *The Herring Gull's World.* Collins: London.

Tinbergen, N. and Kuenen, D. J. (1957). Feeding behaviour in young thrushes. In Schillar, C. H. (ed.), *Instinctive Behaviour: Development of a Modern Concept.* Methuen: London, 209–36.

Tinbergen, N. and Perdeck, A. C. (1950). On the stimulus situation releasing the begging response in the newly-hatched herring-gull chick (*Larus argentatus* Pont). *Behaviour, 3,* 1–39.

Tinkelpaugh, O. L. (1928). An experimental study of representative factors in monkeys. *Journal of Comparative Psychology, 8,* 197–236.

Todorov, J. C., Hanna, E. S. and Bittencourt de Sa, M. C. N. (1984). Frequency versus magnitude of reinforcement: new data with a different procedure. *Journal of the Experimental Analysis of Behaviour, 41,* 157–67.

Tolman, E. C. (1932). *Purposive Behaviour in Animals and Man.* Century: New York.

Tolman, E. C. (1948). Cognitive maps in rats and men. *Psychological Review, 55,* 189–208.

Tolman, E. C. (1959). Principles of purposive behaviourism. In Koch, S. (ed.), *Psychology: A Study of a Science, Vol. 2.* McGraw-Hill: New York, 92–157.

Tolman, E. C. and Honzik, C. H. (1930a). 'Insight' in rats. *University of California Publications in Psychology, 4,* 215–232.

Tolman, E. C. and Honzik, C. H. (1930b). Introduction and removal of reward, and maze learning in rats. *University of California Publications in Psychology, 4,* 257–75.

Tolman, E. C., Ritchie, B. F. and Kalish, D. (1946). Studies in spatial learning: I. Orientation and the short cut. *Journal of Experimental Psychology, 36,* 13–24.

Tolman, E. C., Ritchie, B. F. and Kalish, D. (1947). Studies in spatial learning: V. Response learning versus place learning by the non-correction method. *Journal of Experimental Psychology, 37,* 285–92.

Trapold, M. A. (1970). Are expectancies based upon different positive reinforcing events discriminably different?. *Learning and Motivation, 1,* 129–40.

Twitmeyer, E. B. (1902/1974). A study of the knee jerk. *Journal of Experimental Psychology, 103,* 1047–66.

Urcioli, P. J. (1977). Transfer of oddity from sample performance in pigeons. *Journal of the Experimental Analysis of Behaviour, 27,* 195–202.

Urcioli, P. J. and Zentall, T. R. (1986). Retrospective coding in pigeons' delayed matching-to-sample. *Journal of Experimental Psychology: Animal Behaviour Processes, 12,* 69–770.

Van der Wall, S. B. (1982). An experimental analysis of cache recovery in Clark's nutcracker. *Animal Behaviour, 30,* 84–94.

Vaughan, Jr., W. and Greene, S. L. (1984). Pigeon visual memory capacity. *Journal of Experimental Psychology: Animal Behaviour Processes, 10,* 256–71.

Wagner, A. R. (1976). Priming in STM: an information-processing mechanism for self-generated or retrieval-generated depression in performance. In Tighe, T. J. and Leaton, R. N. (eds). *Habituation.* Lawrence Erlbaum Associates: Hillsdale, New Jersey, 95–128.

Wagner, A. R. (1978). Expectancies and the priming of STM. In Hulse, S. H., Fowler, H. and Honik, W. K. (eds). *Cognitive Processes in Animal Behaviour*. Lawrence Erlbaum Associates: Hillsdale, New Jersey, 177–209.

Wagner, A. R. (1979). Habituation and memory. In Dickinson, A. and Boakes, R. A. (eds). *Mechanisms of Learning and Motivation*. Lawrence Erlbaum: Hillsdale, New Jersey, 53–82.

Wagner, A. R. (1981). SOP: a model of automatic memory processing in animal behaviour. In Spear, N. and Miller, R. R. (eds). *Information Processing in Animals*. Lawrence Erlbaum Associates: Hillsdale, New Jersey, 5–47.

Walker, J. A. and Olton, D. S. (1979). Spatial memory following fimbria-fornix lesions: independent of time for stimulus processing. *Physiology and Behaviour*, *23*, 11–15.

Walker, J. A., and Olton, D. S. (1984). Fimbria-fornix lesions impair spatial working memory but not cognitive mapping. *Behavioural Neuroscience*, *98*, 226–42.

Walker, S. F. (1983a). *Animal Thought*. Routledge & Kegan Paul: London.

Walker, S. F. (1983b). The pros and cons of having a word for it. *Behavioural and Brain Sciences*, *6*, 156–7.

Walker, S. F. (1984). *Learning Theory and Behaviour Modification*. Methuen: London.

Walker, S. F. (1986). The evolution and dissolution of language. In Ellis, A. W. (ed.). *Progress in the Psychology of Language, Vol. 3*. Lawrence Erlbaum Associates: London, 5–48.

Walker, S. F. and Hurwitz, H. M. B. (1970). Effects of relative reinforcer duration on concurrent response rates. *Psychonomic Science*, *22*, 45–7.

Walker, S. F., Schnelle, J. and Hurwitz, H. M. B. (1970). Rates of concurrent responses and reinforcer duration. *Psychonomic Science*, *21*, 173–5.

Warden, C. J. (1931). *Animal Motivation Studies. The Albino Rat*. Columbia University Press: New York.

Warner, L. H. (1927). A study of sex behaviour in the white rat by means of the obstruction method. *Comparative Psychology Monographs*, *4*, No. 22.

Warner, L. H. (1928a). A study of hunger behaviour in the white rat by means of the obstruction method. *Journal of Comparative Psychology*, *8*, 273–99.

Warner, L. H. (1928b). A study of thirst behaviour in the white rat by means of the obstruction method. *Journal of Genetic Psychology*, *35*, 178–92.

Warren, J. M. (1965). Primate learning in comparative perspective. In Schrier, A. M., Harlow, H. F. and Stollnitz, F. (eds). *Behaviour of Nonhuman Primates, Vol. 1*. Academic Press: New York, 249–81.

Warren, J. M. (1973) Learning in vertebrates. In Dewsbury, D. A. and Rethlingshafer, D. A. (eds). *Comparative Psychology: A Modern Survey*. McGraw-Hill: New York, 471–509.

Wasserman, E. A. (1981). Response evocation in autoshaping. In Locurto, C. M., Terrace H. S. and Gibbon, J. (eds). *Autoshaping and Conditioning Theory*. Academic Press: London, 21–54.

Waters, R. S. and Wilson, W. A. (1976). Speech perception by rhesus monkeys: the voicing distinction in synthesized labial and velar stop consonants. *Perception and Psychophysics*, *19*, 285–9.

Watson, J. B. (1907). Kinesthetic and organic sensations: their role in the reactions of the white rat. *Psychological Review Monographs*, *8*, no. 2.

Watson, J. B. (1914/1967). *Behaviour: An Introduction to Comparative Psychology*. Holt, Rinehart & Winston: London.

Watson, J. B. (1931). *Behaviourism*. Kegan Paul, Trench & Trubner: London.

Weidman, U. (1961). The stimuli eliciting begging responses in gulls and terns. *Animal Behaviour*, *9*, 115–16.

Weinberger, N. M., Gold, P. E. and Sternberg, B. B. (1984). Epinephrine enables Pavlovian fear conditioning under anesthesia. *Science*, *223*, 605–7.

Weiskrantz, L. (1974). The interaction between occipital and temporal cortex in vision: an overview. In Schmitt, F. O. and Worden, F. G. (eds). *The Neurosciences: Third Study Program*. MIT Press: London, 189–204.

Weiskrantz, L. (1977). Trying to bridge some neuropsychological gaps between monkey and man. *British Journal of Psychology*, *68*, 431–45.

Weiskrantz, L. (1985). Introduction: categorization, cleverness and consciousness. *Philosophical Transactions of the Royal Society*, B, *308*, 3–19.

Weiss, J. M. (1968). Effects of coping responses on stress. *Journal of Comparative and Physiological Psychology*, *65*, 251–60.

Weiss, J. M. (1971). Effects of coping behaviour in different warning signal conditions on stress pathology in rats. *Journal of Comparative and Physiological Psychology*, *77*, 1–13.

Weiss, J. M. and Glazer, H. I. (1975). Effects of acute exposure to stressors on subsequent avoidance-escape behaviour. *Psychosomatic Medicine*, *37*, 499–521.

Weiss, S. J. (1971). Discrimination training and stimulus compounding consideration of non-reinforcement and response differentiation consequence of s^D. *Journal of the Experimental Analysis of Behaviour*, *15*, 387–402.

Weissman, R. G., Wasserman, E. A., Dodd, P. D. W. and Larew, M. B. (1980). Representation and retention of two-event sequences in pigeons. *Journal of Experimental Psychology: Animal Behaviour Processes*, *6*, 312–25.

Wexler, K. (1982). A principle theory for language acquisition. In Wanner, E. and Gleitman, L. R. (eds), *Language Acquisition: The State of the Art*. Cambridge University Press, 288–315.

Wilcoxon, H., Dragoin, W. and Kral, P. (1971). Illness-induced aversions in rat and quail: relative salience of visual and gustatory cues. *Science*, *171*, 826–8.

Williams, D. R. (1981). Biconditional behaviour: conditioning without constraint. In Locurto, C. M., Terrace, H. S. and Gibbon, J. (eds). *Autoshaping and Conditioning Theory*. Academic Press: London, 55–99.

Williams, D. R. and Williams, H. (1969). Auto-maintenance in the pigeon: sustained pecking despite contingent non-reinforcement. *Journal of the Experimental Analysis of Behaviour*, *12*, 511–20.

Williams, J. H. (1950). *Elephant Bill*. Hart-Davis: London.

Wilson, B., Mackintosh, N. J. and Boakes, R. A. (1985). Transfer of relational rules in matching and oddity learning by pigeons and corvids. *Quarterly Journal of Experimental Psychology*, *378*, 313–22.

Wilson, E. O. (1975). *Sociobiology*. Harvard University Press: Cambridge, Mass.

Wise, K. L., Wise, L. A. and Zimmermann, R. R. (1974). Piagetian object permanence in the infant rhesus monkey. *Developmental Psychology*, *10*, 429–37.

Wolpe, J. (1958). *Psychotherapy by Reciprocal Inhibition*. Stanford Universeity Press.

Woodard, W. T., Schoel, W. M. and Bitterman, M. E. (1971) Reversal learning with singly presented stimuli in pigeons and goldfish. *Journal of Comparative and Physiological Psychology*, *76*, 460–7.

Woodruff, G., Premack, D. and Kennel, K. (1978). Conservation of liquid and solid quantity by the chimpanzee. *Science*, *202*, 991–4.

Woods, S. C. (1976). Conditioned hypoglycemia. *Journal of Comparative and Physiological Psychology*, *90*, 1164–8.

Woods, S. C. and Kulkosky, P. J. (1976). Classically conditioned changes of blood glucose level. *Psychosomatic Medicine*, *38*, 201–19.

Wright, A. A., Santiago, H. C. and Sands, S. F. (1983). On the nature of the primacy effect in memory processing: a reply to Gaffan. *Animal Learning and Behaviour*, *11*, 148–50.

Wright, A. A., Santiago, H. C. and Sands, S. F. (1984a). Monkey memory: *same/different* concept learning, serial probe recognition acquisition, and probe delay effects on the serial position function. *Journal of Experimental Psychology: Animal Behaviour Processes*, *10*, 513–29.

Wright, A. A., Santiago, H. C., Sands, S. F. and Urcioli, P. J. (1984b). Pigeon and monkey serial probe recognition: acquisition strategies, and serial position effects. In Roitblat, H. L., Bever, T. G. and Terrace, H. S. (eds). *Animal Cognition*. Lawrence Erlbaum Associates: London, 353–73.

Wright, D. L., French, G. M. and Riley, D. A. (1968). Similarity responding by monkeys in a matching-to-sample task. *Journal of Comparative and Physiological Psychology*, *65*, 191–6.

Yamaguchi, H. (1961). The effect of continuous, partial, and varied magnitude reinforcement on acquisition and extinction. *Journal of Experimental Psychology, 61*, 319–21.

Yarczower, M. (1971). Stimulus control during conditional discrimination. *Journal of the Experimental Analysis of Behaviour, 16*, 89–94.

Yates, A. (1980). *Biofeedback and the Modification of Behaviour.* Plenum Press: New York.

Yates, F. A. (1966). *The Art of Memory.* Routledge & Kegan Paul: London.

Yeo, C. H. (1979). The anatomy of the vertebrate nervous system: an evolutionary and developmental perspective. In Oakley, D. A. and Plotkin, H. (eds). *Brain Behaviour and Evolution.* Methuen: London, 28–51.

Zeiler, M. D. (1971) Eliminating behaviour with reinforcement. *Journal of the Experimental Analysis of Behaviour, 16*, 400–3.

Zentall, D. B. Hogan, D. E., Edwards, C. A. and Hearst, E. (1980). Oddity learning in the pigeon as a function of the number of incorrect alternatives. *Journal of Experimental Psychology: Animal Behaviour Processes, 6*, 278–89.

Ziriax, J. M. and Silberberg, A. (1984). Concurrent variable-interval variable-ratio schedules can provide only weak evidence for matching. *Journal of the Experimental Analysis of Behaviour, 41*, 83–100.

Zurif, G. E. (1970). A comparison of variable-ratio and variable-interval schedules of reinforcement. *Journal of the Experimental Analysis of Behaviour, 13*, 369–74.

Subject Index

abstract mental codes, possibilities of in primates, 348
acquired distinctiveness of cues, 268
acquisition of conditioned reflexes, 60
after-images, 81–2
airblast, as aversive stimulus, 230
amydala, 205, 313
analogical reasoning, 346–8
analysers, and selective attention in discrimination, 261, 266, 275, 279, 283
analysers, in Pavlov's theories, 57
analysers, switching in of, differentiation from arousal, 283
analysis and synthesis, elementary and higher types, 64, 92
analytic and synthetic distinction, 15–17
animal cognition, 30–31
Anthropoidea, definition of, 332
anticipation, anticipatory reflexes, 114–15; 355
anticipatory goal response, 175–6
anxiety, and stress, 243–4
ape-training experiments, interpretation of, 341
apes, classification of, 332–3
aphasia, 337
Aplysia californica, classical conditioning in, 66–9, 99; habituation in, 38, 47–50;

instrumental conditioning in, 158; and higher vertebrates, 92
appetitive vs aversive motivation, 203–5
approach-avoidance gradients, 211–12
Aristotle, 4–6, 168–9, 191–2
arousal, vs attention, 282–3; conditioned to external cues, 162; in elation and hope, 242; and habituation, 40, 54; and selective attention; 40, 265; and self-sustaining aversive stimuli, 231
articulatory loop, and human verbal learning, 326
associability, of stimuli, 107, 110–13, 279
associations, evolution of mechanisms of, 237; of ideas, 11–13; vs reference, 335; types of, 195–202
attention, 41; to aversive events, 89, 249–50; and backward conditioning, 88; and conditional discrimination, 276; in conditioning, theories of, 279–82; and level of representation, 95–7; in learning sets, 273; sharpening of, 285–6; Thorndike's assessment of, 122; *see also* selective attention
attentiveness, nonspecific, 269

instrumental learning, schedules
of reinforcement
opponent processes, in
conditioning, 76, 82, 102
optimal foraging, 181, 186–8
orienting reflex, or response, 43, 52,
107
overtraining reversal effect, 262
oyster-catcher, 24–5

Papez circuit, 204; *see also* limbic
system
parrot, vocal answers to questions
by, 344
partial reinforcement effect, 183
pattern recognition, 290, and
search images, 25–6
Pavlov, I. (1849–1936),
experiments, 58–63, 180, 184,
255, 265; method of contrasts,
265, 275, 285–6; theories, 56–8,
165–6, 265
Pavlovian conditioning, *see* classical
conditioning
pay-offs, in classical conditioning,
179–82; in instrumental
learning, 174–82, 186–78, 191,
196
peak shift, 255–8
perception, and conditioning, 80–3
perceptual complexity, 50, 66, 284;
and discrimination learning,
287–9; and level of
representation, 95
perceptual learning, 41, 284
perceptual systems, evolution of,
290
picture stimuli, discrimination of,
294–300
place-learning, 141–5, 305
placement studies, 151
Plato, 1–5, 9, 31–2
play, in young mammals, 54
pleasure/pain principle, 177, 179,
203, 205–8, 215–16
polymorphous concept, 292, 300
post-ingestional consequences, 125,
187

preparatory vs consummatory
conditioning, 102
preparedness for formation of
associations, 236–7;
Thorndike's view, 122
presolution reversal, 261
presynaptic facilitation, 68, 115
primacy effect, 326–7
primates, classification of, 332–3;
abstracting of rules by, 278–9;
and learning sets, 269–74;
possibilities of abstract mental
codes in, 348: *see also*
chimpanzees, monkeys
priming of stimulus
representations, 111–12
proactive interference, 318; and
serial position effect, 323–4, 327
probe delay, and serial position
effect, 328
problem box, as used by
Thorndike, 119
procedural versus declarative
representations, 145
productive vs receptive skills,
335–6, 341
proprioception, 200–1, 141
prosimians, 333
prospective vs. retrospective
coding, 320, 322
protodeclarative, 336
psychosomatic factors, 77
punishment, conclusions, 250–1;
lasting effects of, 210; Skinner's
and Thorndike's doubts about,
208–9; and self-punishment,
247–50
pyriform cortex, 205
Pythagoras' Theorem, 1–4, 14

R-R associations, 201
R-R* associations, 200
R-S associations, 200
R-S* associations, 198–9
radial maze, 143–5, 306–9
rationalist views, 4
rats, mouse killing by, 240

Bibliographic Index

In some ways this is an animal
learning book that wants to argue
for limited usability of Animal learning
in formulating theories of beh-
Even states that altho ~~superficial~~
behavioral change may be similar across
many species & many responses doesn't
mean that physiol/psych? mediation
is same ———